A Field Guide to the
National Parks of East Africa

The Peterson Identification System
The system of identification in this Field Guide is based
on the original system devised by Roger Tory Peterson,
which emphasises comparative patterns and makes use of arrows
to point out the most important field marks.

A Field Guide
to the National Parks
of East Africa

JOHN G. WILLIAMS

with 16 colour plates and
16 black and white plates
by Rena Fennessy

Collins
ST JAMES'S PLACE
LONDON

Third Impression 1970
Fourth   ,,   1972

ISBN 0 00 212103 4

© *John G. Williams 1967*
Printed in Great Britain
Collins Clear-Type Press
London and Glasgow

Contents

6

Part 2
The Mammals of the National Parks of East Africa   166

Part 3

The Rarer Birds of the National Parks of East Africa 230

Plates

Introduction

A Field Guide to the National Parks of East Africa has two main aims. The first of these is to assist the user in identifying the mammals and birds to be encountered in our faunal reserves, and secondly it is a reference guide to help in planning an East African holiday to the best possible advantage. In this context the author will always be pleased to meet or hear from naturalist visitors and to advise on itineraries.

This Field Guide is divided into three sections. In the first the National Parks, Game Reserves and other areas of special zoological importance and tourist appeal are detailed, each with a list of its mammals and birds. The second section is a guide to the mammals of East Africa with their diagnostic field characters and distributions. The last section is a field guide to the rarer and more local East African birds, those species not described or illustrated in my earlier *A Field Guide to the Birds of East and Central Africa*. The presentation of both the mammal and bird sections is in systematic order. In the lists of birds occurring in the National Parks those species which were described in my earlier Field Guide are given a page reference with an asterisk (e.g., *75). Numbers without the asterisk are references to the present volume—to plates if in bold type, otherwise to pages.

It is the author's pleasure to record his deep appreciation and gratitude to the Directors and Staff of the National Parks and Game Departments in Kenya, Tanzania and Uganda, and to numerous professional hunters in those countries, without whose active co-operation this book would not have been written. He also extends his warmest thanks to friends in Africa and overseas who have assisted in many ways. The author is especially indebted to Mrs. R. M. Fennessy, the talented Kenya wildlife artist, whose portraiture of mammals and birds so enhances the value of this book.

Kenya, Tanzania and Uganda are unique: no other region in the world has so much to offer the visitor. I hope that readers take away with them unforgettable memories of our wildlife, and that their experiences here foment a growing concern for wildlife conservation throughout the world.

P.O. Box 729
Nairobi, Kenya

John G. Williams

Part 1

The National Parks,
Game Reserves
and other faunal areas

Kenya

Kenya boasts eleven faunal reserves designated as National Parks, National Reserves and Game Reserves administered by County Councils. These are Aberdare National Park, Lake Nakuru National Park, Mount Kenya National Park, Nairobi National Park, Tsavo National Park, Marsabit National Reserve, Amboseli Masai Game Reserve, Mara Masai Game Reserve, Meru Game Reserve, Samburu Game Reserve and Isiolo Game Reserve.

The distinction between a National Park and a Game Reserve, broadly speaking, is that in the former complete protection of fauna and flora is the paramount purpose and human utilisation of the land is precluded. In the Game Reserves preservation of wild life is a primary purpose but human activities such as the grazing of cattle are sometimes allowed. It is fitting to pay tribute to the pastoral tribes, peoples who have lived in harmony with wild life from time immemorial, and to their wise Councils who now have set aside these Game Reserves where their wild life heritage may be preserved.

In addition to the faunal National Parks there are three other Parks which are mainly of historical and archaeological importance. These are:

Fort Jesus National Park which protects the seventeenth-century Portuguese fort at Mombasa, overlooking the Indian Ocean.

Gedi National Park which protects one of the most outstanding thirteenth-century ruined Arab cities.

Olorgesailie National Park, in the Great Rift Valley, which preserves a Pleistocene living-site of hand-axe man, with his artifacts and associated prehistoric mammal fossils exhibited *in situ*.

These National Parks are also not without their zoological interest, which will be detailed later in this section.

ABERDARE NATIONAL PARK

The Aberdare National Park, established in 1950, comprises an area of 228 square miles. This includes the moorlands and part of the forest of the Aberdare Mountains, for the most part over 10,000 feet. The famous Treetops Hotel, twelve miles from Nyeri, is situated in a salient of the Park

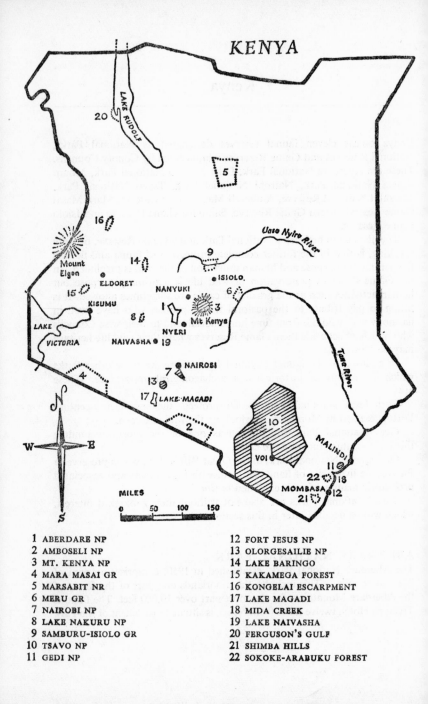

KENYA

1 ABERDARE NP
2 AMBOSELI NP
3 MT. KENYA NP
4 MARA MASAI GR
5 MARSABIT NR
6 MERU GR
7 NAIROBI NP
8 LAKE NAKURU NP
9 SAMBURU-ISIOLO GR
10 TSAVO NP
11 GEDI NP

12 FORT JESUS NP
13 OLORGESAILIE NP
14 LAKE BARINGO
15 KAKAMEGA FOREST
16 KONGELAI ESCARPMENT
17 LAKE MAGADI
18 MIDA CREEK
19 LAKE NAIVASHA
20 FERGUSON'S GULF
21 SHIMBA HILLS
22 SOKOKE-ARABUKU FOREST

which extends down the eastern side of the range to the lower edge of the forest.

The Park is readily accessible from Nyeri and Naro Moru on the eastern side, the road crossing the Park and connecting with the road from Naivasha and North Kinangop on the west.

The Aberdare Mountains are part of the central highlands of Kenya, running roughly north-south between Nairobi and Thomson's Falls. In altitude the range rises to some 12,900 feet. The mountain slopes, especially on the eastern and western flanks, are covered with heavy forest with tree ferns in places giving way to a bamboo-hargenia zone at higher levels.

Deep ravines cut through the forested inclines, through which hidden trout streams flow and waterfalls cascade down hundreds of feet of rock face. Above the forest stretch miles of open moorlands, broken by lichen-covered rocky outcrops, hills and crags, thickets of giant heath and tussock-grass bogs.

To appreciate the full glory of this very beautiful Park, camping is recommended at one of the several approved sites. The hour or so immediately following dawn is the most rewarding time to look for game, and it is then that one has the best chance of suddenly coming upon that shy and elusive animal the Bongo. The upper bamboo zone and hypericum scrub is its favourite habitat.

In the forest are Red Duiker, Suni, Bushbuck—some of the old males on the Aberdares are nearly black—Elephant, Buffalo, Giant Forest Hog, Leopard—all black examples have been recorded—and Colobus monkey.

Eland occur on the open moorlands. The moorland thickets are the home of Bush Duiker and Black-fronted Duiker, and Black Rhino are by no means rare. The Aberdare moorlands is a good locality for Serval, and both the normal spotted and melanistic animals may be seen.

Bird life is abundant and varied. Perhaps the most conspicuous group is the sunbirds. Four species may be seen—Tacazze Sunbird, brilliant metallic violet and bronze with a black belly; Golden-winged Sunbird, scintillating coppery-bronze with golden yellow edged wings and tail; the emerald green Malachite Sunbird, and the tiny Double-collared Sunbird with metallic green upperparts and throat and scarlet chest band.

Game birds include Jackson's and Scaly Francolins in the forest and the very local Montane Francolin on the moorlands. Birds of prey are specially interesting and Crowned and Ayres' Hawk Eagles, Mountain Buzzard, Rufous-breasted Sparrow Hawk and African Goshawk are usually to be seen.

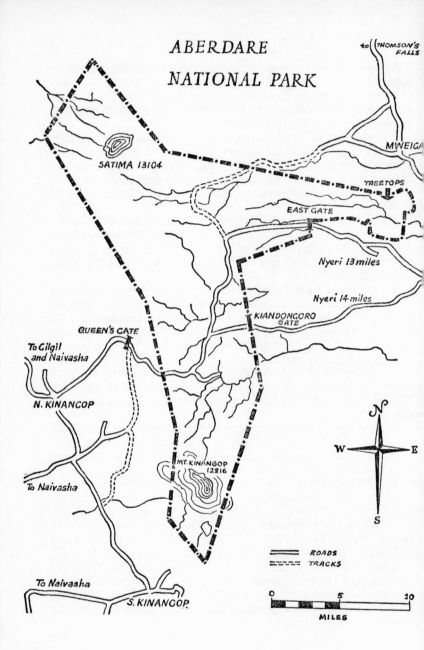

ABERDARE
NATIONAL PARK

to THOMSON'S FALLS

MWEIGA

SATIMA 13104

TREETOPS

EAST GATE

Nyeri 13 miles

Nyeri 14 miles

KIANDONGORO GATE

QUEEN'S GATE

To Gilgil and Naivasha

N. KINANGOP

To Naivasha

MT. KINANGOP 12816

To Naivasha

S. KINANGOP

ROADS
TRACKS

0   5   10
MILES

Some characteristic birds of the higher moorlands are the Scarlet-tufted Malachite Sunbird—but much rarer here than in the alpine zone of Mount Kenya—the tame and confiding Mountain or Hill Chat, Augur Buzzard, Slender-billed Chestnut-wing Starling and White-naped Raven.

MAMMALS OF ABERDARE NATIONAL PARK

Giant White-toothed Shrew
Mole Shrew Mainly in bamboo zone, where they burrow just below surface of ground
Rousette Fruit Bat In caves in forest: attracted to fruiting fig trees
Hollow-faced Bat
Banana Bat or **African Pipistrelle**
Greater Galago
Black-faced Vervet
Blue or **Sykes' Monkey**
Olive Baboon
Black and White Colobus
Hunting Dog Probably spasmodic visitors
Black-backed or **Silver-backed Jackal**
Side-striped Jackal
Zorilla
Clawless Otter Not uncommon along trout streams, but rarely seen. Feeds on fresh-water crabs
African Civet

Bush or **Large-spotted Genet**
African Palm Civet
Marsh Mongoose
Slender or **Black-tipped Mongoose**
White-tailed Mongoose
Spotted Hyaena
African Wild Cat
Serval Not uncommon on moorlands: melanistic examples sometimes seen
Golden Cat Reputed to occur, but not yet confirmed
Lion Rare
Leopard
Ant Bear Occurs at lower levels
Tree Hyrax
Rock Hyrax
African Elephant
Black Rhinoceros
Giant Forest Hog Often seen at Treetops
Bush Pig Common but shy: not often seen

Blue Duiker
Bush Duiker
Klipspringer
Suni
Steinbok
Common Waterbuck
Bohor Reedbuck
Chanler's Reedbuck
Impala
Bongo Found mainly in upper bamboo zone; very shy and elusive. Has been recorded at Treetops
Bushbuck
Eland
African Buffalo
African Hare
Porcupine
Bush Squirrel
African Dormouse
Crested Rat
Giant Rat
Kenya Mole Rat Their presence indicated by the earth mounds thrown up by the animals whilst digging

BIRDS OF ABERDARE NATIONAL PARK

N.B. Numbers in bold type following a bird's name are references to the PLATES and those in ordinary type to PAGES. Numbers preceded by an asterisk are references to the author's *Field Guide to the Birds of East and Central Africa*, and indicate the page in that book on which the bird in question is described.

Little Grebe *20 Recorded at Treetops
Long-tailed Cormorant *21 Treetops
Black-headed Heron *23 Treetops
Yellow-billed Egret *25 Treetops

Little Egret *25
Buff-backed Heron or **Cattle Egret *26**
Hammerkop *28
Wood Ibis or **Yellow-billed Stork *31** Treetops
Sacred Ibis *31 Treetops
Hadada Ibis *34

Green Ibis *34 A rare forest species. Frequents swampy glades in forest
Yellow-billed Duck *38 Treetops
African Black Duck *38 On streams in forest

Garganey Teal *38 Treetops

Red-billed Duck *39 Treetops

Egyptian Goose *41 Treetops

Secretary Bird *42 Recorded on moorlands

Ruppell's Griffon Vulture *42

White-backed Vulture *43

Hooded Vulture *43

Peregrine *45

Lanner *45

European Kestrel *47

Lesser Kestrel *50

Cuckoo Falcon *67 An uncommon species in forest

European Black Kite *51

African Black Kite *51

Black-shouldered Kite *51 Spasmodic visitor to moorlands

Verreaux's Eagle *54

Steppe Eagle *55

Ayres' Hawk Eagle *56 Sometimes seen soaring above forest

Crowned Hawk Eagle *57 Uncommon in forest

Long-crested Hawk Eagle *57

Lammergeyer *44 Rare visitor. Not known to breed

Steppe Buzzard *62 In some years a common winter visitor; in other years seldom seen

Eastern Steppe Buzzard *62 Rare winter visitor or passage migrant

Mountain Buzzard *62 Not uncommon in forest

Augur Buzzard *63

Rufous-breasted Sparrow Hawk *66

Great Sparrow Hawk *66

African Goshawk *67

Montagu's Harrier *68 Winter visitor and passage migrant to moorlands

Pallid Harrier *69 Winter visitor and passage migrant to moorlands

European Marsh Harrier *69 Winter visitor. Rare

Montane Francolin 14 Scrub and moorlands above forest

Scaly Francolin *74 Forest species

Jackson's Francolin *74 Forest and bamboo zones

Cape Quail *76 Uncommon on moorlands

African Crake *79 Spasmodic visitor moorlands. Rarely seen

Peters' Finfoot *86 Rare. Streams at lower altitudes

Crowned Crane *86 Treetops

Black-winged Plover *99 Spasmodic visitor to moorlands

European Common Snipe *104

Great Snipe *104 Mainly passage migrant April/May in moorland bogs

Jack Snipe *104 Rare winter visitor. High altitude bogs

Ruff *106 Treetops

Green Sandpiper *107 Winter visitor. Mountain streams

Wood Sandpiper *107 Treetops

Greenshank *109 Treetops

Marsh Sandpiper *108 Treetops

Olive Pigeon *119 Forest Common

Bronze-naped Pigeon *119 Forest

Pink-breasted Dove *120

Red-eyed Dove *120

Ring-necked Dove *120 Treetops

Laughing Dove *121 Treetops

Tambourine Dove *122

Emerald-spotted Wood Dove *121

Lemon Dove 16 Rare. Forest at lower levels

Green Pigeon *122

Red-chested Cuckoo *123 Treetops

Emerald Cuckoo *125 Treetops, and low level forest

Didric Cuckoo *125

Klaas' Cuckoo *126

White-browed Coucal *126 Treetops

Hartlaub's Turaco *131 Not uncommon in forest

Red-headed Parrot *133 Forest

European Roller *135 Uncommon passage migrant. Treetops

Lilac-breasted Roller *136 Treetops

Broad-billed Roller *137 Lower level forest

Pied Kingfisher *137 Treetops

Giant Kingfisher *138 On forest streams. Feeds largely on fresh-water crabs

Malachite Kingfisher *138 Treetops

European Bee-eater *140 Uncommon visitor. Treetops

Cinnamon-chested Bee-eater 19 Forest glades

Silvery-cheeked Hornbill *147 Forest

Crowned Hornbill *149 Treetops

Ground Hornbill *150 Treetops

White-headed Wood Hoopoe *152 Forest

Cape Grass Owl *153 Swampy hollows on moorlands

African Marsh Owl *154 Moorlands

Mackinder's Eagle Owl 15 Crags and cliffs above forest

Spotted Eagle Owl *155

Verreaux's Eagle Owl *155
Treetops
European Nightjar *156
Migrant. Treetops
Abyssinian Nightjar *157
Pennant-wing Nightjar
*158 Rare visitor. Tree-
tops
Speckled Mousebird *159
Treetops
Narina's Trogon *163
Forest
Bar-tailed Trogon *163
Forest
Golden-rumped Tinker-bird
*168 Treetops
Greater Honeyguide *170
Treetops. Uncommon
Fine-banded Woodpecker
*172 Forest
Nyanza Swift *174
Alpine Swift *175
Mottled Swift *175
Mountain Wagtail *183
Forest streams
Red-capped Lark *182
Moorlands
Blue-headed Wagtail and
races *184 Moorlands on
spring migration
Richard's Pipit *184
Red-throated Pipit *185
Sharpe's Longclaw *186
Moorlands
Dark-capped Bulbul *188
Treetops
Fischer's Greenbul *189
Treetops
Olive-breasted Mountain
Greenbul 21
Yellow-whiskered Greenbul
*189
European Spotted Fly-
catcher *190 Treetops.
Migrant
Dusky Flycatcher *190
Treetops
White-eyed Slaty Fly-
catcher *191 Treetops
Mountain Yellow Fly-
catcher 278
Chin-spot Flycatcher *194
Treetops

Paradise Flycatcher *195
Treetops
Olive Thrush *196
Abyssinian Ground Thrush
10 Bamboo zone
European Common Wheat-
ear *198
Isabelline Wheatear *198
Pied Wheatear *198
Capped Wheatear *198
Uncommon. Moorlands
Hill or Mountain Chat 23
Alpine zone
Stonechat *200
Ruppell's Robin Chat *201
Robin Chat *201
White-starred Bush Robin
*203 Common in bam-
boo zone
Blackcap Warbler *204
Treetops
European Sedge Warbler
290 Treetops
Cinnamon Bracken War-
bler *204
Greater Swamp Warbler 24
Treetops
European Willow Warbler
*205
Brown Woodland Warbler
*205
Grey Apalis 24
Black-breasted Apalis *206
Chestnut-throated
Apalis 24
Grey-backed Camaroptera
*210
Wing-snapping Cisticola 24
Alpine grasslands
Hunter's Cisticola 24
Common in moorland
thickets
Tinkling Cisticola 25
Moorland bogs
European Swallow *212
African Sand Martin *214
African Rock Martin *214
Black Rough-wing Swallow
*215
White-headed Rough-wing
Swallow *215
Purple-throated Cuckoo
Shrike *215

Grey Cuckoo Shrike *216
Drongo *216 Treetops
Fiscal Shrike *219 Tree-
tops
Tropical Boubou *222
Forest
Black-backed Puff-back
*223 Treetops
Black-fronted Bush Shrike
26 Forest trees and creep-
ers
Doherty's Bush Shrike *224
Lower forest: frequents
undergrowth
White-breasted Tit *226
Black-headed Oriole *227
Black-winged Oriole 302
High level forest
Pied Crow *230 Treetops
White-naped Raven *230
Violet-backed Starling
*232 Treetops
Sharpe's Starling *232
Blue-eared Glossy Star-
ling *232 Treetops
Slender-billed Chestnut-
wing Starling 29 Alpine
moorlands and waterfalls,
below which it nests
Superb Starling *235
Treetops
Red-billed Oxpecker *235
Treetops
Kikuyu White-eye *238
Malachite Sunbird *239
Scarlet-tufted Malachite
Sunbird 30 High moor-
lands
Tacazze Sunbird *242
Bronzy Sunbird *242
Treetops
Golden-winged Sunbird
*243
Variable Sunbird *244
Treetops
Eastern Double-collared
Sunbird *245
Northern Double-collared
Sunbird 30 Treetops
Amethyst Sunbird *245
Treetops
Scarlet-chested Sunbird
*246 Treetops

Olive Sunbird 30 Lower altitudes in forest
Collared Sunbird *247
Spectacled Weaver *255 Treetops
Reichenow's Weaver *258
Brown-capped Weaver 31 Forest
Red-naped Widow-bird *262 Treetops
Long-tailed Widow-bird *263 Open bushy moorland

Bronze Mannikin *264 Treetops
Grey-headed Negro Finch 32 Treetops
Abyssinian Crimson-wing 32 Common in bamboo zone
Yellow-bellied Waxbill *266
Waxbill *266 Treetops
Black-headed Waxbill 28 Forest glades
Red-cheeked Cordon-bleu *266

Brimstone Canary *268
Yellow-crowned Canary 28 Upper edges of forest and bamboo zone
Thick-billed Seed-eater 28 Forest undergrowth
Oriole Finch 340 Forest. Uncommon
African Citril 339 Treetops
Golden-breasted Bunting *270

AMBOSELI MASAI GAME RESERVE

Amboseli is justly famous both for its big game—rhino are perhaps the biggest attraction—and for its great scenic beauty.

The 1,259 square miles of this Game Reserve embody five main wild life habitats, plus a generally dry lake-bed, Lake Amboseli, from which it takes its name. These are open plains; extensive stands of yellow-barked acacia woodland; rocky, lava strewn thorn-bush country; swamps and marshes; and at the western end of the Reserve, above Namanga, the massif of Oldoinyo Orok rising to over 8,300 feet and still for the most part zoologically unexplored.

The landscape is everywhere dominated by the glistening, majestic snow-cap of Kilimanjaro immediately to the south—Africa's highest mountain (19,340 feet)—a fitting back-drop to a wild region where the pastoral Masai and their cattle have lived in harmony with wild creatures for many a century.

Amboseli may be reached from Nairobi by two main routes. The first is to Athi River and thence along the main Kajiado-Namanga-Arusha road, turning left through the Game Reserve main gate at Namanga to Ol Tukai Lodge, forty-seven miles on. Total distance from Nairobi is 150 miles. The second route is from Nairobi along the main Mombasa road to some ten miles past Emali, then branching right and following the main Loitokitok road: approximately forty miles along this road it forks right and the Lodge is twenty miles farther on. Total mileage from Nairobi is 142 miles. Accommodation is available at Amboseli New Lodge, Ol Tukai Lodge, Ol Tukai Tented Camp and the Namanga Hotel. Camp sites are also available.

The main game-viewing area of Amboseli lies in the eastern half of the Reserve, in the vicinity of Ol Tukai Lodge and lakes Engoni Naibor and Loginya. Here a network of roads and tracks opens up a wild life paradise.

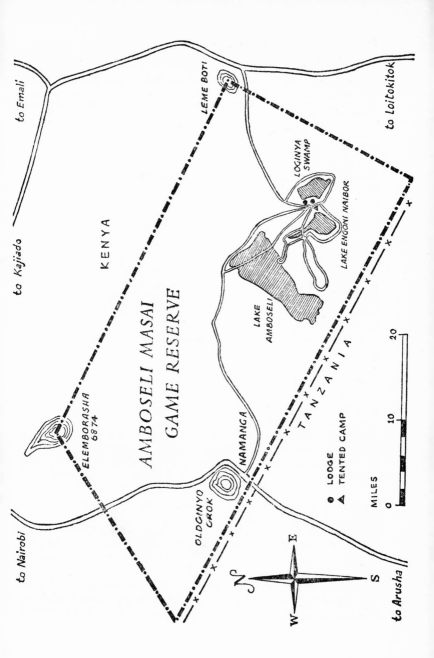

to Emali

to Kajiado

to Nairobi

to Loitokitok

LEME BOTI

KENYA

AMBOSELI MASAI
GAME RESERVE

ELEMBORASHA
6874

LOGINYA
SWAMP

LAKE ENGONI NAIBOR

LAKE
AMBOSELI

TANZANIA

NAMANGA

OLDOINYO
OROK

● LODGE
▲ TENTED CAMP

MILES
0   10   20

N
W   E
S

to Arusha

Elephant, Black Rhino, Lion, Leopard, Cheetah, Masai Giraffe and Buffalo may all be encountered during a single morning's drive of fifty or sixty miles, together with plains game such as Common Zebra, Eland, Coke's Hartebeest, White-bearded Gnu, Common Waterbuck, Thomson's and Grant's Gazelles and Impala.

In the dry bush country towards Namanga, and in the arid area en route to Emali, two especially interesting antelopes may be found: the long-necked Gerenuk—often called the "Giraffe-necked Antelope"—and the Fringe-eared Oryx. Smaller mammals always in evidence include Black-faced Vervet Monkey and Yellow Baboon, Black-backed Jackals, Spotted Hyaena and Bat-eared Foxes. The last may often be seen basking in the sun outside their dens on the open plains.

Bird life is equally abundant, especially in the vicinity of the lakes and swamps where a great variety of water birds may be seen. That rarity in East Africa, the Madagascar Squacco Heron, turns up at fairly regular intervals and the plover with the habits of a lily-trotter, the Long-toed Lapwing, is a resident in small numbers. Sandgrouse of three species, Yellow-throated, Chestnut-bellied and Black-faced, water in their hundreds during the dry season, announcing their arrival at their favourite drinking place with far-carrying "gutta, gutta, gutta" flock calls.

Birds of prey are very well represented. Including the six species of vultures no less than forty-seven different kinds have been recorded from Amboseli, amongst which are two great rarities, the Teita Falcon and the Southern Banded Harrier Eagle.

Around the lodges and tented camp, visitors will see flocks of a yellow weaver-bird with a patch of chestnut on the nape. This is the extremely local Taveta Golden Weaver, which outside of Amboseli may rightly be considered a rare bird. But the bird which quickly draws attention to itself on account of its brilliant plumage and fearless behaviour—it will alight on your table and partake of bread and cake crumbs—is the Superb Glossy Starling.

MAMMALS OF AMBOSELI MASAI GAME RESERVE

Spectacled Elephant Shrew Generally frequents low bush at edge of acacia woodland
Short-snouted Elephant Shrew Inhabits open plains where patches of low bush exist
East African Hedgehog
Giant White-toothed Shrew

Rousette Fruit Bat Attracted to fruiting fig trees
Epauletted Fruit Bat Attracted to fruiting fig trees
White-bellied Tomb Bat
Hollow-faced Bat
False Vampire Bat Colonies often found in disused Masai huts
Yellow-winged Bat Hangs in acacia trees and bushes by day
Lander's Horseshoe Bat
Lesser Leaf-nosed Bat
Banana Bat or African Pipistrelle
Yellow-bellied Bat
Angola Free-tailed Bat Inhabits roofs of huts and lodges

White-bellied Free-tailed Bat
Bush Baby Frequents acacia woodland
Black-faced Vervet
Blue or Sykes' Monkey
Yellow Baboon
Hunting Dog
Golden Jackal The rarest of the jackals at Amboseli
Black-backed or Silver-backed Jackal
Side-striped Jackal
Bat-eared Fox Often seen basking outside holes on open plains
Zorilla Seen usually at dusk
Ratel or Honey Badger Rarely seen
African Civet
Neumann's or Small-spotted Genet
Bush or Large-spotted Genet
Marsh Mongoose
Dwarf Mongoose

Large Grey Mongoose
Slender or Black-tipped Mongoose
White-tailed Mongoose
Banded Mongoose
Aard-wolf Rarely seen: nocturnal
Spotted Hyaena
Striped Hyaena Rare
Cheetah
Caracal
African Wild Cat
Serval
Lion
Leopard
Ant Bear Nocturnal: rarely seen
Tree Hyrax
Rock Hyrax
African Elephant
Black Rhinoceros
Burchell's or Common Zebra
Hippopotamus
Warthog
Masai Giraffe
Coke's Hartebeest or Kongoni

White-bearded Gnu or Wildebeest
Red Duiker Much rarer than Bush Duiker.
Bush Duiker
Klipspringer
Steinbok
Kirk's Dik-Dik
Common Waterbuck
Bohor Reedbuck
Impala
Thomson's Gazelle
Grant's Gazelle
Gerenuk
Fringe-eared Oryx
Bushbuck
Lesser Kudu
Eland
African Buffalo
African Hare
Porcupine Nocturnal: seldom seen
Striped Ground Squirrel
Unstriped Ground Squirrel
Bush Squirrel
Spring Hare
African Dormouse
Kenya Mole Rat

BIRDS OF AMBOSELI MASAI GAME RESERVE

Masai Ostrich *19 Not uncommon on the plains
Little Grebe *20
White-necked Cormorant *20 Uncommon visitor
Long-tailed Cormorant *21
African Darter *21
White Pelican *22
Pink-backed Pelican *22 Spasmodic visitors in varying numbers
Grey Heron *23
Black-headed Heron *23
Goliath Heron *23
Purple Heron *24
Great White Egret *24
Yellow-billed Egret *25
Little Egret *25
Buff-backed Heron or Cattle Egret *26

Squacco Heron *26
Madagascar Squacco Heron *26 A non-breeding visitor in small numbers. Generally observed in Loginya swamps
Green-backed Heron *26
Night Heron *27
Little Bittern *27
Dwarf Bittern *27
(The best place to look for herons and egrets is in the swamps below Observation Hill and along the edges of Loginya swamp east of Ol Tukai Lodge.)
Hammerkop *28
White Stork *29 Winter visitor and passage migrant in flocks of varying numbers

European Black Stork *29 Rare winter visitor
Woolly-necked Stork *29 Rare visitor
Abdim's Stork *29 Spasmodic visitor, sometimes in large flocks. Plains
Open-bill Stork *30 Visitor in small numbers
Saddle-bill Stork *30 Resident in small numbers. Usually seen in Loginya Swamp
Marabou Stork *31
Wood Ibis or Yellow-billed Stork *31
Sacred Ibis *31
Hadada Ibis *34
Glossy Ibis *34 Rare visitor
African Spoonbill *34

Greater Flamingo *35
Lesser Flamingo *35 Flamingos occur as vagrants, never in large numbers
White-backed Duck *36
African Pochard *37
Tufted Duck *37 Rare winter visitor
European Shoveler *37
Yellow-billed Duck *38
Garganey Teal *38
Hottentot Teal *39
Red-billed Duck *39
European Pintail *39
White-faced Tree Duck *40 Uncommon visitor
Fulvous Tree Duck *40
Knob-billed Goose *41
Egyptian Goose *41
Spur-winged Goose *41
Secretary Bird *42
Ruppell's Griffon Vulture *42
White-backed Vulture *43
Lappet-faced Vulture *43
White-headed Vulture *43
Egyptian Vulture *44
Hooded Vulture *43
Peregrine *45 Visitor in small numbers
Lanner *45 Visitor in small numbers, but commoner than Peregrine
Teita Falcon *46 Rare visitor. Has habit of perching high in dead acacia trees
European Hobby *46 Uncommon spring passage migrant
European Kestrel *47 Winter visitor
Greater or White-eyed Kestrel *47 Resident in small numbers, mainly Namanga area
Lesser Kestrel *50 Winter visitor and passage migrant
Pygmy Falcon *51 Most frequent acacia bush country towards Namanga
European Black Kite *51
African Black Kite *51

Black-shouldered Kite *51
Bat Hawk *46 Occurs near Namanga. Probably overlooked on account of its crepuscular habits
Honey Buzzard *62 Rare visitor, usually in April/May
Steppe Eagle *55 Winter visitor in small numbers. Has habit of perching on ground on open plains
Tawny Eagle *54
Wahlberg's Eagle *55
African Hawk Eagle *55
Booted Eagle 232 Rare winter visitor
Martial Eagle *56
Crowned Hawk Eagle *57 Recorded a few times: usually immature birds
Long-crested Hawk Eagle *57
Lizard Buzzard *57
Brown Harrier Eagle *55, *58
Black-chested Harrier Eagle *58
Southern Banded Harrier Eagle *58 Single record of pair in acacia woodland south of Observation Hill
Grasshopper Buzzard *58 Non-breeding visitor Mainly in bush country on Emali road
Bateleur *59
African Fish Eagle *59
Steppe Buzzard *62 Winter visitor in varying numbers
Augur Buzzard *63
Little Sparrow Hawk *63
Shikra *66
Gabar Goshawk *67
Pale Chanting Goshawk *68
Montagu's Harrier *68
Pallid Harrier *69
European Marsh Harrier *69
African Marsh Harrier *69
Harrier Hawk *70

Osprey *70 Rare visitor
Coqui Francolin *71
Crested Francolin *71
Shelley's (Greywing) Francolin *72
Yellow-necked Spurfowl *76
Harlequin Quail *76
Helmeted Guinea-fowl *77
Vulturine Guinea-Fowl *78
Kaffir Rail *79 Sometimes seen in swamp near Simek Causeway
Black Crake *79
Moorhen *83
Red-knobbed Coot *83
Crowned Crane *86
Kori Bustard *87
Jackson's Bustard *88 Plains. The rarest of the Amboseli bustards
White-bellied Bustard *88
Buff-crested Bustard *89 Not uncommon in dry bush country
Black-bellied Bustard *89
Hartlaub's Bustard *89
Spotted Stone Curlew *89
Water Dikkop *90
African Jacana *90
Ringed Plover *91
Little Ringed Plover *91
Kittlitz's Sand Plover *94
Three-banded Plover *94
Caspian Plover *95 Winter visitor in flocks. Open plains
Grey Plover *95 Rare winter visitor
Crowned Lapwing *98
Senegal Plover *98 Rare visitor in small numbers. Open plains
Blacksmith Plover *100
Long-toed Lapwing *101 Swamps. Walks on floating aquatic vegetation in manner of jacana
Avocet *101
Black-winged Stilt *102
Painted Snipe *103
European Common Snipe *104

Dark-capped Bulbul *188
Northern Brownbul 21
European Spotted Flycatcher *190
Dusky Flycatcher *190
Banded Tit-Flycatcher 22
Grey Flycatcher *191
South African Black Flycatcher *191
Silverbird *194
Chin-spot Flycatcher *194
Black-throated Wattle-eye *195
Paradise Flycatcher *195
Olive Thrush *196
Bare-eyed Thrush *196/197
Occurs in arid bush country
European Rock Thrush *197
European Common Wheatear *198
Isabelline Wheatear *198
Pied Wheatear *198
Schalow's Wheatear *198
Found near Namanga
Capped Wheatear *198
Cliff Chat 23   Occurs on Oldoinyo Orok
Anteater Chat *199
European Whinchat *200
White-browed Robin Chat *200
Red-capped Robin Chat *201
Robin Chat *201
Spotted Morning Warbler *202
Red-back Scrub Robin *202
White-winged Scrub Robin *202
White-throated Robin 23
Single record near Ol Tukai: may be overlooked
European Nightingale 286
Winter visitor in small numbers
Sprosser 286   Winter visitor, commoner than nightingale
European Whitethroat 290
Garden Warbler *204
Blackcap Warbler *204

Barred Warbler 290
Great Reed Warbler 287
Passage migrant in spring
European Sedge Warbler 290
Greater Swamp Warbler 24
Resident in small numbers
European Willow Warbler *205
Grey Wren Warbler *205
Black-breasted Apalis *206
Red-faced   Apalis   24
Occurs in arid bush areas
Grey-capped Warbler *206
Buff-bellied Warbler *207
Crombec *207
Red-faced Crombec *207
Yellow-bellied Eremomela *207
Grey-backed Camaroptera *210
Pectoral-patch Cisticola *210
Rattling Cisticola *211
Winding Cisticola 294
Tawny-flanked Prinia *211
European Swallow *212
Angola Swallow *212
Wire-tailed Swallow *212
Red-rumped Swallow *213
Mosque Swallow *213
Striped Swallow *213
Grey-rumped Swallow *213
European   Sand   Martin *214
African Sand Martin *214
Banded Martin *214
African Rock Martin *214
Occurs near Namanga
Black Rough-wing Swallow *215
White-headed Rough-wing Swallow *215
Black Cuckoo Shrike *215
Drongo *216
Straight-crested   Helmet Shrike *217
White-crowned Shrike *218
Northern Brubru *219
Grey-backed Fiscal *220
Lesser Grey Shrike *220
Passage   migrant   late March/April

Fiscal Shrike *219   Namanga area
Teita Fiscal   *220   Dry bush country
Long-tailed Fiscal *220
Red-backed Shrike *221
Red-tailed Shrike *221
Slate-coloured Boubou *222
Tropical Boubou *222
Undergrowth in acacia woodland
Black-backed Puff-back *223
Black-headed Bush Shrike *223
Brown-headed Bush Shrike *223
Sulphur-breasted Bush Shrike *224
Grey-headed Bush Shrike *225
Rosy-patched Shrike *225
Grey Tit *225
White-breasted Tit *226
Red-throated Tit 27
African Penduline Tit *226
European Golden Oriole *227
African Golden Oriole *227
Black-headed Oriole *227
Pied Crow *230
White-naped Raven *230
Wattled Starling *231
Often perch on zebra in manner of oxpeckers
Violet-backed Starling *232
Blue-eared Glossy Starling *232
Ruppell's Long-tailed Starling *233
Red-winged Starling *234
Namanga area
Fischer's Starling 29
Hildebrandt's Starling *235
Superb Starling *235
Red-billed Oxpecker *235
Yellow White-eye *238
Bronzy   Sunbird   *242
Namanga area
Beautiful Sunbird (black-bellied race) *243
Mariqua Sunbird *244

Variable Sunbird *244
Amethyst Sunbird *245
Mainly in Namanga area
Scarlet-chested Sunbird
*246 Mainly in Namanga
area
Hunter's Sunbird 30 Main-
ly in dry bush in eastern
section
Olive Sunbird 30 Occurs
around Namanga
Collared Sunbird *247
Kenya Violet-backed Sun-
bird 29
Buffalo Weaver *248
White-headed Buffalo
Weaver *249
White-browed Sparrow
Weaver *249
Grey-headed Social Weaver
*250
Kenya Rufous Sparrow
* 250
Swahili Sparrow 322
Parrot-billed Sparrow 322
Chestnut Sparrow 31
Yellow-spotted Petronia 29
Speckle-fronted Weaver 29
Layard's Black-headed
Weaver *251
Speke's Weaver *251
Masked Weaver *252
Vitelline Masked Weaver
*252
Chestnut Weaver *253
Taveta Golden Weaver 31

Black-necked Weaver *254
Spectacled Weaver *255
Holub's Golden Weaver
*255
Reichenow's Weaver *258
Near Namanga
Grosbeak Weaver *259
Swamps
Red-headed Weaver *259
Red-billed Quelea *259
Cardinal Quelea *260
Yellow Bishop *261
Yellow-crowned Bishop 32
Spasmodic in appearance:
turns up in swampy hol-
lows in years when heavy
rains have fallen
Fan-tailed Widow-bird *262
White-winged Widow-bird
*262
Bronze Mannikin *264
Silver-bill 27
Grey-headed Silver-bill 27
Frequents dry acacia bush
Cut-throat *264
Quail Finch 27 Frequents
marshy spots on open
plains
Parasitic Weaver 336
Spasmodic in appearance:
occurs only in seasons of
heavy rains
Green-winged Pytilia *264
African Fire Finch *265
Common around Nam-
anga

Jameson's Fire Finch *265
Red-billed Fire Finch *265
Yellow-bellied Waxbill
*266
Waxbill *266
Crimson-rumped Waxbill
*266
Black-cheeked Waxbill 28
Black-faced Waxbill 28
Red-cheeked Cordon-bleu
*266
Blue-capped Cordon-bleu
*267
Purple Grenadier *267
Purple Indigo-finch 28
Pin-tailed Whydah *267
Steel-blue Whydah *267
Dry bush country near
Namanga
Fischer's Straw-tailed
Whydah *267
Paradise Whydah *268
Yellow-fronted Canary
*269
White-bellied Canary 28
Brimstone Canary *268
Kenya Grosbeak Canary
340
Yellow-rumped Seed-eater
*269
Streaky Seed-eater *269
Golden-breasted Bunting
*270
Cinnamon-breasted Rock
Bunting *270

MOUNT KENYA NATIONAL PARK

The Mount Kenya National Park was established in 1949 and covers an area of 227 square miles, the park boundary being the 11,000 feet contour. It comprises small sections of the higher forest and bamboo-hypericum zone, alpine moorlands, glaciers, tarns and glacial moraines. It is dominated by the twin peaks of the mountain, Batian (17,058 feet) and Nelion (17,022 feet).

The visitor to the Mount Kenya National Park does not need to be an experienced mountaineer, and access to the alpine moorlands is easy via the Sirimon Track which branches to the right off the main Nanyuki-Isiolo road a few miles north of Nanyuki: but a four-wheel-drive vehicle is necessary to negotiate the rough surface and steep inclines. The trail passes through magnificent stands of juniper and podocarpus before reaching the high altitude bamboo forest with mighty gorges, sylvan glades and trout streams. Elephant and Buffalo are common, and Black Rhino exist but are not often seen. In the early morning there are always Bushbuck and Bush Duiker in evidence and the expectation of Leopard and the elusive Bongo if one is very lucky.

Birds are not over abundant in the forest, but sometimes Ayres' Hawk Eagle and the Crowned Hawk Eagle may be seen soaring over their hunting grounds. The Red-headed Parrot and Hartlaub's Turaco frequent fruiting podocarpus trees, whilst two forest francolins, Jackson's Francolin and Scaly Francolin, scuttle away into the undergrowth as your vehicle approaches. The rare Mount Kenya race of the Green Ibis feeds in marshy forest glades and another great rarity, the Abyssinian Long-eared Owl, has been recorded from the high forest near the Sirimon Track.

The high altitude forest merges into the bamboo zone, and this in turn changes into hypericum scrub before the moorlands are reached. When in flower the hypericum trees are a glory of golden yellow blossoms and alive with brightly hued sunbirds.

Two interesting small mammals live in this zone. Here and there in the glades there are large "mole hills" thrown up by some fossorial animal—the giant Mount Kenya Mole Rat. In more shady places, and especially where moss grows on the ground, slightly raised earth outlines the tunnels of another burrower: it is the Mount Kenya Mole Shrew, a species known only from this mountain although a closely related form occurs on the Aberdare range.

The flora of the alpine moorlands of Mount Kenya is outstanding with its giant Senecios, Lobelias and Heaths and many colourful true alpines. Two species of giant Lobelias are common, the narrow, feathery-leafed *Lobelia telekii* and the broad leafed *Lobelia keniensis*. Scarlet-tufted Malachite Sunbirds feed at the half-hidden blossoms and Slender-billed Chestnut-wing Starlings search the plant for the thin-shelled snails which make their home there. Among the smaller plants are a tiny mauve crocus-like flower, *Romulea keniensis*, two terrestrial orchids, a *Disa* and a *Habenaria*, and an orange flowered gladiolus, *Gladiolus watsonioides*.

The most interesting larger mammal on the Mount Kenya moorlands is the Black-fronted Duiker, which is local but by no means rare. Among the birds are the Montane Francolin, the tame, almost robin-like Mountain Chat and the finest of East African owls, Mackinder's Eagle Owl. Alpine Swifts nest on certain crags, often associated with a much rarer species the Scarce Swift.

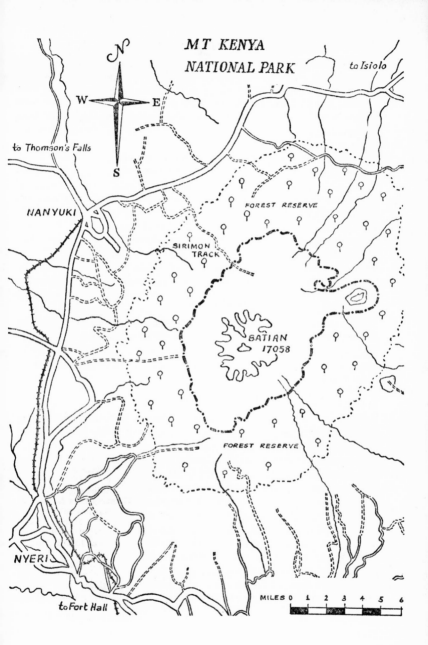

MT KENYA
NATIONAL PARK

N
W   E
S

to Isiolo

to Thomson's Falls

NANYUKI

FOREST RESERVE

SIRIMON
TRACK

BATIAN
17058

FOREST RESERVE

NYERI

to Fort Hall

MILES 0   1   2   3   4   5   6

Expeditions on the mountain, using mules as pack animals, are organised by a firm specialising in mountain safaris, and if you are a mountaineer use of the alpine huts can be booked through the Mountain Club of Kenya. For the visitor who just wishes to spend a day or so on the mountain, first class hotel accommodation is available in and near Nanyuki, 123 miles north of Nairobi.

MAMMALS OF MOUNT KENYA NATIONAL PARK

Mole Shrew Burrows just below surface of ground in bamboo zone
Banana Bat or African Pipistrelle Recorded from high level forest
Sykes' Monkey Occurs in forest just below bamboo zone.
Olive Baboon
Black and White Colobus
Hunting Dog
Black-backed or Silver-backed Jackal
Side-striped Jackal
Clawless Otter In streams in forest
African Civet
Bush or Large-spotted

Genet
Slender or Black-tipped Mongoose
Spotted Hyaena
African Wild Cat
Serval
Lion Reputed to occur at times, but no recent records
Leopard
Tree Hyrax
Rock Hyrax
African Elephant In forest
Black Rhinoceros In forest
Burchell's or Common Zebra
Giant Forest Hog
Bush Pig

Red Duiker In forest
Black-fronted Duiker In bamboo zone and on moorlands
Bush Duiker
Klipspringer
Suni
Chanler's Reedbuck Reputed to occur
Bongo Extremely shy and seldom seen: mainly in upper levels of forest and in bamboo zone
Bushbuck
African Buffalo In forest
Porcupine
African Dormouse
Crested Rat
Mt. Kenya Mole Rat

BIRDS OF MOUNT KENYA NATIONAL PARK

White Stork *29 Once recorded on alpine moorlands
Green Ibis *34 Occurs in meadows bordering mountain streams in forest. Rare
African Black Duck *38 Occurs on mountain streams and tarns
Secretary Bird *42 Has been recorded on moorlands. Rare
Ruppell's Griffon Vulture *42
Peregrine *45
Lanner *45
European Kestrel *47
Lesser Kestrel *50 Occurs in small numbers on

moorlands during migration
Cuckoo Falcon *67 In forest
European Black Kite *51
African Black Kite *51 Probably migrants. Occur spasmodically on moorlands and above forest
Verreaux's Eagle *54
Steppe Eagle *55
Ayres' Hawk Eagle *56 In forest
Crowned Hawk Eagle *57 In forest
Long-crested Hawk Eagle *57
Lammergeyer *44 Seen from time to time and may nest

Steppe Buzzard *62
Eastern Steppe Buzzard *62 Rare
Mountain Buzzard *62
Augur Buzzard *63
Rufus-breasted Sparrow Hawk *66 Occurs in forest and bamboo zone
Great Sparrow Hawk *66
African Goshawk *67
Montagu's Harrier *68
Pallid Harrier *69
European Marsh Harrier *69 The three harriers occur on the moorlands during migration: rare at other times
Montane Francolin 14 On moorlands
Scaly Francolin *74

Jackson's Francolin *74
Cape Quail *76
Black-winged Plover *99
Uncommon visitor to moorlands
European Common Snipe *104
Great Snipe *104 Mainly on spring migration
African Snipe *104
Jack Snipe *104 Rare winter visitor and passage migrant
Green Sandpiper *107
Greenshank *109
Olive Pigeon *119 Forest species
Bronze-naped Pigeon *119
Pink-breasted Dove *120
Red-eyed Dove *120
Lemon Dove 16
Green Pigeon *122
Red-chested Cuckoo *123
Emerald Cuckoo *125
Klaas' Cuckoo *126
Hartlaub's Turaco *131 In forest
Red-headed Parrot *133 In forest
Giant Kingfisher *138 On forest streams
Cinnamon-chested Bee-eater 19 In forest
Silvery-cheeked Hornbill *147 In forest
Crowned Hornbill *149
White-headed Wood Hoo-poe *152
Cape Grass Owl *153 In marshy hollows on moor-lands
Abyssinian Long-eared Owl 15 Occurs rarely in both upper forest and bamboo zone, and in thickets on moorlands
African Marsh Owl *154 Moorlands
African Wood Owl *154 In forest
Mackinder's Eagle Owl 15 Occurs along cliffs on

moorlands: several pairs live in Teleki Valley
Abyssinian Nightjar *157
Golden-rumped Tinker-bird *168
Fine-banded Woodpecker *172
Nyanza Swift *174
Scarce Swift 16 Probably nests in crags on alpine moorlands
Alpine Swift *175
Mottled Swift *175
Mountain Wagtail *183 Occurs on streams
European Grey Wagtail *183
Red-throated Pipit *185
Abyssinian Hill Babbler 21
Dark-capped Bulbul *188
Olive-breasted Mountain Greenbul 21
Yellow-whiskered Greenbul *189
Dusky Flycatcher *190
White-eyed Slaty Fly-catcher *191
Mountain Yellow Fly-catcher 278
Black-throated Wattle-eye *195
Paradise Flycatcher *195
Olive Thrush *196
Orange Ground Thrush 282 Occurs mainly on eastern side of mountain
Abyssinian Ground Thrush 23
European Rock Thrush *197 Uncommon mi-grant
Little Rock Thrush *197
European Common Wheat-ear *198
Capped Wheatear *198
Hill or Mountain Chat 23
Stonechat *200
Ruppell's Robin Chat *201
Robin Chat *201
White-starred Bush Robin *203 Common in bam-boo zone

Blackcap Warbler *204
Cinnamon Bracken Warb-ler *204
European Willow Warbler *205
Brown Woodland Warbler *205
Grey Apalis 24
Black-throated Apalis *206
Chestnut-throated Apalis 24
Hunter's Cisticola 24
European Swallow *212 Uncommon on migration
African Sand Martin *214
African Rock Martin *214
Black Rough-wing Swallow *214
White-headed Rough-wing Swallow *215
Tropical Boubou *222 Sometimes reaches upper levels of forest
White-breasted Tit *226
Black-winged Oriole 302
White-naped Raven *230
Sharpe's Starling *232
Slender-billed Chestnut-wing Starling 29
Kenrick's Starling 308
Kikuyu White-eye *238
Malachite Sunbird *239
Scarlet-tufted Malachite Sunbird 30
Tacazze Sunbird *242
Golden-winged Sunbird *243
Eastern Double-collared Sunbird *245
Reichenow's Weaver *258
Brown-capped Weaver 31
Grey-headed Negro Finch 32
Abyssinian Crimson-wing 32 Common in bamboo zone
Yellow-bellied Waxbill *266
Black-headed Waxbill 28
Yellow-crowned Canary 28
Streaky Seed-eater *269
Thick-billed Seed-eater 28
Oriole Finch 340

MARA MASAI GAME RESERVE

The Mara Game Reserve, an area of some 700 square miles, was established in 1961. Its southern boundary is contiguous with Tanzania's Serengeti National Park, and it is divided into two sections. The inner reserve of 200 square miles has been developed on the lines of a National Park, no intrusion of human settlement being allowed, while the outer remains an undeveloped area where local Masai are permitted to pasture their cattle but which is otherwise undisturbed.

The Mara country is world famous for its vast assemblages of plains game together with their associated predators. It is perhaps the only region left in Kenya where the visitor may see animals in the same super-abundance as existed a century ago.

The Reserve extends from the edge of the Loita Hills in the east to the Mara Triangle and the base of the Siria Escarpment in the west. The inner section, with its network of roads specially constructed for game watching, embraces the area around the Keekorok Lodge and westwards to the Mara River.

Everything is big in Mara. It is a country of breath-taking vistas, a panorama of vast rolling plains and rounded hills, of intermittent groves of acacia woodlands and dense thickets of scrub. The whole is bisected by the Mara River and its tributaries which are margined by luxuriant riverine forest. And in every direction, there are the seemingly endless herds of game animals.

Mara possesses the largest population of lions to be found in Kenya, and also boasts large herds of Topi and a small population of Roan Antelope, animals not found in any other Kenya National Park or Reserve. Elephants are common and the traveller is often held up by "elephants on the road."

Among the great variety of other large beasts are Buffalo, Black Rhino, Hippopotamus, Leopard, Cheetah, Common Zebra, Coke's Hartebeest, White-bearded Gnu, Oribi, Warthog, and Thomson's and Grant's Gazelles.

The bird life of Mara is as profuse as its mammalian fauna. The red-winged Schalow's Turaco with its attenuated white-tipped crest is common along the numerous wooded watercourses, and in the more extensive riverine forest there is also Ross's Turaco. The Mara River is also the home of the great orange-buff African Fishing Owl and of flocks of wary Crested Guinea-fowl.

On the open plains there is a variety of bustards including the large

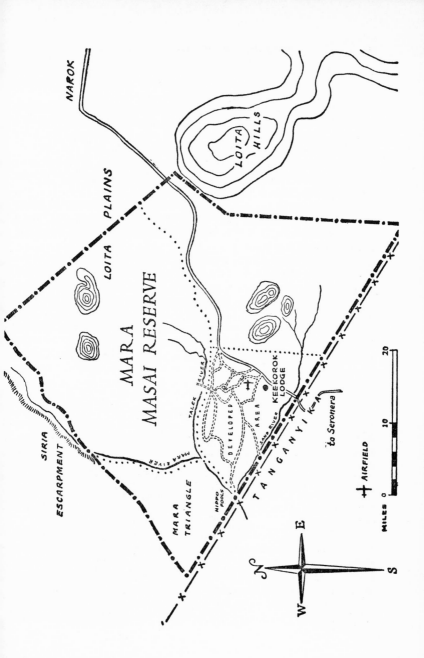

Jackson's Bustard and the black-bellied Hartlaub's Bustard. The latter during nuptial display soars high in the air, then with rigid wings descends slowly to earth like a pricked balloon.

Birds of prey are abundant, and no less than fifty-three different species have so far been recorded. Secretary Birds are a common sight as they stalk sedately over the grasslands, and in the sky there are always vultures and that effortless flier the Bateleur.

Accommodation in Mara Game Reserve is at Keekorok Lodge, which is 165 miles from Nairobi on a road quite negotiable by saloon cars. The route is via the Nairobi-Naivasha road, turning left at mile thirty-five; thence to Narok, sixty-four miles, and then sixty-six miles to the Lodge through some of the best game country in Kenya. In the undeveloped part of the Mara Reserve a limited number of camp sites are available, but the numbers of campers allowed into the reserve is strictly limited to avoid disturbance to the game.

MAMMALS OF MARA MASAI GAME RESERVE

Spectacled Elephant Shrew
East African Hedgehog
Giant White-toothed Shrew
Straw-coloured Fruit Bat
Rousette Fruit Bat
Epauletted Fruit Bat
Pale-bellied Fruit Bat
Hollow-faced Bat
False Vampire Bat
Yellow-winged Bat
Lander's Horseshoe Bat
Lesser Leaf-nosed Bat
Banana Bat or African Pipistrelle
Yellow-bellied Bat
Angola Free-tailed Bat
White-bellied Free-tailed Bat
Greater Galago
Bush Baby
Black-faced Vervet
Blue or Sykes' Monkey
Red-tailed or White-nosed Monkey
Patas Monkey
Olive Baboon
Black and White Colobus
Lesser Ground Pangolin
Hunting Dog
Golden Jackal

Black-backed or Silver-backed Jackal
Side-striped Jackal
Bat-eared Fox
Zorilla
Ratel or Honey Badger
Clawless Otter
African Civet
Neumann's or Small-spotted Genet
Bush or Large-spotted Genet
African Palm Civet
Marsh Mongoose
Dwarf Mongoose
Large Grey Mongoose
Slender or Black-tipped Mongoose
White-tailed Mongoose
Banded Mongoose
Aard-wolf
Spotted Hyaena
Striped Hyaena
Cheetah
African Wild Cat
Serval
Lion
Leopard
Ant Bear
Tree Hyrax
Rock Hyrax

African Elephant
Black Rhinoceros
Burchell's or Common Zebra
Hippopotamus
Giant Forest Hog
Warthog
Bush Pig
Masai Giraffe
Coke's Hartebeest or Kongoni
White-bearded Gnu or Wildebeest
Topi
Red Duiker
Blue Duiker
Bush Duiker
Klipspringer
Suni
Oribi
Steinbok
Kirk's Dik-Dik
Defassa Waterbuck
Bohor Reedbuck
Impala
Thomson's Gazelle
Grant's Gazelle Some examples approach the race *robertsi* with outward growing horns
Roan Antelope

Bushbuck
Eland
African Buffalo
African Hare
Cane Rat

Porcupine
Striped Ground Squirrel
Unstriped Ground Squirrel
Bush Squirrel
Giant Forest Squirrel

Spring Hare
African Dormouse
Kenya Mole Rat

BIRDS OF MARA MASAI GAME RESERVE

Masai Ostrich *19
Little Grebe *20
Long-tailed Cormorant *21
African Darter *21
Black-headed Heron *23
Yellow-billed Egret *25
Little Egret *25
Buff-backed Heron or
Cattle Egret *26
Squacco Heron *26
Green-backed Heron *26
Not uncommon on well-
wooded rivers
Night Heron *27
Hammerkop *28
White Stork *29
European Black Stork *30
Single birds recorded most
years
Woolly-necked Stork *29
Rare
Abdim's Stork *29 Num-
bers vary greatly
Open-bill Stork *30 Un-
common
Saddle-bill Stork *30
Marabou Stork *31
Wood Ibis or Yellow-billed
Stork *31
Sacred Ibis *31
Hadada Ibis *34
African Black Duck *38
Garganey Teal *38
Hottentot Teal *39
Red-billed Duck *39
Knob-billed Goose *41
Egyptian Goose *41
Spur-winged Goose *41
Secretary Bird *42
Ruppell's Griffon Vulture
*42
White-backed Vulture *43
Lappet-faced Vulture *43
White-headed Vulture *43
Egyptian Vulture *44

Hooded Vulture *43
Peregrine *45
Lanner *45
European Hobby *46
Mainly spring passage mi-
grant
African Hobby *46 Rare
European Kestrel *47
White-eyed Kestrel *47
Occurs on open plains with
scattered thorn trees
Lesser Kestrel *50
Grey Kestrel *50
Pygmy Falcon *51
Cuckoo Falcon *67
Occurs in thick riverine
forest. Uncommon
European Black Kite *51
African Black Kite *51
Black-shouldered Kite *51
Bat Hawk *46 Recorded
on the Mara River, hunt-
ing bats over the water,
and near Keekorok Lodge
Honey Buzzard *62 Rare
winter visitor
Steppe Eagle *55
Tawny Eagle *54
Wahlberg's Eagle *55
African Hawk Eagle *55
Rare resident
Booted Eagle 232 Rare
winter visitor
Martial Eagle *56 Occurs
in open country with
scattered trees
Crowned Hawk-eagle *57
Occurs in riverine forest
Long-crested Hawk-eagle
*57
Lizard Buzzard *57
Brown Harrier Eagle *55,
*58
Black-chested Harrier
Eagle *58

Banded Harrier Eagle *58
One record from Mara
River
Bateleur *59
African Fish Eagle *59
Lammergeyer *44 Rare
visitor
Steppe Buzzard *62
Eastern Steppe Buzzard
*62 Rare winter visitor
Augur Buzzard *63
Little Sparrow Hawk *63
Ovampo Sparrow Hawk
*66 Rare: two records
only
Great Sparrow Hawk *66
Shikra *66
African Goshawk *67
Mainly in riverine forest
Gabar Goshawk *67
Pale Chanting Goshawk
*68
Dark Chanting Goshawk
*68
Montagu's Harrier *68
Pallid Harrier *69
European Marsh Harrier
*69
African Marsh Harrier *69
Uncommon visitor
Harrier Hawk *70
Osprey *70 Rare: a few
records from the Mara
River
Coqui Francolin *71
Crested Francolin *71
Shelley's (Grey-wing)
Francolin *72
Hildebrandt's Francolin
*73 Common around
Keekorok Lodge
Scaly Francolin *74
Forest
Yellow-necked Spurfowl
*76

Cape Quail *76

Harlequin Quail *76

Blue Quail *77 Uncommon and local. Mainly in western area of Reserve

Helmeted Guinea-fowl *77

Crested Guinea-fowl *78 In thick riverine forest. Uncommon

European Corn Crake *79 Uncommon passage migrant

African Crake *79 Occurs in long grass. Uncommon

Black Crake *79

White-spotted Pygmy Crake *82 Recorded in forest along Mara River

Peters' Finfoot *86

Crowned Crane *86

Kori Bustard *87

Jackson's Bustard *88

White-bellied Bustard *88

Black-bellied Bustard *89 Rarer than Hartlaub's Bustard

Hartlaub's Bustard *89

Spotted Stone Curlew *90

Water Dikkop *90 Occurs along all the rivers. Mainly nocturnal

African Jacana *90

Little Ringed Plover *91 Uncommon migrant

Kittlitz's Sand Plover *94

Three-banded Plover *94

Caspian Plover *95 Numbers vary from year to year. Sometimes present in large flocks on open plains

Crowned Lapwing or Plover *98

Senegal Plover *98

Black-winged Plover *99 Uncommon visitor

Blacksmith Plover *100

Brown-chested Wattled Plover *99 Recorded but not confirmed: probably rare visitor. Often associates with Senegal Plover on open plains

Wattled Plover *100 Uncommon

Avocet *101 Vagrant in years of heavy rains

Black-winged Stilt *102 Uncommon

Painted Snipe *103

European Common Snipe *104

Great Snipe *104 Spring migrant in small numbers

African Snipe *104

Ruff *106

Common Sandpiper *107

Green Sandpiper *107 Found on rivers and streams

Wood Sandpiper *107

Temminck's Courser *110

Two-banded Courser *111

Heuglin's Courser *110

Bronze-winged Courser *98, *111

Pratincole *111

Button Quail *116

Chestnut-bellied Sandgrouse *117

Black-faced Sandgrouse *118

Yellow-throated Sandgrouse *118

Speckled Pigeon *119

Olive Pigeon *119 In riverine forest. Uncommon

Red-eyed Dove *120

Mourning Dove *121

Ring-necked Dove *120

Laughing Dove *121

Namaqua Dove *121

Tambourine Dove *122

Blue-spotted Wood Dove *122 Mainly in western part of Reserve

Emerald-spotted Wood Dove *121

Green Pigeon *122

European Cuckoo *123

African Cuckoo *123

Red-chested Cuckoo *123

Black Cuckoo *124

Great-spotted Cuckoo *124

Levaillant's Cuckoo *124

Black and White Cuckoo *124

Emerald Cuckoo *125

Didric Cuckoo *125

Klaas' Cuckoo *126

Blue-headed Coucal *127

Senegal Coucal 238 In western areas of Reserve. Uncommon in bush country

White-browed Coucal *126

Green Coucal or Yellowbill *127 Lives in creeper festooned trees in riverine forest

Schalow's Turaco 17 Not uncommon in riverine forest

Ross's Turaco *131 Recorded in riverine forest along Mara River

Eastern Grey Plantaineater 17

White-bellied Go-awaybird *132

Bare-faced Go-away-bird 17

Brown Parrot *134

European Roller *135

Lilac-breasted Roller *136

Rufous-crowned Roller *136

Broad-billed Roller *137

Pied Kingfisher *137

Giant Kingfisher *138 Recorded on Mara River

Malachite Kingfisher *138

Pygmy Kingfisher *139

Woodland Kingfisher *139

Brown-hooded Kingfisher 5

Grey-headed Kingfisher *140

Striped Kingfisher *140

European Bee-eater *140

Madagascar Bee-eater 19 Uncommon visitor in small numbers

Blue-cheeked Bee-eater 19 Winter visitor and passage migrant. Often associated with European Bee-eater

White-throated Bee-eater *142

Little Bee-eater *142
Cinnamon-chested Bee-eater 19 Forested areas
Blue-breasted Bee-eater 19
White-fronted Bee-eater *143
Black and White-casqued Hornbill *147
Grey Hornbill *147
Red-billed Hornbill *148
Von der Decken's Hornbill *149
Crowned Hornbill *149
Ground Hornbill *150
European Hoopoe *151 Uncommon passage migrant
African Hoopoe *151
Green Wood Hoopoe *152
Scimitar-bill*153
Abyssinian Scimitar-bill *152
African Marsh Owl *154
African Wood Owl *154
African Scops Owl *154
White-faced Scops Owl *154
Pearl-spotted Owlet *155
Spotted Eagle Owl *155
Verreaux's Eagle Owl *155
African Fishing Owl *156 Recorded from the Mara River. Rare
European Nightjar *156
Dusky Nightjar *157
Freckled Nightjar *157 Frequents rocky outcrops
Plain Nightjar *157
White-tailed Nightjar *158 Uncommon. Frequents marshy places
Gaboon Nightjar *158
Pennant-wing Nightjar *158 Uncommon migrant August/September
Long-tailed Nightjar *158
Speckled Mousebird *159
Blue-naped Mousebird *162
Narina's Trogon *163 Inhabits riverine forest. Not uncommon

Double-toothed Barbet *164 Frequents fruiting fig trees
Black-billed Barbet 19 Uncommon. Mainly in western parts of Reserve
White-headed Barbet *165
Brown-throated Barbet *166
Spotted-flanked Barbet *166
Red-fronted Barbet 20 Inhabits acacia woodland
Grey-throated Barbet *166
Yellow-spotted Barbet 20 Rare. In forest along Mara River
Red-fronted Tinker-bird *167
Lemon-rumped Tinker-bird *168
Red and Yellow Barbet *169
D'Arnaud's Barbet *169
Yellow-billed Barbet 20 In forest along Mara River
Greater Honey-guide *170 Common. Bird often attracted by knocking a short length of wood against a tree trunk
Scaly-throated Honey-guide *171
Lesser Honey-guide *171
Wahlberg's Honey-guide *171 Inhabits acacia bush
Cassin's Honey-guide *172 Inhabits riverine forest
Nubian Woodpecker *172
Cardinal Woodpecker *173
Brown-backed Woodpecker *173
Bearded Woodpecker *173
Grey Woodpecker *174
Red-breasted Wryneck *174 Often found in Euphorbia trees
Nyanza Swift *174
Mottled Swift *175
Little Swift *175
White-rumped Swift *175
Palm Swift *178

Boehm's Spinetail *175 One record from country towards Sand River
African Broadbill *179 Occurs in forest along Mara River. Not common
Singing Bush Lark 266
Northern White-tailed Bush Lark 16
Red-winged Bush Lark *180
Rufous-naped Lark *180
Flappet Lark *181
Fawn-coloured Lark 266
Fischer's Sparrow Lark *182
Red-capped Lark *182
African Pied Wagtail *183
Mountain Wagtail *183
Well's Wagtail *183
European Grey Wagtail *183
Blue-headed Wagtail and races *184 Common winter visitors and passage migrants
Long-billed Pipit *185
Plain-backed Pipit 21
Richard's Pipit *184
Tree Pipit *185
Red-throated Pipit *185
Yellow-throated Longclaw *186
Pangani Longclaw *186
Rosy-breasted Longclaw *186 On open plains
Arrow-marked Babbler *187
Black-lored Babbler *187
Northern Pied Babbler *187
Rufous Chatterer *187
Dark-capped Bulbul *188
Bristle-bill 21 In riverine forest along Mara River
Fischer's Greenbul *189
Yellow-whiskered Greenbul *189
European Spotted Flycatcher *190
Dusky Flycatcher *190
Ashy Flycatcher *191
Banded Tit-Flycatcher 22
Brown Tit-Flycatcher 278

Masked Weaver *252
Vitelline Masked Weaver *252
Little Weaver 31
Chestnut Weaver *253
Black-necked Weaver *254
Spectacled Weaver *255
Holub's Golden Weaver *255
Vieillot's Black Weaver *255
Black-billed Weaver 31
Uncommon in riverine forest
Reichenow's Weaver *258
Grosbeak Weaver *259
Red-headed Weaver *259
Red-billed Quelea *259
Red-headed Quelea *260
Uncommon and local. Mainly in western area of Reserve
Cardinal Quelea *260
Red Bishop *260

Black-winged Bishop *261
Yellow Bishop *261
Fan-tailed Widow-bird *262
White-winged Widow-bird *262
Red-naped Widow-bird *262
Jackson's Widow-bird *263
Bronze Mannikin *264
Black and White Mannikin 27
Silver-bill 27
Grey-headed Silver-bill 27
Grey-headed Negro Finch 32
Cut-throat *264
Quail Finch 27
Parasitic Weaver 336
Rare: very few records
Green-backed Twin-spot 335 Occurs in riverine forest. Shy and easily overlooked
Green-winged Pytilia *264

African Fire Finch *265
Red-billed Fire Finch *265
Yellow-bellied Waxbill *266
Waxbill *266
Crimson-rumped Waxbill *266
Red-cheeked Cordon-bleu *266
Purple Grenadier *267
Purple Indigo-bird 28
Pin-tailed Whydah *267
Paradise Whydah *268
Yellow-fronted Canary *269
White-bellied Canary 28
Brimstone Canary *268
Yellow-rumped Seed-eater *269
Streaky Seed-eater *269
Golden-breasted Bunting *270
Cinnamon-breasted Rock Bunting *270

MARSABIT NATIONAL RESERVE

Marsabit National Reserve, an area of some 800 square miles in Kenya's Northern Region, consists of a forested mountain which rises like an oasis in the midst of a desert wilderness, a spectacular group of volcanic craters of which Gof Bongoli is the largest and most dramatic, foothills of rugged grandeur and black lava desert which boasts an impressive list of rare and little-known birds.

Apart from the fascination of visiting a wild and remote region which is still "off the map" to most visitors, the great attractions at Marsabit are its Elephants and its Greater Kudu. This Reserve is one of the very few places where one can still be reasonably certain of seeing elephant with tusks of 100 lbs. and over. Prior to 1960 Greater Kudu also were abundant on Marsabit, but in that year they were greatly reduced by an outbreak of rinderpest. Now, however, their numbers are beginning to build up again and one can be tolerably sure of seeing the animals.

Reticulated Giraffe are common on the mountain, where they have taken to spending much of their time in the forest—a most unlikely habitat for giraffe.

Other interesting animals at Marsabit include the Striped Hyaena—the maniac cackle of its laughing cry is spine-chilling if you are under canvas—

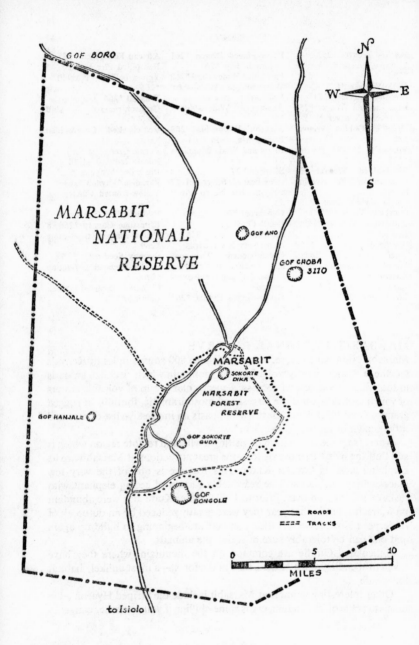

GOF BORO

N
W E
S

MARSABIT
NATIONAL
RESERVE

GOF ANO

GOF CHOBA
3110

MARSABIT

SOKORTE
DIKA

MARSABIT
FOREST
RESERVE

GOF HANJALE

GOF SOKORTE
GUDA

GOF BONGOLE

ROADS
TRACKS

0   5   10

MILES

to Isiolo

and its smaller relative the insectivorous Aard-wolf. The Caracal also occurs, but is seldom seen except on a nocturnal trip into the edge of the Dida Galgalla desert—itself a most rewarding experience.

Some of the craters come within the forest zone, and one, which fills with water during seasons of favourable rains, is the aptly named Lake Paradise made famous by the early films and writings of Martin Johnson and Vivien de Wattville. Most of the water-birds so far recorded at Marsabit have been observed around this lake or at the crater swamp adjacent to Marsabit Lodge.

Immediately north of Marsabit lies that most inhospitable of terrains, the black lava wastes of the great Dida Galgalla desert. A buffer zone of sandy soil with plentiful acacia trees and bush lies between it and the mountain. This area is the home of many ornithological rarities, from the majestic black-faced Heuglin's Bustard and immaculate Somali Ostrich to Swallow-tailed Kites, most graceful of their tribe, Cream-coloured Coursers in abundance, pale green Somali Bee-eaters and the supposedly rare Masked Lark which is the commonest bird in the black lava wastes.

On Marsabit there is always the chance of seeing something really special in the birds of prey line—fifty-two different ones have been recorded—and it is probable that the Lammergeyer nests on the towering cliffs of Gof Bongoli or one of the other craters.

The distance from Isiolo to Marsabit is 168 miles, in other words 348 miles north of Nairobi. As the visitor to Marsabit will have to travel over indifferent roads north of Isiolo and through normally waterless country there are a number of strictly enforced rules with which he must comply. A permit to enter the area must be obtained from Provincial Headquarters at Isiolo; parties must travel in at least two suitable vehicles, and they must be completely self-contained as regards fuel, water and food.

Accommodation at Marsabit is limited to the Marsabit Forest Lodge, sited in the forest near the edge of a shallow crater: the Lodge provides two double bedrooms with beds and mattresses, but not bed linen, and extra (camp) beds are also available. The lodge is run on a "do it yourself" principle, and the visitor must provide and cook his own food. There are camp sites for those who prefer to stay under canvas.

MAMMALS OF MARSABIT NATIONAL RESERVE

Spectacled Elephant Shrew	Pale-bellied Fruit Bat	Lander's Horseshoe Bat
In dry scrub at lower altitudes	White-bellied Tomb Bat	Lesser Leaf-nosed Bat
	Hollow-faced Bat	Banana Bat or African
East African Hedgehog	False Vampire Bat	Pipistrelle
Rousette Fruit Bat	Yellow-winged Bat	Yellow-bellied Bat
Epauletted Fruit Bat	In acacia thickets	Angola Free-tailed Bat

White-bellied Free-tailed Bat
Black-faced Vervet
Blue or Sykes' Monkey
Patas Monkey Reputed to occur but not confirmed
Olive Baboon
Black and White Colobus Reputed to occur, but no recent records
Lesser Ground Pangolin
Hunting Dog
Golden Jackal
Black-backed or Silver-backed Jackal
Side-striped Jackal
Bat-eared Fox
Zorilla
Ratel or Honey Badger
African Civet
Neumann's or Small-spotted Genet
Bush or Large-spotted Genet
Dwarf Mongoose

Large Grey Mongoose
Slender or Black-tipped Mongoose
White-tailed Mongoose
Banded Mongoose
Aard-wolf
Spotted Hyaena
Striped Hyaena
Cheetah Uncommon
Caracal
African Wild Cat
Serval
Lion
Leopard
Ant Bear
African Elephant
Black Rhinoceros
Grevy's Zebra
Warthog
Reticulated Giraffe
Bush Duiker
Klipspringer
Suni
Guenther's Dik-Dik
Grant's Gazelle The race *petersi* in which fawn body

colour extends to root of tail; horns almost parallel
Gerenuk
Beisa Oryx
Bushbuck
Greater Kudu
Lesser Kudu
African Buffalo
African Hare
Porcupine
Striped Ground Squirrel
Unstriped Ground Squirrel
Bush Squirrel
East African Red Squirrel Reputed to occur but not confirmed
Spring Hare Reputed to occur but not confirmed
African Dormouse
Giant Rat
Kenya Mole Rat A mole rat of unknown species occurs on Marsabit
Naked Mole Rat

BIRDS OF MARSABIT NATIONAL RESERVE

Somali Ostrich *19
Little Grebe *20 Recorded on Lake Paradise
Purple Heron *24 Recorded on Lake Paradise
Buff-backed Heron or Cattle Egret *26
Squacco Heron *26
White Stork *29
European Black Stork *30
Abdim's Stork *29
Saddle-bill Stork *30 Rare
Marabou Stork *31
Wood Ibis or Yellow-billed Stork *31
Sacred Ibis *31
Hadada Ibis *34
African Pochard *37 Spasmodic visitor
European Shoveler *37
Yellow-billed Duck *38
Garganey Teal *38
Hottentot Teal *39
Red-billed Duck *39

European Pintail *39
Fulvous Tree Duck *40
Knob-billed Goose *41
Egyptian Goose *41
Spur-wing Goose *41
The numbers of water birds at Marsabit depend on the water level in Lake Paradise: during the occasional years of heavy rains wild-fowl occur commonly
Secretary Bird *42 Rare
Ruppell's Griffon Vulture *42
White-backed Vulture *43
Lappet-faced Vulture *43
White-headed Vulture *43
Egyptian Vulture *44
Hooded Vulture *43
Peregrine *45
Lanner *45
European Hobby *46 Spring migrant

Eastern Red-footed Falcon *50 Occurs on spring migration in small numbers. Usually associated with migrating Lesser Kestrels
European Kestrel *47
African Kestrel *47 Resident in small numbers
White-eyed Kestrel *47
Fox Kestrel *47 Uncommon visitor
Lesser Kestrel *50
Pygmy Falcon *51
Swallow-tailed Kite *54 Spasmodic visitor. Sometimes nests at edge of Dida Galgalla desert north of Marsabit
European Black Kite *51
African Black Kite *51
Black-shouldered Kite *51
Honey Buzzard *62 Uncommon on spring migration

Steppe Eagle *55
Tawny Eagle *54 The very pale cream-coloured phase occurs
African Hawk Eagle *55
Booted Eagle 232 Uncommon migrant and winter visitor
Martial Eagle *56
Crowned Hawk Eagle *57 Reputed to occur but not confirmed
Long-crested Hawk Eagle *57
Lizard Buzzard *57
Brown Harrier Eagle *55, *58
Black-chested Harrier Eagle *58
Spotted Eagle *55 Rare visitor
Lesser Spotted Eagle *55 Rare visitor
Grasshopper Buzzard *58
Bateleur Eagle *59
Lammergeyer *44 Uncommon, but may breed in the cliffs of Gof Bongoli
Steppe Buzzard *62
Eastern Steppe Buzzard *62 Rare visitor
Mountain Buzzard *62 Resident in small numbers
Long-legged Buzzard 232 Rare visitor
Augur Buzzard *63
Rufous-breasted Sparrow Hawk *66
Great Sparrow Hawk *66
Shikra *66
African Goshawk *67
Gabar Goshawk *67
Pale Chanting Goshawk *68
Montagu's Harrier *68
Pallid Harrier *69
European Marsh Harrier *69
Harrier Hawk *70
Crested Francolin *71
Scaly Francolin *74
Yellow-necked Spurfowl *76

Harlequin Quail *76
Stone Partridge *77
Tufted Guinea-fowl *77
Vulturine Guinea-fowl *78
European Corn Crake *79 Uncommon spring migrant
Crowned Crane *86
Kori Bustard *87
Heuglin's Bustard *88 Rare on Marsabit, but common in the Dida Galgalla desert immediately to the north
Buff-crested Bustard *89
Hartlaub's Bustard *89
European Stone Curlew *90 Rare winter visitor
Senegal Stone Curlew *90
Spotted Stone Curlew *89
Caspian Plover *95
Crowned Plover *98
Spurwing Plover *99 Lake Paradise
Blackhead Plover *100
Black-winged Stilt *102
Ruff *106 Uncommon visitor to Lake Paradise
Common Sandpiper *107 Lake Paradise
Wood Sandpiper *107 Lake Paradise
Greenshank *109 Uncommon visitor to Lake Paradise
Cream-coloured Courser *110
Temminck's Courser *110 Much less common than the Cream-coloured Courser
Heuglin's Courser *110
Bronze-winged Courser *98, *111
Pratincole *111 Uncommon visitor to Lake Paradise
Button Quail *116
Chestnut-bellied Sandgrouse *117
Black-faced Sandgrouse *118

Lichtenstein's Sandgrouse *118
Speckled Pigeon *119
Olive Pigeon *119
Pink-breasted Dove *120
Red-eyed Dove *120
Mourning Dove *121
Ring-necked Dove *120
Laughing Dove *121
Namaqua Dove *121
Tambourine Dove *122
Emerald-spotted Wood Dove *121
Bruce's Green Pigeon *122
European Cuckoo *123 Spring migrant
African Cuckoo *123
Red-chested Cuckoo *123
Black Cuckoo *124
Great Spotted Cuckoo *124
Black and White Cuckoo *124
Emerald Cuckoo *125
Didric Cuckoo *125
Klaas' Cuckoo *126
Blue-headed Coucal *127
White-Browed Coucal* 126
Hartlaub's Turaco *131
White-bellied Go-away-bird *132
European Roller *135
Lilac-breasted Roller *136
Rufous-crowned Roller *136
Broad-billed Roller *137
Pygmy Kingfisher *139
Grey-headed Kingfisher *140
Striped Kingfisher *140
European Bee-eater *140
Madagascar Bee-eater 19
Blue-cheeked Bee-eater 19
Carmine Bee-eater *141 Spasmodic visitor, sometimes common
White-throated Bee-eater *142
Little Bee-eater *142
Cinnamon-chested Bee-eater 19
Somali Bee-eater 19 Common in the Dida Galgalla desert north of Marsabit

MERU GAME RESERVE

The Meru Game Reserve, an area of some 700 square miles to the north-east of Mount Kenya, possesses several special attractions for the visitor. Firstly it is part of the domain made famous by Elsa the lioness, whose association with this wild and lovely country is well known through Joy Adamson's books. An excursion to Elsa's camp on the Ura River in the south of the Reserve is well worth while.

Secondly, a section of the Reserve has been designated as a wilderness area, in which there are no roads. The energetic visitor who would explore must proceed on foot, escorted by an experienced ranger guide and with porters to carry camping equipment and food. Such an expedition furnishes the opportunity to experience the pleasures, and perhaps some of the hazards, of a foot safari as it was at the beginning of the century. Approaching elephant, rhino and buffalo under these conditions is a very different proposition to viewing the animals from the safety of a motor vehicle.

The third novelty Meru has to offer is its introduced White Rhinos—the only Park or Reserve in Kenya to possess these animals.

Meru Reserve ranges from 3,400 feet in the foothills of the Nyambeni range, its northern boundary, to less than 1,000 feet on the Tana River in the south-eastern sector. The area is well watered, the main rivers being the Rojerwero, Ura and Tana; all three are margined by dense riverine forest or magnificent stands of dom and raphia palms. Most of the Reserve is covered by bush of varying densities, Combretum bush prevailing in the northern section and Commiphora in the south. The north-eastern quadrant is open dom palm country, grassland and acacia woods, and in the extreme north there is a small patch of rain forest, an outlier of the Ngaia forest.

A well-planned network of roads ensures excellent game-viewing and big game commonly includes Elephant, Black Rhinoceros, Hippopotamus, plentiful in the Rojerwero and Tana Rivers, Reticulated Giraffe, Grevy's and Common Zebra, Grant's Gazelle, Lesser Kudu and Gerenuk. Lion, Leopard and Cheetah may be found and Beisa Oryx are quite plentiful. In addition to game viewing on land, a motor boat suitable for four passengers plus crew is available for anyone wishing to explore the country from the rivers. This is perhaps the best way to locate the shy Peters' Finfoot, a very elusive bird to seek from the river banks.

Birds are abundant and colourful. In dom palm areas the Red-necked Falcon is often to be seen. There are at least three species of Coursers, but

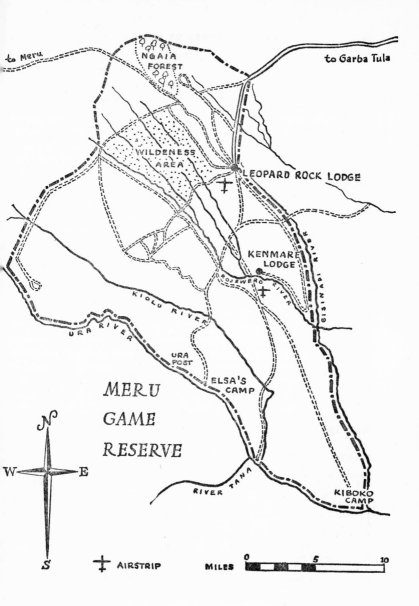

to Meru

to Garba Tula

NGAIA FOREST

WILDENESS AREA

LEOPARD ROCK LODGE

KENMARE LODGE

ROJEWERO RIVER

GISINDI RIVER

KIOLU RIVER

URA RIVER

URA POST

ELSA'S CAMP

MERU GAME RESERVE

RIVER TANA

KIBOKO CAMP

N
W   E
S

✝ AIRSTRIP

MILES 0   5   10

N.P.E.A.

D

one, Heuglin's Courser, is seldom observed on account of its nocturnal habits. The African Fishing Owl almost certainly occurs on the Tana River and campers in this part of the Reserve should listen for its loud blood-curdling cry; an unforgettable sound. Those remarkable birds the honey-guides are represented by four species, and the rare Brown-backed Wood-pecker frequents fig trees along the rivers. The resplendent Golden-breasted Starling is often encountered in flocks, but is usually shy and difficult to approach.

In the acacia woodlands along some of the rivers lives the smallest of the long-tailed Sunbirds, the diminutive Smaller Black-bellied Sunbird, which gathers insects and nectar from the branches of red-flowered parasitic Loranthus growing in the trees.

Accommodation in the Meru Reserve includes Kenmare Safari Lodge with full hotel facilities, and the Leopard Rock Lodge which provides shelter, beds and cooking facilities only. Kenmare Lodge is situated on the Rojerwero River: Leopard Rock Lodge is farther north near the rocky outcrop from which it takes its name. In addition there are camp sites, near the Leopard Rock and in the south on the Tana River.

There are two routes to the Meru Reserve from Nairobi. The first is the main road via Nyeri, Nanyuki and Meru: the second is a dry weather route via Embu to Meru.

From Meru the road is through Mathara and Kangeta towards Maua. After Kangeta and some three miles along the Maua road a left turn on to the Kinna road leads to the Game Reserve gate, where instructions will be given on how to reach Leopard Rock or Kenmare Lodge. The road from Meru is well signposted.

In addition to access by road the visitor can fly to airstrips at Leopard Rock Lodge and at Kenmare Lodge.

MAMMALS OF MERU GAME RESERVE

Spectacled Elephant Shrew	Banana Bat or African	Olive Baboon
East African Hedgehog	Pipistrelle	Lesser Ground Pangolin
Giant White-toothed Shrew	Yellow-bellied Bat	Rare
Rousette Fruit Bat	Angola Free-tailed Bat	Hunting Dog Spasmodic
Epauletted Fruit Bat	White-bellied Free-tailed	visitor
Pale-bellied Fruit Bat	Bat	Black-backed or Silver-
White-bellied Tomb Bat	Flat-headed Free-tailed Bat	backed Jackal
Hollow-faced Bat	Not yet recorded but	Side-striped Jackal
False Vampire Bat	certain to occur	Zorilla
Yellow-winged Bat Hangs	Greater Galago	Ratel or Honey Badger
in acacia thickets during	Bush Baby	Clawless Otter
day	Black-faced Vervet	African Civet
Lander's Horseshoe Bat	Blue or Sykes' Monkey	Neumann's or Small-
Lesser Leaf-nosed Bat	Patas Monkey	spotted Genet

Bush or Large-spotted Genet
Marsh Mongoose
Dwarf Mongoose
Large Grey Mongoose
Banded Mongoose
Aard-wolf
Spotted Hyaena
Striped Hyaena
Cheetah
Caracal
African Wild Cat
Serval
Lion
Leopard
Ant Bear
Tree Hyrax
Rock Hyrax
African Elephant
Black Rhinoceros
Square-lipped or White

Rhinoceros Introduced animals
Grevy's Zebra
Burchell's or Common Zebra
Hippopotamus
Warthog
Bush Pig
Reticulated Giraffe
Coke's Hartebeest or Kongoni
Blue Duiker
Bush Duiker
Suni
Oribi
Steinbok
Kirk's Dik-Dik
Common Waterbuck
Bohor Reedbuck
Impala
Grant's Gazelle

Gerenuk
Beisa Oryx
Bushbuck
Lesser Kudu
Eland
African Buffalo
African Hare
Cane Rat
Porcupine
Striped Ground Squirrel
Unstriped Ground Squirrel
Bush Squirrel
East African Red Squirrel
Riverine woodland along Tana River
Spring Hare
African Dormouse
Giant Rat
Naked Mole Rat

BIRDS OF MERU GAME RESERVE

Somali Ostrich *19
Little Grebe *20
Long-tailed Cormorant *21
African Darter *21
Black-headed Heron *23
Buff-backed Heron or Cattle Egret *26
Green-backed Heron *26 Along rivers
Hammerkop *28
White Stork *29 Spasmodic visitor
Abdim's Stork *29 Uncommon visitor
Marabou Stork *31
Wood Ibis or Yellow-billed Stork *31
Sacred Ibis *31 Uncommon
Hadada Ibis *34
African Black Duck *38
Egyptian Goose *41
Secretary Bird *42
Ruppell's Griffon Vulture *42
White-backed Vulture *43
Lappet-faced Vulture *43
White-headed Vulture *43

Egyptian Vulture *44
Hooded Vulture *43
Lanner *45
Red-necked Falcon *46 Associated with palms. Recorded from north-eastern sector of Reserve
European Kestrel *47
Lesser Kestrel *50
Pygmy Falcon *51
European Black Kite *51
African Black Kite *51
Black-shouldered Kite *51
Steppe Eagle *55
Tawny Eagle *54
Wahlberg's Eagle *55
African Hawk Eagle *55
Martial Eagle *56
Long-crested Hawk Eagle *57
Lizard Buzzard *57
Brown Harrier Eagle *55, *58
Black-chested Harrier Eagle *58
Grasshopper Buzzard *58
Bateleur *59
African Fish Eagle *59
Palm-nut Vulture *44

Steppe Buzzard *62 Uncommon winter visitor
Little Sparrow Hawk *63
Shikra *66
Gabar Goshawk *67
Pale Chanting Goshawk *68
Montagu's Harrier *68
Pallid Harrier *69
European Marsh Harrier *69 The three harriers are most frequent during spring migration
Harrier Hawk *70
Crested Francolin *71
Yellow-necked Spurfowl *76
Harlequin Quail *76
Tufted Guinea-fowl *77
Kenya Crested Guinea-fowl *78
Vulturine Guinea-fowl *78
Kaffir Rail *79
Black Crake *79
Peters' Finfoot *86 On thickly wooded rivers and streams
Crowned Crane *86
Kori Bustard *87

Chestnut-headed Sparrow Lark *182
Fischer's Sparrow Lark *182
Red-capped Lark *182
African Pied Wagtail *183
Blue-headed Wagtail *184 Various races occur on spring migration
Richard's Pipit *184
Yellow-throated Longclaw *186
Scaly Babbler 21 Occurs along Tana River. Rare
Northern Pied Babbler *187
Rufous Chatterer *187
Dark-capped Bulbul *188
White-eared Bulbul 21 Found at lower altitudes near Tana River
Northern Brownbul 21
European Spotted Flycatcher *190
Dusky Flycatcher *190
Ashy Flycatcher *191
Banded Tit-Flycatcher 22
Grey Flycatcher *191
South African Black Flycatcher *191
Chin-spot Flycatcher *194
Pygmy Puff-back Flycatcher 22
Black-throated Wattle-eye *195
Paradise Flycatcher *195
Bare-eyed Thrush *196, 197
European Rock Thrush *197
European Common Wheatear *198
Isabelline Wheatear *198
Pied Wheatear *198
Capped Wheatear *198
White-browed Robin Chat *200
Red-capped Robin Chat *201
Morning Warbler *202 Associated with stands of palms
Spotted Morning Warbler *202

Red-backed Scrub Robin *202
White-winged Scrub Robin *202
European Nightingale 286
Sprosser 286
Garden Warbler *204
Blackcap Warbler *204
Barred Warbler 290
Olive-tree Warbler 290
Great Reed Warbler 287 Uncommon passage migrant in spring
European Marsh Warbler 290 Spring passage migrant
European Sedge Warbler 290
European Willow Warbler *205
Grey Wren Warbler *205
Black-breasted Apalis *206
Red-faced Apalis 24
Grey-capped Warbler *206 Occurs in riverine thickets
Buff-bellied Warbler *207
Crombec *207
Yellow-bellied Eremomela *207
Grey-backed Camaroptera *210
Rattling Cisticola *211
Winding Cisticola 294
Tiny Cisticola 294
Ashy Cisticola 294
European Swallow *212
Angola Swallow *212
Wire-tailed Swallow *212
Red-rumped Swallow *213
Striped Swallow *213
European Sand Martin *214
African Sand Martin *214
Banded Martin *214
Black Cuckoo Shrike *215
Drongo *216
Straight-crested Helmet Shrike *217
Chestnut-fronted Shrike *218
White-crowned Shrike *218
Northern Brubru *219

Lesser Grey Shrike *220 Spring passage migrant
Fiscal Shrike *219
Teita Fiscal *220
Long-tailed Fiscal *220
Red-backed Shrike *221
Red-tailed Shrike *221
Slate-coloured Boubou *222
Tropical Boubou *222
Black-backed Puff-back *223
Puff-back Shrike 300
Black-headed Bush Shrike *223
Brown-headed Bush Shrike *223
Three-streaked Bush Shrike 26
Sulphur-breasted Bush Shrike *224
Grey-headed Bush Shrike *225
Rosy-patched Shrike *225
Grey Tit *225
Mouse-coloured Penduline Tit 27
European Golden Oriole *227
Black-headed Oriole *227
White-naped Raven *230
Fan-tailed Raven *230
Wattled Starling *231
Violet-backed Starling *232
Blue-eared Glossy Starling *232
Ruppell's Long-tailed Starling *233
Golden-breasted Starling *234
Fischer's Starling 29
Hildebrandt's Starling *235
Superb Starling *235
Red-billed Oxpecker *235
Yellow White-eye *238
Smaller Black-bellied Sunbird 30
Mariqua Sunbird *244
Variable Sunbird *244
Hunter's Sunbird 30
Collared Sunbird *247
Kenya Violet-backed Sunbird 29

Buffalo Weaver *248
White-headed Buffalo Weaver *249
White-browed Sparrow Weaver *249
Grey-headed Social Weaver *250
Black-capped Social Weaver 27
Kenya Rufous Sparrow *250
Parrot-billed Sparrow 322
Chestnut Sparrow 31
Yellow-spotted Petronia 27
Speckle-fronted Weaver 27
Layard's Black-headed Weaver *251
Masked Weaver *252
Vitelline Masked Weaver *252

Chestnut Weaver *253
Black-necked Weaver *254
Spectacled Weaver *255
Golden Weaver 31
Grosbeak Weaver *259
Red-headed Weaver *259
Red-billed Quelea *259
Cardinal Quelea *260
Red Bishop *260
Yellow Bishop *261
White-winged Widow-bird *262
Bronze Mannikin *264
Grey-headed Silver-bill 27
Cut-throat *264
Green-winged Pytilia *264
African Fire Finch *265
Jameson's Fire Finch *265
Red-billed Fire Finch *265

Waxbill *266
Red-cheeked Cordon-bleu *266
Purple Grenadier *267
Purple Indigo-bird 28
Pin-tailed Whydah *267
Steel-blue Whydah *267
Fischer's Straw-tailed Whydah *267
Paradise Whydah *268
Yellow-fronted Canary *269
Yellow-rumped Seed-eater *269
Somali Golden-breasted Bunting *270
Cinnamon-breasted Rock Bunting *270

NAIROBI NATIONAL PARK

Nairobi National Park is unique. Nowhere else in the world does there exist a wild life reserve with such a variety of animals and birds so close to a major city. Only four miles separate the centre of Nairobi from the Park where game animals, and the large carnivores which prey upon them, exist to-day in the splendour and abundance of half a century ago.

The area of Nairobi National Park is a little over forty-four square miles. Though of such small dimensions compared with other faunal reserves in East and Central Africa, Nairobi Park possesses a diversity of environments. Each of these has its own special animals and birds. Over much of the Park open plains country predominates, with or without scattered acacia bush. There is a section of highland forest in which crotons, Kenya olive, muhugu, ekebergia, markhamia and Cape chestnut are some of the characteristic trees; and a permanent river with fringing riverine forest mainly Yellow-barked Acacia, *Acacia xanthophloea*, the "fever tree" of the early explorers. Also there are stretches of broken bush country and deep, rocky valleys and gorges with scrub and long grass. The comparatively recent construction of dams has added a further type of habitat, favourable to certain birds previously uncommon or even unrecorded.

The main entrance to Nairobi National Park is off the Langata Road, Nairobi, and thence along a road which traverses a sector of forest before reaching the expanse of plains beyond. Anywhere in the Park an abund-

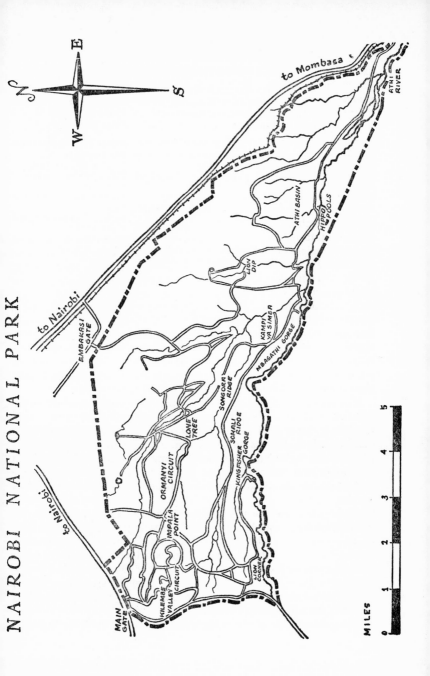

NAIROBI NATIONAL PARK

ance of animal and bird life can be seen throughout the day, but the ideal time for a visit is shortly after dawn. At that hour there is a good chance of seeing some of the nocturnal species, not usually encountered before they disappear into their daytime hideouts.

It is perhaps unnecessary to suggest that the visitor to the Nairobi National Park—and this applies equally to parks elsewhere in East and Central Africa—should proceed slowly, with frequent stops to scan the immediate surroundings through binoculars. Many of the rarely-seen animals may be discovered in apparently deserted places by dint of slow progress and diligent searching.

The large game animals are obviously Nairobi Park's main attraction and many such may be seen, from Lion, Leopard and Cheetah to Masai Giraffe, Zebra and Hippo. A few Black Rhino occur, but they are secretive and keep mainly to the forested parts where they are not often observed. Elephants are not found in the Park and the Buffalo is also absent, except for the odd straggler from the nearby Ngong Hills, and some introduced semi-tame animals.

It is among the ungulates that the greatest abundance of animals is found. Impala, Coke's Hartebeest (usually called Kongoni), Wildebeest and Eland can all be considered common, as also Thomson's Gazelle and Grant's Gazelle. These two species may be distinguished at all ages by the extent of white on the buttocks: in Thomson's gazelle the white stops below the root of the tail; in Grant's gazelle the white extends above the base of the tail and on to the rump.

The variety of bird life in Nairobi National Park may be gauged by the fact that more species of birds have been observed there than have been recorded in the British Isles. But birds are not always present in very large numbers. Much depends on the season of the year—northern migrants pass through during late March and in April; on whether rains have been plentiful or poor, recent or remote; and upon the availability of food for both insectivorous and frugivorous birds and of suitable prey for raptorials.

Birds of prey are much in evidence, from the stately Secretary Bird— two or three pairs nest and are resident—to Martial, Crowned, Tawny and Bateleur Eagles, six species of vultures and a variety of buzzards and hawks. The Augur Buzzard, identified by its red tail and chequered black and white wing patch, is the most common raptor. During March and early April many Montagu's, European Marsh and Pallid Harriers may be seen moving northwards in loose parties, and flocks of migrating Common and Lesser Kestrels are also in evidence.

That associate of vultures, king of the scavenging birds, the Marabou

Stork is common around the Park dams and is extremely tame and confiding. They often rest on their tarsi in a most comical, clown-like manner.

Game birds are represented by Helmeted Guinea-fowl and Yellow-
necked Spurfowl which are common in open country alongside Shelley's
(Greywing) Francolin, and by Scaly Francolins in the forest area. In some
years Harlequin Quails are extremely abundant in the grasslands and
their far-carrying "pleet, pleet, pleet, pleet" can be heard on all sides. The
larger Cape Quail is an uncommon visitor.

Two endemic African bird families, the Turacos and the Mousebirds,
are represented by Hartlaub's Turaco—a pigeon-sized bird with a long
broad tail, mainly green and blue-black plumage and vivid red flight
feathers—and by the Speckled and Blue-naped Mousebirds or Colies.
Mousebirds are drab coloured, very long-tailed birds of gregarious habits.
The blue-naped species has a patch of turquoise-blue on the back of the
head and long, wire-like tail feathers. It occurs in acacia country while
the Speckled Mousebird keeps to bush near the forest edge.

The largest living bird in the world, the Ostrich, is common on the
plains. During the nesting season the male's neck and thighs take on a
bright pink hue. Other large birds often encountered are the Crowned
Crane, Kori Bustard, Ground Hornbill, European White Stork, Abdim's
Stork, Egyptian Goose, Black-necked Heron—seen more frequently on
dry land, where it accounts for many rodents, than in swampy places—
and the Wood Ibis or Yellow-billed Stork.

Sunbirds are much in evidence when the flowers they visit are in blos-
som. They favour especially the bushy, orange-flowered Leonotis and a
greenish-yellow crotolaria bush. Among the commoner species are
Bronzy, Variable, Malachite, Amethyst, Collared and the gem-like black-
bellied Beautiful Sunbird. Weaver-birds and their allies are also well
represented. The commonest species are the black-backed Reichenow's
Weaver and the mottled-backed Speke's Weaver. The former nests singly
while the latter builds colonies in isolated acacia trees.

In the more bushy grasslands the Red-naped Widow-bird is numerous
and in years of good grass the related Jackson's Widow-bird appears, the
male of which constructs dancing rings in the grass wherein to perform
to the female.

MAMMALS OF NAIROBI NATIONAL PARK

Short-snouted Elephant Shrew	Epauletted Fruit Bat	Lander's Horseshoe Bat
East African Hedgehog	White-bellied Tomb Bat	Banana Bat or African Pipistrelle
Giant White-toothed Shrew	Hollow-faced Bat	Yellow-bellied Bat
Rousette Fruit Bat	False Vampire Bat	Angola Free-tailed Bat
	Yellow-winged Bat	

White-bellied Free-tailed Bat
Greater Galago
Bush Baby
Black-faced Vervet
Sykes' Monkey
Olive Baboon
Black and White Colobus Occurs in adjacent Ngong Hills forest
Hunting Dog
Black-backed or Silver-backed Jackal
Side-striped Jackal
Bat-eared Fox
Zorilla
Ratel or Honey Badger
Clawless Otter Recorded at Hippo Pools at dusk
African Civet
Neumann's or Small-spotted Genet
Bush or Large-spotted Genet Melanistic examples sometimes occur
African Palm Civet
Marsh Mongoose
Dwarf Mongoose

Slender or Black-tipped Mongoose
White-tailed Mongoose
Aard-wolf Rare
Spotted Hyaena
Striped Hyaena Rare
Cheetah
Caracal
African Wild Cat
Serval
Lion
Leopard
Ant Bear
Tree Hyrax
Rock Hyrax
Black Rhinoceros
Burchell's or Common Zebra
Hippopotamus
Warthog
Masai Giraffe
Coke's Hartebeest or Kongoni
White-bearded Gnu or Wildebeest
Bush Duiker
Klipspringer
Suni
Steinbok

Kirk's Dik-dik
Common Waterbuck
Defassa Waterbuck (Animals showing intermediate characters between Common and Defassa Waterbuck have been recorded)
Bohor Reedbuck
Chanler's Reedbuck A small herd exists in the Sosian Gorge
Impala
Thomson's Gazelle
Grant's Gazelle
Bushbuck
Eland
African Buffalo Introduced animals
African Hare
Cane Rat
Porcupine
Striped Ground Squirrel
Bush Squirrel
Spring Hare
African Dormouse
Giant Rat
Kenya Mole Rat

BIRDS OF NAIROBI NATIONAL PARK

Masai Ostrich *19
Little Grebe *20
White-necked Cormorant *20
Long-tailed Cormorant *21
White Pelican *22
Pink-backed Pelican *22 Pelicans are visitors in small numbers
Grey Heron *23
Black-headed Heron *23 Common
Goliath Heron *23 Uncommon
Purple Heron *24 Uncommon
Great White Egret *24 Uncommon
Yellow-billed Egret *25
Little Egret *25

Buff-backed Heron or Cattle Egret *26
Squacco Heron *26
Green-backed Heron *26 Occurs along Athi River
Night Heron *27 May be heard flying over at dusk, but rarely seen in Park
Dwarf Bittern *27 A nocturnal species which is rarely seen: has been picked up dead in Park after striking wires
Hammerkop *28
White Stork *29 Spasmodic visitor. Sometimes in large flocks
European Black Stork *30 Single birds recorded from time to time

Abdim's Stork *29 Spasmodic visitor
Open-bill Stork *30 Uncommon
Saddle-bill Stork *30 Two records
Marabou Stork *31
Wood Ibis or Yellow-billed Stork *31
Sacred Ibis *31
Hadada Ibis *34
African Spoonbill *34
Greater Flamingo *35
Lesser Flamingo *35 Flamingos turn up from time to time as stragglers on dams
White-backed Duck *36
African Pochard *37
European Shoveler *37
Yellow-billed Duck *38

African Black Duck *38
A few residents on Athi River

Garganey Teal *38
Hottentot Teal *39
Red-billed Duck *39
European Pintail *39
Fulvous Tree Duck *40
Knob-billed Goose *41
Egyptian Goose *41
Spur-winged Goose *41
Uncommon visitor
Secretary Bird *42
Ruppell's Griffon Vulture *42
White-backed Vulture *43
Lappet-faced Vulture *43
White-headed Vulture *43
Egyptian Vulture *44
Hooded Vulture *43
Peregrine *45 Rare visitor
Lanner *45
European Hobby *46
Mainly passage migrant late April
European Kestrel *47
White-eyed Kestrel *47
Uncommon resident, Plains
Lesser Kestrel *50
Cuckoo Falcon *67 Resident small numbers, forest area
European Black Kite *51
African Black Kite *51
Black-shouldered Kite *51
Honey Buzzard *62 Uncommon winter visitor and migrant
Steppe Eagle *54
Tawny Eagle *54
Wahlberg's Eagle *55
Uncommon visitor
Ayres' Hawk Eagle *56
Single record, forest area
Martial Eagle *56
Crowned Hawk Eagle *57
Long-crested Hawk Eagle *57
Lizard Buzzard *57
Brown Harrier Eagle *55, *58 Uncommon visitor

Black-chested Harrier Eagle *58
Bateleur *59
African Fish Eagle *59
Sometimes seen Athi River
Lammergeyer *44 Rare visitor
Steppe Buzzard *62
Eastern Steppe Buzzard *62 Rare winter visitor
Augur Buzzard *63
Little Sparrow Hawk *63
Uncommon. Resident in forest
Ovampo Sparrow Hawk *66 Rare resident
Great Sparrow Hawk *66
Uncommon resident, forest
African Goshawk *67
Gabar Goshawk *67
Pale Chanting Goshawk *68
Montagu's Harrier *68
Pallid Harrier *69
European Marsh Harrier *69
African Marsh Harrier *69
Harrier Hawk *70
Osprey *70 Rare visitor
Shelley's (Greywing) Francolin *72
Scaly Francolin *74 Occurs in forest
Yellow-necked Spurfowl *76
Cape Quail *76
Harlequin Quail *76
Helmeted Guinea-fowl *77
European Corn Crake *79
Probably common migrant but not often seen
African Crake *79 Occurs in thick cover near dams. Not often seen.
Black Crake *79 Common on dams and along Athi River
Striped Crake 14 Probably occurs on dams as species recorded several times in Nairobi

Purple Gallinule *82
Straggler
Moorhen *83
Lesser Moorhen *83 Rare
Red-knobbed Coot *83
Uncommon visitor
Peters' Finfoot *86 Rare resident, Athi River
Crowned Crane *86
Kori Bustard *87
White-bellied Bustard *88
Hartlaub's Bustard *89
Spotted Stone Curlew *89
African Jacana *90
Ringed Plover *91
Little Ringed Plover *91
Kittlitz's Sand Plover *94
Three-banded Plover *94
Caspian Plover *95 Winter visitor in small flocks. Frequents short-grassed open plains
Crowned Lapwing or Plover *98
Black-winged Plover *99
Blacksmith Plover *100
Avocet *101 Uncommon visitor
Black-winged Stilt *102
Painted Snipe *103
European Common Snipe *104
Great Snipe *104 Uncommon spring migrant
African Snipe *104
Curlew Sandpiper *105
Little Stint *105
Ruff *106
Common Sandpiper *107
Green Sandpiper *107
Wood Sandpiper *107
Spotted Redshank 14 Uncommon winter visitor
Marsh Sandpiper *108
Greenshank *109
Temminck's Courser *110
Pratincole *111
Uncommon visitor
Button Quail *116
Spasmodic visitor
Black-faced Sandgrouse *118

Yellow-throated Sand-grouse *118
Speckled Pigeon *119
Olive Pigeon *119
Pink-breasted Dove *120
Red-eyed Dove *120
Ring-necked Dove *120
Laughing Dove *121
Namaqua Dove *121
Tambourine Dove *122
Emerald-spotted Wood Dove *121
Green Pigeon *122
European Cuckoo *123
Mainly spring migrant
African Cuckoo *123
Red-chested Cuckoo *123
Black Cuckoo *124
Great-spotted Cuckoo *124
Black and White Cuckoo *124
Emerald Cuckoo *125
Didric Cuckoo *125
Klaas' Cuckoo *126
Mainly in forest area
White-browed Coucal *126
Hartlaub's Turaco *131
White-bellied Go-away-bird *132
European Roller *135
Lilac-breasted Roller *136
Rufous-crowned Roller *136
Broad-billed Roller *137
Pied Kingfisher *137
Giant Kingfisher *138 Occurs along Athi River
Malachite Kingfisher *138
Pygmy Kingfisher *139
Grey-headed Kingfisher *140
Striped Kingfisher *140
European Bee-eater *140
White-throated Bee-eater *142
Little Bee-eater *142
Cinnamon-chested Bee-eater 19 Occurs in forest
White-fronted Bee-eater *143
Silvery-cheeked Hornbill *147
Grey Hornbill *147

Red-billed Hornbill *148
Von der Decken's Hornbill *149
Crowned Hornbill *149
Mainly in forest area
Ground Hornbill *150
Uncommon
European Hoopoe *151
African Hoopoe *151 Un-common. Acacia country
Green Wood Hoopoe *152
White-headed Wood Hoo-poe *152
Abyssinian Scimitar-bill *152
African Barn Owl *153
Uncommon resident
African Marsh Owl *154
African Wood Owl *154
Occurs in forest area
Pearl-spotted Owlet *155
Spotted Eagle Owl *155
Verreaux's Eagle Owl *155
European Nightjar *156
Dusky Nightjar *157
Plain Nightjar *157 Un-common visitor
Abyssinian Nightjar *157
Long-tailed Nightjar *158
Speckled Mousebird *159
Blue-naped Mousebird *162
Narina's Trogon *163
Uncommon resident, for-est area
White-headed Barbet *165
Spotted-flanked Barbet *166
Red-fronted Barbet 20
Red-fronted Tinker-bird *167
Golden-rumped Tinker-bird *168 Occurs forest area
Red and Yellow Barbet *169
D'Arnaud's Barbet *169
Greater Honey-guide *170
Best located by its call, a loud and distinct "weet-ear, weet-ear" repeated over and over again
Scaly-throated Honey-guide *171 Rare

Lesser Honey-guide *171
Wahlberg's Honey-guide *171 Occurs acacia woodland
Cassin's Honey-guide *172
Occurs forest area
Nubian Woodpecker *172
Cardinal Woodpecker *173
Bearded Woodpecker *173
Grey Woodpecker *174
Nyanza Swift *174
Mottled Swift *175
Little Swift *175
White-rumped Swift *175
Horus Swift *178 Un-common visitor
Northern White-tailed Bush Lark 16 Inhabits long grass
Rufous-naped Lark *180
Fawn-coloured Lark 266
Uncommon
Short-tailed Lark 16 Oc-curs on plains near Athi River
Fischer's Sparrow Lark *182
Red-capped Lark *182
African Pied Wagtail *183
Wells' Wagtail *183
Blue-headed Wagtail and races *184 Winter visitor and passage migrant. Common
Long-billed Pipit *185
Richard's Pipit *184
Tree Pipit *185
Red-throated Pipit *185
Yellow-throated Longclaw *186
Pangani Longclaw *186
Rosy-breasted Longclaw *186
Black-lored Babbler *187
Northern Pied Babbler *187
Dark-capped Bulbul *188
Fischer's Greenbul *189
Yellow-whiskered Greenbul *189
European Spotted Fly-catcher *190
Dusky Flycatcher *190
Banded Tit-Flycatcher 22

LAKE NAKURU NATIONAL PARK

Lake Nakuru, the world-famous haunt of flamingos, is a shallow alkaline lake in Kenya's Rift Valley, some twenty-four square miles in extent, immediately south of Nakuru township. A first-class tarmac highway connects Nairobi with Nakuru, the ninety-seven-mile road link passing down the forested Kikuyu Escarpment with fine views over the Kedong Valley and Mounts Suswa and Longonot, then north-westwards past Lakes Naivasha and Elmenteita. From Nakuru the route to the lake is well signposted.

The National Park comprises the lake and its immediate surrounds. The landscape is picturesque, areas of sedge, marsh and grasslands alternating with rocky cliffs and outcrops, stretches of yellow-barked acacia woodland and on the eastern perimeter rocky hillsides covered with a forest of grotesque-looking Euphorbia trees—all set against a background of hilly, broken country.

The Park was created in 1960 chiefly as a bird sanctuary. At times vast concentrations of more than a million flamingos live on the lake, forming what the famous ornithologist, Roger Tory Peterson, has described as "the most fabulous bird spectacle in the world." But flamingos are unpredictable creatures, and not always to be found on Lake Nakuru in such vast numbers. The lake water-levels derive from rainfall, and the inflow of the tiny Njoro River fluctuates greatly. As conditions and food supplies alter, so do the numbers of flamingos present. However, even when the flamingo population is at low ebb there is always a wealth of bird-life to be observed on Lake Nakuru, both water-birds and those species which favour the habitats surrounding the lake. At present, nearly four hundred species have been recorded within the area of the Park.

Although Lake Nakuru National Park is primarily a bird sanctuary, the number of animals to be encountered is not inconsiderable. A small herd of Hippopotamus lives among the reeds in the north-eastern corner,

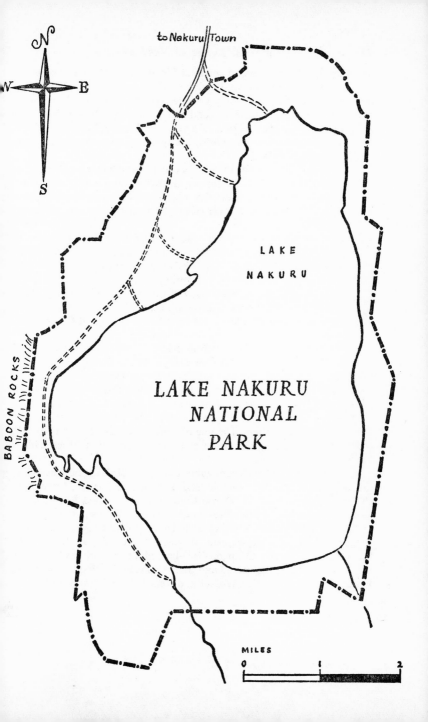

to Nakuru Town

N
W E
S

LAKE
NAKURU

BABOON ROCKS

LAKE NAKURU
NATIONAL
PARK

MILES
0   1   2

where springs have created a series of hippo pools. The lake shore is a good place to observe Bohor Reedbuck; these animals are often flushed from high grass or sedge in which they sleep during the day. Bushbuck may be seen at the edge of the acacia woodland, especially at dawn and towards dusk. Lake Nakuru is the home of a very rare bat, the Long-eared Leaf-nosed Bat (*Hipposideros megalotis*), a tiny orange-buff species with ears half the length of its body.

Both Lesser and Greater Flamingos occur abundantly as non-breeding visitors on Lake Nakuru, the former vastly the more numerous. In addition there is a great variety of other water birds including two interesting ducks, the Cape Wigeon, a lover of brackish waters, and the stiff-tailed Maccoa Duck.

Several species of plovers are resident, Blacksmith Plover, Spurwing Plover, Crowned Plover, Kittlitz's Sand Plover and Three-banded Plover; and many northern-breeding shore birds occur along the margins of the lake as winter visitors. During the spring migration their numbers are augmented by passage migrants, many of which are in full-summer plumage. Among these are flocks of Little Stints, Curlew Sandpipers, Marsh Sandpipers and Greenshanks, smaller parties of Wood and Green Sandpipers and sometimes a few Black-tailed Godwits.

Birds of prey are always much in evidence, including five species of vultures, Lanner, Long-crested Hawk Eagle, Augur Buzzard, Brown and Black-chested Harrier Eagles, Fish Eagle, Gabar Goshawk and Harrier Hawk. During the winter months and on migration further species appear, the following being common: European and Lesser Kestrels, European Black Kite, Steppe Eagle, Steppe Buzzard, and Montagu's, Pallid and European Marsh Harriers. The line of cliffs known as "Baboon Rocks", which rise above the western shore, is the home of a pair of majestic black Verreaux's Eagles.

In the acacia woodlands contiguous to the lake birds are numerous and the following species are characteristic: Red-chested Cuckoo, Levaillant's Cuckoo, Emerald Cuckoo, Didric Cuckoo, Lilac-breasted Roller, Grey-headed Kingfisher, Little Bee-eater, African Hoopoe, Pearl-spotted Owlet, Verreaux's Eagle Owl, Greater Honey-guide, Grey Woodpecker, Rattling Cisticola, Grey-capped Warbler, White-browed Robin-chat, Black Cuckoo Shrike, Drongo, Grey-backed Fiscal, Tropical Boubou, White-breasted Tit, Blue-eared and Superb Glossy Starlings, Bronzy and Variable Sunbirds, Speke's Weaver and Red-cheeked Cordon-bleu.

MAMMALS OF LAKE NAKURU NATIONAL PARK

Spectacled Elephant Shrew
Giant White-toothed Shrew
Rousette Fruit Bat
Epauletted Fruit Bat
White-bellied Tomb Bat
Hollow-faced Bat
False Vampire Bat
Yellow-winged Bat
Lander's Horseshoe Bat
Lesser Leaf-nosed Bat
Long-eared Leaf-nosed Bat
African Trident Bat
African Mouse-eared Bat
Banana Bat or African Pipistrelle
Yellow-bellied Bat
Angola Free-tailed Bat
Bush Baby
Black-faced Vervet
Blue or Sykes' Monkey
Olive Baboon
Black and White Colobus
Lesser Ground Pangolin Rare
Hunting Dog Very uncommon visitor

Black-backed or Silver-backed Jackal
Side-striped Jackal
Bat-eared Fox
Zorilla
Ratel or Honey Badger Rare
African Civet
Neumann's or Small-spotted Genet
Bush or Large-spotted Genet
Marsh Mongoose
Dwarf Mongoose
Slender or Black-tipped Mongoose
White-tailed Mongoose
Aard-wolf Rare
Spotted Hyaena
Cheetah Rare
African Wild Cat
Serval
Lion Rare
Leopard Rare
Ant Bear
Tree Hyrax

Rock Hyrax
Burchell's or Common Zebra
Hippopotamus
Masai Giraffe
Bush Duiker
Klipspringer
Steinbok
Kirk's Dik-dik
Defassa Waterbuck
Bohor Reedbuck
Chanler's Reedbuck
Impala
Thomson's Gazelle
Grant's Gazelle
Bushbuck
Eland
African Buffalo Rare
African Hare
Cane Rat
Porcupine
Bush Squirrel
Spring Hare
African Dormouse
Giant Rat
Kenya Mole Rat

BIRDS OF LAKE NAKURU NATIONAL PARK

Great-crested Grebe *19
Black-necked Grebe *20
Little Grebe *20
White-necked Cormorant *20
Long-tailed Cormorant *21
African Darter *21
White Pelican *22
Pink-backed Pelican *22
Grey Heron *23
Black-headed Heron *23
Goliath Heron *23 Rare visitor
Purple Heron *24 Recorded a few times near Hippo pools
Great White Egret *24
Yellow-billed Egret *25
Little Egret *25
Reef Heron *25 Two examples in dark plumage phase were present on lake in late 1965 and early 1966

Buff-backed Heron or Cattle Egret *26
Squacco Heron *26
Green-backed Heron *26 Recorded mouth of Njoro River
Night Heron *27
Little Bittern *27 Uncommon
Dwarf Bittern *27 Rare
Hammerkop *28
White Stork *29 Spasmodic visitor and passage migrant
European Black Stork *30 Rare winter visitor
Abdim's Stork *29 Uncommon visitor
Saddle-bill Stork *30 Uncommon
Marabou Stork *31
Wood Ibis or Yellow-billed Stork *31

Sacred Ibis *31
Hadada Ibis *34
Glossy Ibis *34
African Spoonbill *34
Greater Flamingo *35
Lesser Flamingo *35
Maccoa Duck *36
African Pochard *37
Tufted Duck *37 Uncommon winter visitor
European Shoveler *37
Yellow-billed Duck *38 Uncommon
Garganey Teal *38
Cape Wigeon *39 Common resident
Hottentot Teal *39
Red-billed Duck *39
Gadwall *38 Rare winter visitor
European Wigeon *38 Uncommon winter visitor

European Teal *39 Rare winter visitor
European Pintail *39
White-faced Tree Duck *40 Uncommon
Fulvous Tree Duck *40
Knob-billed Goose *41
Egyptian Goose *41
Spur-wing Goose *41 Uncommon
Secretary Bird *42
Ruppell's Griffon Vulture *42
White-backed Vulture *43
Lappet-faced Vulture *43
White-headed Vulture *43
Egyptian Vulture *44
Hooded Vulture *43 Vultures are spasmodic visitors in small numbers
Peregrine *45 Uncommon
Lanner *45
European Hobby *46 Mainly spring passage migrant
African Hobby *46 Rare
European Kestrel *47
White-eyed Kestrel *47
Lesser Kestrel *50
European Black Kite *51
African Black Kite *51
Black-shouldered Kite *51
Bat Hawk *46 Honey Buzzard *62 Uncommon winter visitor and passage migrant
Verreaux's Eagle *54 Pair resident on Baboon Rocks cliffs
Steppe Eagle *55
Tawny Eagle *54
Wahlberg's Eagle *55
Booted Eagle 232 Rare winter visitor
Martial Eagle *56 Uncommon visitor
Long-crested Hawk Eagle *57
Lizard Buzzard *57
Brown Harrier Eagle *55, *58

Black-chested Harrier Eagle *58
Bateleur *59
African Fish Eagle *59
Steppe Buzzard *62
Eastern Steppe Buzzard *62 Rare winter visitor
Augur Buzzard *63
Little Sparrow Hawk *63 Occurs in acacia belt on western side of lake
Great Sparrow Hawk *66
African Goshawk *67
Gabar Goshawk *67
Montagu's Harrier *68
Pallid Harrier *69
European Marsh Harrier *69
African Marsh Harrier *69
Harrier Hawk *70
Coqui Francolin *71
Hildebrandt's Francolin *73
Yellow-necked Spurfowl *76
Cape Quail *76
Harlequin Quail *76
Helmeted Guinea-fowl *77
Kaffir Rail *79 Recorded at Hippo pools
European Corn Crake *79 Uncommon migrant
African Crake *79
Black Crake *79 Occurs at Hippo pools
Purple Gallinule *82 Uncommon
Allen's Gallinule *82 One record
Moorhen *83
Lesser Moorhen *83 Uncommon
Red-knobbed Coot *83
Crowned Crane *86
Jackson's Bustard *88 Rare
White-bellied Bustard *88
Spotted Stone Curlew *89
Ringed Plover *91
Little Ringed Plover *91
Kittlitz's Sand Plover *94
Three-banded Plover *94

Caspian Plover *95 Uncommon visitor
Grey Plover *95
Crowned Lapwing or Plover *98
Black-winged Plover *99
Spurwing Plover *99
Blacksmith Plover *100 ✓
Avocet *101
Black-winged Stilt *102
Painted Snipe *103
European Common Snipe *104
Great Snipe *104
African Snipe *104
Curlew Sandpiper *105
Little Stint *105
Temminck's Stint *105 Uncommon winter visitor
Ruff *106
Common Sandpiper *107
Green Sandpiper *107
Wood Sandpiper *107
Redshank *106 Rare winter visitor
Spotted Redshank 14 Uncommon winter visitor
Marsh Sandpiper *108
Greenshank *109
Black-tailed Godwit 14 Uncommon winter visitor
Curlew *109 Uncommon winter visitor
Temminck's Courser *110
Pratincole *111
Lesser Black-backed Gull *114 Winter visitor in small numbers
Grey-headed Gull *114 ✓
Gull-billed Tern *115 ✓
White-winged Black Tern *115
Whiskered Tern *115
African Skimmer *116 Spasmodic visitor in small numbers
Button Quail *116
Speckled Pigeon *119
Pink-breasted Dove *120
Red-eyed Dove *120
Ring-necked Dove *120
Laughing Dove *121
Namaqua Dove *121

Streaky Seed-eater *269   Golden-breasted Bunting   Cinnamon-breasted Rock
African Citril 339   *270   Bunting *270

SAMBURU-ISIOLO GAME RESERVES

The Samburu and Isiolo Game Reserves are the most accessible of the
Northern Frontier faunal sanctuaries, 213 miles from Nairobi, thirty-
three miles north of Isiolo township, over good roads. For those who prefer to travel by air there is a landing strip near the Samburu Game Reserve
Lodge.

The Samburu Reserve covers an area of forty square miles on the
northern bank of the Uaso Nyiro River, with a river frontage of ten miles.
The adjoining Isiolo Game Reserve of seventy-five square miles lies on the
southern bank of the same ten-mile stretch. A bridge across the Uaso
Nyiro a couple of miles upstream of the Samburu Lodge connects the two
Reserves, and it is convenient to treat them as a single unit.

In addition to the rugged splendour of its landscape the very name
"Northern Frontier Province" conjures up an atmosphere of mystery and
adventure. It is indeed a vast and little visited region, where travelling,
even nowadays, is tough and where the nomadic tribes have changed
little over the centuries. The two Reserves provide a worthy introduction
to this most colourful part of Kenya.

Permanent water available from the ten miles of river ensures that an
abundance of wild life exists in the Reserves at all times. The main attractions are Reticulated Giraffe, Grevy's Zebra, Beisa Oryx, the blue-necked
Somali Ostrich and crocodiles in the river. Elephant are plentiful and
Black Rhinoceros, Lion, Leopard, Cheetah, Gerenuk, Buffalo and the
two species of hyaenas are to be seen. Among the smaller mammals the
Ground Squirrel is abundant and tame.

For such a relatively small area the bird life is strikingly numerous and
colourful; there is no difficulty in seeing well over a hundred species of
birds in a single day. Perhaps the most impressive sight is the immense
flocks of Tufted and Vulturine Guinea-fowls which make their way each
afternoon to the river-bank to drink, the latter resplendent with white-
streaked necks and brilliant blue underparts.

Buffalo Springs, in the Isiolo Game Reserve, with its pools and streams
of fresh water, is the drinking place in the dry season for literally thousands
of sandgrouse and doves, in addition to a galaxy of smaller birds.

The tiny Pygmy Falcon is common, the males blue-grey and white, the
females with a mahogany-brown mantle. At a distance, when perched high
in some acacia tree, they distinctly resemble shrikes. The giant amongst

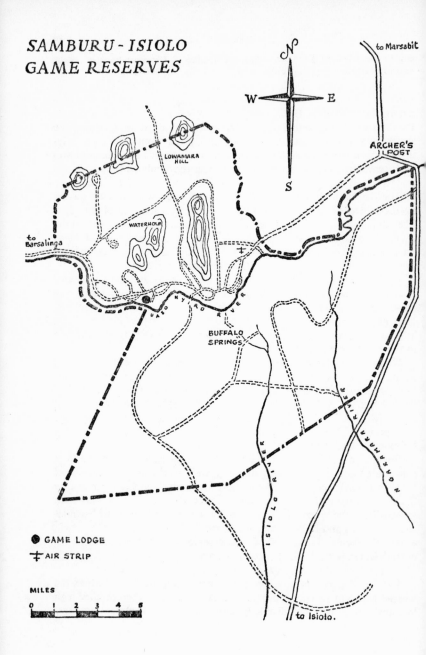

SAMBURU - ISIOLO
GAME RESERVES

to Marsabit

N
W E
S

to Barsalinga

LOWAMARA
HILL

WATERHOLE

ARCHER'S
POST

UASO NYIRO RIVER

BUFFALO
SPRINGS

ISIOLO RIVER

NGARRAMARA RIVER

● GAME LODGE
✛ AIR STRIP

MILES
0 1 2 3 4 5

to Isiolo.

eagles the Martial Eagle is often seen, usually perched high on some vantage point, alert for dik-dik or guinea-fowl.

Accommodation with all amenities is at the Samburu Game Lodge, sited on the edge of the Uaso Nyiro River below giant acacias and dom palms. Camping sites are available in both Reserves. The Lodge is built on the camp site of one of the most famous of the old time elephant hunters, Arthur Newmann. The visitor may find it fitting, whilst taking a "sundowner," to contemplate the austerity endured by the early hunters and explorers contrasted with the comfort of a present-day safari!

MAMMALS OF SAMBURU-ISIOLO GAME RESERVES

Spectacled Elephant Shrew
Rousette Fruit Bat
Epauletted Fruit Bat
Pale-bellied Fruit Bat
White-bellied Tomb Bat
Hollow-faced Bat
False Vampire Bat
Yellow-winged Bat
Lander's Horseshoe Bat
Lesser Leaf-nosed Bat
Banana Bat or African Pipistrelle
Yellow-bellied Bat
Angola Free-tailed Bat
White-bellied Free-tailed Bat
Greater Galago
Bush Baby
Black-faced Vervet
Blue or Sykes' Monkey
Olive Baboon
Hunting Dog
Golden Jackal
Black-backed or Silver-backed Jackal
Side-striped Jackal
Bat-eared Fox
Zorilla
Ratel or Honey Badger
Clawless Otter Rare

African Civet
Neumann's or Small-spotted Genet
Bush or Large-spotted Genet
Marsh Mongoose
Dwarf Mongoose
Large Grey Mongoose
Slender or Black-tipped Mongoose
White-tailed Mongoose
Banded Mongoose
Aard-wolf
Spotted Hyaena
Striped Hyaena
Cheetah
Caracal
African Wild Cat
Serval
Lion
Leopard
Tree Hyrax
Rock Hyrax
African Elephant
Black Rhinoceros
Grevy's Zebra
Burchell's or Common Zebra
Hippopotamus
Warthog

Reticulated Giraffe
Red Duiker
Blue Duiker
Bush Duiker
Klipspringer
Steinbok
Kirk's Dik-dik
Guenther's Dik-dik
Common Waterbuck Intermediates between Common and Defassa Waterbuck have been recorded on Uaso Nyiro River
Impala
Grant's Gazelle
Gerenuk
Beisa Oryx
Bushbuck
Lesser Kudu
Eland
African Buffalo
African Hare
Porcupine
Striped Ground Squirrel
Unstriped Ground Squirrel
Bush Squirrel
East African Red Squirrel
Spring Hare
African Dormouse
Naked Mole Rat

BIRDS OF SAMBURU-ISIOLO GAME RESERVES

Somali Ostrich *19
Little Grebe *20
Long-tailed Cormorant *21
African Darter *21
Grey Heron *23

Black-headed Heron *23
Goliath Heron *23
Great White Egret *24
Little Egret *25
Buff-backed Heron or Cattle Egret *26

Green-backed Heron *26
Night Heron *27
Hammerkop *28
White Stork *29 Rare visitor

Woolly-necked Stork *29
Uncommon visitor
Abdim's Stork *29 Spasmodic visitor: sometimes in flocks
Open-bill Stork *30 Single record
Saddle-bill Stork *30 Uncommon
Marabou Stork *31
Wood Ibis or Yellow-billed Stork *31
Sacred Ibis *31
Hadada Ibis *34
Egyptian Goose *41
Secretary Bird *42
Ruppell's Griffon Vulture *42
White-backed Vulture *43
Lappet-faced Vulture *43
White-headed Vulture *43
Egyptian Vulture *44
Hooded Vulture *43
Peregrine *45
Lanner *45
European Hobby *46 Spring passage migrant
Red-necked Falcon *46 Rare
European Kestrel *47
White-eyed Kestrel *47
Lesser Kestrel *50
Pygmy Falcon *51
Swallow-tailed Kite *54 Rare visitor
European Black Kite *51
African Black Kite *51
Black-shouldered Kite *51
Bat Hawk *46 One recorded near Samburu Lodge
Honey Buzzard *62 Rare visitor
Verreaux's Eagle *54
Steppe Eagle *55
Tawny Eagle *54
Wahlberg's Eagle *55
African Hawk Eagle *55 Rare
Booted Eagle 232 Rare visitor
Martial Eagle *56

Long-crested Hawk Eagle *57
Lizard Buzzard *57
Brown Harrier Eagle *55, *58
Black-chested Harrier Eagle *58
Lesser Spotted Eagle *55 Rare winter visitor
Grasshopper Buzzard *58 Uncommon visitor
Bateleur *59
African Fish Eagle *59
Lammergeyer *44 Rare visitor
Steppe Buzzard *62
Little Sparrow Hawk *63
Shikra *66
Gabar Goshawk *67
Pale Chanting Goshawk *68
Montagu's Harrier *68
Pallid Harrier *69
European Marsh Harrier *69
Harrier Hawk *70
Osprey *70 Rare visitor
Crested Francolin *71
Yellow-necked Spurfowl *76
Harlequin Quail *76
Stone Partridge *77 Occurs on rocky hills
Tufted Guinea-fowl *77
Vulturine Guinea-fowl *78
Crowned Crane *86 Uncommon visitor
Kori Bustard *87
Heuglin's Bustard *88 Uncommon
Buff-crested Bustard *89
Spotted Stone Curlew *89
Water Dikkop *90
Little Ringed Plover *91
Three-banded Plover *94
Caspian Plover *95 Rare visitor
Crowned Lapwing or Plover *98
Senegal Plover *98 Uncommon visitor

Blackhead Plover *100 Mainly nocturnal: often on airstrip at dusk
Common Sandpiper *107
Green Sandpiper *107
Greenshank *109
Cream-coloured Courser *110
Temminck's Courser *110
Two-banded Courser *111
Heuglin's Courser *110
Bronze-winged Courser *98, *111
Pratincole *111 Uncommon
Button Quail *116
Chestnut-bellied Sand-grouse *117
Black-faced Sandgrouse *118
Lichtenstein's Sandgrouse *118
Speckled Pigeon *119
Red-eyed Dove *120
Mourning Dove *121
Ring-necked Dove *120
Laughing Dove *121
Namaqua Dove *121
Tambourine Dove *122
Emerald-spotted Wood Dove *121
Green Pigeon *122
European Cuckoo *123
African Cuckoo *123
Red-chested Cuckoo *123
Black Cuckoo *124
Great-spotted Cuckoo *124 Uncommon
Levaillant's Cuckoo *124
Black and White Cuckoo *124
Emerald Cuckoo *125
Didric Cuckoo *125
Klaas' Cuckoo *126
White-browed Coucal *126
White-bellied Go-away-bird *132
Orange-bellied Parrot *133 Uncommon
Brown Parrot *134
European Roller *135
Lilac-breasted Roller *136
Rufous-crowned Roller *136

Robin Chat *201
Spotted Morning Warbler *202
Red-backed Scrub Robin *202
White-winged Scrub Robin *202
White-throated Robin 23 Rare winter visitor
European Nightingale 286
Sprosser 286
Garden Warbler *204
Blackcap Warbler *204
Barred Warbler 290
Olive-tree Warbler 290
European Sedge Warbler 290
European Willow Warbler *205
Grey Wren Warbler *205
Black-breasted Apalis *206
Red-faced Apalis 24
Buff-bellied Warbler *207
Crombec *207
Yellow-bellied Eremomela *207
Yellow-vented Eremomela *210
Grey-backed Camaroptera *210
Pectoral-patch Cisticola *210
Rattling Cisticola *211
Tiny Cisticola 294
Ashy Cisticola 294
Tawny-flanked Prinia *211
European Swallow *212
Angola Swallow *212
Ethiopian Swallow *212 Uncommon
Wire-tailed Swallow *212
Red-rumped Swallow *213
Striped Swallow *213
Grey-rumped Swallow *213 Uncommon
European Sand Martin *214
African Sand Martin *214
Banded Martin *214
African Rock Martin *214
Black Rough-wing Swallow *214 Uncommon visitor
Black Cuckoo Shrike *215

Drongo *216
White-crowned Shrike *218
Northern Brubru *219
Lesser Grey Shrike *220 Mainly spring passage migrant
Somali Fiscal *220 Rare visitor
Teita Fiscal *220
Long-tailed Fiscal *220
Red-backed Shrike *221
Red-tailed Shrike *221
Slate-coloured Boubou *222
Tropical Boubou *222
Black-backed Puff-back *223
Black-headed Bush Shrike *223
Three-streaked Bush Shrike 27
Sulphur-breasted Bush Shrike *224
Grey-headed Bush Shrike *225
Rosy-patched Shrike *225
Grey Tit *225
White-breasted Tit *226
Mouse-coloured Penduline Tit 27
European Golden Oriole *227 Mainly spring passage migrant
Black-headed Oriole *227
Dwarf or Lesser Brown-necked Raven 26
White-naped Raven *230
Fan-tailed Raven *230
Wattled Starling *231
Violet-backed Starling *232 Spasmodic visitor
Magpie Starling 29 Uncommon visitor in small numbers
Blue-eared Glossy Starling *232
Black-breasted Glossy Starling 29 Uncommon visitor
Ruppell's Long-tailed Starling *233
Golden-breasted Starling *234
Hildebrandt's Starling *235

Superb Starling *235
Yellow-billed Oxpecker *238
Red-billed Oxpecker *235
Yellow White-eye *238
Smaller Black-bellied Sunbird 30 Rare
Shining Sunbird 30 Rare visitor
Mariqua Sunbird *244
Variable Sunbird *244
Hunter's Sunbird 30
Collared Sunbird *247
Kenya Violet-backed Sunbird 29
Buffalo Weaver *248
White-headed Buffalo Weaver *249
White-browed Sparrow Weaver *249
Donaldson-Smith's Sparrow Weaver *249
Grey-headed Social Weaver *250
Black-capped Social Weaver 27
Kenya Rufous Sparrow *250
Grey-headed Sparrow *250
Swahili Sparrow 322
Chestnut Sparrow 31
Yellow-spotted Petronia 27
Speckle-fronted Weaver 27
Layard's Black headed-Weaver *251
Masked Weaver *252
Vitelline Masked Weaver *252
Chestnut Weaver *253
Black-necked Weaver *254
Spectacled Weaver *255
Golden Weaver 31
Red-headed Weaver *259
Red-billed Quelea *259
Cardinal Quelea *260
Yellow Bishop *261
Fire-fronted Bishop 32 Appears in years of heavy rains when there is abundant grass
White-winged Widow-bird *262 Spasmodic visitor
Bronze Mannikin *262

Silver-bill 27
Grey-headed Silver-bill 27
Cut-throat *264
Green-winged Pytilia *264
African Fire Finch *265
Jameson's Fire Finch *265
Red-billed Fire Finch *265
Waxbill *266
Red-cheeked Cordon-bleu *266

Blue-capped Cordon-bleu *267
Purple Grenadier *267
Purple Indigo-bird 28
Pin-tailed Whydah *267
Steel-blue Whydah *267
Fischer's Straw-tailed Whydah *267
Paradise Whydah *268

Yellow-fronted Canary *269
White-bellied Canary 28
Yellow-rumped Seed-eater *269
Somali Golden-breasted Bunting *270
Cinnamon-breasted Rock Bunting *270

TSAVO NATIONAL PARK

The Tsavo National Park, a vast arid region of 8,034 square miles, is Kenya's largest wild life stronghold. The Park comprises a diversity of habitats, open plains alternating with savannah bush and semi-desert scrub; acacia woodlands; rocky ridges and outcrops, and more extensive ranges and isolated hills; belts of riverine vegetation; palm thickets; and on the Chyulu Hills extension area, mountain forest.

The Park, which lies roughly half-way between the coast and Nairobi, is bisected by the main Nairobi-Mombasa road and railway. That portion lying north and east of the road is designated Tsavo Park East; that to the south and west, Tsavo Park West. The Park is watered by two permanent rivers, the Tsavo River which flows through Tsavo Park West and the Athi River which crosses a corner of Tsavo Park East. The two unite above Lugard Falls to become the Galana River. The Voi River, to the south, is not permanent.

Mainly on account of the difficult waterless nature of much of the terrain, parts of the Park have not yet been developed for visitors. These include the uninhabited scrub desert north of the Galana River and the southern portion of Tsavo Park West, south of the Voi-Taveta road.

Most of the Park is made up of basement gneisses and schists, but part of the western sector is of recent volcanic origin, including the Chyulu Hills extension. Here may be seen many lava flows and cones, such as Shitani, near Kilaguni Lodge, which is a perfect example of a recent volcano. This volcanic zone also contains the famous Mzima Springs, where some fifty million gallons of sparkling crystal-clear water gush out daily from below a lava ridge. Hippopotamus and shoals of Barbel live in the springs and provide a dramatic spectacle. The water is so clear that every action of these huge aquatic beasts under the water, and of their attendant piscine scavengers, may be watched from the lookouts or through the plate-glass windows of the submerged observation chamber.

Downstream from the springs is a dense and luxuriant stand of wild date palms and Raphia palms, the latter with immense fronds of up to thirty feet long. It is not unusual to spot the rare and elusive Peters' Fin-foot swimming between the fronds where these touch the water.

One of the other great spectacles of Tsavo Park, perhaps its greatest, is Mudanda Rock between Voi and Manyani. This mile-long outcrop is a water catchment area which supplies a natural dam at its base. In the dry season hundreds of elephants come daily to drink and bathe. From a safe vantage point just above the water visitors may sit and watch the activities of the great beasts below them.

The Lugard Falls on the Galana River, twenty-five miles from Voi, are remarkable for the fantastic shapes of the water-worn rocks. The river disappears into a rocky gorge so narrow in one part that it is possible to stand astride the cleft with the Falls immediately below.

At present there is a network of over 500 miles of roadways in the Tsavo Park, passing through much of the best game viewing areas and following the rivers where there is the greatest concentration of game during the dry season. Specially rewarding circuits are those along the Galana River from Lugard Falls to Sobo, southwards to Aruba and then northwest to Mudanda Rock; and from Kilaguni Lodge to Tsavo Gate, along a stretch of the Tsavo River.

Elephants in large herds are the number one attraction at Tsavo. For those who like to indulge in game watching without effort, what could be pleasanter than to recline in a comfortable chair on the veranda of Kilaguni Lodge, a cold drink at hand, and watch the elephants take their refreshment from the waterhole a hundred yards or so away.

Tsavo is also a good place to see one of our most beautiful antelopes, the Lesser Kudu with spiral horns and white striped coat. Whilst you may come across these graceful animals almost anywhere, the dry bush along the Galana River is their favourite haunt. Other animals likely to be encountered are Black Rhinoceros, Buffalo, Common Waterbuck, Eland, Gerenuk, Fringe-eared Oryx and Impala.

Birdlife is legion in the Park and the visitor is constantly meeting with new species. One of the most conspicuous is the White-headed Buffalo Weaver, brownish-black and white with a startling vivid red rump when it flies. Starlings are numerous, including the brilliantly plumaged Golden-breasted Starling and the rare but duller Fischer's Starling. Hornbills are another prevalent group of birds, eight species occur in the Park. Birds of prey, Bustards, Sunbirds and Weaver-birds are other families well represented. Hole-nesting birds—starlings, parrots, barbets and rollers—are often associated with the thick-trunked Baobab trees which are such a feature of the landscape.

Accommodation in the Tsavo National Park includes Kilaguni Lodge,

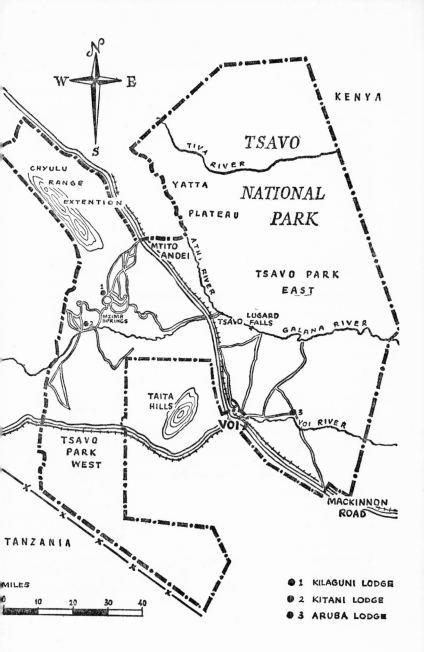

N

W E

S

CHYULU
RANGE
EXTENTION

TSAVO

KENYA

TIVA RIVER

YATTA

PLATEAU

NATIONAL
PARK

MTITO
ANDEI

ATHI RIVER

1

MZIMA
SPRINGS

2

TSAVO PARK
EAST

TSAVO
FALLS

LUGARD
FALLS

GALANA RIVER

TAITA
HILLS

VOI

3

VOI RIVER

TSAVO
PARK
WEST

MACKINNON
ROAD

TANZANIA

MILES

0   10   20   30   40

● 1 KILAGUNI LODGE
● 2 KITANI LODGE
● 3 ARUBA LODGE

twenty-two miles from Mtito Andei, with full catering facilities and amenities. In the western sector Kitani Lodge and Murka Lodge provide shelter and bedding may be hired but visitors must provide their own food. Aruba Safari Lodge with full catering and hotel facilities is in Tsavo Park East, twenty-two miles from Voi. In addition there are certain camping sites in the Park which may be used with the permission of the Park Warden. Outside the Park accommodation is available at hotels at Mtito Andei and at Voi. Main roads connect Tsavo National Park with Nairobi and Mombasa, and for those who travel by air there are landing fields at Kilaguni Lodge, Aruba and elsewhere.

MAMMALS OF TSAVO NATIONAL PARK

Spectacled Elephant Shrew
East African Hedgehog
Giant White-toothed Shrew
Rousette Fruit Bat
Epauletted Fruit Bat
Pale-bellied Fruit Bat
White-bellied Tomb Bat
Hollow-faced Bat
False Vampire Bat
Yellow-winged Bat
Lander's Horseshoe Bat
Lesser Leaf-nosed Bat
Giant Leaf-nosed Bat Recorded from Galana River
African Trident Bat Recorded from Kilaguni Lodge
Banana Bat or African Pipistrelle
Yellow-bellied Bat
Angola Free-tailed Bat
White-bellied Free-tailed Bat
Flat-headed Free-tailed Bat
Greater Galago
Bush Baby
Black-faced Vervet
Blue or Sykes' Monkey
Yellow Baboon
Lesser Ground Pangolin
Hunting Dog
Golden Jackal
Black-backed or Silver-backed Jackal
Side-striped Jackal
Bat-eared Fox

Zorilla
Ratel or Honey Badger
Clawless Otter
African Civet
Neumann's or Small-spotted Genet
Bush or Large-spotted Genet
African Palm Civet
Marsh Mongoose
Dwarf Mongoose
Large Grey Mongoose
Slender or Black-tipped Mongoose
White-tailed Mongoose
Banded Mongoose
Aard-wolf
Spotted Hyaena
Striped Hyaena
Cheetah
Caracal
African Wild Cat
Serval
Lion
Leopard
Ant Bear
Tree Hyrax
Rock Hyrax
African Elephant
Black Rhinoceros
Grevy's Zebra Reputed to occur in extreme north of Park
Burchell's or Common Zebra
Warthog

Masai Giraffe
Coke's Hartebeest or Kongoni
Hunter's Hartebeest or Hirola Introduced into Park, present status not known
Red Duiker
Blue Duiker
Bush Duiker
Klipspringer
Suni
Steinbok
Kirk's Dik-dik
Common Waterbuck
Bohor Reedbuck
Impala
Grant's Gazelle
Gerenuk
Fringe-eared Oryx
Bushbuck
Lesser Kudu
Eland
African Buffalo
African Hare
Cane Rat
Porcupine
Striped Ground Squirrel
Unstriped Ground Squirrel
Bush Squirrel
East African Red Squirrel
Spring Hare
African Dormouse
Giant Rat
Kenya Mole Rat
Naked Mole Rat

BIRDS OF TSAVO NATIONAL PARK

Masai Ostrich *19 Occurs mainly south of the Galana River
Somali Ostrich *19 Occurs mainly north of the Galana River
Little Grebe *20 Recorded from Aruba and Tsavo River
Long-tailed Cormorant *21
African Darter *21
White Pelican *22
Pink-backed Pelican *22 Pelicans occur from time to time on larger dams
Grey Heron *23
Black-headed Heron *23
Goliath Heron *23
Purple Heron *24 Recorded from Tsavo River
Great White Egret *24
Yellow-billed Egret *25
Black Heron *25 One recorded from Aruba dam
Little Egret *25
Buff-backed Heron or Cattle Egret *26
Squacco Heron *26
Madagascar Squacco Heron *26 Recorded from Mzima Springs
Green-backed Heron *26 Occurs on rivers
Night Heron *27
White-backed Night Heron *27 Probably occurs, as recorded from Lake Jipe on southern border
Little Bittern *27
Dwarf Bittern *27
Hammerkop *28
White Stork *29
European Black Stork *30 Rare winter visitor
Woolly-necked Stork *29
Abdim's Stork *29
Open-bill Stork *30
Saddle-bill Stork *30
Marabou Stork *31
Wood Ibis or Yellow-billed Stork *31

Sacred Ibis *31
Hadada Ibis *34
Glossy Ibis *34 Rare visitor
African Spoonbill *34 Uncommon visitor to dams
European Shoveler *37
Yellow-billed Duck *38
African Black Duck *38 Recorded from Tsavo and Athi Rivers
Garganey Teal *38
Hottentot Teal *39
Red-billed Duck *39
European Pintail *39
White-faced Tree Duck *40
Fulvous Tree Duck *40
Pygmy Goose *40 Rare visitor to dams
Knob-billed Goose *41
Egyptian Goose *41
Spur-winged Goose *41
Secretary Bird *42
Ruppell's Griffon Vulture *42
White-backed Vulture *43
Lappet-faced Vulture *43
White-headed Vulture *43
Egyptian Vulture *44
Hooded Vulture *43
Peregrine *45 Uncommon
Lanner *45
Teita Falcon *46 Rare: has been recorded in the Voi area
European Hobby *46 Occurs mainly as spring passage migrant
African Hobby *46 Recorded from near Chyulu Hills
Sooty Falcon *50 Recorded during autumn migration along the Galana River
Eastern Red-footed Falcon *50 Very uncommon: a few to be seen amongst

flocks of migrating Lesser Kestrels in spring
Red-necked Falcon *46 Occurs along Tsavo and Galana Rivers
European Kestrel *47
African Kestrel *47
White-eyed Kestrel *47
Lesser Kestrel *50
Grey Kestrel *50 Uncommon. Occurs along rivers
Pygmy Falcon *51
Cuckoo Falcon *67 Uncommon. Occurs in forest and well-wooded areas
European Black Kite *51
African Black Kite *51
Black-shouldered Kite *51
Bat Hawk *46 Not uncommon in the Voi area
Honey Buzzard *62 Uncommon winter visitor and passage migrant
Verreaux's Eagle *54 Rare
Steppe Eagle *55
Tawny Eagle *54
Wahlberg's Eagle *55
African Hawk Eagle *55
Ayres' Hawk Eagle *56
Booted Eagle 232 Rare winter visitor
Martial Eagle *56
Crowned Hawk Eagle *57 Occurs in the Chyulu Hills forest
Long-crested Hawk Eagle *57
Lizard Buzzard *57
Brown Harrier Eagle *55, *58
Black-chested Harrier Eagle *58
Lesser Spotted Eagle *55 Rare winter visitor
Grasshopper Buzzard *58 Common visitor between November and March
Bateleur *59
African Fish Eagle *59

Palm-nut Vulture *44
Lammergeyer *44 Rare visitor
Steppe Buzzard *62 Winter visitor in varying numbers
Augur Buzzard *63 Occurs in Chyulu Hills
Little Sparrow Hawk *63
Ovampo Sparrow Hawk *66 Uncommon. Usually found in vicinity of baobab trees
Great Sparrow Hawk *66
Shikra *66
African Goshawk *67
Gabar Goshawk *67
Pale Chanting Goshawk *68
Montagu's Harrier *68
Pallid Harrier *69
European Marsh Harrier *69
African Marsh Harrier *69 Rare
Harrier Hawk *70
Osprey *70 Rare visitoı
Coqui Francolin *71
Crested Francolin *71
Shelley's (Greywing) Francolin *72
Scaly Francolin *74 Occurs on Chyulu Hills
Yellow-necked Spurfowl *76
Cape Quail *76
Harlequin Quail *76
Stone Partridge *77 Reputed to occur on rocky hills north of the Galana River, but not confirmed
Helmeted Guinea-fowl *77
Kenya Crested Guinea-fowl *78
Vulturine Guinea-fowl *78
Kaffir Rail *79 Rarely seen
European Corn Crake *79 Passage migrant, seldom seen
Black Crake *79
Moorhen *83

Red-knobbed Coot *83 Uncommon
Peters' Finfoot *86
Crowned Crane *86
Kori Bustard *87
Jackson's Bustard *88 Rare
White-bellied Bustard *88
Buff-crested Bustard *89
Black-bellied Bustard *89
Hartlaub's Bustard *89
Spotted Stone Curlew *89
Water Dikkop *90
African Jacana *90
Ringed Plover *91
Little Ringed Plover *91
Kittlitz's Sand Plover *94
Three-banded Plover *94
Caspian Plover *95 Winter visitor. Frequents open plains
Crowned Lapwing or Plover *98
Senegal Plover *98
Blacksmith Plover *100
Blackhead Plover *100
Avocet *101
Black-winged Stilt *102
Painted Snipe *103
European Common Snipe *104
Great Snipe *104
African Snipe *104
Curlew Sandpiper *105
Little Stint *105
Ruff *105
Common Sandpiper *107
Green Sandpiper *107
Wood Sandpiper *107
Marsh Sandpiper *108
Greenshank *109
Temminck's Courser *110
Two-banded Courser *99, *111
Heuglin's Courser *110
Bronze-winged Courser *98, *111
Pratincole *111
Button Quail *116
Chestnut-bellied Sandgrouse *117
Black-faced Sandgrouse *118

Yellow-throated Sandgrouse *118
Speckled Pigeon *119
Olive Pigeon *119
Bronze-naped Pigeon *119
Red-eyed Dove *120
Mourning Dove *121
Ring-necked Dove *120
Laughing Dove *121
Namaqua Dove *121
Tambourine Dove *122
Emerald-spotted Wood Dove *121
Green Pigeon *122
European Cuckoo *123
African Cuckoo *123
Red-chested Cuckoo *123
Black Cuckoo *124
Great-spotted Cuckoo *124
Levaillant's Cuckoo *124
Black and White Cuckoo *124
Emerald Cuckoo *125
Didric Cuckoo *125
Klaas' Cuckoo *126
White-browed Coucal *126
Hartlaub's Turaco *131 Occurs in forest on Chyulu Hills
Violet-crested Turaco *131 Rare
White-bellied Go-away-bird *132
Orange-bellied Parrot *133
Brown Parrot *134
European Roller *135
Lilac-breasted Roller *136
Rufous-crowned Roller *136
Broad-billed Roller *137
Pied Kingfisher *137
Giant Kingfisher *138
Half-collared Kingfisher 18 Rare
Malachite Kingfisher *138
Pygmy Kingfisher *139
Brown-hooded Kingfisher 18
Grey-headed Kingfisher *140
Striped Kingfisher *140
European Bee-eater *140
Madagascar Bee-eater 19
Blue-cheeked Bee-eater 19

Violet-backed Starling *232
Abbott's Starling 29 Recorded Chyulu Hills forest
Blue-eared Glossy Starling *232
Black-breasted Glossy Starling 29
Ruppell's Long-tailed Starling *233
Golden-breasted Starling *234
Red-wing Starling *234
Fischer's Starling 29
Hildebrandt's Starling *235
Shelley's Starling *235
Superb Starling *235
Yellow-billed Oxpecker *238
Red-billed Oxpecker *235
Yellow White-eye *238
Bronzy Sunbird *242
Beautiful Sunbird (black-bellied race) *243
Smaller Black-bellied Sunbird 30 Inhabits acacia trees near rivers
Little Purple-banded Sunbird *245
Tsavo Purple-banded Sunbird 30
Violet-breasted Sunbird 313
Mariqua Sunbird *244
Variable Sunbird *244
Eastern Double-collared Sunbird *245 Chyulu Hills forest
Amethyst Sunbird *245
Scarlet-chested Sunbird *246 Chyulu Hills
Hunter's Sunbird 30
Olive Sunbird 30
Collared Sunbird *247
Kenya Violet-backed Sunbird 29
Buffalo Weaver *248

White-headed Buffalo Weaver *249
White-browed Sparrow Weaver *249
Grey-headed Social Weaver *250
Black-capped Social Weaver 27
Kenya Rufous Sparrow *350
Swahili Sparrow 322
Parrot-billed Sparrow 322
Chestnut Sparrow 31
Yellow-spotted Petronia 27
Speckle-fronted Weaver 27
Layard's Black-headed Weaver *251
Masked Weaver *252
Vitelline Masked Weaver *252
Chestnut Weaver *253
Golden Palm Weaver *254
Black-necked Weaver *254
Spectacled Weaver *255
Golden Weaver 31
Holub's Golden Weaver *255
Reichenow's Weaver *258 Chyulu Hills
Grosbeak Weaver *259
Red-headed Weaver *259
Red-billed Quelea *259
Red-headed Quelea *260
Cardinal Quelea *260
Red Bishop *260
Zanzibar Red Bishop *261
Black-winged Bishop *261
Yellow Bishop *261
Fire-fronted Bishop 32
Fan-tailed Widow-bird *262
White-winged Widow-bird *262
Red-collared Widow-bird *262
Bronze Mannikin *264

Rufous-backed Mannikin *264
Silver-bill 27
Grey-headed Silver-bill 27
Cut-throat *264
Quail Finch 27
Parasitic Weaver 336
Peters' Twin-spot 28 Occurs in dense cover: easily overlooked
Green-winged Pytilia *264
African Fire Finch *265
Jameson's Fire Finch *265
Red-billed Fire Finch *265
Yellow-bellied Waxbill *266
Waxbill *266
Black-cheeked Waxbill 28
Red-cheeked Cordon-bleu *266
Blue-capped Cordon-bleu *267
Purple Grenadier *267
Purple Indigo-bird 28
Pin-tailed Whydah *267
Steel-blue Whydah *267
Fischer's Straw-tailed Whydah *267
Paradise Whydah *268
Yellow-fronted Canary *269
White-bellied Canary 28
Brimstone Canary *268
Kenya Grosbeak Canary 340
Yellow-rumped Seed-eater *269
Streaky Seed-eater *269
Golden-breasted Bunting *270
Somali Golden-breasted Bunting *270
Cinnamon-breasted Rock Bunting *270

GEDI NATIONAL PARK

The Gedi National Park, situated on the Kenya coast twelve miles south of Malindi, is a ruined city of Islamic origin dating from the thirteenth century. The Great Mosque, portions of the palace and other dwellings have been partly restored, and deep wells cleared of vegetation which formerly choked them. An information centre displays some of the more spectacular finds which have been made and details what is known of the city's history.

The Gedi ruins are set in the midst of tall coastal forest and have much of interest to the naturalist, especially the colony of the uncommon Mottled-throated Spinetail, a swift which nests in the disused wells. The following interesting mammals and birds may be seen.

MAMMALS OF GEDI NATIONAL PARK

Yellow-rumped Elephant Shrew	Bush Baby	Dwarf Mongoose
	Sykes' Monkey	Red Duiker
Epauletted Fruit Bat	Black-faced Vervet Monkey	Blue Duiker
False Vampire Bat	Yellow Baboon	Suni
Greater Galago	Black and White Colobus	Bush Squirrel

BIRDS OF GEDI NATIONAL PARK

Cuckoo Falcon *67	Crowned Hornbill *149	Zanzibar Puff-back Shrike 26
Crowned Hawk Eagle *57	Narina's Trogon *163	Nicator 26
Southern Banded Harrier Eagle *58	Mottled-throated Spinetail *175	Black-breasted Glossy Starling 29
Little Sparrow Hawk *63	Boehm's Spinetail *175	Mouse-coloured Sunbird 30
Kenya Crested Guinea-fowl *78	Scaly Babbler 21	Plain-backed Sunbird 320
Green Pigeon *122	East Coast Akalat 283	Dark-backed Weaver 31
Fischer's Turaco *130	Eastern Bearded Scrub Robin 23	Peters' Twin-spot 28
Brown-headed Parrot *134	Retz's Red-billed Shrike *218	
Trumpeter Hornbill *146		
Silvery-cheeked Hornbill *147	Chestnut-fronted Shrike *218	

FORT JESUS NATIONAL PARK

Fort Jesus, a seventeenth century Portuguese fort overlooking the Indian Ocean at Mombasa, was designated a National Park in 1958. Much reconstruction work has been carried out and a historical museum established, in which displays illustrate the culture of the coast from the thirteenth to the nineteenth century.

Two birds of special note may be seen at the Fort. During the day the Indian House Crow is common and at dusk the Bat Hawk is often observed.

OLORGESAILIE NATIONAL PARK

Olorgesailie National Park is a fifty-two-acre prehistoric living site of hand-axe man, forty-two miles from Nairobi on the Nairobi-Magadi road. It has been developed as a field museum with hand axes and other tools preserved *in situ*, together with fossils of associated extinct mammals.

The site was developed during the early 1940s by the famous Kenya prehistorian Dr. L. S. B. Leakey and Mrs. Leakey. Later excavations in 1962-63 have revealed parts of a number of camps and living floors at different levels, and these are now exhibited exactly as they were un-covered. Olorgesailie has been acclaimed as one of the most important sites of this period of culture in the world.

In addition to its archaeological importance, Olorgesailie and the country surrounding the site is of great zoological interest. The following notable mammals and birds occur there.

MAMMALS OF OLORGESAILIE NATIONAL PARK

Spectacled Elephant Shrew	Neumann's or Small-spotted Genet	Lion
Olive Baboon	Aard-wolf	Leopard
Ratel or Honey Badger	Striped Hyaena	Black Rhinoceros
African Civet	Caracal	Klipspringer

BIRDS OF OLORGESAILIE NATIONAL PARK

Lanner *45	Heuglin's Courser *110	Beautiful Sunbird (Black-bellied race) *243
African Hawk Eagle *55	Button Quail *116	
Martial Eagle *56	Black-faced Sandgrouse *118	Steel-blue Whydah *267
Gabar Goshawk *67		Fischer's Straw-tailed Whydah *267
Pale Chanting Goshawk *68	White-throated Bee-eater *142	Paradise Whydah *268
Buff-crested Bustard *89	Wahlberg's Honey-Guide *171	
Two-banded Courser *111		

Important Faunal Areas
outside National Parks and Game Reserves

Not all of Kenya's wild life exists within the boundaries of National Parks and Game Reserves. The following are some localities of special interest to the naturalist.

LAKE BARINGO. Lake Baringo, one of Kenya's Rift Valley lakes, north of Nakuru, possesses two major ornithological attractions. These are Gibraltar Island with the largest nesting colony of Goliath Herons in East Africa, and the escarpment immediately west of Campi ya Samaki on the western side of the lake, the home of Verreaux's Eagle, the rare Bristle-crowned Starling and Hemprich's Hornbill. Birds generally are abundant in the acacia woodland bordering the lake and include Curly-crested Helmet Shrikes, Silver-bird, Grey-headed Silver-bill and Grey-headed Bush Shrike.

KAKAMEGA FOREST. The Kakamega Forest lying east of Kakamega township is an area of immense ornithological interest. The forest is West African in character and many birds occur there that are not found elsewhere in Kenya. Characteristic species include the following:

Bat Hawk *46
Crowned Hawk Eagle *57
Ross's Turaco *131
Great Blue Turaco *132
Eastern Grey Plantain-eater 17
Grey Parrot 17
Blue-headed Bee-eater 19
Black and White-casqued Hornbill *147
Red-chested Owlet *147
Narina's Trogon *163
Bar-tailed Trogon *163
Double-toothed Barbet *164
Grey-throated Barbet *166
Yellow-spotted Barbet 20
Moustached Green Tinkerbird *167
Speckled Barbet *168
Thick-billed Honey-guide 20
Cassin's Honey-guide *172
Brown-eared Woodpecker 20
Buff-spotted Woodpecker 20

Yellow-crested Woodpecker 20
Sabine's Spinetail 16
African Broadbill *179
Bristle-bill 21
Honey-guide Greenbul 274
Joyful Greenbul 271
Shrike Flycatcher 279
Wattle-eye Flycatcher *195
Chestnut Wattle-eye *195
Jameson's Wattle-eye 22
Yellow-bellied Wattle-eye 280
Black-headed Paradise Flycatcher *196
Blue-shouldered Robin Chat 23
Equatorial Akalat 23
Brown-chested Alethe 23
Uganda Woodland Warbler 290
Black-faced Rufous Warbler 25
Petit's Cuckoo Shrike 25
Velvet-mantled Drongo 25
Square-tailed Drongo *217

Mackinnon's Grey Shrike *220
Pink-footed Puff-back Shrike 300
Doherty's Bush Shrike *224
Grey-green Bush Shrike 301
Dusky Tit *226
Waller's Chestnut-wing Starling 308
Stuhlmann's Starling 308
Orange-tufted Sunbird 29
Green-throated Sunbird 30
Blue-throated Brown Sunbird 30
Grey-chinned Sunbird 29
Green Hylia 27
Dark-backed Weaver 31
Vieillot's Black Weaver *255
Brown-capped Weaver 31
Yellow-mantled Weaver 31
Red-headed Malimbe *258
Red-headed Blue-bill 32
Oriole Finch 340

KONGELAI ESCARPMENT. The Kongelai Escarpment immediately north of Kapenguria is an easy day's trip from Kitale. Around Kapenguria at 7,500 feet the Spotted Creeper (*248) is fairly numerous and is often a member of a mixed bird party with various tits, orioles, flycatchers and weavers. The Escarpment road, which drops to 4,500 feet at the Suam River, is an extremely rich bird locality with some 300 species recorded.

Special species include White-crested Turaco, Eastern Grey Plantain-eater, Senegal Coucal, Yellow-billed Shrike, Stone Partridge, Lesser Blue-eared Starling, Curly-crested Helmet Shrike and Jackson's Hornbill.

LAKE MAGADI. This is a shallow alkaline lake in southern Kenya just north of the Tanzanian border and seventy miles from Nairobi. Water birds are abundant including the Chestnut-banded Sand Plover which is not found elsewhere in Kenya. The road to Magadi passes over the south-eastern end of the Ngong Hills at 7,000 feet, and then drops in a series of "steps" down the eastern wall of the Rift Valley until the 2,000 feet level at the lake is reached. As Magadi is a concession area permission to visit the lake must be obtained from the Magadi Soda Company.

Some of the more interesting mammals and birds found in this area are listed below:

Short-snouted Elephant Shrew	Cheetah	Bush Duiker
Black-faced Vervet	Caracal	Klipspringer
Olive Baboon	African Wild Cat	Steinbok
Bat-eared Fox	Lion	Kirk's Dik-dik
Zorilla	Leopard	Impala
Ratel or Honey Badger	Ant Bear	Grant's Gazelle
African Civet	Rock Hyrax	Gerenuk
Neumann's or Small-spotted Genet	Black Rhinoceros	Fringe-eared Oryx
Aard-wolf	Common Zebra	Porcupine
Spotted Hyaena	Warthog	Striped Ground Squirrel
Striped Hyaena	Masai Giraffe	Bush Squirrel
	Coke's Hartebeest	
	White-bearded Gnu	

Masai Ostrich *19	Peregrine *45	Bronze-winged Courser *98, *111
White Pelican *22	Lanner *45	Pratincole *111
Pink-backed Pelican *22	African Hawk Eagle *55	White-bellied Go-away-bird *132
Grey Heron *23	Brown Harrier Eagle *55, *58	Singing Bush Lark 266
Goliath Heron *23	Pale Chanting Goshawk *68	Rosy-patched Shrike *225
Dwarf Bittern *27 Breeds in the fresh water swamps immediately south of Magadi	Kori Bustard *87	Beautiful Sunbird (black-bellied race) *243
Saddle-bill Stork *30	White-bellied Bustard *88	Kenya Violet-backed Sunbird 29
African Spoonbill *34	Buff-crested Bustard *89	Steel-blue Whydah *267
Greater Flamingo *35	Spotted Stone Curlew *89	Fischer's Straw-tailed Whydah *267
Lesser Flamingo *35 Usually in very large numbers at southern end of lake. Breeding recorded	Chestnut-banded Sand Plover *91, *94	Paradise Whydah *268
Cape Wigeon *39	Two-banded Courser *111	Kenya Grosbeak Canary 340
	Temminck's Courser *110	
	Heuglin's Courser *110	

MIDA CREEK. Mida Creek is a vast expanse of almost land-locked tidal mudflats a few miles south of Gedi National Park, and is one of the best localities in East Africa wherein to study the spring migration of waders. Here from late March until early May, migrating flocks of Little Stints, Curlew Sandpipers, Sanderlings, Turnstones, Greenshanks, Terek Sandpipers, Whimbrels, Curlews, Great and Mongolian Sand Plovers and Grey Plovers assemble briefly in their flight northwards. Many are in the full glory of their breeding plumage.

The belt of mangrove swamp which fringes this tidal basin offers ideal concealment from which to watch or photograph shore birds at close quarters. Besides the northern migrants Mida Creek is also one of the few places on the Kenya coast where Crab Plovers may be seen. Other interesting birds to be encountered are Osprey, Caspian Tern, Sooty Gull, and Lesser Crested Tern: whilst the mangrove trees offer perches for Carmine, Madagascar and European Bee-eaters.

LAKE NAIVASHA AND HELL'S GATE. Fresh-water Lake Naivasha, only fifty miles from Nairobi, is a bird-watcher's paradise. It is also the most beautiful of Kenya's Rift Valley lakes with its fringing banks of feathery-headed papyrus, secluded lagoons and channels, vast expanses of blue water-lilies and the Crescent Island Wildlife Sanctuary. Waterbirds exist in great variety and abundance.

Fish Eagles and Ospreys are resident, herons and egrets are well represented, Lily-trotters, Purple Gallinules, Red-knobbed Coots and Black Crakes are everywhere. African Marsh Harriers and the three migrant harriers are often seen sailing just above the reed beds, hunting the little *Hyperolius* tree-frogs which form the bulk of their diet.

Some eight miles south east of Lake Naivasha are the towering cliffs of the Hell's Gate gorge, with their resident pair of Lammergeyers, several Verreaux's Eagles, colonies of Ruppell's Griffon Vultures and other notable birds.

In addition to its birds the following mammals are also found at Naivasha and Hell's Gate:

Black-faced Vervet	Marsh Mongoose	Klipspringer Hell's Gate
Olive Baboon	White-tailed Mongoose	Steinbok
Black-backed and Side-striped Jackals	Aard-wolf	Kirk's Dik-dik
	Serval	Defassa Waterbuck
Bat-eared Fox	Rock Hyrax	Bohor Reedbuck
Zorilla	Common Zebra	Chanler's Reedbuck
Clawless Otter	Hippopotamus	Impala
African Civet	Masai Giraffe	Thomson's Gazelle
Small-spotted Genet	Coke's Hartebeest	Grant's Gazelle
Large-spotted Genet	Bush Duiker	Bushbuck

African Buffalo Hell's
Gate
African Hare

Porcupine
Striped Ground Squirrel
Bush Squirrel

Spring Hare Numerous
on Crescent Island
African Mole Rat

BIRDS

Masai Ostrich *19
Great-crested Grebe *19
Black-necked Grebe *20
Little Grebe *20
White-necked Cormorant
*20
Long-tailed Cormorant *21
African Darter *21
White Pelican *22
Pink-backed Pelican *22
Grey Heron *23
Black-headed Heron *23
Goliath Heron *23
Purple Heron *24
Great White Egret *24
Yellow-billed Egret *25
Black Heron *25 Rare
visitor
Little Egret *26
Buff-backed Heron or Cattle
Egret *26
Squacco Heron *26
Night Heron *27
Little Bittern *27
Dwarf Bittern *27
Hammerkop *28
White Stork *29
European Black Stork *30
Rare visitor
Abdim's Stork *29
Open-bill Stork *30
Saddle-bill Stork *30
Rare visitor
Marabou Stork *31
Wood Ibis or Yellow-billed
Stork *31
Sacred Ibis *31
Hadada Ibis *34
Glossy Ibis *34
African Spoonbill *34
Greater Flamingo *35
Lesser Flamingo *35
Flamingos are spasmodic
visitors only
Maccoa Duck *36
White-backed Duck *36
African Pochard *37
European Shoveler *37

Yellow-billed Duck *38
African Black Duck *38
Garganey Teal *38
Cape Wigeon *39 Rare
visitor
Hottentot Teal *39
Red-billed Duck *39
European Pintail *39
Fulvous Tree Duck *40
Pygmy Goose *40 Un-
common
Knob-billed Goose *41
Egyptian Goose *41
Spur-winged Goose *41
Secretary Bird *42
Ruppell's Griffon Vulture
*42
White-backed Vulture *43
Lappet-faced Vulture *43
White-headed Vulture *43
Egyptian Vulture *44
Hooded Vulture *43
Peregrine *45
Lanner *45
European Hobby *46
European Kestrel *47
African Kestrel *47 Hell's
Gate
White-eyed Kestrel *47
Lesser Kestrel *50
European Black Kite *51
African Black Kite *51
Black-shouldered Kite *51
Bat Hawk *46
Verreaux's Eagle *54
Steppe Eagle *55
Tawny Eagle *54
Martial Eagle *56 Rare
visitor
Long-crested Hawk Eagle
*57
Brown Harrier Eagle *55,
*58
Black-chested Harrier
Eagle *58
Lesser Spotted Eagle *55
Bateleur *59
African Fish Eagle *59

Lammergeyer *44 Hell's
Gate
Steppe Buzzard *62
Augur Buzzard *63
Little Sparrow Hawk *63
Gabar Goshawk *67
Montagu's Harrier *68
Pallid Harrier *69
European Marsh Harrier
*69
African Marsh Harrier
*69
Harrier Hawk *70
Osprey *70
Hildebrandt's Francolin
*73 Hell's Gate
Yellow-necked Spurfowl
*76
Cape Quail *76
Harlequin Quail *76
Helmeted Guinea-fowl *77
Kaffir Rail *79
Black Crake *79
Purple Gallinule *82
Moorhen *83
Red-knobbed Coot *83
Crowned Crane *86
African Jacana or Lily-
trotter *90
Ringed Plover *91
Little Ringed Plover *91
Kittlitz's Plover *94
Three-banded Plover *94
Caspian Plover *95
Crowned Lapwing or Plover
*98
Black-winged Plover *99
Spurwing Plover *100
Blacksmith Plover *100
Avocet *101
Black-winged Stilt *102
Painted Snipe *103
European Common Snipe
*104
Great Snipe *104
African Snipe *104
Curlew Sandpiper *105
Little Stint *105

Yellow-bellied Waxbill *266
Waxbill *266
Crimson-rumped Waxbill *266
Red-cheeked Cordon-bleu *266

Purple Grenadier *267
Purple Indigo-bird 28
Pin-tailed Whydah *267
Brimstone Canary *268
Yellow-rumped Canary *269
Streaky Seed-eater *269

Golden-breasted Bunting *270
Cinnamon-breasted Rock Bunting *270

FERGUSON'S GULF, LAKE RUDOLF. Ferguson's Gulf, some forty miles north east of Lodwar, Turkana, on the western shores of Lake Rudolf possesses an extremely rich avifauna. This is the one locality in Kenya where, in the spring, one may observe Black-tailed Godwits and Spotted Redshanks in full breeding plumage. Between March and early May it is also an exceptional locality for the northwards movement of European passage migrants. Vast numbers of various races of Blue-headed and Yellow Wagtails move through in waves, together with huge flocks of Marsh Sandpipers and other waders. Birds of prey are abundant in the locality: in some years Swallow-tailed Kites are very common, even breeding in colonies in isolated groups of acacia trees between the Gulf and Lodwar.

Central Island in Lake Rudolf may be reached from Ferguson's Gulf. This island with its crater lakes is the nesting area of large colonies of waterbirds (and of crocodiles) and Lesser Flamingos are reputed to breed there also. African Skimmers nest in April/May on the black lava sand beaches.

Mammals are not well represented but the general region is rich in many species of bats, including the rare Mouse-tailed Bat: it is not at all unlikely that new species remain to be discovered.

Some of the special birds which occur in the Ferguson's Gulf area include:

Reef Heron *25
Teita Falcon *46
Fox Kestrel *47
Swallow-tailed Kite *54
Bat Hawk *46
Osprey *70 Nests on Central Island
Heuglin's Bustard *88
Senegal Stone Curlew *90
Spotted Redshank 14

Black-tailed Godwit 14
Cream-coloured Courser *110
Pratincole *111
Caspian Tern *115 Nests on Central Island
Little Tern 236
African Skimmer *116
Abyssinian Roller 18
Carmine Bee-eater *141

Jackson's Hornbill *149
Abyssinian Ground Hornbill *150
Star-spotted Nightjar 260
Curly-crested Helmet Shrike *217
Pygmy Sunbird 30
Shining Sunbird 30
Somali Sparrow 322
Yellow-crowned Bishop 32

SHIMBA HILLS. The Shimba Hills, near Kwale and south of Mombasa, is rolling park-like country where open grasslands alternate with patches of coastal rain forest. The locality is important as the only habitat in Kenya of the Sable Antelope. These animals are quite numerous and are relatively tame. Elephant, lion and leopard also occur, but are not often seen. Other noteworthy mammals are:

Knob-bristled Forest Elephant Shrew	Black-faced Vervet	Blue Duiker
Black and Red Elephant Shrew	Sykes' Monkey	Bush Duiker
	Yellow Baboon	Suni
Greater Galago	Black and White Colobus	Bushbuck
Bush Baby	Serval	
	Red Duiker	

BIRDS

Cuckoo Falcon *67	Green Barbet *167	Square-tailed Drongo *217
Honey Buzzard *62	Green Tinker-bird *167	Retz's Red-billed Shrike *218
African Hawk Eagle *55	Greater Honey-guide *170	Chestnut-fronted Shrike *218
Crowned Hawk Eagle *57	Little Spotted Woodpecker 20	Zanzibar Puff-back Shrike 26
Southern Banded Harrier Eagle *58	Golden-tailed Woodpecker *173	Four-coloured Bush Shrike *224
Palm-nut Vulture *44	Boehm's Spinetail *175	Nicator 26
Red-necked Spurfowl *75	African Broadbill *179	Black-breasted Glossy Starling 29
Kenya Crested Guinea-fowl *78	African Pitta *179 Rare	Plain-backed Sunbird 320
Fischer's Turaco *130	Pangani Longclaw *186	Dark-backed Weaver 31
Carmine Bee-eater *141	Little Yellow Flycatcher 278	Zanzibar Red Bishop *261
Trumpeter Hornbill *146	Cape Puff-back Flycatcher *194	Peters' Twin-spot 28
Silvery-cheeked Hornbill *147	East Coast Akalat 283	Green-backed Twin-spot 335
Narina's Trogon *163	Green-backed Camaroptera *210	
Black-collared Barbet *164	Croaking Cisticola 294	
Brown-breasted Barbet *165		

SOKOKE-ARABUKU FOREST. The coastal Sokoke Forest runs parallel to the coast-line north of Mombasa from above Kilifi to Gedi. It is the home of two outstandingly interesting and rare mammals—the Zanzibar or Aders' Duiker and the Yellow-rumped Elephant Shrew—and of many rare and local birds. Amongst these is the recently discovered Morden's Owlet (*Otus ireneae*), a species smaller even than the African Scops Owl with finely vermiculated underparts.

Other special birds which occur in the Sokoke-Arabuku forest are:

Southern Banded Harrier Eagle *58	Green Tinker-bird *167	Mottled-throated Spinetail *175
Fischer's Turaco *130	Golden-tailed Woodpecker *173	African Pitta *179
Green Barbet *167	Boehm's Spinetail *175	Sokoke Pipit 268

Scaly Babbler **21**
Little Yellow Flycatcher
278
East Coast Akalat 283
Retz's Red-billed Shrike
*218

Chestnut-fronted Shrike
*218
Zanzibar Puff-back Shrike
26
Four-coloured Bush Shrike
*224

Nicator **26**
Amani Sunbird **29**
Plain-backed Sunbird 320
Clarke's Weaver **31**

Tanzania

Tanzania possesses five National Parks, the Ngorongoro Conservation Area which includes the famous Ngorongoro Crater, and a number of Game Reserves of which some may in future be designated National Parks.

Best known among Tanzania's faunal reserves is the Serengeti National Park of 5,600 square miles, perhaps the most famous game area in the world. Lake Manyara National Park is noted for its birdlife and for tree-climbing lions. The Ngurdoto Crater National Park, sited between Mounts Kilimanjaro and Meru, has the small but beautiful Ngurdoto Crater where the wildlife exists without disturbance from man. Two recently created sanctuaries are the Mikumi National Park, within easy reach of Dar-es-Salaam; and the Ruaha National Park, a vast region of over 5,000 square miles where Greater Kudu are common. These two parks are as yet relatively undeveloped, but their future potential is very great and Ruaha may well become the premier National Park in East Africa.

LAKE MANYARA NATIONAL PARK

Although Lake Manyara National Park covers an area of only 123 square miles, its terrain is so diverse that its mammal and bird lists are most impressive. The Park includes the northern and most of the western parts of the lake and its shores with a westward expansion to the top of the Rift Valley wall where the Lake Manyara Hotel is sited. Large areas of ground-water forest with giant fig and mahogany trees alternate with acacia woodland and more open places, all well watered. A network of roads and tracks gives the visitor maximum game and bird viewing opportunities. The tree-climbing Lions of Manyara—like the tree-climbing Lions of Ishasha in the Queen Elizabeth Park, Uganda—are famous for this departure from normal lion behaviour. In Manyara it is probably due to an abundance of tsetse and other flies: the lions have found that in an arboreal resting place the torment of biting flies is less.

In the Queen Elizabeth Park a different explanation must be sought: there the lions apparently climb trees as vantage points in order to see over the tall grass.

Numbers of Elephant are resident in the Park. Buffalo are common

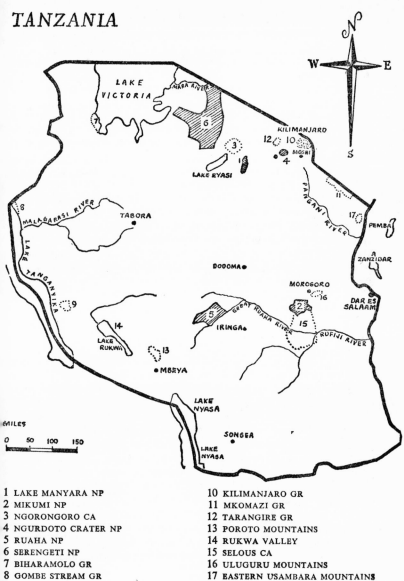

TANZANIA

1 LAKE MANYARA NP
2 MIKUMI NP
3 NGORONGORO CA
4 NGURDOTO CRATER NP
5 RUAHA NP
6 SERENGETI NP
7 BIHARAMOLO GR
8 GOMBE STREAM GR
9 KATAVI PLAIN GR

10 KILIMANJARO GR
11 MKOMAZI GR
12 TARANGIRE GR
13 POROTO MOUNTAINS
14 RUKWA VALLEY
15 SELOUS CA
16 ULUGURU MOUNTAINS
17 EASTERN USAMBARA MOUNTAINS

96 NATIONAL PARKS OF EAST AFRICA

and herds of 300-400 have been recorded. Black Rhinoceros are often seen. Leopards occur in most places and it is not unusual to come across them in the early morning or late evening: like the lions, they may be seen resting in trees.

Manyara is noted for its wealth of birdlife. At times the lake is visited by many thousands of Lesser Flamingos, together with a sprinkling of the larger species. Maccoa Ducks and White-backed Ducks are resident, and the beautiful little Pygmy Goose is sometimes observed. The Chestnut-banded Sand Plover, a bird with a very restricted distribution in East Africa, is found on mudflats and sandy areas. Over thirty different birds of prey have been recorded in the Park, including the Palm-nut Vulture and Ayres' and Crowned Hawk Eagles.

Lake Manyara National Park is seventy-six miles south-west of Arusha via the Great north Road; at Makuyuni a right turn leads after twenty-five miles to the village of Mto-wa-Mbu: the Park entrance is a little over a mile past the village. Accommodation is available at the Lake Manyara Hotel, sited on the top of the Rift Wall with spectacular views over the lake. Official camping sites are available near the Park boundary.

MAMMALS OF LAKE MANYARA NATIONAL PARK

Spectacled Elephant Shrew
Giant White-toothed Shrew
Straw-coloured Fruit Bat
Epauletted Fruit Bat
White-bellied Tomb Bat
Hollow-faced Bat
False Vampire Bat
Yellow-winged Bat
Lander's Horseshoe Bat
Lesser Leaf-nosed Bat
Banana Bat or African Pipistrelle
Yellow-bellied Bat
Angola Free-tailed Bat
White-bellied Free-tailed Bat
Greater Galago
Bush Baby
Black-faced Vervet
Sykes' Monkey
Olive Baboon
Black-backed Jackal

Side-striped Jackal
Bat-eared Fox
Zorilla
Ratel or Honey Badger
Clawless Otter
African Civet
Small-spotted Genet
Large-spotted Genet
African Palm Civet
Marsh Mongoose
Dwarf Mongoose
Black-tipped Mongoose
Banded Mongoose
Spotted Hyaena
Lion
Leopard
Ant Bear
Tree Hyrax
Rock Hyrax
African Elephant
Black Rhinoceros
Common Zebra

Hippopotamus
Warthog
Masai Giraffe
Coke's Hartebeest
Red Duiker
Bush Duiker
Klipspringer
Suni
Kirk's Dik-dik
Common Waterbuck
Bohor Reedbuck
Impala
Bushbuck
African Buffalo
African Hare
Cane Rat
Porcupine
Striped Ground Squirrel
Bush Squirrel
African Dormouse

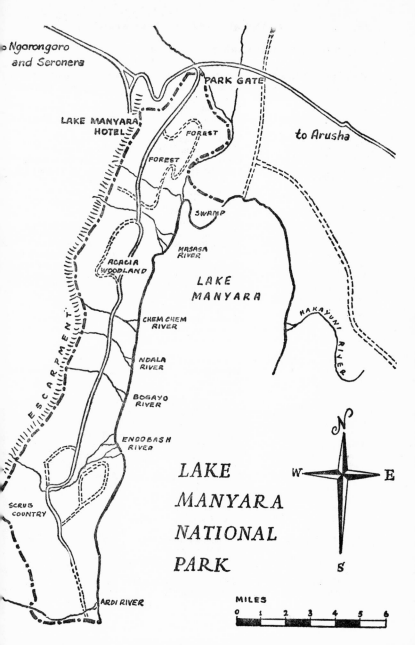

Ngorongoro and Seronera

PARK GATE

LAKE MANYARA HOTEL

FOREST

FOREST

to Arusha

SWAMP

MASASA RIVER

ACACIA WOODLAND

LAKE MANYARA

HAKAYUNI RIVER

CHEM CHEM RIVER

NDALA RIVER

BOGAYO RIVER

ESCARPMENT

ENDOBASH RIVER

SCRUB COUNTRY

LAKE
MANYARA
NATIONAL
PARK

N
W — E
S

ARDI RIVER

MILES
0 1 2 3 4 5 6

N.P.E.A.

G

BIRDS OF LAKE MANYARA NATIONAL PARK

Masai Ostrich *19
Great-crested Grebe *19
Little Grebe *20
Long-tailed Cormorant *21
White Pelican *22
Pink-backed Pelican *22
Grey Heron *23
Black-headed Heron *23
Goliath Heron *23
Purple Heron *24
Great White Egret *24
Yellow-billed Egret *25
Black Heron *25
Little Egret *25
Buff-backed Heron or Cattle Egret *26
Squacco Heron *26
Green-backed Heron *26
Night Heron *27
Dwarf Bittern *27
Hammerkop *28
White Stork *29
European Black Stork *30 Rare visitor
Abdim's Stork *29
Open-bill Stork *30
Saddle-bill Stork *30
Marabou Stork *31
Wood Ibis or Yellow-billed Stork *31
Sacred Ibis *31
Hadada Ibis *34
Glossy Ibis *34
African Spoonbill *34
Greater Flamingo *35
Lesser Flamingo *35
Maccoa Duck *36
White-backed Duck *36
African Pochard *37
European Shoveler *37
Yellow-billed Duck *38
African Black Duck *38 On streams
Garganey Teal *38
Cape Wigeon *39
Hottentot Teal *39
Red-billed Duck *39
European Pintail *39
Pygmy Goose *40
Knob-billed Goose *41
Egyptian Goose *41

Spur-winged Goose *41
Secretary Bird *42
Ruppell's Griffon Vulture *42
White-backed Vulture *43
Lappet-faced Vulture *43
White-headed Vulture *43
Egyptian Vulture *44
Hooded Vulture *43
Lanner *45
European Hobby *46
African Hobby *46
European Kestrel *47
Lesser Kestrel *50
Pygmy Falcon *51
Cuckoo Falcon *67 Rare
European Black Kite *51
African Black Kite *51
Black-shouldered Kite *51
Steppe Eagle *55 Uncommon winter visitor
Tawny Eagle *54
Wahlberg's Eagle *55
Ayres' Hawk Eagle *56
Martial Eagle *56
Crowned Hawk Eagle *57
Long-crested Hawk Eagle *57
Lizard Buzzard *57
Black-chested Harrier Eagle *58
Bateleur *59
African Fish Eagle *59
Palm-nut Vulture *44
Steppe Buzzard *62
Augur Buzzard *63
Little Sparrow Hawk *63
Ovampo Sparrow Hawk *66 Rare
Great Sparrow Hawk *66
Shikra *66
African Goshawk *67
Gabar Goshawk *67
Pale Chanting Goshawk *68
Montagu's Harrier *68
Pallid Harrier *69
European Marsh Harrier *69
African Marsh Harrier *69
Harrier Hawk *70

Osprey *70
Crested Francolin *71
Hildebrandt's Francolin *73
Red-necked Spurfowl *75
Yellow-necked Spurfowl *76
Cape Quail *76
Harlequin Quail *76
Helmeted Guinea-fowl *77
Crested Guinea-fowl *78
African Crake *79
Black Crake *79
Purple Gallinule *82
Moorhen *83
Lesser Moorhen *83
Red-knobbed Coot *83
Crowned Crane *86
Black-bellied Bustard *89
Hartlaub's Bustard *89
Spotted Stone Curlew *89
Water Dikkop *90
African Jacana *90
Ringed Plover *91
Little Ringed Plover *91
White-fronted Sand Plover *91
Chestnut-banded Sand Plover *91, *94
Kittlitz's Sand Plover *94
Three-banded Plover *94
Caspian Plover *95
Crowned Lapwing or Plover *98
Blacksmith Plover *100
Long-toed Lapwing *101
Avocet *101
Black-winged Stilt *102
Painted Snipe *103
European Common Snipe *104
Great Snipe *104
African Snipe *104
Curlew Sandpiper *105
Little Stint *105
Sanderling *105 Rare visitor
Ruff *106
Terek Sandpiper *106 Uncommon
Common Sandpiper *107

European Common Wheatear *198
Pied Wheatear *198
Capped Wheatear *198
Cliff Chat 23
White-browed Robin Chat *200
Red-capped Robin Chat *201
Spotted Morning Warbler *202
Red-backed Scrub Robin *202
White-winged Scrub Robin *202
Sprosser 286
Blackcap Warbler *204
Lesser Swamp Warbler 287
Black-breasted Apalis *206
Red-faced Crombec *207
Grey-backed Camaroptera *210
Rattling Cisticola *211
Winding Cisticola 294
Croaking Cisticola 294
Tawny-flanked Prinia *211
European Swallow *212
Wire-tailed Swallow *212
Mosque Swallow *213
Striped Swallow *213
African Sand Martin *214
Banded Martin *214
African Rock Martin *214
Black Rough-wing Swallow *214
Black Cuckoo Shrike *215
Drongo *216
Straight-crested Helmet Shrike *217
White-crowned Shrike *218
Lesser Grey Shrike *220
Long-tailed Fiscal *220

Grey-backed Fiscal *220
Red-backed Shrike *221
Red-tailed Shrike *221
Magpie Shrike *221
Slate-coloured Boubou *222
Black-backed Puff-back *223
Brown-headed Bush Shrike *223
Sulphur-breasted Bush Shrike *224
White-breasted Tit *226
African Golden Oriole *227
European Golden Oriole *227
Black-headed Oriole *227
Pied Crow *230
White-naped Raven *230
Wattled Starling *231
Violet-backed Starling *232
Blue-eared Glossy Starling *232
Red-wing Starling *234
Hildebrandt's Starling *235
Superb Starling *235
Yellow-billed Oxpecker *238
Red-billed Oxpecker *235
Yellow White-eye *238
Bronzy Sunbird *242
Beautiful Sunbird (black-bellied race) *243
Golden-winged Sunbird *243
Variable Sunbird *244
Amethyst Sunbird *245
Scarlet-chested Sunbird *246
Collared Sunbird *247
Kenya Violet-backed Sunbird 29
Buffalo Weaver *248

White-headed Buffalo Weaver *249
Rufous-tailed Weaver 31
Grey-headed Sparrow *250
Yellow-spotted Petronia 27
Masked Weaver *252
Vitelline Masked Weaver *252
Golden-backed Weaver *253
Chestnut Weaver *253
Spectacled Weaver *255
Grosbeak Weaver *259
Red-headed Weaver *259
Red-billed Quelea *259
Cardinal Quelea *260
Red Bishop *260
Black Bishop 32
Fan-tailed Widow-bird *262
Red-collared Widow-bird *262
Rufous-backed Mannikin *264
Peters' Twin-spot 28
Green-winged Pytilia *264
Jameson's Fire Finch *265
Red-billed Fire Finch *265
Waxbill *266
Crimson-rumped Waxbill *266
Red-cheeked Cordon-bleu *266
Purple Indigo-bird 28
Pin-tailed Whydah *267
Steel-blue Whydah *267
Fischer's Straw-tailed Whydah *267
Paradise Whydah *268
Streaky Seed-eater *269

MIKUMI NATIONAL PARK

Mikumi National Park, a faunal reserve of some 450 square miles, is situated 183 miles from Dar es Salaam astride the main road to Iringa. All but the last twenty miles of this road are macadamised. Picturesque wooded hills form a border to the Mkata River flood plains, one of the main sections of the Park and the haunt of many Elephant and Buffalo. There are also areas of brachystegia woodlands, broken by

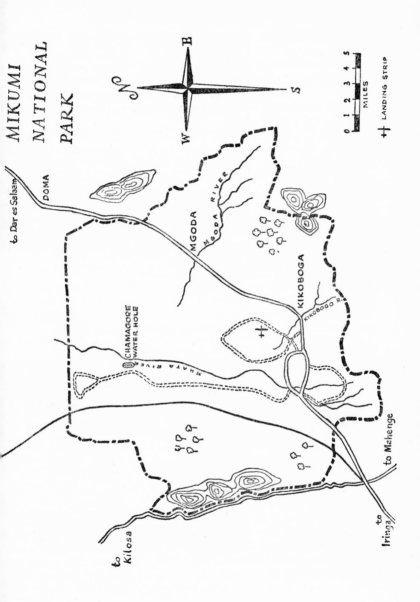

MIKUMI NATIONAL PARK

to Dar es Salaam

DOMA

MGODA

MGODA RIVER

CHAMAGORE WATER HOLE

MUATA RIVER

KIKOBOGA

KIKOBOGA R.

to Kilosa

to Mahenge

to Iringa

N
E
W
S

0 1 2 3 4 5
MILES

LANDING STRIP

glades and transient watercourses. Game animals and birds are abundant.

The mammals most frequently encountered are Lion, Hippopotamus, Masai Giraffe, Common Zebra, Impala, Warthog and Wildebeest. Present though less common are Greater Kudu, Black Rhinoceros, Cheetah, Leopard, Common Waterbuck, Bohor Reedbuck, Lichtenstein's Hartebeest and Sable Antelope.

Birdlife is extremely varied, many colourful and interesting species occurring in Mikumi National Park which are not found in the more northern Parks. Species of special note include White-backed Night Heron, Dickinson's Kestrel (in brachystegia woodlands), Bronze-winged Courser, Delalande's Green Pigeon, Violet-crested Turaco, Brown-necked Parrot, Racquet-tailed Roller, Boehm's Bee-eater, Pale-billed Hornbill, Spotted-throated Woodpecker, Angola Rock Thrush, White-headed Black Chat, White-breasted Cuckoo Shrike, Ashy Starling and Shelley's Double-collared Sunbird which frequents a red-flowered Loranthus parasitic on brachystegia trees.

Mikumi is most accessible from Dar-es-Salaam—an easy three and a half hours' drive. It may also be reached from Iringa, 135 miles along the Iringa-Morogoro road. Permanent tented accommodation is available at the Mikumi Game Camp, and there are camping sites within the Park. An airstrip close to the tented camp is maintained for light aircraft.

MAMMALS OF MIKUMI NATIONAL PARK

Spectacled Elephant Shrew	Dwarf Mongoose	Red Duiker
Epauletted Fruit Bat	Banded Mongoose	Bush Duiker
Hollow-faced Bat	Spotted Hyaena	Common Waterbuck
Lesser Leaf-nosed Bat	Cheetah	Bohor Reedbuck
Yellow-bellied Bat	Serval	Impala
White-bellied Free-tailed Bat	Lion	Sable Antelope
Bush Baby	Leopard	Bushbuck
Black-faced Vervet	Ant Bear	Greater Kudu
Yellow Baboon	Rock Hyrax	African Buffalo
Hunting Dog	African Elephant	African Hare
Black-backed Jackal	Black Rhinoceros	Cane Rat
Bat-eared Fox	Common Zebra	Porcupine
Ratel	Hippopotamus	Striped Ground Squirrel
Small-spotted Genet	Warthog	Bush Squirrel
Large-spotted Genet	Masai Giraffe	Spring Hare
	Wildebeest	African Dormouse

BIRDS OF MIKUMI NATIONAL PARK

Long-tailed Cormorant *21
White Pelican *22
Pink-backed Pelican *22
Black-headed Heron *23
Goliath Heron *23
Yellow-billed Egret *25
Black Heron *25
Little Egret *25
Buff-backed Heron or
Cattle Egret *26
Squacco Heron *26
Green-backed Heron *26
White-backed Night Heron *27
Hammerkop *28
White Stork *29
Open-bill Stork *30
Saddle-bill Stork *30
Marabou Stork *31
Wood Ibis or Yellow-billed Stork *31
Sacred Ibis *31
Hadada Ibis *34
African Spoonbill *34
Red-billed Duck *39
Pygmy Goose *40
Egyptian Goose *41
Knob-billed Goose *41
Secretary Bird *42
White-backed Vulture *43
European Hobby *46
Mainly spring migrant
Red-necked Falcon *46
European Kestrel *47
Lesser Kestrel *50
Dickinson's Kestrel *50
Cuckoo Falcon *67
African Black Kite *51
Black-shouldered Kite *51
Tawny Eagle *54
Wahlberg's Eagle *55
Martial Eagle *56
Lizard Buzzard *57
Black-chested Harrier Eagle *58
Bateleur *59
African Fish Eagle *59
Little Sparrow Hawk *63
Ovampo Sparrow Hawk *66

Great Sparrow Hawk *66
Shikra *66
Gabar Goshawk *67
Dark Chanting Goshawk *68
Montagu's Harrier *68
Pallid Harrier *69
European Marsh Harrier *69
African Marsh Harrier *69
Harrier Hawk *70
Coqui Francolin *71
Shelley's (Greywing) Francolin *72
Red-necked Spurfowl *76
Harlequin Quail *76
Helmeted Guinea-fowl *77
Black Crake *79
Crowned Crane *86
Black-bellied Bustard *89
Spotted Stone Curlew *89
Water Dikkop *90
African Jacana *90
Little Ringed Plover *91
Kittlitz's Sand Plover *94
Three-banded Plover *94
Crowned Lapwing or Plover *98
Blacksmith Plover *100
Painted Snipe *103
Ruff *106
Common Sandpiper *107
Green Sandpiper *107
Wood Sandpiper *107
Greenshank *109
Temminck's Courser *110
Bronze-winged Courser *98, *111
Pratincole *111
Red-eyed Dove *120
Ring-necked Dove *120
Laughing Dove *121
Namaqua Dove *121
Tambourine Dove *122
Emerald-spotted Wood Dove *121
Delalande's Green Pigeon 237
European Cuckoo *123
African Cuckoo *123
Red-chested Cuckoo *123

Levaillant's Cuckoo *124
Black and White Cuckoo *124
Emerald Cuckoo *125
Didric Cuckoo *125
White-browed Coucal *126
Violet-crested Turaco *131
Bare-faced Go-away-bird 17
Brown-necked Parrot 17
Brown Parrot *134
Yellow-collared Lovebird *135
European Roller *135
Racquet-tailed Roller 18
Lilac-breasted Roller *136
Rufous-crowned Roller *136
Broad-billed Roller *137
Pied Kingfisher *137
Half-collared Kingfisher 18
Malachite Kingfisher *138
Pygmy Kingfisher *139
Grey-headed Kingfisher *140
Striped Kingfisher *140
European Bee-eater *140
Madagascar Bee-eater 19
Southern Carmine Bee-eater 19
White-throated Bee-eater *142
Boehm's Bee-eater 19
Little Bee-eater *142
Swallow-tailed Bee-eater *146
Trumpeter Hornbill *146
Grey Hornbill *147
Crowned Hornbill *149
Pale-billed Hornbill *148
Ground Hornbill *150
African Hoopoe *151
Green Wood Hoopoe *152
Scimitar-bill *153
African Marsh Owl *154
African Wood Owl *154
African Scops Owl *154
Pearl-spotted Owlet *155
Verreaux's Eagle Owl *155
European Nightjar *156
Freckled Nightjar *157
Plain Nightjar *157

Shelley's Double-collared Sunbird 313
Variable Sunbird *244
Southern Double-collared Sunbird 30
Amethyst Sunbird *245
Scarlet-chested Sunbird *246
Olive Sunbird 30
Collared Sunbird *247
Violet-backed Sunbird *247
Spotted Creeper *248
White-headed Buffalo Weaver *249
White-browed Sparrow Weaver *249
Grey-headed Sparrow *250
Yellow-throated Petronia 323
Layard's Black-headed Weaver *251
Masked Weaver *252
Golden-backed Weaver *253
Black-necked Weaver *254
Spectacled Weaver *255

Holub's Golden Weaver *255
Grosbeak Weaver *259
Red-headed Weaver *259
Red-billed Quelea *259
Red-headed Quelea *260
Cardinal Quelea *260
Red Bishop *260
Black-winged Bishop *261
Yellow Bishop *261
Fan-tailed Widow-bird *262
Yellow-mantled Widow-bird 32
White-winged Widow-bird *262
Red-collared Widow-bird *262
Bronze Mannikin *264
Rufous-backed Mannikin *264
Magpie Mannikin 331
Grey-headed Silver-bill 27
Urungu Seed-cracker 333
Quail Finch 27
Peters' Twin-spot 28

Green-winged Pytilia *264
Jameson's Fire Finch *265
Red-billed Fire Finch *265
Yellow-bellied Waxbill *266
Waxbill *266
Zebra Waxbill 337
Angola Cordon-bleu *267
Red-cheeked Cordon-bleu *266
Purple Grenadier *267
Purple Indigo-bird 28
Pin-tailed Whydah *267
Fischer's Straw-tailed Whydah *267
Paradise Whydah *268
Yellow-fronted Canary *269
Brimstone Canary *268
Streaky-headed Seed-eater 340
Three-streaked Bunting 28
Golden-breasted Bunting *270
Cinnamon-breasted Rock Bunting *270

NGORONGORO CRATER CONSERVATION AREA

The Ngorongoro Conservation Area of 2,500 square miles was established in 1959. Previously, most of the area and the famous Ngorongoro Crater had formed part of the now contiguous Serengeti National Park. The dual purpose of the Conservation Area is to conserve the region's natural resources and also to safeguard the interests of the indigenous Masai inhabitants, who continue to reside there with their herds of cattle.

The Ngorongoro Crater is one of the most spectacular game haunts in Africa: it is also one of the biggest craters or more correctly calderas in the world, over nine miles across, 2,000 to 2,500 feet deep and covering 102 square miles. The approach road at 7,500 feet skirts the rim of the crater affording many breathtaking scenic views over the crater floor thousands of feet below.

Entry into the crater is by way of the Lerai Descent, an extremely steep and winding road down the slopes of the crater wall—negotiable only by four-wheel-drive vehicles. The caldera bottom is mainly open grassy plains with alternating fresh and brackish-water lakes, swamps and two patches of dense acacia woodlands called the Lerai and Laindi Forests.

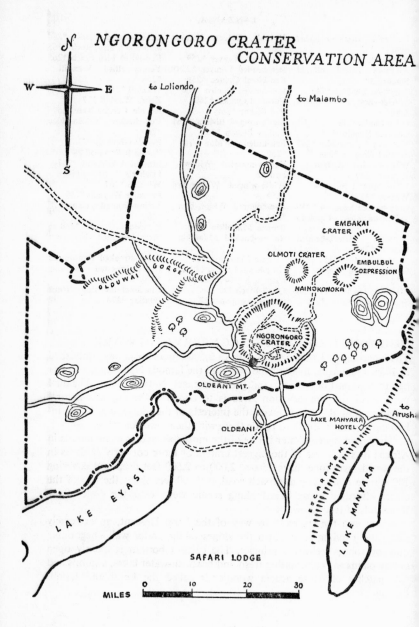

NGORONGORO CRATER CONSERVATION AREA

N
W — E
S

to Loliondo

to Malambo

EMBAKAI CRATER

OLMOTI CRATER

EMBULBUL DEPRESSION

OLDUVAI GORGE

NAINOKONOKA

NGORONGORO CRATER

OLDEANI MT.

LAKE MANYARA HOTEL

to Arusha

OLDEANI

ESCARPMENT

LAKE EYASI

LAKE MANYARA

SAFARI LODGE

MILES
0   10   20   30

Game animals and birds are abundant inside the crater. All of the so-called "Big Five" may be seen—Elephant, Lion, Black Rhinoceros, Hippopotamus and Buffalo. Other species commonly encountered are Cheetah, Eland, Grant's and Thomson's Gazelles, Common Zebra, a super-abundance of Spotted Hyaena, Hunting Dog, and, if one is lucky, Leopard.

Among the notable birds are Lammergeyer, Verreaux's Eagle and Egyptian Vulture, which make their home in the highest cliffs of the crater wall; the beautiful Rosy-breasted Longclaw, which appears on the plains after rains; and flocks of Lesser and Greater Flamingos which are spasmodic visitors to the crater lakes. The European Black Stork is sometimes seen; usually one or two winter in the crater.

In the highland forest on the crater rim two sunbirds are specially noticeable, the long-tailed Golden-winged Sunbird and the smaller Eastern Double-collared Sunbird. At dusk the Abyssinian Nightjar is often seen or heard—the call is a long-drawn-out "Pee-oo-wee."

From Arusha the distance to the Crater Lodge is 112 miles; the road passes the entrance to Lake Manyara National Park, thence on to the Mbulu Plateau, through the farming country of Karatu and Oldeani and into the highland forest to the rim of the crater. From Seronera, headquarters of the Serengeti National Park, to the crater is eighty-seven miles, first over miles of open plains and light acacia woodlands and then into the hill country west of the crater. This road passes famous Olduvai Gorge, where remains of prehistoric man were discovered. For those who wish to visit Ngorongoro Crater by air there is a 5,000 foot airstrip on the crater floor, suitable for light aircraft.

Accommodation is available at the Ngorongoro Crater Lodge, situated at nearly 8,000 feet on the crater rim, near the Lerai entrance road.

MAMMALS OF NGORONGORO CRATER CONSERVATION AREA

Rousette Fruit Bat
Epauletted Fruit Bat
Hollow-faced Bat
False Vampire Bat
Lesser Leaf-nosed Bat
Yellow-bellied Bat
Angola Free-tailed Bat
Black-faced Vervet
Olive Baboon
Hunting Dog
Golden Jackal
Black-backed Jackal
Side-striped Jackal
Bat-eared Fox

Ratel or Honey Badger
African Civet
Small-spotted Genet
Large-spotted Genet
Marsh Mongoose
Dwarf Mongoose
Banded Mongoose
Spotted Hyaena
Cheetah
African Wild Cat
Serval
Lion
Leopard
Rock Hyrax

African Elephant
Black Rhinoceros
Common Zebra
Hippopotamus
Giant Forest Hog In forest on crater rim
Warthog
Masai Giraffe
Coke's Hartebeest
White-bearded Gnu or Wildebeest
Bush Duiker
Klipspringer
Common Waterbuck

Bohor Reedbuck
Impala
Thomson's Gazelle
Grant's Gazelle

Bushbuck
Eland
African Buffalo
African Hare

Porcupine
Bush Squirrel
Giant Rat

BIRDS OF NGORONGORO CRATER CONSERVATION AREA

Masai Ostrich *19
Little Grebe *20
Long-tailed Cormorant *21
White Pelican *22
Pink-backed Pelican *22
Grey Heron *23
Black-headed Heron *23
Goliath Heron *23
Great White Egret *24
Yellow-billed Egret *25
Little Egret *25
Buff-backed Heron or
Cattle Egret *26
Squacco Heron *26
Hammerkop *28
White Stork *29
European Black Stork
*30
Abdim's Stork *29
Open-bill Stork *30
Saddle-bill Stork *30
Marabou Stork *31
Wood Ibis or Yellow-billed
Stork *31
Sacred Ibis *31
Hadada Ibis *34
African Spoonbill *34
Greater Flamingo *35
Lesser Flamingo *35
White-backed Duck *36
African Pochard *37
European Shoveler *37
Yellow-billed Duck *38
African Black Duck *38
Garganey Teal *38
Hottentot Teal *39
Red-billed Duck *39
Cape Wigeon *39
European Teal *39 Rare
visitor
European Pintail *39
Fulvous Tree Duck *40
Knob-billed Goose *41
Egyptian Goose *41
Spur-winged Goose *41
Secretary Bird *42

Ruppell's Griffon Vulture
*42
White-backed Vulture *43
Lappet-faced Vulture *43
White-headed Vulture *43
Egyptian Vulture *44
Hooded Vulture *43
Peregrine *45
Lanner *45
European Kestrel *47
Lesser Kestrel *50
European Black Kite *51
African Black Kite *51
Black-shouldered Kite *51
Verreaux's Eagle *54
Steppe Eagle *55
Tawny Eagle *54
Martial Eagle *56
Long-crested Hawk Eagle
*57
Black-chested Harrier
Eagle *58
Bateleur *59
African Fish Eagle *59
Lammergeyer *44
Steppe Buzzard *62
Augur Buzzard *63
Gabar Goshawk *67
Montagu's Harrier *68
Pallid Harrier *69
European Marsh Harrier
*69
African Marsh Harrier
*69
Yellow-necked   Spurfowl
*76
Helmeted Guinea-fowl *77
Crowned Crane *86
Kori Bustard *87
Little Ringed Plover *91
Kittlitz's Sand Plover *94
Three-banded Plover *94
Caspian Plover *95
Crowned   Lapwing   or
Plover *98
Senegal Plover *98

Blacksmith Plover *100
Avocet *101
Black-winged Stilt *102
Painted Snipe *103
European Common Snipe
*104
African Snipe *104
Curlew Sandpiper *105
Little Stint *105
Ruff *106
Common Sandpiper *107
Green Sandpiper *107
Wood Sandpiper *107
Marsh Sandpiper *108
Greenshank *109
Temminck's Courser *110
Pratincole *111
White-winged Black Tern
*115
Red-eyed Dove *120
Ring-necked Dove *120
Laughing Dove *121
Namaqua Dove *121
Emerald-spotted Wood
Dove *121
Green Pigeon *122
European Cuckoo *123
African Cuckoo *123
Red-chested Cuckoo *123
Black Cuckoo *124
Great-spotted Cuckoo *124
Didric Cuckoo *125
White-browed Coucal *126
White-bellied Go-away-bird
*132
Lilac-breasted Roller *13
Pied Kingfisher *137
Malachite Kingfisher *138
Pygmy Kingfisher *139
Grey-headed   Kingfisher
*140
Striped Kingfisher *140
European Bee-eater *140
Little Bee-eater *142
Grey Hornbill *147
Crowned Hornbill *149

African Hoopoe *151
Green Wood Hoopoe *152
Scimitar-bill *153
African Marsh Owl *154
Pearl-spotted Owlet *155
Spotted Eagle Owl *155
Verreaux's Eagle Owl *155
European Nightjar *156
Plain Nightjar *157
Abyssinian Nightjar *157
Long-tailed Nightjar *158
Speckled Mousebird *159
Nubian Woodpecker *172
Cardinal Woodpecker *173
Brown-backed Woodpecker *173
Nyanza Swift *174
Mottled Swift *175
Fischer's Sparrow Lark *182
Red-capped Lark *182
African Pied Wagtail *183
Blue-headed Wagtail and races *184
Richard's Pipit *184
Yellow-throated Longclaw *186
Rosy-breasted Longclaw *186
Dark-capped Bulbul *188
European Spotted Flycatcher *190
Grey Flycatcher *191
White-eyed Slaty Flycatcher *191
South African Black Flycatcher *191
Chin-spot Flycatcher *194
Black-throated Wattle-eye *195
Paradise Flycatcher *195
European Rock Thrush *197
Little Rock Thrush *197
European Common Wheatear *198
Isabelline Wheatear *198
Pied Wheatear *198
Schalow's Wheatear *198
Capped Wheatear *198
Cliff Chat 23

Anteater Chat *199
Stonechat *200
European Whinchat *200
Robin Chat *201
European Willow Warbler *205
Black-breasted Apalis *206
Grey-backed Camaroptera *210
Rattling Cisticola *211
Winding Cisticola 294
Tawny-flanked Prinia *211
European Swallow *212
Angola Swallow *212
Red-rumped Swallow *213
Striped Swallow *213
Grey-rumped Swallow *213
European Sand Martin *214
African Sand Martin *214
Banded Martin *214
African Rock Martin *214
Black Rough-wing Swallow *214
Black Cuckoo Shrike *215
Drongo *216
White-crowned Shrike *218
Northern Brubru *219
Grey-backed Fiscal *220
Lesse Grey Shrike *220
Fiscal Shrike *219
Long-tailed Fiscal *220
Red-backed Shrike *221
Red-tailed Shrike *221
Magpie Shrike *221
Slate-coloured Boubou *222
Tropical Boubou *222
Black-headed Bush Shrike *223
Sulphur-breasted Bush Shrike *224
White-breasted Tit *226
Black-headed Oriole *227
Pied Crow *230
Cape Rock *230
White-naped Raven *230
Wattled Starling *231
Blue-eared Glossy Starling *232
Red-wing Starling *234
Superb Starling *235

Red-billed Oxpecker *235
Bronzy Sunbird *242
Golden-winged Sunbird *243
Mariqua Sunbird *244
Variable Sunbird *244
Eastern Double-collared Sunbird *245
Scarlet-chested Sunbird *246
Collared Sunbird *247
White-browed Sparrow Weaver *249
Rufous-tailed Weaver 31
Grey-headed Social Weaver *250
Kenya Rufous Sparrow *250
Yellow-spotted Petronia 27
Speckle-fronted Weaver 27
Masked Weaver *252
Chestnut Weaver *253
Red-billed Quelea *259
Cardinal Quelea *260
Red Bishop *260
Yellow Bishop *261
Fan-tailed Widow-bird *262
White-winged Widow-bird *262
Bronze Mannikin *264
Cut-throat *264
Quail Finch 27
Green-winged Pytilia *264
Red-billed Fire Finch *265
Waxbill *266
Red-cheeked Cordon-bleu *266
Purple Grenadier *267
Purple Indigo-bird 28
Pin-tailed Whydah *267
Paradise Whydah *268
Yellow-fronted Canary *269
Brimstone Canary *268
Yellow-breasted Seed-eater *269
Streaky Seed-eater *269
Golden-breasted Bunting *270
Cinnamon-breasted Rock Bunting *270

NGURDOTO CRATER NATIONAL PARK

Considering that the Ngurdoto Crater National Park embraces an area of only twenty square miles and is less than half an hour's drive from Arusha, it is remarkable for its range of habitats—a miniature volcanic crater, highland rain forest, acacia woodland and a string of crater lakes—and for the range of game animals and birds which occur there. In addition on a clear day there are spectacular views of both Mount Kilimanjaro and Mount Meru from strategically placed lookouts on Ngurdoto Crater rim.

Game animals in great quantity will not be seen in this Park, but Black Rhinoceros, Elephant, Buffalo, Masai Giraffe and other animals live in the crater and may be viewed through binoculars from the several ideally placed vantage points around the rim. The crater itself, one and a half miles across, is a sanctuary within a sanctuary, open only to the wild creatures which inhabit it and where man is completely excluded.

The Momela crater lakes at the northern end of the Park are visited by herds of Elephant, Masai Giraffe, the odd Black Rhinoceros and other animals, and it is here that Bushbuck sometimes emerge from cover in the early morning and late evening.

In the forested parts of the Park, Black and White Colobus and Blue Monkeys are often observed, and if one is fortunate the Crowned Hawk Eagle—ogre of the monkey population—may also be seen.

Greater and Lesser Flamingos and a host of other water-birds occur on the Momela lakes and offer many photographic opportunities. The beautiful Narina's Trogon is found in the forests, but is shy and often overlooked, and is best located by its call—a series of soft coos all on one note. The African Broadbill and the deep green Broad-ringed White-eye are other interesting birds found in this forest habitat.

To reach Ngurdoto Crater National Park from Arusha one follows the main Arusha-Moshi road to mile thirteen, there turning left into a signposted gravel road towards Ngare Nanyuki; and after nine miles a short branch road to the right leads to the Park's crater gate. If travelling from Nairobi one takes a sign-posted turning to the left twenty-four miles before Arusha, from then on following signboards which lead to the Momela Gate. For those wishing to spend some days in the Park, accommodation is provided at the Momela Game Lodge.

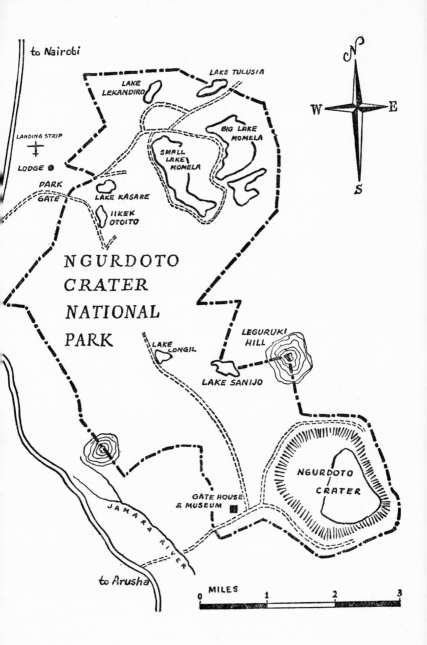

MAMMALS OF NGURDOTO CRATER NATIONAL PARK

Giant White-toothed Shrew
Rousette Fruit Bat
Epauletted Fruit Bat
White-bellied Tomb Bat
Hollow-faced Bat
False Vampire Bat
Yellow-winged Bat
Banana Bat
Yellow-bellied Bat
Angola Free-tailed Bat
White-bellied Free-tailed Bat
Greater Galago
Bush Baby
Black-faced Vervet
Blue Monkey
Olive Baboon
Black and White Colobus
Black-backed Jackal

Side-striped Jackal
Zorilla
African Civet
Large-spotted Genet
African Palm Civet
Marsh Mongoose
Black-tipped Mongoose
Spotted Hyaena
Serval
Leopard
Ant Bear
Tree Hyrax
Rock Hyrax
African Elephant
Black Rhinoceros
Common Zebra
Hippopotamus
Giant Forest Hog
Warthog

Bush Pig
Masai Giraffe
Red Duiker
Blue Duiker
Bush Duiker
Suni
Kirk's Dik-dik
Common Waterbuck
Bohor Reedbuck
Impala
Bushbuck
African Buffalo
African Hare
Porcupine
Bush Squirrel
Giant Rat
Kenya Mole Rat

BIRDS OF NGURDOTO CRATER NATIONAL PARK

Great-crested Grebe *19
Little Grebe *20
Long-tailed Cormorant *21
White Pelican *22
Pink-backed Pelican *22
Grey Heron *23
Black-headed Heron *23
Purple Heron *24
Great White Egret *24
Yellow-billed Egret *25
Buff-backed Heron or Cattle Egret *26
Squacco Heron *26
Night Heron *27
Little Bittern *27
Hammerkop *28
White Stork *29 Spasmodic visitor
Saddle-bill Stork *30
Marabou Stork *31
Wood Ibis or Yellow-billed Stork *31
Sacred Ibis *31
Hadada Ibis *34
African Spoonbill *34
Greater Flamingo *35
Lesser Flamingo *35
Maccoa Duck *36
White-backed Duck *36
African Pochard *37

European Shoveler *37
Yellow-billed Duck *38
Garganey Teal *38
Cape Wigeon *39
Hottentot Teal *39
Red-billed Duck *39
European Pintail *39
White-faced Tree Duck *40
Fulvous Tree Duck *40
Knob-billed Goose *41
Egyptian Goose *41
Spur-winged Goose *41
White-backed Vulture *43
Peregrine *45
Lanner *45
European Kestrel *47
Cuckoo Falcon *67
African Black Kite *51
Black-shouldered Kite *51
Ayres' Hawk Eagle *56 Rare
Martial Eagle *56
Crowned Hawk Eagle *57
Long-crested Hawk Eagle *57
Bateleur *59
African Fish Eagle *59
Palm-nut Vulture *44
Mountain Buzzard *62
Augur Buzzard *63

Little Sparrow Hawk *63
Great Sparrow Hawk *66
African Goshawk *67
Gabar Goshawk *67
Harrier Hawk *70
Shelley's (Greywing) Francolin *72
Hildebrandt's Francolin *73
Scaly Francolin *74
Helmeted Guinea-fowl *77
Black Crake *79
Moorhen *83
Lesser Moorhen *83
Red-knobbed Coot *83
Crowned Crane *86
African Jacana *90
Ringed Plover *91
Little Ringed Plover *91
Kittlitz's Sand Plover *94
Three-banded Plover *94
Crowned Lapwing or Plover *98
Black-winged Plover *99
Blacksmith Plover *100
Avocet *101
Black-winged Stilt *102
European Common Snipe *104
African Snipe *104

Bronzy Sunbird *242
Beautiful Sunbird *243
Golden-winged Sunbird *243
Variable Sunbird *244
Amethyst Sunbird *245
Scarlet-chested Sunbird *246
Olive Sunbird 30
Collared Sunbird *247
Speke's Weaver *251
Chestnut Weaver *253
Golden Palm Weaver *254
Taveta Golden Weaver 31

Spectacled Weaver *255
Reichenow's Weaver *258
Grosbeak Weaver *259
Red-headed Weaver *259
Red-billed Quelea *259
Cardinal Quelea *260
Yellow Bishop *261
Red-naped Widow Bird *262
Bronze Mannikin *264
Rufous-backed Mannikin *264
Grey-headed Negro Finch 32

Jameson's Fire Finch *265
Yellow-bellied Waxbill *266
Waxbill *266
Crimson-rumped Waxbill *266
Pin-tailed Whydah *267
Streaky Seed-eater *269
Thick-billed Seed-eater 28
African Citril 339
Golden-breasted Bunting *270

RUAHA NATIONAL PARK

The Ruaha National Park, most recently created of Tanzanian Parks—it was gazetted in 1964—is a vast, still comparatively unexplored game and bird sanctuary covering 5,000 square miles; it is only a little smaller than the better-known Serengeti National Park. Mainly on account of its geographical position this most outstanding Park is at present little visited although it is readily accessible by air, being less than four hours' flying time from Nairobi. A landing strip suitable for light aircraft exists at Park headquarters at Msembe: or one can fly to Iringa and motor the remaining seventy miles to the Park.

The Ruaha National Park lies between two large rivers, the Njombe and the Ruaha: the latter flows for a hundred miles along the entire eastern border, first through rugged gorges and rocky broken country then through lush plains where it is flanked by palm thickets and tall acacia woodland. During the dry season, from June to November, there is a concentration of game along the river, herds of Elephant, Giraffe, Buffalo and Impala and numerous Greater Kudu. Crocodiles may be seen basking on the many sandbanks.

The hinterland varies from mountains to undulating plateau country at an altitude around 3,000 feet. There are stretches of brachystegia woodland, the home of Roan and Sable Antelope and Lichtenstein's Hartebeest, and bush country where Lesser Kudu occur. There are also areas of open grassland, an abundance of rocky hills and in the south the zoologically unexplored massif of Ngalambulwa Mountain which rises to 5,250 feet.

Three main areas have so far been opened up for game viewing, the really spectacular Ruaha River drive of great scenic beauty where Greater Kudu are common and tame, the Mdonya woodlands circuit where Sable and Roan Antelope and Lichtenstein's Hartebeest may be encountered, and the Mbage-Mwagusi track for Elephants.

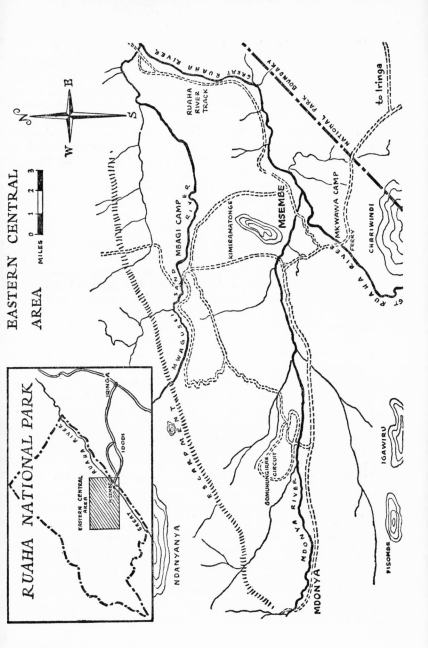

RUAHA NATIONAL PARK

EASTERN CENTRAL
AREA

MILES
0 1 2 3

Access roads to other areas of special interest are under construction or being planned. Among the special facilities available at Ruaha—which should be introduced in other National Parks—are the several photographic hides and tree-houses strategically placed to overlook habitual game watering points.

Perhaps Ruaha's greatest charm is the fact that it is a completely unspoiled African wilderness. Its future potential is very great and of all the East African faunal preserves it is the Park of the future. To visit it during the early days of its development is a unique experience.

There is an impressive array of game animals in the Ruaha National Park. It is the largest Elephant sanctuary in Tanzania, and it is the only East African Park where one may be certain of seeing and photographing Greater Kudu. Among the carnivora Lion, Leopard, Cheetah, Hunting Dog, Spotted Hyaena and Bat-eared Fox are all possibles.

Bird life is abundant and the Park is one of the few places in Africa where the rare raptorial Eleanora's Falcon may be encountered: migrating flocks have been recorded in December and January. The brachystegia woodland is the home of Dickinson's Kestrel, Violet-crested Turaco, Pale-billed Hornbill and Racquet-tailed Roller. Along the more heavily wooded sections of the Ruaha River is found the giant Pel's Fishing Owl.

The Park is reached from Iringa, seventy miles, via Mloa (by-passing Idoli), and across the Ruaha River by ferry within the Park at Ibuguziwa. From Dar-es-Salaam to the Park is 386 miles, by way of Morogoro and Iringa. Do-it-yourself rondaval accommodation is available near Park headquarters. Camping is permitted in demarcated areas in the Park

MAMMALS OF RUAHA NATIONAL PARK

Rousette Fruit Bat	Blue Monkey	Cheetah
Epauletted Fruit Bat	Yellow Baboon	Caracal
White-bellied Tomb Bat	Hunting Dog	African Wild Cat
Hollow-faced Bat	Black-backed Jackal	Serval
False Vampire Bat	Side-striped Jackal	Lion
Yellow-winged Bat	Bat-eared Fox	Leopard
Lesser Leaf-nosed Bat	Ratel or Honey Badger	Ant Bear
Giant Leaf-nosed Bat	African Civet	Tree Hyrax
Banana Bat	Small-spotted Genet	Rock Hyrax
Yellow-bellied Bat	Large-spotted Genet	African Elephant
Angola Free-tailed Bat	African Palm Civet	Black Rhinoceros
White-bellied Free-tailed Bat	Marsh Mongoose	Common Zebra
Greater Galago	Dwarf Mongoose	Hippopotamus
Bush Baby	Large Grey Mongoose	Warthog
Black-faced Vervet	Aard-wolf Rare	Masai Giraffe
	Spotted Hyaena	Lichtenstein's Hartebeest

Bush Duiker
Klipspringer
Kirk's Dik-dik
Common Waterbuck
Bohor Reedbuck
Impala
Grant's Gazelle

Sable Antelope
Roan Antelope
Bushbuck
Greater Kudu
Lesser Kudu
Eland
African Buffalo

African Hare
Cane Rat
Porcupine
Bush Squirrel
Spring Hare
African Dormouse

BIRDS OF RUAHA NATIONAL PARK

Little Grebe *20
Long-tailed Cormorant *21
African Darter *21
White Pelican *22
Pink-backed Pelican *22
Black-headed Heron *23
Goliath Heron *23
Great White Egret *24
Yellow-billed Egret *25
Little Egret *25
Buff-backed Heron or Cattle Egret *26
Green-backed Heron *26
Hammerkop *28
White Stork *29
European Black Stork *30
Woolly-necked Stork *29
Abdim's Stork *29
Open-bill Stork *30
Saddle-bill Stork *30
Marabou Stork *31
Wood Ibis or Yellow-billed Stork *31
Sacred Ibis *31
Hadada Ibis *34
African Black Duck *38
Red-billed Duck *39
Knob-billed Goose *41
Egyptian Goose *41
Spur-winged Goose *41
Secretary Bird *42
White-backed Vulture *43
Hooded Vulture *43
Lanner *45
European Hobby *46
Eleonora's Falcon 231
Red-necked Falcon *46
European Kestrel *47
Lesser Kestrel *50
Grey Kestrel *50
Dickinson's Kestrel *50
Cuckoo Falcon *67
European Black Kite *51
African Black Kite *51

Black-shouldered Kite *51
Bat Hawk *46
Tawny Eagle *54
Wahlberg's Eagle *55
African Hawk Eagle *55
Martial Eagle *56
Crowned Hawk Eagle *57
Long-crested Hawk Eagle *57
Lizard Buzzard *57
Brown Harrier Eagle *55, *58
Black-chested Harrier Eagle *58
Southern Banded Harrier Eagle *58
Bateleur *59
African Fish Eagle *59
Palm-nut Vulture *44
Little Sparrow Hawk *63
Ovampo Sparrow Hawk *66
Great Sparrow Hawk *66
Shikra *66
African Goshawk *67
Gabar Goshawk *67
Dark Chanting Goshawk *68
Montagu's Harrier *68
Pallid Harrier *69
European Marsh Harrier *69
Harrier Hawk *70
Coqui Francolin *71
Shelley's Francolin *72
Hildebrandt's Francolin *73
Red-necked Spurfowl *75
Harlequin Quail *76
Helmeted Guinea-fowl *77
Crested Guinea-fowl *78
Black Crake *79
Moorhen *83
Peters' Finfoot *86

Crowned Crane *86
Jackson's Bustard *88
Black-bellied Bustard *89
Spotted Stone Curlew *89
Water Dikkop *90
African Jacana *90
Kittlitz's Sand Plover *94
Three-banded Plover *94
Crowned Lapwing or Plover *98
Senegal Plover *98
Blacksmith Plover *100
White-headed Plover *100
Wattled Plover *100
Long-toed Lapwing *101
Painted Snipe *103
African Snipe *104
Ruff *106
Common Sandpiper *107
Green Sandpiper *107
Wood Sandpiper *107
Greenshank *109
Temminck's Courser *110
Bronze-winged Courser *98, *111
Pratincole *111
African Skimmer *116
Button Quail *116
Yellow-throated Sandgrouse *118
Speckled Pigeon *119
Olive Pigeon *119
Red-eyed Dove *120
Mourning Dove *121
Ring-necked Dove *120
Laughing Dove *121
Namaqua Dove *121
Tambourine Dove *122
Emerald-spotted Wood Dove *121
Delalande's Green Pigeon 237
European Cuckoo *123
African Cuckoo *123

Red-capped Robin Chat *201
Robin Chat *201
Morning Warbler *202
Red-backed Scrub Robin *202
Blackcap Warbler *204
European Sedge Warbler 290
Lesser Swamp Warbler 287
European Willow Warbler *205
Barred Wren Warbler 24
Fan-tailed Warbler 24
Red-faced Crombec *207
Yellow-bellied Eremomela
Green-cap Eremomela *210
Grey-backed Camaroptera *210
Wing-snapping Cisticola 24
Pectoral-patch Cisticola *210
Rattling Cisticola *211
Winding Cisticola 294
Croaking Cisticola 294
Tawny-flanked Prinia *211
Moustache Warbler 25
European Swallow *212
Angola Swallow *212
Blue Swallow 25
Wire-tailed Swallow *212
Red-rumped Swallow *213
Mosque Swallow *213
Striped Swallow *213
Grey-rumped Swallow *213
European Sand Martin *214
African Sand Martin *214
Banded Martin *214
African Rock Martin *214
Black Rough-wing Swallow *214
Eastern Rough-wing Swallow *215
White-headed Rough-wing Swallow *215
Black Cuckoo Shrike *215
White-breasted Cuckoo Shrike *216
Grey Cuckoo Shrike *216
Drongo *216
Square-tailed Drongo *217

Straight-crested Helmet Shrike *217
Retz's Red-billed Shrike *218
White-crowned Shrike *218
Black-browed Brubru *219
Grey-backed Fiscal *220
Lesser Grey Shrike *220
Uhehe Fiscal *220
Souza's Shrike 26
Red-backed Shrike *221
Magpie Shrike *221
Slate-coloured Boubou *222
Tropical Boubou *222
Black-backed Puff-back *222
Black-headed Bush Shrike *223
Brown-headed Bush Shrike *223
Blackcap Bush Shrike *223
Sulphur-breasted Bush Shrike *224
Black-fronted Bush Shrike 26
Grey-headed Bush Shrike *225
Nicator 26
Grey Tit *225
Black Tit *226
Cinnamon-breasted Tit *226
African Penduline Tit *226
European Golden Oriole *227
African Golden Oriole *227
Black-headed Oriole *227
Pied Crow *230
Wattled Starling *231
White-winged Babbling Starling 26
Violet-backed Starling *232
Blue-eared Starling *232
Lesser Blue-eared Starling *232
Ruppell's Long-tailed Starling *233
Ashy Starling 29
Red-wing Starling *234
Superb Starling *235
Yellow-billed Oxpecker *238

Red-billed Oxpecker *235
Yellow White-eye *238
Green White-eye *239
Bronzy Sunbird *242
Beautiful Sunbird (black-bellied race) *243
Copper Sunbird 30
Little Purple-banded Sunbird *245
Mariqua Sunbird *244
Variable Sunbird *244
Southern Double-collared Sunbird 30
Amethyst Sunbird *245
Scarlet-chested Sunbird *246
Olive Sunbird 30
Collared Sunbird *247
Spotted Creeper *248
White-headed Buffalo Weaver *249
White-browed Sparrow Weaver *249
Grey-headed Sparrow *250
Swahili Sparrow 322
Yellow-throated Petronia 323
Layard's Black-headed Weaver *251
Masked Weaver *252
Golden-backed Weaver *253
Dark-backed Weaver 31
Spectacled Weaver *255
Golden Weaver 31
Holub's Golden Weaver *255
Bertram's Weaver 327
Grosbeak Weaver *259
Red-headed Weaver *259
Red-billed Quelea *259
Red-headed Quelea *260
Cardinal Quelea *260
Red Bishop *260
Black-winged Bishop *261
Yellow Bishop *261
Fan-tailed Widow-bird *262
Yellow-mantled Widow-bird 32
White-winged Widow-bird *262
Red-collared Widow-bird *262

Bronze Mannikin *264
Rufous-backed Mannikin *264
Magpie Mannikin 331
Grey-headed Silver-bill 27
Quail Finch 27
Locust Finch 335
Parasitic Weaver 336
Peters' Twin-spot 28
Green-backed Twin-spot 335
Orange-winged Pytilia 336
Green-winged Pytilia *264

African Fire Finch *265
Jameson's Fire Finch *265
Red-billed Fire Finch *265
Yellow-bellied Waxbill *266
Waxbill *266
Zebra Waxbill 337
Fawn-breasted Waxbill 337
Lavender Waxbill 337
Angola Cordon-bleu *267
Red-cheeked Cordon-bleu *266
Purple Grenadier *267
Purple Indigo-bird 28

Pin-tailed Whydah *267
Paradise Whydah *268
Broad-tailed Paradise Whydah *268
Yellow-fronted Canary *269
Brimstone Canary *268
Streaky-headed Seed-eater 340
Three-streaked Bunting 28
Golden-breasted Bunting *270
Cinnamon-breasted Rock Bunting *270

SERENGETI NATIONAL PARK

Serengeti, the largest and best known of Tanzania's National Parks, covers an area of over 5,600 square miles. Its northern boundary abuts Kenya's Mara Masai Game Reserve, whilst its western extension known as the "corridor" reaches to within five miles of Lake Victoria.

In this world-famous wild life sanctuary there still exists the greatest and most spectacular concentration of game animals found anywhere in the world.

Most of the Serengeti is vast open plains with lofty rocky outcrops giving character to the landscape. There are also acacia and savannah woodland and scrub, forested and well-treed rivers, and the occasional swamp and small lake. In altitude Serengeti varies between 3,000 and 6,000 feet: Park headquarters at Seronera is at 5,000 feet.

In addition to its vast herds of Wildebeest, Common Zebra, Thomson's Gazelle and other plains game, Serengeti is renowned for its lion population. It is not at all unusual to see forty or more lions in a single day, including several superbly maned old males. Leopards are relatively numerous and are to be found during the daytime resting in trees along the Seronera River.

During May and June, or sometimes earlier, there is a remarkable migration of game animals, chiefly Zebra and Wildebeest, away from their usual haunts on the central plains and into the corridor. The animals converge and then move westwards, six to ten abreast in winding columns several miles long. This movement has its following of carnivora, ready to dispose of the weaklings and stragglers.

The remarkable "robertsi" race of Grant's Gazelle with extremely wide-branched horns is found in the western sector of the Park. Other interesting animals include all three species of Jackal, Striped Hyaena and Aard-wolf.

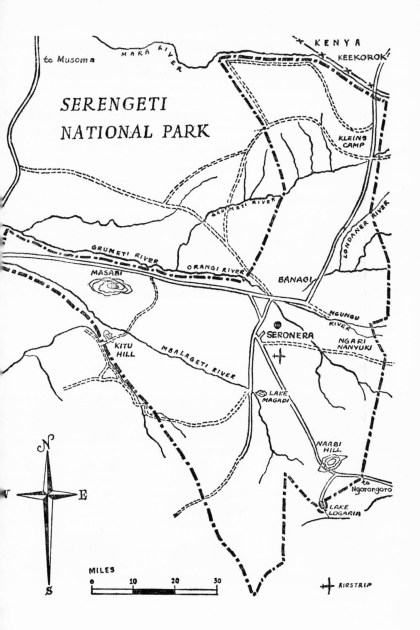

to Musoma

MARA RIVER

KENYA
KEEKOROK

SERENGETI
NATIONAL PARK

KLEINS
CAMP

GRUMETI RIVER

LONDANER RIVER

GRUMETI RIVER

ORANGI RIVER

MASABI

BANAGI

NGUNGU
RIVER

SERONERA

NGARI
NANYUKI

KITU
HILL

MBALAGETI RIVER

LAKE
MAGADI

NAABI
HILL

to Ngorongoro

LAKE
LOGARIA

N

W   E

S

MILES
0   10   20   30

AIRSTRIP

Nobody, at whatever level of interest in ornithology, can fail to notice the wealth of bird life in Serengeti. Colourful rollers, bee-eaters, kingfishers and sunbirds are common, whilst amongst larger species birds of prey, game birds and waterfowl are well represented.

Species of special note include the extremely local Grey-breasted Spurfowl, the rare Brown-chested Wattled Plover which is sometimes found associated with flocks of Senegal Plover on the open plains, the large brownish Rufous-tailed Weaver, Schalow's Turaco which inhabits riverine forest and the Little Tawny Pipit and the Red-throated Tit which are quite common around Seronera Lodge.

The most usual route to the Serengeti National Park and one suitable for saloon cars is from Arusha via Lake Manyara and Ngorongoro. From Arusha to Seronera is 198 miles; from Ngorongoro ninety miles. It is also possible to visit Serengeti from Keekorok via Sand River and Klein's Camp, a distance of about ninety-five miles. Airstrips exist at Seronera and elsewhere in the Park and East African Airways maintain an air service from Nairobi to Seronera.

Accommodation with all facilities is available at Seronera Lodge, where there are also nine official camp sites. Special permission must be obtained to camp elsewhere in the Park.

MAMMALS OF SERENGETI NATIONAL PARK

Spectacled Elephant Shrew	Black-backed Jackal ✓	Lion ✓
East African Hedgehog	Side-striped Jackal	Leopard
Giant White-toothed Shrew	Bat-eared Fox	Ant Bear
Rousette Fruit Bat	Zorilla	Tree Hyrax
Epauletted Fruit Bat	African Striped Weasel	Rock Hyrax ✓
Pale-bellied Fruit Bat	Ratel or Honey Badger	African Elephant
White-bellied Tomb Bat	Clawless Otter	Black Rhinoceros
Hollow-faced Bat	African Civet	Common Zebra ✓
False Vampire Bat	Small-spotted Genet	Hippopotamus
Yellow-winged Bat	Large-spotted Genet	Warthog
Lander's Horseshoe Bat	African Palm Civet	Bush Pig
Lesser Leaf-nosed Bat	Marsh Mongoose ✓	Masai Giraffe
Banana Bat	Dwarf Mongoose	Coke's Hartebeest or Kongoni
Yellow-bellied Bat	Large Grey Mongoose	
Angola Free-tailed Bat	Black-tipped Mongoose	White-bearded Gnu or Wildebeest
Greater Galago	White-tailed Mongoose	
Bush Baby	Banded Mongoose	Topi ✓
Black-faced Vervet	Aard-wolf	Red Duiker
Blue or Sykes' Monkey	Spotted Hyaena ✓	Blue Duiker
Patas Monkey	Striped Hyaena ✓	Bush Duiker
Olive Baboon	Cheetah	Klipspringer
Black and White Colobus	Caracal	Suni
Hunting Dog	African Wild Cat	Oribi
Golden Jackal	Serval	Steinbok

Kirk's Dik-dik
Common Waterbuck ✓
Defassa Waterbuck
Bohor Reedbuck
Chanler's Reedbuck Recorded Banagi Hill
Impala ✓
Thomson's Gazelle ✓
Grant's Gazelle Western

race *robertsi* in western corridor; nominate race elsewhere
Roan Antelope
Fringe-eared Oryx
Bushbuck
Lesser Kudu
Eland
African Buffalo ✓

African Hare
Cane Rat
Porcupine
Bush Squirrel
Spring Hare
African Dormouse
Giant Rat
Kenya Mole Rat

BIRDS OF SERENGETI NATIONAL PARK

Masai Ostrich *19
Great-crested Grebe *19
Little Grebe *20
Long-tailed Cormorant *21
African Darter *21
White Pelican *22
Pink-backed Pelican *22
Black-headed Heron *23
Goliath Heron *23
Great White Egret *24
Yellow-billed Egret *25
Little Egret *25
Buff-backed Heron or Cattle Egret *26
Squacco Heron *26
Green-backed Heron *26
Little Bittern *27
Hammerkop *28
White Stork *29
European Black Stork *30
Woolly-necked Stork *29
Abdim's Stork *29
Open-bill Stork *30
Saddle-bill Stork *30
Marabou Stork *31
Wood Ibis or Yellow-billed Stork *31
Sacred Ibis *31
Hadada Ibis *34
African Spoonbill *34
Greater Flamingo *35
Lesser Flamingo *35
Maccoa Duck *36
African Pochard *37
Yellow-billed Duck *38
African Black Duck *38
Garganey Teal *38
Cape Wigeon *39
Hottentot Teal *39
Red-billed Duck *39
White-faced Tree Duck *40
Fulvous Tree Duck *40

Knob-billed Goose *41
Egyptian Goose *41
Spur-winged Goose *41
Secretary Bird *42
Ruppell's Griffon Vulture *42
White-backed Vulture *43
Lappet-faced Vulture *43
White-headed Vulture *43
Egyptian Vulture *44
Hooded Vulture *43
Lanner *45
European Hobby *46
White-eyed Kestrel *47
European Kestrel *47
African Kestrel *47
Lesser Kestrel *50
Pygmy Falcon *51
European Black Kite *51
African Black Kite *51
Black-shouldered Kite *51
Bat Hawk *46
Verreaux's Eagle *54
Steppe Eagle *55
Tawny Eagle *54
Wahlberg's Eagle *55
African Hawk Eagle *55
Ayres' Hawk Eagle *56
Martial Eagle *56
Long-crested Hawk Eagle *57
Lizard Buzzard *57
Brown Harrier Eagle *55, *58
Black-chested Harrier Eagle *58
Bateleur *59
African Fish Eagle *59
Steppe Buzzard *62
Augur Buzzard *63
Little Sparrow Hawk *63
Shikra *66

Gabar Goshawk *67
Pale Chanting Goshawk *68
Dark Chanting Goshawk *68
Montagu's Harrier *68
Pallid Harrier *69
European Marsh Harrier *69
Harrier Hawk *70
Coqui Francolin *71
Crested Francolin *71
Shelley's (Greywing) Francolin *72
Red-necked Spurfowl *75
Grey-breasted Spurfowl *75
Cape Quail *76
Harlequin Quail *76
Helmeted Guinea-fowl *7
Crested Guinea-fowl *78
African Crake *79
Black Crake *79
Crowned Crane *86
Kori Bustard *87
Jackson's Bustard *88
White-bellied Bustard *88
Black-bellied Bustard *89
Hartlaub's Bustard *89
Spotted Stone Curlew *90
Water Dikkop *90
African Jacana *90
Ringed Plover *91
Chestnut-banded Sand Plover *91, *94
Kittlitz's Sand Plover *94
Three-banded Plover *94
Caspian Plover *95
Crowned Lapwing or Plover *98
Senegal Plover *98
Black-winged Plover *99
Blacksmith Plover *100

Arrow-marked Babbler *187

Black-lored Babbler *187

Rufous Chatterer *187

Dark-capped Bulbul *188

European Spotted Flycatcher *190

Dusky Flycatcher *190

Ashy Flycatcher *191

Banded Tit-Flycatcher 22

Pale Flycatcher *190

Grey Flycatcher *191

South African Black Flycatcher *191

Silverbird *194

Chin-spot Flycatcher *194

Wattle-eye *195

Paradise Flycatcher *195

European Rock Thrush *197

European Common Wheatear *198

Capped Wheatear *198

Cliff Chat 23

Sooty Chat *200

White-browed Robin Chat *200

Red-backed Scrub Robin *202

White-throated Robin 23

Garden Warbler *204

Blackcap Warbler *204

Great Reed Warbler 287

European Sedge Warbler 290

European Willow Warbler *205

Black-breasted Apalis *206

Fan-tailed Warbler 24

Buff-bellied Warbler *207

Red-faced Crombec *207

Yellow-bellied Eremomela *207

Grey-backed Camaroptera *210

Pectoral-patch Cisticola *210

Rattling Cisticola *211

Croaking Cisticola 294

Tiny Cisticola 294

Winding Cisticola 294

Tawny-flanked Prinia *211

Moustache Warbler 25

European Swallow *212

Angola Swallow *212

Wire-tailed Swallow *212

Red-rumped Swallow *213

Mosque Swallow *213

Striped Swallow *213

Banded Martin *214

African Rock Martin *124

Black Rough-wing Swallow *214

Black Cuckoo Shrike *215

Drongo *216

Straight-crested Helmet Shrike *217

White-crowned Shrike *218

Northern Brubru *219

Grey-backed Fiscal *220

Lesser Grey Shrike *220

Fiscal Shrike *219

Red-backed Shrike *221

Red-tailed Shrike *221

Magpie Shrike *221

Black-headed Gonolek *221

Slate-coloured Boubou *222

Tropical Boubou *222

Black-backed Puff-back *223

Black-headed Bush Shrike *223

Sulphur-breasted Bush Shrike *224

Grey-headed Bush Shrike *225

White-breasted Tit *226

Red-throated Tit 27

African Penduline Tit *226

Black-headed Oriole *227

Cape Rook *230

White-naped Raven *230

Wattled Starling *231

Violet-backed Starling *232

Blue-eared Glossy Starling *232

Ruppell's Long-tailed Starling *233

Ashy Starling 29

Hildebrandt's Starling *235

Superb Starling *235

Yellow-billed Oxpecker *238

Red-billed Oxpecker *235

Malachite Sunbird *239

Bronzy Sunbird *242

Beautiful Sunbird (black-bellied race) *243

Golden-winged Sunbird *243

Little Purple-banded Sunbird *244

Mariqua Sunbird *244

Variable Sunbird *244

Scarlet-chested Sunbird *246

Green-headed Sunbird *246

Olive Sunbird 30

Collared Sunbird *247

Violet-backed Sunbird *247

Kenya Violet-backed Sunbird 29

Buffalo Weaver *248

White-headed Buffalo Weaver *249

White-browed Sparrow Weaver *249

Rufous-tailed Weaver 31

Grey-headed Social Weaver *250

Kenya Rufous Sparrow *250

Swahili Sparrow 322

Chestnut Sparrow 31

Yellow-spotted Petronia 27

Speckle-fronted Weaver 27

Masked Weaver *252

Vitelline Masked Weaver *252

Chestnut Weaver *253

Black-necked Weaver *254

Spectacled Weaver *255

Holub's Golden Weaver *255

Vieillot's Black Weaver *255

Grosbeak Weaver *259

Red-headed Weaver *259

Red-billed Quelea *259

Red-headed Quelea *260

Cardinal Quelea *260

Red Bishop *260

Black-winged Bishop *261

Black Bishop 32

Yellow Bishop *261

Fan-tailed Widow-bird *262

Yellow-mantled Widow-bird 32
White-winged Widow-bird *262
Bronze Mannikin *264
Black and White Mannikin 27
Grey-headed Silver-bill 27
Grey-headed Negro Finch 32
Cut-throat *264
Quail Finch 27
Green-winged Pytilia *264
African Fire Finch *265

Jameson's Fire Finch *265
Red-billed Fire Finch *265
Yellow-bellied Waxbill *266
Waxbill *266
Black-cheeked Waxbill 28
Red-cheeked Cordon-bleu *266
Blue-capped Cordon-bleu *267
Purple Grenadier *267
Purple Indigo-bird 15
Pin-tailed Whydah *267
Steel-blue Whydah *267

Fischer's Straw-tailed Whydah *267
Paradise Whydah *268
Yellow-fronted Canary *269
White-bellied Canary 28
Brimstone Canary *268
Streaky Seed-eater *269
Golden-breasted Bunting *270
Cinnamon-breasted Rock Bunting *270

Game Reserves

Variety is the keynote of Tanzania's Game Reserves which range in terrain from lakeshore to the top of Africa's highest mountain. In each there exist species of animals and birds not to be encountered elsewhere in the country.

For the visitor prepared to disregard the nuisance of tsetse flies a visit to the Biharamulo Game Reserve in north-western Tanzania is a very well-worth-while safari. An expedition to the Chimpanzee Reserve on the Gombe Stream, accessible only by fisherman's boat from Kigoma, is also something of an adventure.

Farther afield the Katavi Plain Reserve, south of the Ugalla River game country, has the atmosphere of unspoiled Africa: but again tsetse flies may be a little troublesome. Finally there is majestic Mount Kilimanjaro where in transit up the forested slopes, there is always the chance of seeing that elusive rarity the dark coloured Abbot's Duiker.

BIHARAMULO GAME RESERVE

The Biharamulo Game Reserve is an area of 450 square miles on the south-western shores of Lake Victoria, east of the Mwanza-Bukoba road in north-western Tanzania. It was established in 1959. A rich mammal and bird fauna is present but for the visitor the area has the inconvenience of being spasmodically troubled by tsetse fly.

This Reserve comprises thickly wooded, undulating country ranging in altitude from 3,700 feet at lake-shore to 5,000 feet inland. It is mainly covered with heavy brachystegia and acacia woodlands, interspersed with more open areas, the home of Lichtenstein's Hartebeest, Sable Antelope, Southern Reedbuck and Sharpe's Grysbok. Crocodile and Hippopotamus occur in the lake-shore section.

Bird life is abundant and there are many unusual and rare species, including the following:

Rufous-bellied Heron *26
Grey Kestrel *50
Bat Hawk *46
Ring-necked Francolin *72
White-spotted Pygmy Crake *82
Long-toed Lapwing *101
Bronze-winged Courser *98, *111
Afep Pigeon *119

Blue-breasted Kingfisher 18
Black-billed Barbet 19
Red-faced Barbet 19
Snowy-headed Robin Chat *201
Lesser Blue-eared Glossy Starling *233
Splendid Glossy Starling *233

Red-chested Sunbird 30
Copper Sunbird 30
Green-throated Sunbird 30
Blue-throated Brown Sunbird 30
Orange Weaver 31
Slender-billed Weaver 31
Weyn's Weaver 327
Black-bellied Seed-cracker 32

GOMBE STREAM GAME RESERVE

The Gombe Stream Game Reserve on the north-eastern shore of Lake Tanganyika, north of Kigoma, was established in 1945 mainly for the protection of the Chimpanzee population which exists there. It comprises sixty-one square miles of lake-shore and precipitous mountain country, well watered and with dense forest. Access is by boat from Kigoma. In addition to the Chimpanzees there are Red Colobus, Buffalo, Defassa Waterbuck, Bushbuck and Leopard.

Among the notable birds recorded from the Gombe Stream Reserve are:

African Hobby *46
Grey Kestrel *50
Bat Hawk *46
Palm-nut Vulture *44
Forbes' Plover *94
Afep Pigeon *119
Yellow-bill or Green Coucal *127
Shining-blue Kingfisher 18
Blue-breasted Kingfisher 18

Double-toothed Barbet *164
Hairy-breasted Barbet *165
Grey-throated Barbet *166
Yellow-spotted Barbet 20
Yellow-billed Barbet 20
African Broadbill *179
Equatorial Akalat 23
Splendid Glossy Starling *233

Purple-headed Glossy Starling 29
Red-chested Sunbird 30
Superb Sunbird 30
Green-throated Sunbird 30
Northern Brown-throated Weaver 31
Red-headed Malimbe *258
Red-headed Blue-bill 32

KATAVI PLAIN GAME RESERVE

The Katavi Plain Game Reserve of 720 square miles lies between the Ugalla River and the south-eastern shores of Lake Tanganyika in south-western Tanzania; it was established in 1951. Extensive open grassy plains alternate with brachystegia woodland, acacia bush country and lakes and swamps. The mammalian fauna includes large herds of Elephant and Buffalo besides Hippopotamus, Southern Reedbuck, Topi, Eland, Roan Antelope, Defassa Waterbuck, Common Zebra, Lion and Leopard.

The area is rich in water-birds and birds of prey. The following species of special note have been recorded:

Black Heron *25	Swallow-tailed Bee-eater *146	Blue Swallow 25
Rufous-bellied Heron *26		White-breasted Cuckoo Shrike *216
Dwarf Bittern *27	Pale-billed Hornbill *148	
Pygmy Goose *40	Fiery-necked Nightjar 16	White-winged Babbling Starling 26
Dickinson's Kestrel *50	Pennant-wing Nightjar *158	
Forbes' Plover *94		Yellow-throated Petronia 323
Go-away-bird 17	Red-faced Mousebird *162	
Brown-necked Parrot 17	Black-backed Barbet 20	Tanganyika Masked Weaver 324
Boehm's Bee-eater 19	African Pitta *179	

KILIMANJARO GAME RESERVE

Kilimanjaro Game Reserve covers an area of 720 square miles of Africa's highest mountain, extending from the 6,000 feet contour to the summit at 19,340 feet. At lower altitudes the Reserve consists of mountain rain forest, giving way to scrub—there is no bamboo zone on Kilimanjaro—then alpine moorland and finally icefields.

Easiest access to the mountain is from Marangu on the southern slopes, whence the Marangu mountain track, passable for four-wheel-drive vehicles, leads to the upper edge of the forest at 9,500 feet.

The most interesting mammal in the mountain forest is Abbot's Duiker, an extremely local and uncommon antelope restricted to a few mountain forests in northern Tanzania. In addition Elephant, Buffalo, Black Rhinoceros, Eland, Leopard, Black and White Colobus and Blue Monkey occur in the Reserve.

Of special note among Kilimanjaro birds in the alpine zone are Lammergeyer, Mountain Chat and Scarlet-tufted Malachite Sunbird; among forest species the following warrant enumeration:

Green Ibis *34	Bar-tailed Trogon *163	Golden-winged Sunbird *243
Cuckoo Falcon *67	White-eared Barbet *166	
Rufous-breasted Sparrow Hawk *66	Olive Woodpecker 20	Eastern Double-collared Sunbird *245
	Black-fronted Bush Shrike 26	
Hartlaub's Turaco *131		Olive Sunbird 30
Cinnamon-breasted Bee-eater 19	Abbot's Starling 29	Dark-backed Weaver 31
	Kenrick's Starling 308	Abyssinian Crimson-wing 32
Silvery-cheeked Hornbill *147	Broad-ringed White-eye 26	
	Malachite Sunbird *239	Oriole Finch 340
Narina's Trogon *163	Tacazze Sunbird *242	

MKOMAZI GAME RESERVE

Mkomazi Game Reserve, an area of 1,350 square miles in north-eastern Tanzania, adjoins a portion of the southern boundary of Kenya's Tsavo National Park: in effect it is a southern extension of that Park. The country is very arid, open plains and thornbush with isolated rocky hills.

The fauna includes Elephant, Black Rhinoceros, Buffalo, Lion, Leopard, Lesser Kudu, Gerenuk and Fringe-eared Oryx.

Bird life is more in evidence than big game and the following species are noteworthy:

Red-necked Falcon *46
Pygmy Falcon *51
Wahlberg's Eagle *56
Martial Eagle *56
Lizard Buzzard *57
Brown Harrier Eagle *55, *58
Grasshopper Buzzard *58
Ovampo Sparrow Hawk *66
Shikra *66
Buff-crested Bustard *89

Heuglin's Courser *110
Button Quail *116
Carmine Bee-eater *141
Trumpeter Hornbill *146
Silvery-cheeked Hornbill *147
Yellow-billed Hornbill *148
Donaldson-Smith's Night-jar *156
Brown-breasted Barbet *165

Retz's Red-billed Shrike *218
Four-coloured Bush Shrike *224
Golden-breasted Starling *234
Hunter's Sunbird 30
Kenya Violet-backed Sunbird 29
Dark-backed Weaver 31
Paradise Whydah *268

TARANGIRE GAME RESERVE

The Tarangire Game Reserve is an area of 525 square miles of arid acacia thornbush and thicket in north-eastern Tanzania, north of Mount Meru, adjoining the main Nairobi-Arusha road.

Among the big game which occurs in this Reserve are Elephant, Black Rhinoceros, Buffalo, Fringe-eared Oryx, Common Zebra, Eland, Coke's Hartebeest, White-bearded Gnu, Lesser Kudu, Impala and Common Waterbuck.

Birds are abundant and the following striking species have been recorded:

Masai Ostrich *19
Secretary Bird *42
White-headed Vulture *43
Lappet-faced Vulture *43
Pygmy Falcon *51
African Hawk Eagle *55
Martial Eagle *56
Black-chested Harrier Eagle *58
Bateleur *59

Pale Chanting Goshawk *68
Buff-crested Bustard *89
Spotted Stone Curlew *89
Two-banded Courser *111
Heuglin's Courser *110
Button Quail *116
Yellow-throated Sandgrouse *118
Great-spotted Cuckoo *124

White-throated Bee-eater *142
Yellow-billed Hornbill *148
Von der Decken's Hornbill *149
Abyssinian Scimitar-bill *152
African Scops Owl *154
Singing Bush Lark 266
Pangani Longclaw *186

I

Sulphur-breasted Bush Shrike *224
Grey-headed Bush Shrike *225
Rosy-patched Shrike *225
Golden-breasted Starling *234
Beautiful Sunbird (Black-bellied race) *243
Kenya Violet-backed Sunbird 29

Buffalo Weaver *248
White-headed Buffalo Weaver *249
Grey-headed Social Weaver *250
Yellow-spotted Petronia 27
Speckle-fronted Weaver 27
Taveta Golden Weaver 31
Red Bishop *260
Grey-headed Silver-bill 27
Quail Finch 27

Green-winged Pytilia *264
Blue-capped Cordon-bleu *267
Steel-blue Whydah *267
Fischer's Straw-tailed Whydah *267
Paradise Whydah *268
Kenya Grosbeak Canary 340

Other Faunal Localities

In addition to the National Parks and Game Reserves enumerated above, there exist in Tanzania a number of other zoologically important localities. Among these haunts of rare and little-known animals and birds are the following:

POROTO MOUNTAINS, MBEYA DISTRICT, SOUTHERN TANZANIA

This is a good locality for the ornithologist. The striking, long-tailed, yellow-shouldered Marsh Widow-bird is found in the marshy hollows in the valleys. Forest patches on these mountains and on adjacent Mount Rungwe possess a rich avifauna including:

African Hobby *46
Cuckoo Falcon *67
Ayres' Hawk Eagle *56
Southern Banded Harrier Eagle *58

Livingstone's Turaco *127
Half-collared Kingfisher 18
Green Barbet *167
Stierling's Woodpecker 264
Olive Woodpecker 20

Boehm's Spinetail *175
White-chested Alethe 286
Yellow-throated Woodland Warbler 290
Blue Swallow 25

THE RUKWA VALLEY, NORTH-WEST OF MBEYA, SOUTHERN TANZANIA

The famous game country of the Rukwa Valley is relatively inaccessible and can be visited only in the dry season and with sturdy four-wheel-drive vehicles.

Large herds of Puku exist in the area, alongside concentrations of Topi, Eland and Buffalo. Lichtenstein's Hartebeest, Southern Reedbuck, Impala, Elephant, Defassa Waterbuck, Roan Antelope, Greater Kudu, Common Zebra, Masai Giraffe, Hippopotamus and Lion also occur. Sitatunga are found in the swamps to the west of the Rukwa.

Two remarkable genetic mutations have been reported from the Rukwa Valley, albino giraffe and a dark coloured zebra marked with spots instead of stripes.

Bird life abounds in the Rukwa Valley and some 400 different species have been recorded. Amongst the more important are:

Black Heron *25	Pygmy Goose *40	Tanganyika Masked
White-backed Night Heron *27	Red-necked Falcon *46	Weaver 324
	Kaffir Rail *79	Quail Finch 27
Rufous-bellied Heron *26	Wattled Crane *87	
Glossy Ibis *34 Nests in colonies	Boehm's Bee-eater 19	
	Anchieta's Sunbird 29	

THE SELOUS CONTROLLED AREA

The Selous Controlled Area is a southern extension of the Mikumi National Park, covering some 11,000 square miles, and is predominantly an elephant reserve. The area is mainly brachystegia woodlands with grassy flood-plains and some dense forest patches: much of it is inaccessible.

In addition to Elephant there are Hippopotamus, Buffalo, Wildebeest, Lichtenstein's Hartebeest, Sable Antelope, Greater Kudu, Eland, Lion and Leopard. Bird life is similar to that found in the Mikumi National Park.

ULUGURU MOUNTAINS, MOROGORO DISTRICT, EASTERN TANZANIA

The forests of the Uluguru Mountains, immediately south of Morogoro, support a varied avifauna, including three species which occur nowhere else. These are Mrs. Moreau's Warbler (*Scepomycter winifredae*), 4″, a thickset olive-grey warbler with a chestnut head and chest; the Black-cap Shrike (*Malaconotus alius*), 8″, a heavy bush shrike, green above, yellowish-green below with a black cap and heavy black bill; and Loveridge's Sunbird (*Cinnyris loveridgei*). Other interesting species recorded from the Uluguru forests are:

African Black Duck *38	Bronze-naped Pigeon *119	Green-headed Oriole 303
Ayres' Hawk Eagle *56	Livingstone's Turaco *127	Uluguru Violet-backed Sunbird 319
Southern Banded Harrier Eagle *58	Half-collared Kingfisher 18	
Palm-nut Vulture *44	Usambara Nightjar 260	Bertram's Weaver 327
Rufous-breasted Sparrow Hawk *66	Bar-tailed Trogon *163	Red-faced Crimson-wing 32
	Olive Woodpecker 20	Oriole Finch 340
Crested Guinea-fowl *78	Sharpe's Akalat 283	
	White-chested Alethe 286	

EASTERN USAMBARA MOUNTAINS, NORTH-EASTERN TANZANIA

The forests of the Eastern Usambara Mountains, in extreme north-eastern Tanzania, are readily accessible from Tanga and Amani. Among the few mammals occurring is the rare Abbot's Duiker which is sometimes seen in the early morning.

The locality boasts three endemic bird species, namely the Naduk Eagle Owl (*Bubo vosseleri*), 26", a pale rufous-buff eagle owl with barred underparts and well-developed ear tufts; the Usambara Alethe (*Alethe montana*), 5", a plump robin-like bird, olivaceous brown above, greyish and white below, with a rufous streak from the base of the bill to above the eye; and the Usambara Weaver (*Hyphanturgus nicolli*). Other notable birds are:

Cuckoo Falcon *67
Southern Banded Harrier Eagle *58
Palm-nut Vulture *44
Great Sparrow Hawk *66
Bronze-naped Pigeon *119
Lemon Dove 16
Fischer's Turaco *130
Half-collared Kingfisher 18
Trumpeter Hornbill *146
Silvery-cheeked Hornbill *147
Usambara Nightjar 260
Narina's Trogon *163

Bar-tailed Trogon *163
White-eared Barbet *166
Green Barbet *167
Green Tinkerbird *167
Orange Ground Thrush 282
Sharpe's Akalat 283
White-chested Alethe 286
Square-tailed Drongo *217
Retz's Red-billed Shrike *218
Chestnut-fronted Shrike *218
Black-fronted Bush Shrike 26

Green-headed Oriole 303
Sharpe's Starling *232
Abbott's Starling 29
Kenrick's Starling 308
Banded Green Sunbird 319
Uluguru Violet-backed Sunbird 319
Amani Sunbird 29
Dark-backed Weaver 31
Usambara Red-headed Blue-bill 332
Red-faced Crimson-wing 32
Oriole Finch 304

Uganda

Uganda possesses three National Parks, the Queen Elizabeth Park in western Uganda between Lakes Edward and George; the Murchison Falls Park farther north, astride the Victoria Nile and bounded on the west by Lake Albert; and the recently established Kidepo Valley National Park in the wilds of north-eastern Karamoja.

Each of these National Parks lies within a distinct zoological region and each has a fauna complementing the others. The three together provide a remarkably complete cross-section of the wild life of Uganda. In character they are quite unlike any other of East Africa's faunal preserves.

The Queen Elizabeth National Park, immediately to the south of the snow-capped "Mountains of the Moon"—the Ruwenzori Range—is a region of lush green vegetation and rolling grassy plains, of great lakes and swamps and stretches of imposing tropical forest—outliers of the great forests of the Congo. It includes the Kazinga Channel joining Lake Edward to Lake George, where in a launch one can approach to within feet of elephant and buffalo at the water's edge. To the north there is an extensive zone of old volcanic craters and crater lakes, with superb scenic views of the Ruwenzori Mountains. In the Kigezi section—famous for its tree-climbing lions and vast herds of topi—the Ishasha River boundary abuts the Congo Parc de Kivu, previously known as the Parc National Albert.

Murchison Falls National Park has the attraction of the famous waterfall from which it derives its title. The launch trip on the Victoria Nile to the foot of the Falls is a highlight of a visit to East Africa; the river banks are lined with big game animals and some of the largest crocodiles in Africa bask on sand-bars in the river. Fishing is allowed in the Nile, both above and below the Falls, for Nile Perch which run up to 160 lb. weight or more. Most of Murchison Park is open rolling grasslands, with areas of savannah woodland, an isolated forest where chimpanzees are found, and forest strips along the river.

Uganda's most recently gazetted Park, the Kidepo Valley National Park, is situated in what used to be one of the most inaccessible and wild parts of the country, north-eastern Karamoja. An extensive road construction programme now enables anyone to visit this supremely beautiful country of wide sand rivers, forests of borassus palms and rugged mountain terrain, all unusually rich in mammals and birds.

133

UGANDA

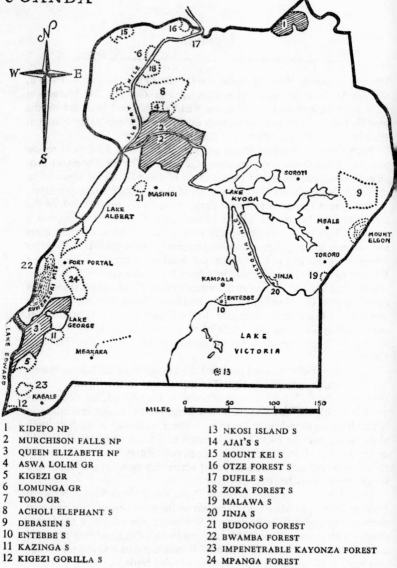

1 KIDEPO NP	13 NKOSI ISLAND S
2 MURCHISON FALLS NP	14 AJAI'S S
3 QUEEN ELIZABETH NP	15 MOUNT KEI S
4 ASWA LOLIM GR	16 OTZE FOREST S
5 KIGEZI GR	17 DUFILE S
6 LOMUNGA GR	18 ZOKA FOREST S
7 TORO GR	19 MALAWA S
8 ACHOLI ELEPHANT S	20 JINJA S
9 DEBASIEN S	21 BUDONGO FOREST
10 ENTEBBE S	22 BWAMBA FOREST
11 KAZINGA S	23 IMPENETRABLE KAYONZA FOREST
12 KIGEZI GORILLA S	24 MPANGA FOREST

KIDEPO VALLEY NATIONAL PARK

The Kidepo Valley National Park, an area of 486 square miles in the remote north-eastern corner of Uganda, was established in March, 1962. Its thirty miles long north-western boundary abuts the Sudan border. The Kidepo basin lies in mountainous country at an altitude of between 3,000 and 4,000 feet. It is encircled by wooded hills and dominated by Mount Morongole on its eastern flank and by the forested hogsback of Lotuke in the Sudan, peaks which rise to over 9,000 feet. Here exists some of the wildest and most magnificent scenery to be found in East Africa, completely unsullied by civilisation.

The Park straddles the Kidepo and Larus Rivers and their tributaries, which during periods of rain flow northwards into the Sudan. For the greater part of the year most of the Kidepo Park water courses are dry, with the exception of the upper reaches of the Larus River which has some permanent surface water derived from the Napore Hills.

Much of the Park is arid savannah and acacia country with stands of borassus palms, broken by numerous sand rivers which make road construction difficult and which are often a barrier to anything other than four-wheel-drive vehicles. In the western section of the Park there is relatively more water and a greater abundance of wild life: this part of the Kidepo is being developed.

The most rewarding time to visit the Kidepo Park is during the dry season, between December and early April. During the rainy seasons in April-May and July-August, travel is difficult and game difficult to locate on account of the long grass.

A number of game animals occur in the Kidepo National Park which are not found in either of the other Uganda National Parks. These include Lesser Kudu, usually found in the eastern sector of the Park, Bright's Gazelle (a race of Grant's Gazelle), Eland, Zebra, Roan Antelope, Klipspringer, Kirk's Dik-dik, Chanler's Mountain Reedbuck and Cheetah. Greater Kudu occur on the Morongole Massif, but their presence actually in the Park has not been confirmed.

Most numerous species are Jackson's Hartebeest, Oribi, Rothschild's Giraffe, Buffalo, Elephant, Bush Duiker, Eland, Common Zebra and Bright's Gazelle. Other species, such as Roan Antelope, the two Reedbuck, Klipspringer and Bushbuck are less common and more local. Black Rhinoceros, Lion, Leopard and Cheetah are present in small numbers.

Bird life is abundant and varied, and the area is especially rich in birds of prey, both resident species and northern migrants. Abyssinian Ground

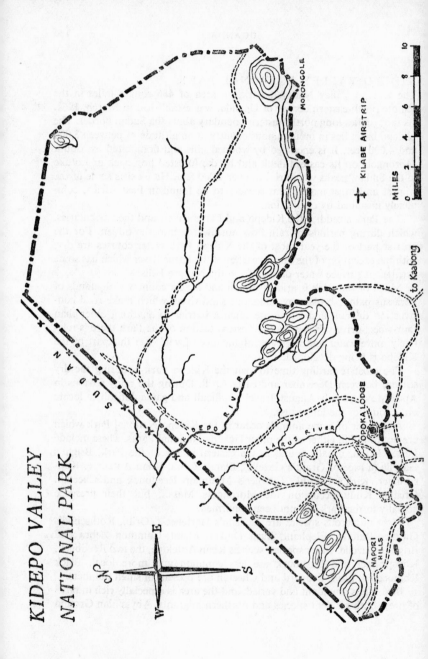

KIDEPO VALLEY
NATIONAL PARK

SUDAN

KIDEPO RIVER

LARUS RIVER

NAPORI HILLS

MORONGOLE

KILABE AIRSTRIP

OPOKA LODGE

to Kaabong

MILES

0   2   4   6   8   10

Hornbills are not uncommon and the remarkable Standard-wing Nightjar breeds in the Kidepo. Other specially noteworthy birds are Blue Quail, Stone Partridge, Four-banded Sandgrouse, White-crested Turaco, Rose-ringed Parakeet, Abyssinian Roller, Swallow-tailed Bee-eater, Fan-tailed Raven and Piapiac.

There are two alternative road routes to the Kidepo Park; one via Moroto, Kotido and Kaabong, and the other from Gulu via Kitgum, Rom and Karenga. A landing strip suitable for light aircraft exists at Kalabe, near Kidepo Lodge and the Park Headquarters at Opoka Hill. Accommodation is available in a series of cool safari lodges of Italian design, operated on the self-service principle.

MAMMALS OF KIDEPO NATIONAL PARK

Spectacled Elephant Shrew
Rousette Fruit Bat
Epauletted Fruit Bat
Pale-bellied Fruit Bat
Mouse-tailed Bat
White-bellied Tomb Bat
Hollow-faced Bat
False Vampire Bat
Yellow-winged Bat
Lander's Horseshoe Bat
Lesser Leaf-nosed Bat
Yellow-bellied Bat
Angola Free-tailed Bat
Flat-headed Free-tailed Bat
Bush Baby
Black-faced Vervet
Patas Monkey
Olive Baboon
Black-backed Jackal
Side-striped Jackal
Bat-eared Fox
Small-spotted Genet

Large-spotted Genet
Percival's Dwarf Mongoose
Large Grey Mongoose
White-tailed Mongoose
Banded Mongoose
Aard-wolf
Spotted Hyaena
Striped Hyaena
Cheetah
Caracal
African Wild Cat
Lion
Leopard
Ant Bear
Tree Hyrax
Rock Hyrax
African Elephant
Black Rhinoceros
Common Zebra
Warthog
Rothschild's Giraffe
Jackson's Hartebeest

Bush Duiker
Klipspringer
Oribi
Kirk's Dik-dik
Defassa Waterbuck
Bohor Reedbuck
Chanler's Reedbuck
Bright's Gazelle
Roan Antelope
Bushbuck
Greater Kudu Probably occurs
Lesser Kudu
Eland
African Buffalo
African Hare
Porcupine
Unstriped Ground Squirrel
Bush Squirrel
African Dormouse

BIRDS OF KIDEPO NATIONAL PARK

Ostrich *19
Long-tailed Cormorant *21
Black-headed Heron *23
Buff-backed Heron or
Cattle Egret *26
Green-backed Heron *26
Hammerkop *28
White Stork *29
Abdim's Stork *29
Open-bill Stork *30
Saddle-bill Stork *30

Marabou Stork *31
Sacred Ibis *31
Knob-billed Goose *41
Secretary Bird *42
Ruppell's Griffon Vulture *42
White-backed Vulture *43
Lappet-faced Vulture *43
White-headed Vulture *43
Egyptian Vulture *44
Hooded Vulture *43

Peregrine *45
Lanner *45
Teita Falcon *46 Not yet recorded but probably occurs
European Hobby *46
Saker *46 Sight records but not yet confirmed
Red-necked Falcon *46
European Kestrel *47
African Kestrel *47

Fox Kestrel *47
Lesser Kestrel *50
Grey Kestrel *50
Pygmy Falcon *51
Swallow-tailed Kite   *54
Not yet recorded but
certain to occur
European Black Kite *51
African Black Kite *51
Black-shouldered Kite *51
Verreaux's Eagle *54
Steppe Eagle *55
Tawny Eagle *54
Wahlberg's Eagle *55
African Hawk Eagle *55
Booted Eagle 232
Martial Eagle *56
Long-crested Hawk Eagle
*57
Lizard Buzzard *57
Brown Harrier Eagle *55,
*58
Grasshopper Buzzard *58
Bateleur *59
Palm-nut Vulture *44
Lammergeyer *44 Not
yet recorded but probably
occurs
Steppe Buzzard *62
Long-legged Buzzard 232
Sight record but not yet
confirmed
Augur Buzzard *63
Little Sparrow Hawk *63
Shikra *66
Gabar Goshawk *67
Pale Chanting Goshawk
*68
Dark Chanting Goshawk
*68
Montagu's Harrier *68
Pallid Harrier *69
European Marsh Harrier
*69
Harrier Hawk *70
Crested Francolin *71
Shelley's (Greywing) Fran-
colin *72
Heuglin's Francolin *73
Yellow-necked Spurfowl
*76
Harlequin Quail *76
Blue Quail *77

Stone Partridge *77
Tufted Guinea-fowl *77
Black Crake *79
Kori Bustard *87
Jackson's Bustard *88
White-bellied Bustard *88
Black-bellied Bustard *89
Hartlaub's Bustard *89
Spotted Stone Curlew *89
African Jacana *90
Ringed Plover *91
Kittlitz's Sand Plover *94
Caspian Plover *95
Spurwing Plover *99
Wattled Plover *100
Blackhead Plover *100
Green Sandpiper *107
Temminck's Courser *110
Bronze-winged Courser
*98, *111
Button Quail *116
Four-banded Sandgrouse
*118
Speckled Pigeon *119
Red-eyed Dove *120
Mourning Dove *121
Ring-necked Dove *120
Vinaceous Dove 237
Laughing Dove *121
Namaqua Dove *121
Black-billed Wood Dove
237
Bruce's Green Pigeon *122
European Cuckoo *123
African Cuckoo *123
Red-chested Cuckoo *123
Black Cuckoo *124
Great Spotted Cuckoo
*124
Black and White Cuckoo
*124
Levaillant's Cuckoo *124
Didric Cuckoo *125
White-browed Coucal *126
White-crested Turaco *131
White-bellied Go-away-bird
*132
Brown Parrot *134
Rose-ringed Parrakeet 243
European Roller *135
Abyssinian Roller 18
Rufous-crowned Roller
*136

Broad-billed Roller *137
Grey-headed   Kingfisher
*140
Striped Kingfisher *140
Little Bee-eater *142
Swallow-tailed   Bee-eater
*146
Grey Hornbill *147
Red-billed Hornbill *148
Jackson's Hornbill *149
Abyssinian Ground Horn-
bill *150
European Hoopoe *151
Senegal Hoopoe *151
Green Wood Hoopoe *152
Abyssinian   Scimitar-bill
*152
African Scops Owl *154
White-faced   Scops   Owl
*154
Pearl-spotted Owlet *155
Spotted Eagle Owl *155
Verreaux's Eagle Owl *155
European Nightjar *156
Freckled Nightjar *157
Plain Nightjar *157
Standard-wing   Nightjar
*159
Long-tailed Nightjar *159
Speckled Mousebird *159
Blue-naped Mousebird *162
Double-toothed   Barbet
*164
Black-billed Barbet 19
Spotted-flanked   Barbet
*166
Red-fronted Barbet 20
Red and Yellow Barbet
*169
D'Arnaud's Barbet *169
Greater Honey-guide *170
Nubian Woodpecker *172
Cardinal Woodpecker *173
Bearded Woodpecker *173
Nyanza Swift *174
Scarce Swift 16
Mottled Swift *175
Palm Swift *178
Flappet Lark *181
Red-winged   Bush   Lark
*180
African Pied Wagtail *183
Richard's Pipit *184

Yellow-throated Longclaw *186

Rufous Chatterer *187

Dark-capped Bulbul *188

Dusky Flycatcher *190

Little Grey Flycatcher 22

Silverbird *194

Paradise Flycatcher *195

Olive Thrush *196

European Rock Thrush *197

European Common Wheatear *198

Isabelline Wheatear *198

Pied Wheatear *198

Cliff Chat 23

Sooty Chat *200

Spotted Morning Warbler *202

Barred Warbler 290

European Willow Warbler *205

Grey Wren Warbler *205

Fan-tailed Warbler 24

Black-breasted Apalis *206

Grey-capped Warbler *206

Buff-bellied Warbler *207

Crombec *207

Yellow-bellied Eremomela *207

Grey-backed Camaroptera *210

Rattling Cisticola *211

Foxy Cisticola 295

Winding Cisticola 294

Croaking Cisticola 294

Tawny-flanked Prinia *211

European Swallow *214

European Sand Martin *214

Banded Martin *214

African Rock Martin *214

White-headed Rough-wing Swallow *215

Black Cuckoo Shrike *215

Drongo *216

Curly-crested Helmet Shrike *217

White-crowned Shrike *218

Northern Brubru *219

Red-backed Shrike *221

Red-tailed Shrike *221

Black-headed Bush Shrike *223

Sulphur-breasted Bush Shrike *224

Grey-headed Bush Shrike *225

White-breasted Tit *226

Mouse-coloured Penduline Tit 27

African Golden Oriole *227

Black-headed Oriole *227

Fan-tailed Raven *230

Piapiac *231

Wattled Starling *231

Violet-backed Starling *232

Blue-eared Glossy Starling *232

Bronze-tailed Starling 29

Lesser Blue-eared Starling *232

Ruppell's Long-tailed Starling *233

Superb Starling *235

Yellow-billed Oxpecker *238

Beautiful Sunbird *243

Pygmy Sunbird 30

Copper Sunbird 30

Mariqua Sunbird *244

Scarlet-chested Sunbird *246

Buffalo Weaver *248

White-headed Buffalo Weaver *249

White-browed Sparrow Weaver *249

Chestnut-crowned Sparrow Weaver 321

Grey-headed Social Weaver *250

Grey-headed Sparrow *250

Yellow-spotted Petronia 27

Speckle-fronted Weaver 27

Northern Masked Weaver 234

Masked Weaver *252

Chestnut Weaver *253

Black-necked Weaver *254

Spectacled Weaver *255

Red-headed Weaver *259

Red-billed Quelea *259

Cardinal Quelea *260

Red Bishop *260

Yellow Bishop *261

Black-winged Bishop *261

White-winged Widow-bird *262

Bronze Mannikin *264

Silver-bill 27

Cut-throat *264

Green-winged Pytilia *264

Red-billed Fire Finch *265

Crimson-rumped Waxbill *266

Red-cheeked Cordon-bleu *266

Purple Grenadier *267

Pin-tailed Whydah *267

Paradise Whydah *268

Yellow-fronted Canary *269

White-bellied Canary 28

Yellow-rumped Seed-eater *269

Golden-breasted Bunting *270

Cinnamon-breasted Rock Bunting *270

MURCHISON FALLS NATIONAL PARK

Murchison Falls National Park, an area of 1,557 square miles in north-western Uganda, is Uganda's largest faunal reserve. It was gazetted in 1952. The Park, bounded on the west by Lake Albert and the Albert Nile, is bisected by the Victoria Nile. At the Murchison Falls in the centre of the Park the latter forces its way through a rock cleft some twenty feet wide, falling in a spectacular cascade to the lower reaches of the river below. The great feature of this sector of the Nile is its large crocodile population, probably the largest concentration of these reptiles still left in Africa.

Much of the Murchison Falls Park is vast undulating grassy plains, over which the famed Elephant herds wander at will. The Elephant population has been estimated to number between 4,000 and 8,000 beasts. Locally there are areas of savannah woodlands, some isolated forest patches such as the Rabongo Forest where Chimpanzees may be found, and strips of riverine forest along some sections of the Victoria Nile.

The most developed part of the Park with the best network of motorable tracks is immediately west of Paraa, the Park Headquarters, and includes what is known as the Buligi Circuit. This track follows the shore of the Albert Nile to its confluence with the Victoria Nile, an area especially prolific in water birds and where the rare Whale-headed Stork has been recorded. Mammals also are abundant, especially Elephant, Uganda Kob, Jackson's Hartebeest and Oribi. Both the White and the Black Rhinoceros may be encountered.

A road system opens more distant parts of the Park to visitors, especially rewarding routes being the access road right to the edge of the Murchison Falls on the south bank, and the road north of the Victoria Nile to Chobe just above the picturesque Karuma Falls. This extremely attractive section of the river is dotted with well-treed islets. The district is noted for its Rothschild's Giraffe and Black Rhinoceros.

The highlight of any visit to Murchison Park is the seven-mile launch trip from Paraa upstream to the foot of the Falls. Hippopotamus and Crocodiles are to be seen in abundance, and Elephant, Buffalo and the odd Black Rhinoceros line the water's edge, paying little heed to the boat and allowing a very near approach and unlimited photographic opportunities. There is a veritable bewilderment of bird life: it is not at all unusual to see sixty or more species on a single trip, ranging from stately Saddle-bill Storks and Goliath Herons to brilliant Malachite Kingfishers, Red-throated Bee-eaters and graceful Wattled Plovers.

Fishing is permitted in the waters of the Nile which lie within the Park and Nile Perch of up to 150 to 200 lbs. are to be caught. The most popular sections of the river for Nile Perch spinning are in the slack water at the foot of the Murchison Falls and in pools below the Karuma Falls at Chobe.

Accommodation is available in two modern hotels in the Park, the Paraa Safari Lodge on a northern bluff overlooking the Victoria Nile, and

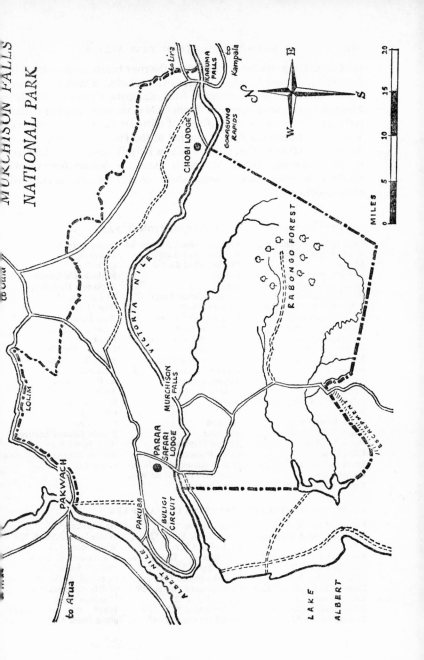

MURCHISON FALLS
NATIONAL PARK

the Chobe Lodge on the north bank of the river below the Karuma Falls. Camping is allowed in specified places with permission from the Warden. Paraa Safari Lodge is 190 miles from Kampala, fifty-four miles from Masindi, on an all-weather road. From Gulu in the north-east the entrance is through Wangwar Gate, a distance of thirty-six miles. From Arua in the West Nile District the Park is entered at the Pakwach ferry across the Albert Nile, fifty-six miles. Chobe Lodge is 175 miles direct from Kampala, or 211 miles if the road via Masindi is taken. The distance from Gulu to Chobe is fifty-two miles. Landing strips suitable for light aircraft exist close to both lodges.

MAMMALS OF MURCHISON FALLS NATIONAL PARK

East African Hedgehog	Hunting Dog Mainly in north-west of Park	Hippopotamus
Giant White-toothed		Warthog
Shrew	Black-backed Jackal	Bush Pig
Rousette Fruit Bat	Zorilla	Rothschild's Giraffe
Epauletted Fruit Bat	Ratel	Jackson's Hartebeest
Pale-bellied Fruit Bat	Spotted-necked Otter	Red Duiker
White-bellied Tomb Bat	African Civet	Blue Duiker
Hollow-faced Bat	Large-spotted Genet	Bush Duiker
False Vampire Bat	Marsh Mongoose	Oribi
Yellow-winged Bat	Large Grey Mongoose	Uganda Kob
Lander's Horseshoe Bat	Black-tipped Mongoose	Defassa Waterbuck
Lesser Leaf-nosed Bat	White-tailed Mongoose	Bohor Reedbuck
Banana Bat	Banded Mongoose	Bushbuck
Yellow-bellied Bat	Spotted Hyaena	African Buffalo
Angola Free-tailed Bat	African Wild Cat	African Hare
White-bellied Free-tailed	Serval	Bunyoro Rabbit
Bat	Lion	Cane Rat
Black-faced Vervet	Leopard	Porcupine
Red-tailed Monkey	Ant Bear	Striped Ground Squirrel
Patas Monkey	African Elephant	Bush Squirrel
Olive Baboon	Black Rhinoceros	African Dormouse
Black and White Colobus	White Rhinoceros Intro-	Giant Rat
Chimpanzee	duced into Park from West	
Lesser Ground Pangolin	Nile District	

BIRDS OF MURCHISON FALLS NATIONAL PARK

Little Grebe *20	Purple Heron *24	Hammerkop *28
White-necked Cormorant *20.	Great White Egret *24	Whale-headed Stork *28
	Little Egret *25	White Stork *29
Long-tailed Cormorant *21	Buff-backed Heron or	Woolly-necked Stork *29
African Darter *21	Cattle Egret *26	Abdim's Stork *29
White Pelican *22	Squacco Heron *26	Open-bill Stork *30
Pink-backed Pelican *22	Green-backed Heron *26	Saddle-bill Stork *30
Grey Heron *23	Night Heron *27	Marabou Stork *31
Black-headed Heron *23	Little Bittern *27	Wood Ibis or Yellow-
Goliath Heron *23	Dwarf Bittern *27	billed Stork *31

QUEEN ELIZABETH NATIONAL PARK

With its landscape dominated by the snow-capped peaks of the mighty Ruwenzori Range immediately to the north—the famed "Mountains of the Moon" which rise to over 16,500 feet—the Queen Elizabeth National Park posseses a character all its own.

Established in 1952 with an area of 767 square miles, it lies in extreme western Uganda between Lake Edward and Lake George: its south-western and western borders at the Ishasha River and Kayanja adjoin the Congo Parc du Kivu. The Park boasts a remarkable range of habitats—grassy plains, tropical forest, rivers, swamps, lakes and a zone of old volcanic craters, some of great beauty with wooded slopes and deep blue or green lakes hidden in their depths.

Throughout the Park game animals and birds occur in super abund-ance, although there are some unexpected gaps. For instance there are no Rhinoceros, Giraffe, Zebra or Jackson's Hartebeest in the Park, and even more surprising, there are no crocodiles in Lakes George and Edward nor in the Kazinga Channel which connects the two lakes.

The Maramagambo Forest, south of the Kazinga Channel, divides the rolling park-like plains of the Kigezi section from the euphorbia-dotted grasslands of the north. Chimpanzees, Black and White Colobus, a few of the rare Red Colobus, Blue Monkey and Red-tailed Monkey may be seen from the main road which traverses the forest.

The Kigezi parkland—undulating grassy plains with isolated clumps of widely spaced trees—is famous for its lions which have developed a tree-climbing propensity. Here also are large herds of Topi and Uganda Kob, and Giant Forest Hogs are not rare.

In the grassland valley bottoms drainage from surrounding slopes has created several sloughs, beloved by hippos and not infrequently the habitat of the rare Whale-headed Stork. Elsewhere in the Park, this remarkably prehistoric-looking bird may be encountered on the shores of Lake George in the Kamulikwezi Circuit.

Large herds of Elephant and Buffalo are a feature of the Queen Elizabeth Park; certain of the latter, in their paler and more reddish colour, indicate inter-breeding with the red forest buffalo of the Congo. Exceptionally fine specimens of Defassa Waterbuck are found, some of the males carrying the finest horns in Africa. Leopards are by no means rare, but are shy and not often seen.

The launch trip along the Kazinga Channel is a most rewarding experience: to approach within a few feet of Elephants and other animals on the bank is unforgettable. Birds are abundant and colourful, Malachite and Pied Kingfishers abound and pay little heed to the human intruder. The head of the channel, where it joins Lake Edward, is the only known locality of the recently described Uganda Cormorant, an African resident race of the familiar European Cormorant. In the spring large flocks of migrating White-winged Black Terns hawk fly above the water in the manner of swallows. The usual bird count on a single launch trip is between sixty and seventy species.

Near Rutanda Game Scout Post to the north of the Maramagambo are one or two small lakes surrounded by swamp and forest. This is an outstanding bird locality with a great variety of sunbirds, that most beautiful of the bee-eaters, the Black Bee-eater, and Blue-breasted and Shining-blue Kingfishers. For water-birds the mouth of the Nyamagesani River, Pelican Point, is outstanding.

Full hotel accommodation in the Park is available at Mweya Safari Lodge, built on a bluff overlooking Lake Edward and the Kazinga Channel. Park Headquarters is also situated at Mweya. In the south-west

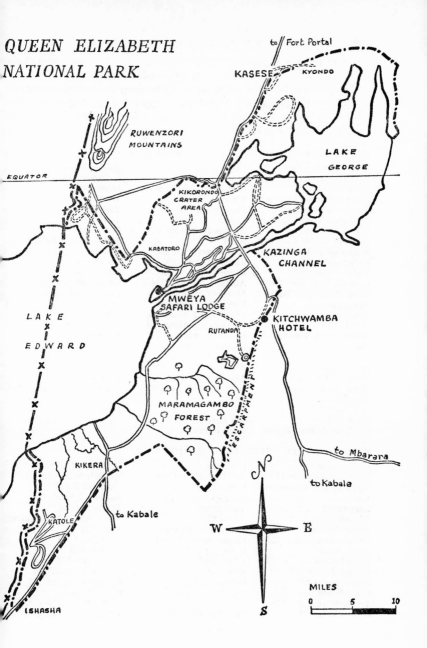

QUEEN ELIZABETH
NATIONAL PARK

to Fort Portal

KASESE   KYONDO

RUWENZORI
MOUNTAINS

EQUATOR

LAKE
GEORGE

KIKORONDO
CRATER
AREA

KABATORO

KAZINGA
CHANNEL

MWEYA
SAFARI LODGE

KITCHWAMBA
HOTEL

RUTANDA

LAKE

EDWARD

MARAMAGAMBO
FOREST

ESCARPMENT

to Mbarara

KIKERA

to Kabale

to Kabale

KATOLE

N

W   E

MILES

0   5   10

S

ISHASHA

sector there is a self-service camp at Ishasha. Official camping sites along the Kazinga Channel exist for those who wish to use them.

From Kampala, either via Masaka and Mbarara or via Fort Portal, the distance to the Queen Elizabeth Park is approximately 290 miles. The Kigezi portion of the Park may be reached from Kabale. The airfield serving the Park is at Kasese.

MAMMALS OF QUEEN ELIZABETH NATIONAL PARK

Otter Shrew May occur in streams in Maramagambo Forest
Straw-coloured Fruit Bat
Rousette Fruit Bat
Epauletted Fruit Bat
Pale-bellied Fruit Bat
Hammer-headed Fruit Bat
White-bellied Tomb Bat
Hollow-faced Bat
Yellow-winged Bat
Lander's Horseshoe Bat
Lesser Leaf-nosed Bat
Banana Bat
Yellow-bellied Bat
Angola Free-tailed Bat
White-bellied Free-tailed Bat
Potto
Bush Baby
Demidoff's Galago
Black-faced Vervet
Blue Monkey
Red-tailed Monkey
Olive Baboon
Black and White Colobus

Red Colobus
Chimpanzee
Lesser Ground Pangolin
Hunting Dog
Side-striped Jackal
Zorilla
African Striped Weasel
Ratel
Spotted-necked Otter
African Civet
Large-spotted Genet
African Palm Civet
Marsh Mongoose
Large Grey Mongoose
Black-tipped Mongoose
White-tailed Mongoose
Banded Mongoose
Spotted Hyaena
African Wild Cat
Serval
Golden Cat Not yet recorded but may occur
Lion
Leopard
Ant Bear
Rock Hyrax

African Elephant
Hippopotamus
Giant Forest Hog
Warthog
Bush Pig
Topi
Red Duiker
Yellow-backed Duiker
Blue Duiker
Bush Duiker
Uganda Kob
Defassa Waterbuck
Bohor Reedbuck
Bushbuck
African Buffalo
African Hare
Cane Rat
Porcupine
Striped Ground Squirrel
Bush Squirrel
Giant Forest Squirrel
Scaly-tailed Flying Squirrel
African Dormouse
Giant Rat

BIRDS OF QUEEN ELIZABETH NATIONAL PARK

Little Grebe *20
Uganda Cormorant 14
White-necked Cormorant *20
Long-tailed Cormorant *21
African Darter *21
White Pelican *22
Pink-backed Pelican *22
Grey Heron *23
Black-headed Heron *23
Goliath Heron *23
Purple Heron *24
Great White Egret *24
Yellow-billed Egret *25
Black Heron *25

Little Egret *25
Buff-backed Heron or Cattle Egret *26
Squacco Heron *26
Madagascar Squacco Heron *26
Green-backed Heron *26
Rufous-bellied Heron *26
Night Heron *27
Little Bittern *27
Dwarf Bittern *27
Hammerkop *28
Whale-headed Stork *28
White Stork *29
European Black Stork *30

Woolly-necked Stork *29
Abdim's Stork *29
Open-bill Stork *30
Saddle-bill Stork *30
Marabou Stork *31
Wood Ibis or Yellow-billed Stork *31
Sacred Ibis *31
Hadada Ibis *34
Glossy Ibis *34
African Spoonbill *34
Greater Flamingo *35
Lesser Flamingo *35
White-backed Duck *36
White-eyed Pochard *37

African Pochard *37
European Shoveler *37
Garganey Teal *38
Hottentot Teal *39
Red-billed Duck *39
European Teal *39
White-faced Tree Duck *40
Fulvous Tree Duck *40
Pygmy Goose *40
Knob-billed Goose *41
Egyptian Goose *41
Spur-winged Goose *41
Ruppell's Griffon Vulture *42
White-backed Vulture *43
Lappet-faced Vulture *43
White-headed Vulture *43
Hooded Vulture *43
Peregrine *45
Lanner *45
European Hobby *46
African Hobby *46
Sooty Falcon *50
European Kestrel *47
Grey Kestrel *50
Cuckoo Falcon *67
African Black Kite *51
Black-shouldered Kite *51
Honey Buzzard *62
Steppe Eagle *55
Tawny Eagle *54
Wahlberg's Eagle *55
Ayres' Hawk Eagle *56
Martial Eagle *56
Crowned Hawk Eagle *57
Long-crested Hawk Eagle *57
Lizard Buzzard *57
Brown Harrier Eagle *55, *58
Black-chested Harrier Eagle *58
Banded Harrier Eagle *58
Grasshopper Buzzard *58
Bateleur *59
African Fish Eagle *59
Palm-nut Vulture *44
Steppe Buzzard *62
Eastern Steppe Buzzard *62
Mountain Buzzard *62
Augur Buzzard *63
Little Sparrow Hawk *63
Great Sparrow Hawk *66

Shikra *66
Gabar Goshawk *67
Montagu's Harrier *68
Pallid Harrier *69
European Marsh Harrier *69
African Marsh Harrier *69
Harrier Hawk *70
Osprey *70
Coqui Francolin *71
Red-wing Francolin *72
Scaly Francolin *74
Red-necked Spurfowl *75
Cape Quail *76
Harlequin Quail *76
Blue Quail *77
Helmeted Guinea-fowl *77
Tufted Guinea-fowl *77
Crested Guinea-fowl *78
African Crake *79
Black Crake *79
Striped Crake 14
White-spotted Pygmy Crake *82
Moorhen *83
Crowned Crane *86
Black-bellied Bustard *89
Water Dikkop *90
African Jacana *90
Ringed Plover *91
Little Ringed Plover *91
White-fronted Sand Plover *91
Kittlitz's Sand Plover *94
Three-banded Plover *94
Caspian Plover *95
Grey Plover *95
Crowned Lapwing or Plover *98
Senegal Plover *98
Spurwing Plover *99
Brown-chested Wattled Plover *99
Wattled Plover *100
Long-toed Lapwing *101
European Oyster-catcher *102
Avocet *101
Black-winged Stilt *102
Painted Snipe *103
European Common Snipe *104
African Snipe *104

Curlew Sandpiper *105
Little Stint *105
Temminck's Stint *105
Sanderling *105
Ruff *106
Turnstone *106
Terek Sandpiper *106
Common Sandpiper *107
Green Sandpiper *107
Wood Sandpiper *107
Redshank *106
Spotted Redshank 14
Marsh Sandpiper *108
Greenshank *109
Black-tailed Godwit 14
Bar-tailed Godwit 14
Curlew *109
Whimbrel *109
Temminck's Courser *110
Bronze-winged Courser *98, *111
Pratincole *111
Lesser Black-backed Gull *114
Grey-headed Gull *114
Gull-billed Tern *115
Caspian Tern *115
White-winged Black Tern *115
Whiskered Tern *115
African Skimmer *116
Button Quail *116
Black-rumped Button Quail *117
Olive Pigeon *119
Afep Pigeon *119
Red-eyed Dove *120
Ring-necked Dove *120
Laughing Dove *121
Namaqua Dove *121
Tambourine Dove *122
Blue-spotted Wood Dove *122
Western Lemon Dove 237
Green Pigeon *122
European Cuckoo *123
African Cuckoo *123
Red-chested Cuckoo *123
Black Cuckoo *124
Levaillant's Cuckoo *124
Black and White Cuckoo *124
Emerald Cuckoo *125

Yellow Bishop *261
Fan-tailed Widow-bird *262
Yellow-shouldered Widow-bird 32
Yellow-mantled Widow-bird 32
White-winged Widow-bird *262
Red-collared Widow-bird *262
Bronze Mannikin *264
Black and White Mannikin 27
Grey-headed Negro Finch 32

Chestnut-breasted Negro Finch 332
Red-headed Blue-bill 32
Black-bellied Seed-cracker 32
Quail Finch 27
Parasitic Weaver 336
Green-backed Twin-spot 335
Green-winged Pytilia *264
African Fire Finch *265
Red-billed Fire Finch *265
Waxbill *266
Zebra Waxbill 337
Fawn-breasted Waxbill 337

Black-crowned Waxbill 28
Red-cheeked Cordon-bleu *266
Purple Indigo-bird 28
Pin-tailed Whydah *267
Yellow-fronted Canary *269
Brimstone Canary *268
Yellow-rumped Seed-eater *269
Golden-breasted Bunting *270
Cinnamon-breasted Rock Bunting *270

Game Reserves and Animal Sanctuaries

In addition to the three National Parks Uganda possesses a number of Game Reserves and Animal Sanctuaries. The difference between "Game Reserve" and "Animal Sanctuary" is that in a Game Reserve human settlement, cultivation and stock grazing are prohibited. In an Animal Sanctuary the animal and bird life is strictly protected and hunting is not allowed, unless under exceptional circumstances and with a special Chief Game Warden's permit; but there is no restriction on human activities such as cultivation of crops and grazing of domestic stock.

Several of Uganda's Animal Sanctuaries have been established for the special purpose of giving protection to a single species. These include the Kigezi Gorilla Sanctuary in extreme south-western Uganda, set up for the protection of the Mountain Gorilla; the Nkosi Island Sitatunga Sanctuary in Lake Victoria; and the several White Rhinoceros Sanctuaries in West Nile.

ASWA LOLIM GAME RESERVE

The Aswa Lolim Game Reserve is an area of forty square miles of savannah grasslands, adjoining the northern border of the Murchison Falls National Park. The Reserve provides essential seasonal grazing for Uganda Kob and contains that animal's territorial breeding grounds.

Elephant, Black Rhinoceros, Jackson's Hartebeest, Bohor Reedbuck, Buffalo, Lion and Leopard occur in this Reserve. Bird life is similar to that found in the Murchison Falls National Park.

KIGEZI GAME RESERVE

The 200 square miles of the Kigezi Game Reserve adjoins the southern boundary of the Queen Elizabeth National Park, and acts as a buffer zone between the Park and the thickly settled areas to the south and east.

It contains open grasslands, park-like savannah woodland and forest. It carries large herds of Elephant, Buffalo and Topi. Uganda Kob, Bushbuck, Giant Forest Hog and Defassa Waterbuck also occur. Bird life is abundant and similar to that of the adjoining Queen Elizabeth Park.

LOMUNGA GAME RESERVE

The Lomunga Game Reserve, an area of approximately thirty-five square miles west of the Albert Nile in West Madi District, was established to give complete protection to a small number of White Rhinoceros found in the area. Other game animals in the Reserve include Elephant, Buffalo, Jackson's Hartebeest, Uganda Kob, Bohor Reedbuck, Hippopotamus, Lion and Leopard.

Notable birds which may be seen include:

Whale-headed Stork *28	White-headed Plover *100	Black-breasted Barbet *164
Woolly-necked Stork *29	Egyptian Plover 14	Violet-backed Sunbird *247
Red-necked Falcon *46	Red-throated Bee-eater 19	
Banded Harrier Eagle *58	Swallow-tailed Bee-eater *146	

TORO GAME RESERVE

The Toro Game Reserve, an area of 202 square miles at the southern end of Lake Albert, contains grassy lakeshore flats, swamps, steep forested escarpments and heavily wooded streams. A large population of Uganda Kob is found here, estimated to number over 10,000, and among other game animals are Elephant, Hippopotamus, Jackson's Hartebeest, Bohor Reedbuck, Giant Forest Hog, Defassa Waterbuck, Lion and Leopard. Limited and strictly controlled hunting is permitted under special permit issued by the Chief Game Warden. Accommodation and guides are available at the Uganda Wildlife Development Lodge on the Wassa River.

In the main the bird life is similar to that found in the Murchison Falls National Park.

Specially interesting species, including some not found in the Murchison Park, are:

African Hobby *46
Brown Harrier Eagle *55,
*58
Banded Harrier Eagle *58

Painted Snipe *103
White-naped Pigeon 16
White-thighed Hornbill 15
Wattled Black Hornbill 15

Pied Hornbill *150
Yellow-spotted Barbet 20
Hartlaub's Marsh Widow-
bird 330

ACHOLI ELEPHANT SANCTUARY

The 1,350 square miles of the Acholi Elephant Sanctuary lies immediately north of Murchison Falls National Park and the Aswa Lolim Game Reserve. Vast tracts of open grassland are intersected by wooded streams. It is an outstanding game area with many Elephant among which are a number of very large tuskers. Black Rhinoceros are present in small numbers, together with Buffalo, Hippopotamus, Jackson's Hartebeest, Defassa Waterbuck, Bushbuck, Uganda Kob, Bohor Reedbuck, Oribi, Lion and Leopard.

The bird life does not differ from that found in similar habitats in the Murchison Falls National Park.

DEBASIEN ANIMAL SANCTUARY

The Debasien Animal Sanctuary in southern Karamoja, eastern Uganda, comprises 760 square miles of more or less arid bush country—the Pian Plains—and the forested massif of Mount Debasien, or Kadam as it is alternatively called, rising in its centre to 10,000 feet.

Game animals occurring in this sanctuary include Buffalo, Rothschild's Giraffe, Greater and Lesser Kudu, Bushbuck, Bohor and Chanler's Reedbuck, Uganda Kob, Giant Forest Hog, Bright's Gazelle, Roan Antelope, Jackson's Hartebeest, Lion and Leopard.

Limited controlled hunting is allowed under special permit from the Chief Game Warden.

Some of the most characteristic birds of the area are:

Ostrich *19
Marabou Stork *31
Secretary Bird *42
Ruppell's Griffon Vulture *42
White-backed Vulture *43
Lanner *45
Wahlberg's Eagle *55
Tawny Eagle *54
Martial Eagle *56
Bateleur *59
Dark Chanting Goshawk *68

Stone Partridge *77
Buff-crested Bustard *89
Spotted Stone Curlew *89
Heuglin's Courser *110
Button Quail *116
White-bellied Go-away-bird *132
Brown Parrot *134
Rufous-crowned Roller *136
Grey-headed Kingfisher *140
Striped Kingfisher *140

European Bee-eater *142
White-throated Bee-eater *142
Red-billed Hornbill *148
Jackson's Hornbill *149
Abyssinian Scimitar-bill *152
Nubian Woodpecker *172
Cardinal Woodpecker *173
Bearded Woodpecker *173
Mottled Swift *175
Spotted Morning Warbler *202

Curly-crested Helmet
Shrike *217
Yellow-billed Shrike 26
Sulphur-breasted Bush
Shrike *224

Lesser Blue-eared Starling
*232
Beautiful Sunbird *243
Mariqua Sunbird *244
Buffalo Weaver *248

White-headed Buffalo
Weaver *249

ENTEBBE ANIMAL AND BIRD SANCTUARY

The twenty square miles of the Entebbe Animal and Bird Sanctuary encompass the township and famous botanical gardens of Entebbe on the shores of Lake Victoria.

In the swamp at the northern end of Entebbe Airport, Sitatunga may sometimes be seen in the early morning or late evening; and the Whale-headed Stork and Rufous-bellied Heron have also been recorded in this locality.

The extensive botanical gardens which run down to the lake shore are extremely rich in birds, including many uncommon species. White-collared Pratincoles may often be seen perched on the Yacht Club jetty, amongst Grey-headed Gulls and Common Sandpipers. Grey Parrots visit flowering Erythrina trees in the early morning to feed on the nectar-rich blossoms. Sunbirds also favour these trees, including the aptly-named Superb Sunbird and the rare Orange-tufted Sunbird. The following are some of the characteristic and more interesting species likely to be encountered:

Little Grebe *20
White-necked Cormorant
*20
Long-tailed Cormorant *21
African Darter *21
Grey Heron *23
Black-headed Heron *23
Goliath Heron *23
Great White Egret *24
Little Egret *25
Hammerkop *28
Abdim's Stork *29
Open-bill Stork *30
Hadada Ibis *34
Knob-billed Goose *41
Pygmy Goose *40
Egyptian Goose *41
Hooded Vulture *43
African Hobby *46
Bat Hawk *46
Long-crested Hawk Eagle
*57
African Fish Eagle *59

Palm-nut Vulture *44
African Marsh Harrier *69
Harrier Hawk *70
Osprey *70
White-spotted Pygmy
Crake *82
Crowned Crane *86
Water Dikkop *90
African Jacana *90
Long-toed Lapwing *101
Afep Pigeon *119
Blue-spotted Wood Dove
*122
Green Pigeon *122
Red-chested Cuckoo *123
Emerald Cuckoo *125
Blue-headed Coucal *127
Ross's Turaco *131
Great Blue Turaco *132
Eastern Grey Plantain-
eater 17
Red-headed Lovebird 4
Broad-billed Roller *137

Pied Kingfisher *137
Giant Kingfisher *138
Malachite Kingfisher *138
Pygmy Kingfisher *139
Woodland Kingfisher *139
Blue-breasted Kingfisher 18
Grey-headed Kingfisher
*140
Striped Kingfisher *140
European Bee-eater *140
Madagascar Bee-eater 19
Blue-breasted Bee-eater 19
Little Bee-eater *142
Black and White-casqued
Hornbill *147
Pied Hornbill *150
African Hoopoe *151
Double-toothed Barbet
*164
Grey-throated Barbet *166
Yellow-spotted Barbet 20
Lemon-rumped Tinker-bird
*168

Yellow-billed Barbet 20
Greater Honey-guide *170
Uganda Spotted Wood-pecker *173
Little Swift *175
White-rumped Swift *175
Palm Swift *178
Bristle-bill 21
Yellow-throated Leaflove 21
Joyful Greenbul 271
Yellow-whiskered Greenbul *189
Swamp Flycatcher *190
Black and White Fly-catcher 279
Wattle-eye Flycatcher *195
Blue Flycatcher *195
Paradise Flycatcher *195
Black-headed Paradise Fly-catcher *196
Snowy-headed Robin Chat *201
Red-shouldered Cuckoo Shrike 297
Drongo *216
Grey-backed Fiscal *220

Black-headed Gonolek *221
Tropical Boubou *222
Puff-back Shrike 300
African Golden Oriole *227
Splendid Glossy Starling *233
Purple-headed Glossy Star-ling 29
Ruppell's Long-tailed Starling *233
Green White-eye *239
Bronzy Sunbird *242
Red-chested Sunbird 30
Copper Sunbird 30
Variable Sunbird *244
Olive-bellied Sunbird 30
Green-throated Sunbird 30
Scarlet-chested Sunbird *246
Green-headed Sunbird *246
Blue-throated Brown Sun-bird 30
Olive Sunbird 30
Collared Sunbird *247
Grey-chinned Sunbird 29
Green Hylia 27

Black-headed Weaver *250
Yellow-collared Weaver *253
Golden-backed Weaver *253
Northern Brown-throated Weaver 31
Orange Weaver 31
Black-necked Weaver *254
Spectacled Weaver *255
Slender-billed Weaver 31
Vieillot's Black Weaver *255
Weyn's Weaver 327
Stuhlmann's Weaver 31
Brown-capped Weaver 31
Red-headed Malimbe *258
Grosbeak Weaver *259
Red-headed Weaver *259
Black-winged Bishop *261
Black Bishop 32
Yellow Bishop *261
Fan-tailed Widow-bird *262
Black-bellied Seed-cracker 32
Pin-tailed Whydah *267

JINJA ANIMAL AND BIRD SANCTUARY

This is another small sanctuary encompassing part of Jinja township and the mouth of the Victoria Nile, an area of about five square miles. Hippopotamus occur in the Nile and at night sometimes wander over the Jinja golf course.

Characteristic birds include:

White-necked Cormorant *20
African Darter *21
Black-headed Heron *23
Hammerkop *28
Hadada Ibis *34
African Hobby *46

Bat Hawk *46
Eastern Grey Plantain-eater 17
Brown Parrot *134
Pied Kingfisher *137
Woodland Kingfisher *139
Striped Kingfisher *140

Grey-headed Kingfisher *140
Double-toothed Barbet *164
Little Swift *175

KAZINGA ANIMAL SANCTUARY

The Kazinga Animal Sanctuary, an area of approximately eighty square miles, abuts the east-central border of the Queen Elizabeth National Park and part of the southern shores of Lake George. It consists of rough grasslands with scattered bush and small clumps of euphorbia and acacia trees.

Animals and birds are the same as those found in a similar habitat in the Park. Elephant, Buffalo, Hippopotamus, Uganda Kob and Defassa Waterbuck are characteristic, and among birds the most noticeable are African Fish Eagle, Crowned Crane, various herons, egrets and storks and numerous weavers.

KIGEZI GORILLA SANCTUARY

The Kigezi Gorilla Sanctuary is situated on Mounts Muhavura and Mgahinga in the Birunga volcanoes, extreme south-west Uganda.

It covers seventeen square miles of forested and bamboo-covered slopes. Accommodation and guides are available at the Travellers Rest Hotel at Kisoro: there is also a mountain camp on the saddle between Muhavura and Mgahinga. A fairly strenuous three or four hours' climb up mountain footpaths is necessary to reach the gorilla habitat.

In addition to the chance of observing Gorillas the forest and bamboo-hypericum zone offer the possibility of seeing the rare Golden Monkey. Other animals which may be encountered are Elephant, Buffalo, Leopard, Bushbuck, Giant Forest Hog, Blue Monkey and Black and White Colobus.

Birds are plentiful and the colourful Ruwenzori Turaco is common though more often heard than seen. Other specially interesting birds include:

Cuckoo Falcon *67
Mountain Buzzard *62
Great Sparrow Hawk *66
Handsome Francolin *75
Western Lemon Dove 237
Bar-tailed Trogon *163
Western Green Tinkerbird *167
Yellow-billed Barbet 20
African Broadbill *179
Mountain Illadopsis 21
Olive-breasted Mountain Greenbul 21
Mountain Yellow Flycatcher 278
Ruwenzori Puff-back Flycatcher 280
Blue Flycatcher *195
Abyssinian Ground Thrush 23
Brown-chested Alethe 23
White-starred Bush Robin *203

Cinnamon Bracken Warbler *204
Red-faced Woodland Warbler 24
Black-collared Apalis *205
Collared Apalis 292
Masked Apalis 292
Black-throated Apalis *206
Chestnut-throated Apalis 24
Grey-capped Warbler *206
White-browed Crombec 24
Luhder's Bush Shrike 26
Doherty's Bush Shrike *224
Stripe-breasted Tit 302
Waller's Chestnut-wing Starling 308
Slender-billed Chestnut wing Starling 29
Scarlet-tufted Malachite Sunbird 30

Greater Double-collared Sunbird 30
Northern Double-collared Sunbird 30
Regal Sunbird 30
Green-headed Sunbird *246
Blue-headed Sunbird 30
Dark-backed Weaver 31
Strange Weaver 326
Brown-capped Weaver 31
Red-faced Crimson-wing 32
Abyssinian Crimson-wing 32
Dusky Crimson-wing 32
Shelley's Crimson-wing 32
Dusky Fire Finch 336
Yellow-bellied Waxbill *266
Black-headed Waxbill 28
Yellow-crowned Canary 28
Streaky Seed-eater *269
Oriole Finch 340

MALAWA SANCTUARY

The Malawa Wildlife Sanctuary a few miles south of Tororo, near the
Kenya border, comprises an area of approximately twelve square miles of
limestone hills, acacia woodland and swamp. The area is primarily of
interest to ornithologists, and the following are some of the outstanding
birds which occur:

White-backed Night Heron *27

Verreaux's Eagle *54 Occurs on nearby Tororo Rock

Banded Harrier Eagle *58

Ross's Turaco *131

Eastern Grey Plantain-eater 17

Bare-faced Go-away-bird 17

Red-headed Lovebird 17

Broad-billed Roller *137

Blue-breasted Bee-eater 19

Ground Hornbill *150

Double-toothed Barbet *164

Black-billed Barbet 19

White-headed Barbet *165

Yellow-fronted Tinker-Bird *168

Greater Honey-guide *170

Brown-backed Woodpecker *173

Blue Flycatcher *195

Blue Swallow 25

Black-headed Gonolek *221

Purple Glossy Starling 29

Splendid Glossy Starling *233

Copper Sunbird 30

Mariqua Sunbird *244

Variable Sunbird *244

Scarlet-chested Sunbird *246

Green-headed Sunbird *246

Red Bishop *260

Black-winged Bishop *261

Fan-tailed Widow-bird *262

Yellow-shouldered Widow-bird 32

Yellow-mantled Widow-bird 32

Hartlaub's Marsh Widow-bird 330

Black-bellied Waxbill 337

NKOSI ISLAND SITATUNGA SANCTUARY

Several of the Sese group of islands in Lake Victoria, south of Entebbe, are
famous as the haunt of the swamp-living antelope the Sitatunga. Nkosi
Island, a southern outlier of the group, has been established as a Sitatunga
Sanctuary. A boat service to the Sese Islands operates from Port Bell near
Entebbe, and it is sometimes possible to hire a Game Department launch
to visit the islands.

Many of the islands including Nkosi are forested and are margined by
extensive areas of swamp. Bird life is abundant, perhaps the most characteristic species being the Grey Parrot: Whale-headed Storks occur locally
in the swamps. Other special birds inhabiting these islands include:

Goliath Heron *23

Purple Heron *24

Night Heron *27

Rufous-bellied Heron *26

Saddle-bill Stork *30

Pygmy Goose *40

Bat Hawk *46

Crowned Hawk Eagle *57

African Fish Eagle *59

African Marsh Harrier *69

Kaffir Rail *79

White-spotted Pygmy Crake *82

Water Dikkop *90

Long-toed Lapwing *101

White-collared Pratincole *111

Afep Pigeon *119

Emerald Cuckoo *125

Blue-headed Coucal *127

Black-billed Turaco *130

Ross's Turaco *131

Great Blue Turaco *132

Eastern Grey Plantain-eater 17

Red-headed Lovebird 17

Broad-billed Roller *137

Giant Kingfisher *138

Blue-breasted Kingfisher 18

Blue-headed Bee-eater 19

Black and White-casqued Hornbill *147

Pied Hornbill *150

Double-toothed Barbet *164

Hairy-breasted Barbet *165
Yellow-spotted Barbet 20
Red-tailed Greenbul *188
Bristle-bill 21
Yellow-throated Leaflove 21
Chestnut Wattle-eye *195
Jameson's Wattle-eye 22
Snowy-headed Robin Chat *201
Petit's Cuckoo Shrike 25
Black-headed Gonolek *221
Grey-green Bush Shrike 301

Splendid Glossy Starling *233
Stuhlmann's Starling 308
Red-chested Sunbird 30
Superb Sunbird 30
Copper Sunbird 30
Green-throated Sunbird 30
Scarlet-chested Sunbird *246
Green-headed Sunbird *264
Blue-throated Brown Sunbird 30

Grey-headed Sunbird 29
Green Hylia 27
Orange Weaver 31
Dark-backed Weaver 31
Weyns' Weaver 327
Hartlaub's Marsh Widowbird 330
Red-headed Blue-bill 32
Black-bellied Seed-cracker 32
Green-backed Twin-spot 335

WEST NILE WHITE RHINOCEROS SANCTUARIES

Four Sanctuaries in West Nile Province established for the protection of the White Rhinoceros together cover a total area of some 250 square miles. These are Mount Kei Sanctuary in the north-west, Otze Forest and Dufile Sanctuaries in the north-east and Ajai's Sanctuary farther south.

Ajai's Sanctuary is the most accessible of these reserves, reached via Pakwach Ferry, Mutir and Inde, and is the best locality in Uganda for seeing and photographing White Rhinoceros. It includes the so-called Ajai's Island a few miles north of Inde and the adjacent swamp and savannah woodland inhabited by the rhino.

Bird life in these sanctuaries is similar to that found in the Murchison Falls National Park.

ZOKA FOREST ELEPHANT SANCTUARY

The Zoka Forest Sanctuary covers approximately eighty square miles on the east side of the Albert Nile in East Madi, embracing the Zoka Forest and the country between the forest and the Nile.

Elephant and Black Rhinoceros occur in the forest, and on the surrounding plains Elephant, Buffalo, Uganda Kob, Jackson's Hartebeest, Defassa Waterbuck, Oribi and Bohor Reedbuck may be found.

Plains and waterside birdlife is similar to that of the Murchison Falls National Park, but the Zoka Forest remains ornithologically unexplored owing to its remoteness and general inaccessibility.

Other Important Faunal Areas

In addition to Uganda's National Parks, Game Reserves and Wildlife Sanctuaries there are four forest regions of great zoological importance, localities where many animals and birds occur which are not found in the Parks and Reserves. Situated in western Uganda, these are the Budongo Forest, the Bwamba Forest, the Impenetrable Kayonza Forest and the Mpanga Forest.

BUDONGO FOREST

The Budongo Forest lying between Masindi and Lake Albert is easy of access, and accommodation is available at a rest house twenty-one miles from Masindi. The forest has been opened up by timber felling operations over many years and a network of forest roads and tracks greatly facilitates bird-watching.

Budongo Forest is famous for its Chimpanzees and is the most accessible locality in East Africa in which to see these apes. Other uncommon animals which live in the Budongo include the curious Scaly-tailed Flying Squirrel, the Tree Pangolin, Potto, Black-fronted Duiker, Blue Duiker, Black and White Colobus and Giant Forest Squirrel. Around the outskirts of the forest the local Bunyoro Rabbit is common and is often to be seen on roads at night.

The bird life of the Budongo Forest is extremely rich and the following outstanding species have been recorded:

Cuckoo Falcon *67
Ayres' Hawk Eagle *56
Crowned Hawk Eagle *57
Crested Guinea-fowl *78
Forest Francolin *74
Nahan's Forest Francolin *74
White-spotted Pygmy Crake *82
Afep Pigeon *119
Western Lemon Dove 237
Black-billed Turaco 17
Ross's Turaco *131
Great Blue Turaco *132
Eastern Grey Plantain-eater 17
Grey Parrot 17
Broad-billed Roller *137
Blue-throated Roller 18
Shining-blue Kingfisher 18
Dwarf Kingfisher 18
Blue-breasted Kingfisher 18
Chocolate-backed Kingfisher 18
White-thighed Hornbill 15
White-headed Wood Hoopoe *152
African Wood Owl *154
White-tailed Nightjar *158
Narina's Trogon *163
Hairy-breasted Barbet *165

Yellow-spotted Barbet 20
Yellow-billed Barbet 20
Greater Honey-guide *170
Cassin's Honey-guide *172
Brown-eared Woodpecker 20
Buff-spotted Woodpecker 20
Yellow-crested Woodpecker 20
Mottled-throated Spinetail *175
Sabine's Spinetail 16
African Broadbill *179
Red-sided Broadbill *179
Green-breasted Pitta *180
Red-tailed Greenbul *188
Bristle-bill 21
Green-tailed Bristle-bill 271
Yellow-throated Leaflove 21
Spotted Greenbul 274
Grey Tit-flycatcher 278
Chestnut-cap Flycatcher 22
Chestnut Wattle-eye *195
Jameson's Wattle-eye 22
Blue Flycatcher *195
Black-headed Paradise Flycatcher *196
Red-tailed Ant Thrush 281
Blue-shouldered Robin Chat 23

Snowy-headed Robin Chat *201
Equatorial Akalat 23
Forest Robin 23
Fire-crested Alethe 283
Brown-chested Alethe 23
Uganda Woodland Warbler 290
Black-capped Apalis 292
White-chinned Prinia 25
Banded Prinia 25
Black-faced Rufous Warbler 25
Red-shouldered Cuckoo Shrike 297
Velvet-mantled Drongo 25
Square-tailed Drongo *217
Pink-footed Puff-back Shrike 300
Nicator 26
Dusky Tit *226
Splendid Glossy Starling *233
Purple-headed Glossy Starling 29
Stuhlmann's Starling 308
Superb Sunbird 30
Olive-bellied Sunbird 30
Green-headed Sunbird *246
Blue-throated Brown Sunbird 30
Grey-chinned Sunbird 29

Violet-backed Sunbird *247 Brown-capped Weaver 31   Red-headed Blue-bill 32
Little Green Sunbird 320   Yellow-mantled Weaver 31 Black-bellied Seed-cracker
Grey-headed Sunbird 29   Crested Malimbe *258   32
Green Hylia 27   Red-headed Malimbe *258   Red-faced Crimson-wing 32
Dark-backed Weaver 31   Grey-headed Negro Finch   Grey-headed Olive-back
Compact Weaver 31   32   338

BWAMBA FOREST

The low-lying Bwamba Forest, the average altitude 2,500 feet, lies at the southern end of the Semliki Valley, flanked on the east by the Ruwenzori Mountains. Ecologically it is part of the great Congo Ituri Forest, and as such contains many species of birds and some mammals not found elsewhere in East Africa.

Habitats vary from almost impenetrable swamp forest to great stands of iron-wood trees and typical low altitude rain forest. The area is well-watered by streams from the Ruwenzori highlands.

Parts of the Bwamba Forest are accessible from Fort Portal, via the Buranga Pass at the northern end of the Ruwenzori Range, down the western escarpment to the hot springs at Mongiro and thence through the eastern edge of the forest to Bundibugyo. A few footpaths extend a short distance into the forest, but in most places elephant and buffalo trails afford the only feasible passage.

Elephant, Buffalo and Leopard are not uncommon, but are not often seen on account of the dense cover. Important among the smaller mammals are Otter Shrew, Potto, Bush Baby and Demidoff's Galago, Black Mangabey, Brazza Monkey, Red-tailed Monkey, Black and White Colobus, small numbers of Chimpanzee, Tree Pangolin, African Palm Civet, Golden Cat, Giant Forest Squirrel and Scaly-tailed Flying Squirrel.

Bird life in Bwamba is outstandingly rich and nearly 400 species have so far been recorded. Mixed bird parties in the tree-tops—a feature of these western Uganda forests—may contain upwards of thirty or forty species. Following is a list of some of the more interesting birds:

African Hobby *46   Western Lemon Dove 237   Chocolate-backed King-
Grey Kestrel *50   Black-billed Turaco 17   fisher 18
Cuckoo Falcon *67   Ross's Turaco *131   Black Bee-eater 19
Bat Hawk *46   Great Blue Turaco *132   White-tailed Hornbill 15
Crowned Hawk Eagle *57   Grey Parrot 17   White-thighed Hornbill 15
Palm-nut Vulture *44   Black-collared Lovebird 17 White-crested Hornbill 15
Western Little Sparrow   Broad-billed Roller *137 Sometimes associates with
Hawk *63   Blue-throated Roller 18   troops of Colobus mon-
Long-tailed Hawk 232   Giant Kingfisher *138   keys, feeding on insects
Scaly Francolin *74   Shining-blue Kingfisher 18 disturbed by the animals
White-naped Pigeon 16   White-breasted Kingfisher Wattled Black Hornbill 15
Often found perched in   18   Pied Hornbill *150
trees around the hot   Dwarf Kingfisher 18   Black Dwarf Hornbill
springs at Mongiro   Blue-breasted Kingfisher 18 255

162 NATIONAL PARKS OF EAST AFRICA

Red-billed Dwarf Hornbill 255
Forest Wood Hoopoe 15
Fiery-necked Nightjar 16
Standard-wing Nightjar *159
Pennant-wing Nightjar *158
Narina's Trogon *163
Double-toothed Barbet *164
Hairy-breasted Barbet *165
Grey-throated Barbet *166
Yellow-throated Tinker-bird *168
Yellow-billed Barbet 20
Spotted Honey-guide 20
Cassin's Honey-guide *172
Green-backed Woodpecker 263
Brown-eared Woodpecker 20
Buff-spotted Woodpecker 20
Uganda Spotted Woodpecker *173
Yellow-crested Woodpecker 20
Elliot's Woodpecker 20
Scarce Swift 16
Alpine Swift *175
Mottled Swift *175
Mottled-throated Spinetail *175
Sabine's Spinetail 16
African Broadbill *179
Red-sided Broadbill *179
Green-breasted Pitta *180
Brown Illadopsis 270
Red-tailed Greenbul *188
White-tailed Greenbul 274
Leaflove 274
Honey-guide Greenbul 274

Xavier's Greenbul 274
Rufous Flycatcher 22
Shrike Flycatcher 279
Chestnut Wattle-eye *195
Jameson's Wattle-eye 22
Yellow-bellied Wattle-eye 280
Blue Flycatcher *195
Blue-headed Crested Flycatcher 281
White-tailed Crested Flycatcher 281
Black-headed Paradise Flycatcher *196
Kurrichane Thrush *196
Blue-shouldered Robin Chat 23
Red-capped Robin Chat *201
Snowy-headed Robin Chat *201
Equatorial Akalat 23
Akalat 283
Forest Robin 23
Fire-crested Alethe 283
Brown-chested Alethe 23
White-chinned Prinia 25
Banded Prinia 25
Black-faced Rufous Warbler 25
Velvet-mantled Drongo 25
Red-billed Shrike 25
Mackinnon's Grey Shrike *220
Luhder's Bush Shrike 26
Grey-green Bush Shrike 301
Nicator 26
Yellow-throated Nicator 301
Black-winged Oriole 302

Western Black-headed Oriole 303
Splendid Glossy Starling *233
Purple-headed Glossy Starling 29
Narrow-tailed Starling 308
Purple-breasted Sunbird 30
Superb Sunbird 30
Copper Sunbird 30
Olive-bellied Sunbird 30
Tiny Sunbird 316
Green-throated Sunbird 30
Scarlet-chested Sunbird *246
Green-headed Sunbird *246
Blue-throated Brown Sunbird 30
Grey-chinned Sunbird 29
Violet-backed Sunbird *247
Little Green Sunbird 320
Grey-headed Sunbird 29
Green Hylia 27
Yellow-mantled Weaver 31
Maxwell's Black Weaver 328
Crested Malimbe *258
Red-headed Malimbe *258
Gray's Malimbe 239
Red-bellied Malimbe 239
Grey-headed Negro Finch 32
Chestnut-breasted Negro Finch 332
White-breasted Negro Finch 332
Red-headed Blue-bill 32
Grant's Blue-bill 332
Black-bellied Seed-cracker 32
Green-backed Twin-spot 335
Black-crowned Waxbill 28

IMPENETRABLE KAYONZA FOREST

The Impenetrable Kayonza Forest of south-western Kigezi is a continuous belt of montane forest characterised by deep river gorges. It ranges in altitude from 4,000 feet to over 8,500 feet. The low level rain forest is designated the Kayonza Forest: this merges into upland rain forest and bamboo, the Impenetrable Forest. This highland section has zoological affinities with the Ruwenzori-Kivu faunistic zone.

Less than twenty years ago the region was inaccessible except on foot, but now a road linking Kabale with the Queen Elizabeth National Park passes through the eastern edge affording some magnificent scenic views.

Among the interesting mammals which may be observed from this road are two rare primates, the Golden Monkey which lives in the high reaches, especially the bamboo zone, and at lower levels Hoest's Monkey. Gorillas exist in the remote western part of the forest, but are not likely to be seen by the casual visitor. Blue Monkey, Black and White Colobus and Red-tailed Monkey are common. The Golden Cat is reputed to occur but this has yet to be confirmed. Other interesting mammals are the fossorial Ruwenzori Golden Mole, Otter Shrew, Hammer-headed Fruit Bat, Potto, Demidoff's Galago, African Striped Weasel, African Civet and Black-fronted Duiker: it is possible that the yellow-backed Duiker also occurs in the Impenetrable Forest.

Birds are numerous and among the most noticeable are Ruwenzori, Black-billed and Great Blue Turacos. Forest birds of prey are well represented including Cuckoo Falcon and Mountain Buzzard, whilst a great rarity, Cassin's Hawk Eagle, has been recorded. Other interesting birds include:

African Black Duck *38
Bat Hawk *46
Crowned Hawk Eagle *57
Rufous-breasted Sparrow Hawk *66
Great Sparrow Hawk *66
Handsome Francolin *75
Crested Guinea-fowl *78
Afep Pigeon *119
Pink-breasted Dove *120
Yellow-bill or Green Coucal *127
Giant Kingfisher *137
Shining-blue Kingfisher 18
Blue-breasted Kingfisher 18
Black Bee-eater 19
White-thighed Hornbill 15
White-headed Wood Hoopoe *152
Red-chested Owlet 259
Narina's Trogon *163
Bar-tailed Trogon *163
Western Green Tinker-bird *167
Yellow-billed Barbet 20
Greater Honey-guide *170

Thick-billed Honey-guide 20
Cassin's Honey-guide *172
Brown-eared Woodpecker 20
Yellow-crested Woodpecker 20
Elliot's Woodpecker 20
African Broadbill *179
African Pitta *179
Green-breasted Pitta *180
Mountain Yellow Flycatcher 278
Rufous Flycatcher 22
Shrike Flycatcher 279
Ruwenzori Puff-back Flycatcher 280
Chestnut Wattle-eye *195
Jameson's Wattle-eye 22
Blue Flycatcher *195
Dusky Crested Flycatcher 281
Grey-winged Robin Chat 282
Equatorial Akalat 23
Fire-crested Alethe 283

Brown-chested Alethe 23
Red-throated Alethe 286
Red-faced Woodland Warbler 24
Masked Apalis 292
White-browed Crombec 31
Black-faced Rufous Warbler 25
Doherty's Bush Shrike *224
Stripe-breasted Tit 302
Black-winged Oriole 302
Sharpe's Starling *232
Waller's Chestnut-wing Starling 308
Stuhlmann's Starling 308
Purple-breasted Sunbird 30
Northern Double-collared Sunbird 30
Regal Sunbird 30
Green-headed Sunbird *246
Blue-headed Sunbird 30
Grey-chinned Sunbird 29
Grey-headed Sunbird 29
Green Hylia 27
Strange Weaver 326

Black-billed Weaver 31   Red-faced Crimson-wing 32   Black-headed Waxbill 28
Brown-capped Weaver 31   Abyssinian Crimson Wing   White-collared Olive-back
Yellow-mantled Weaver 31   32   28
Crested Malimbe *258   Dusky Crimson-wing 32   Yellow-crowned Canary 28
Red-headed Malimbe *258   Shelley's Crimson-wing 32
Red-headed Blue-bill 32   Dusky Fire Finch 336

MPANGA FOREST

The Mpanga Forest, the northern margin of which abuts Fort Portal, is a vast tract of rain forest extending southwards almost to Lake George. In the Fort Portal section part of the forest has been opened up during timber felling operations and is easily accessible.

Elephant and Buffalo occur but it is the smaller mammals which are more frequently seen. The most interesting of these is the Red Colobus which is common: mixed troops of Red and Black and White Colobus are often seen in the tree tops along some of the older less frequented tracks. Chimpanzees are also quite numerous, but usually less fearless than they are in the Budongo Forest. Other interesting mammals include Potto, Demidoff's Galago, Tree Pangolin, African Civet, African Palm Civet, Giant Forest Squirrel and Scaly-tailed Flying Squirrel.

Bird life is less abundant than in the Bwamba and Budongo Forests, but these interesting species occur:

Cuckoo Falcon *67   Brown-eared Woodpecker   Splendid Glossy Starling
Cassin's Hawk Eagle 232   20   *233
Mountain Buzzard *62   Buff-spotted Woodpecker   Narrow-tailed Starling 308
Scaly Francolin *74   20   Superb Sunbird 30
Nahan's Forest Francolin   Yellow-crested Wood-   Orange-tufted Sunbird 29
*74   pecker 20   Green-throated Sunbird 30
Forest Francolin *74   Elliot's Woodpecker 20   Grey-chinned Sunbird 29
Crested Guinea-fowl *78   African Broadbill *179   Grey-headed Sunbird 29
Afep Pigeon *119   Green-breasted Pitta *180   Green Hylia 27
Western Lemon Dove 237   Jameson's Wattle-eye 22   Dark-backed Weaver 31
Black-billed Turaco 17   Red-tailed Ant Thrush 281   Black-billed Weaver 31
Ross's Turaco *131   Grey-winged Robin Chat   Brown-capped Weaver 31
Great Blue Turaco *132   282   Yellow-mantled Weaver 31
Blue-throated Roller 18   Blue-shouldered   Robin   Red-headed Malimbe *258
Shining-blue Kingfisher 18   Chat 23   White-breasted Negro
Blue-breasted Kingfisher 18   Snowy-headed Robin Chat   Finch 332
Blue-headed Bee-eater 19   *201   Red-headed Blue-bill 32
Black Bee-eater 19   Equatorial Akalat 23   Black-bellied Seed-cracker
Pied Hornbill *150   Forest Robin 23   32
Narina's Trogon *163   Fire-crested Alethe 283   Grey-headed   Olive-back
Bar-tailed Trogon *163   Black-faced Rufous War-   338
Hairy-breasted Barbet *165   bler 25   White-collared Olive-back
Western   Green   Tinker-   Velvet-mantled Drongo 25   28
bird *167   Square-tailed Drongo *217
Yellow-billed Barbet 20   Luhder's Bush Shrike 26

Part 2

The Mammals of the
National Parks of East Africa

The Mammals of the National Parks of East Africa

The essential purpose of this guide is to assist the user in identifying various living mammals in the field. This being so, characters given in the descriptions have been confined to the external appearance of the individual species. Details of anatomical and dental structure, of use only when one is handling a dead animal or a museum specimen, have been omitted.

Measurements given under each species indicate the total length, i.e. from tip of nose to end of tail. The tail length is also given when this may be of diagnostic value. In the case of larger mammals the height at shoulder is also given.

All the mammals you are likely to encounter have been described and illustrated, but no attempt has been made to define and figure all the many species in groups such as the shrews, bats and smaller rodents. These, after all, are of primary concern mainly to the specialist mammalogist, and are not likely to be seen by the average field naturalist visiting our National Parks and Faunal Reserves.

The presentation of the groups is in systematic order, commencing with the Insectivores and finishing with the Rodents.

Insectivores: *Insectivora*

Five Families of the Order Insectivora are found in East Africa. These are:

Elephant Shrews

(Macroscelididae)
A group of terrestrial mammals, ranging in length from 6 to 20″, with a long trunk-like, flexible snout. Differ from true shrews in

Fig. 1 *Spectacled Elephant Shrew*

having very large round eyes, upright ears, long hind legs and their generally much larger size. Mainly diurnal.

Golden Moles (Chrysochloridae)
Small burrowing mammals, 4 to 4½″ in length, with cylindrical bodies and blunt pointed muzzles; no visible tail; claws on forefeet well developed for digging. Fur soft and full with a characteristic metallic lustre. Golden moles may be distinguished from mole rats and other fossorial rodents by their lack of rodent-type incisor teeth.

Fig. 2 Stuhlmann's Golden Mole

Hedgehogs (Erinaceidae)
Plump terrestrial mammals, 6 to 8″ in length, with upperparts covered with sharp quills. Nocturnal; often appears after rains.

Fig. 3 East African Hedgehog

Otter Shrews (Potamogalidae)
Streamlined, aquatic insectivores, 8 to 24″ in length, with relatively broad and flattened heads and long powerful flat-sided tails which they use in swimming: feet not webbed. Mainly nocturnal.

Fig. 4 Otter Shrew

Shrews (Soricidae)
Small mouse-like insectivores, 2½ to 8″ in length, with long pointed snouts and soft velvety fur; eyes usually minute; ears small and rounded, often concealed in fur. The shrew family contains some of the smallest mammals in the world.

Fig. 5 Giant White-toothed Shrew

RUFOUS SPECTACLED ELEPHANT SHREW

Elephantulus rufescens   fig. 1

Identification: 10″, tail 4½″. A medium sized elephant shrew, greyish-brown above, tinged rufous on back and head; white below with a white patch above and below the eye. Progresses both by running and by jumping.

Distribution and Habitat: Widespread and locally common in the drier areas of East Africa: perhaps most abundant in northern Karamoja, Uganda.

Allied Species: The Short-snouted Elephant Shrew (*Nasilio brachyrhynchus*) is smaller, 8½″, tail 3½″, with a shorter snout. It occurs on open plains of southern Kenya, and has been recorded near Iringa, Tanzania. The Knob-bristled Forest Elephant Shrew (*Petrodromus sultan*) (p. 192) is a giant edition of the Rufous Spectacled Elephant Shrew, 14″, tail 6″, with knob-tipped bristles on the ventral surface of the tail. It occurs in bush and forest along the Kenya coast, on the Teita Hills in south-eastern Kenya, and in eastern Tanzania, including Zanzibar and Mafia Islands.

YELLOW-RUMPED ELEPHANT SHREW

Rhynchocyon chrysopygus   p. 192

Identification: 20″, tail 8″. Hind legs and proboscis strongly developed. This is one of the larger elephant shrews, bright dark mahogany red, with a golden lower back and rump patch: tail black with white tip.

Distribution and Habitat: Coastal district of Kenya north of Mombasa. Inhabits coastal forests and dense bush. Usually shy and difficult to observe. Not uncommon in the Sokoke-Arabuku forest, Kenya coast. Mainly diurnal; solitary.

Allied Species: The Black and Red Elephant Shrew, *Rhynchocyon petersi*, lacks the yellow rump patch. It occurs in coastal forests of Kenya south of Mombasa, and in eastern Tanzania, including Zanzibar and Mafia Islands.

RUWENZORI GOLDEN MOLE   *Chrysochloris stuhlmanni*   fig. 2

Identification: 4½″. Two of the three fore-claws greatly developed for digging. Uniform deep brown with high metallic gloss; nose naked; no tail or external ears; eyes rudimentary.

Distribution and Habitat: Mountain forests of Ruwenzori and Kigezi, western Uganda; Mount Elgon, western Kenya and Uganda, and the Livingstone Mountains, Poroto Mountains, Rungwe Mountain and Uzungura Mountains, Tanzania. Tunnels in soft forest soil, often near

the surface, when its presence may be detected by the low ridges
pushed up along the line of its burrows.

EAST AFRICAN HEDGEHOG   *Erinaceus pruneri*   fig. 3
Identification: 7-9″. A short-legged plump animal with the crown and
back covered with short, sharp quills, brown with white tips. Forehead,
sides of face and underparts white; foreparts of face black. As a
means of defence when disturbed the hedgehog curls itself into a spiny
ball.
Distribution and Habitat: The hedgehog has a wide distribution in East
Africa, but is extremely local and usually uncommon. An exception is
the Nairobi district, Kenya, where it is abundant. Occurs in a variety of
habitats from dry highland forest to arid bush country. Nocturnal and
usually solitary: most in evidence after rains when plenty of insect food
is available.

OTTER SHREW   *Potamogale velox*   fig. 4
Identification: 20″, tail 8″. A short-limbed aquatic animal with a broad,
flattened head and a powerful, vertically flattened tail: in general appearance much like a miniature otter. Above warm brown with very
dense pale undercoat; underparts white.
Distribution and Habitat: In East Africa known only from mountain
streams on Ruwenzori range and in the Kalinzu Forest, south-western
Kigezi, Uganda. Nocturnal and solitary: inhabits small fast-flowing
rivers and streams. Very rarely encountered, but perhaps not very uncommon where it occurs.

GIANT WHITE-TOOTHED SHREW   *Crocidura occidentalis*   fig. 5
Identification: 9-10″, tail 3½″. Many species of White-toothed or Musk
Shrews (so-called on account of their strong odour) occur in East
Africa, the largest of which is the present species. It is uniform dark
rufous brown. Shrews of the genus *Crocidura* may be distinguished
from the related *Suncus* shrews by their white, not red-brown teeth.
Both groups have the tail shorter than the head and body. Shrews of
the semi-arboreal genus *Sylvisorex* have a tail longer than the head and
body; those of the genus *Surdisorex*, Mole Shrews, two species of
which occur in forest on Mount Kenya and the Aberdare range respectively, are short-tailed shrews which are semi-fossorial in habits
with relatively large forefeet.
Distribution and Habitat: Widely distributed and locally common in
East Africa. Favours edges of swamps and marshes where there is rank

vegetation, but occurs also in damp woodlands and other habitats, often a long way from water. Usually solitary: diurnal and nocturnal.

Bats: *Chiroptera*

Bats are the only mammals which possess real wings and which are capable of sustained flight. They are almost exclusively nocturnal in their habits. The one East African exception is the semi-diurnal Yellow-winged Bat (*Lavia frons*) which roosts in acacia trees and thickets. During overcast and dull weather this bat sometimes forages for insect prey long before dusk.

East African bats are classified into two sub-orders, the Fruit Bats, Megachiroptera, which possess large eyes and a claw on the second as well as on the first finger (fig. 6) and the Insect-eating Bats, Microchiroptera, which have small or minute eyes and a claw on only the first finger (fig. 6).

Fig. 6 *Wahlberg's Fruit Bat*   *Banana Bat*

FRUIT BATS

STRAW-COLOURED FRUIT BAT   *Eidolon helvum* p.180

Identification: 9″, tail ½″, wingspan 30″. This is a large pale yellowish-brown fruit bat with orange-tawny tinge on foreneck: no white tufts at base of ears and no white "epaulets" on shoulders. The Rousette Fruit Bats also lack ear tufts and epaulets, but are smaller and dark brown in colour.

Distribution and Habitat: This is a locally common species found in many localities in Uganda; in Kenya recorded from the coast and from Kakamega; and in north-eastern districts and Bukoba in Tanzania; occurs on both Pemba and Zanzibar. A highly gregarious species, roosting in trees. Sometimes many thousands occupy a single communal roost: one such exists in Kampala, Uganda, in a eucalyptus plantation inside the city boundary.

Allied Species: The Rousette Fruit Bat (*Rousettus aegyptiacus*) is smaller, 5″, uniform dark slate-brown. It occurs in coastal districts of Tanzania and Kenya and in Western Kenya. It is a colony rooster in caves.

EPAULETTED FRUIT BAT   *Epomophorus wahlbergi*   fig. 6

Identification: 5½″, wingspan 20″. A uniform buff-brown fruit bat with white tufts at the base of the ears and in the male a glandular sac, lined with white hairs, on each shoulder—the "epaulets." These epaulets are not always conspicuous as the bat can draw in the glandular pocket so that the white hairs are concealed.

Distribution and Habitat: Widespread but local throughout most of East Africa, including Zanzibar and Pemba Island. Gregarious, roosting in palms and other trees in small groups. Sometimes roosts in caves.

Allied Species: The Pale-bellied Fruit Bat (*Epomops franqueti*) is larger, 7″, wingspan 23″; and has a light abdominal patch. It is common in Uganda and north-western Tanzania. Other species of the genera *Epomophorus* and *Epomops* occur in East Africa, externally much alike. Their certain identification depends upon internal dental and palate structure characters.

HAMMER-HEADED FRUIT BAT *Hypsignathus monstrosus* p. 180

Identification: Male 10½″, female 9″, wingspan 38″, 32″. This is the largest bat found on the African mainland. It is uniform brownish-grey with a slightly paler abdominal patch and inconspicuous white tufts at the base of the ears. The adult male has a large, grotesque-looking head, with a monstrously developed nasal region, pendulous lips, swollen ruffles around the nose and a hairless split chin. Uniform dark grey colour and large size are best field characteristics.

Distribution and Habitat: Local and uncommon in Uganda; perhaps most frequent at Entebbe. Recorded from Kakamega Forest, Western Kenya. A forest bat, far less gregarious than most fruit bats. Usually seen at dusk when flighting to feeding areas.

INSECT-EATING BATS

East African insectivorous bats vary much in external appearance and are classified into eight families:

The **Mouse-tailed Bats** (Rhinopomidae) remarkable for their very long and slender tails extending outside the interfemoral membrane (fig. 7).

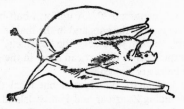

Fig. 7 Mouse-tailed Bat

The **Tomb or Sheath-tailed Bats** (Emballonuridae) in which the tail protrudes from the middle of the interfemoral membrane (fig. 8).

Fig. 8 White-bellied Tomb Bat

The Hollow-faced Bats (Nycteridae) have long, soft grey or brown fur, large ears, a deep frontal groove and a long curiously bifid-tipped tail, enclosed in the interfemoral membrane (fig. 9).

The False Vampires and Yellow-winged Bats (Megadermatidae) lack tails, but possess well developed interfemoral membranes. Ears large; fur long and soft (fig. 10).

Fig. 9 Hollow-faced Bat

Fig. 10 Yellow-winged Bat

The **Horseshoe Bats** (Rhinolophidae) possess a simple tail enclosed in the interfemoral membrane and characteristic horseshoe-like nose leaves. The relatively large ears lack a tragus (fig. 11).

Fig. 11 Lander's Horseshoe Bat

The **Leaf-nosed Bats** (Hipposideridae) resemble the Horseshoe Bats but possess facial appendages of nose-leaf or trident shape (fig. 12).

Fig. 12 Nose-leaf forms: trident shape and normal nose-leaf

The **Mouse-eared and Pipistrelle Bats** and their allies (Vespertilionidae) represent the largest group. They are characterised by their short heads and small nostrils, without nose leaves or other complex structures: tail simple, enclosed in interfemoral membrane (fig. 13).

Fig. 13   *Mouse-eared Bat*

The **Free-tailed Bats** (Molossidae) possess thick-skinned tails (the skin fits loosely over the vertebrae) which project well beyond the edge of the interfemoral membrane. Fur short and dense with a velvet-like lustre: heads thickset (fig. 14).

Fig. 14   *Angola Free-tailed Bat*

MOUSE-TAILED BAT   *Rhinopoma hardwickei*   fig. 7

Identification: 5″, tail 2½″, wingspan 9″. A creamy brown bat easily distinguished by its very long, slender tail which extends far beyond the poorly developed interfemoral membrane. Appears at dusk; flight slower than most insectivorous bats and less erratic.

Distribution and Habitat: In East Africa known from northern Turkana, Kenya, where it is recorded from Central Island and Ferguson's Gulf, Lake Rudolf, and at Lokomorinyang in the extreme north, and at Lake Baringo. Also occurs in north-eastern Karamoja, Uganda. Roosts in colonies in caves; hunts prey usually over water.

WHITE-BELLIED TOMB BAT   *Taphozous mauritianus*   fig. 8
Identification: 4½″, tail ½″, wingspan 14″. Freckled grey above, white below; wings translucent white. Tail protrudes from centre of inter-femoral membrane.
Distribution and Habitat: Wide ranging throughout East Africa out-side forest areas. Roost singly or in small groups in palm trees or in houses, where they cling to walls below roofs. They are less attracted to dark roosting places than most bats. Flight direct and fast.

HOLLOW-FACED BAT   *Nycteris hispida*   fig. 9
Identification: 4″ tail 2″, wingspan 8½″. A small greyish brown bat with long hair, large ears and a tail half the total length. The deep frontal groove, which gives this bat its name, is hidden by the nose-leaves. When resting hangs suspended by its feet.
Distribution and Habitat: Found locally throughout East Africa in all types of habitat. Roosts singly or in small groups in roofs of buildings, in hollow trees or in caves. Flight erratic but not very rapid.

FALSE VAMPIRE BAT   *Megaderma cor*   p. 180
Identification: 3″, wingspan 13″. A grey, long-haired bat with very large ears and long oval nose-leaf; no tail. At rest hangs suspended by feet.
Distribution and Habitat: Found locally outside forest areas throughout East Africa. Roosts in colonies in caves and sometimes large hollow trees such as baobabs.

YELLOW-WINGED BAT   *Lavia frons*   fig. 10
Identification: 3½″, wingspan 15″. A slate-grey, very long-furred bat with very large ears; wings yellowish-orange; no tail. At rest hangs suspended by its feet in acacia trees and bushes. Sometimes hunts by day in overcast weather. Orange wings render it most conspicuous when disturbed.
Distribution and Habitat: The Yellow-winged Bat has a wide distribu-tion in East Africa in acacia woodland and bush country. Roosts singly, or in twos and threes, in thorn trees and bushes.

LANDER'S HORSESHOE BAT   *Rhinolophus landeri*   fig. 11
Identification: 3″, tail 1″, wingspan 11″. Two colour phases occur, the commoner which is uniform grey-brown and one which is bright cinnamon-rufous: muzzle with characteristic horseshoe leaf-nose: ears sharp pointed, without tragus; the male has two patches of

stiffened reddish hairs near the armpits. At rest hangs suspended by feet.

Distribution and Habitat: Widely distributed in East Africa, but uncommon and local. Roosts in caves and large hollow trees; often associated with Lesser Leaf-nosed Bat to which it bears a superficial resemblance.

LESSER LEAF-NOSED BAT   *Hipposideros caffer*   p. 180

Identification: 3″, tail 1″, wingspan 11″. Variable in colour, grey, brown or bright rufous-cinnamon: notched rounded ears without tragus: characteristic leaf-nose (fig. 12). At rest hangs by the feet.

Distribution and Habitat: Common and widespread in East Africa. Roosts in small groups or colonies in caves, buildings, hollow trees and animal burrows.

GIANT LEAF-NOSED BAT   *Hipposideros commersoni*   p. 180

Identification: 5½″, tail ½″, wingspan 25″. One of the largest insectivorous bats in Africa. Relatively short-haired, pale brown with a broad Y-shaped darker band on upperparts. Ears rather narrow and pointed.

Distribution and Habitat: Locally common in coastal districts of Kenya and Tanzania: rare elsewhere. Found in colonies in caves and large hollow trees.

LONG-EARED LEAF-NOSED BAT *Hipposideros megalotis* p. 180

Identification: 3″, tail 1″, wingspan 10″. A small orange-buff, leaf-nosed bat with long ears. Has a resemblance to one of the *Nycteris* bats. At rest hangs suspended from its feet.

Distribution and Habitat: In East Africa known only from Naivasha, Nakuru, Elmenteita and the Kinangop plateau. Enters buildings and caves at night: daytime roosts not known, but probably roofs of buildings. This attractive bat is rare and little known.

Allied Species: The African Trident Bat (*Triaenops afer*) occurs in coastal districts of Kenya and Tanzania. It is a larger species than the Lesser Leaf-nosed Bat with a trident-shaped nose-leaf (fig. 12).

AFRICAN MOUSE-EARED BAT   *Myotis tricolor*   fig. 13

Identification: 4″, tail 1½″, wingspan 13″. A greyish bat with a distinct rufous tinge over upperparts; ears relatively long; muzzle without noseleaves.

Distribution and Habitat: In Kenya known from the Rift Valley and Mount Elgon. Not recorded from Tanzania or Uganda. Roosts singly or in small colonies in holes in caves and in tree holes.

BANANA BAT or AFRICAN PIPISTRELLE

Pipistrellus nanus   fig. 6

Identification: 3″, tail 1″, wingspan 9″. A dark coloured little bat, deep rufous-brown on back; wings black. Ears small; muzzle simple. Appears during early dusk; flight very erratic.

Distribution and Habitat: Widespread and common in East Africa. More frequently seen than many small bats as it appears on the wing well before dark. Roosts singly or in small numbers, in unopened banana leaves or among banana fruits, and in holes in trees and buildings.

YELLOW-BELLIED BAT   *Scotophilus nigrita*   p. 180

Identification: 5″, tail 2″, wingspan 13″. A rich brown bat with bright yellow or brownish-yellow underparts. Ears moderate; muzzle simple without nose-leaves. Wings, face and ears black.

Distribution and Habitat: Locally common in East Africa. Roosts in small groups in holes in trees and in roofs of houses.

ANGOLA FREE-TAILED BAT   *Tadarida condylura*   fig. 14

Identification: 4½″, tail 1½″, wingspan 14″. Upperparts brown or grey-brown, sometimes pale rufous-brown, often speckled white; grey-brown below, often white in centre of abdomen; tufts of brown hairs between ears in male; wings grey-brown. Appears at dusk; flight extremely strong, direct and rapid.

Distribution and Habitat: Widespread and common in Kenya, but local in Uganda, and in Tanzania recorded in south-east and north. Roosts usually in roofs of buildings, sometimes in large colonies.

WHITE-BELLIED FREE-TAILED BAT   *Tadarida limbata* p. 180

Identification: 4″, tail 1″, wingspan 12″. Above dark grey-brown; males with tuft of long hairs between ears; below, chest and flanks grey brown, belly white: wings white, sometimes greyish towards tips. Leaves roost at dusk; flight direct and very rapid.

Distribution and Habitat: A common and widely distributed bat in Kenya and Uganda; in Tanzania mainly in north-eastern and coastal districts; occurs on Zanzibar and Pemba. Roosts in colonies, generally in roofs of buildings, but sometimes in hollow trees and in cliffs.

FLAT-HEADED FREE-TAILED BAT *Platymops barbatogularis* p. 180

Identification: 3½", tail 1", wingspan 10". The striking feature of this group of bats is the marked flattening of the head and body, an adaptation which allows them to live in very narrow rock crevices. They are dark brown above; below warm pale brown with a dark brown stripe down each side: well developed gular sac present in both sexes.

Distribution and Habitat: Known only from Kenya, where recorded from Northern Turkana, Isiolo, West Suk, Lake Baringo, and Maktau and Simba River, Southern Kenya. These bats roost singly or in small scattered colonies in rock fissures of rounded granite hills. They appear at dusk, their flight being direct and rapid.

GIANT FREE-TAILED BAT *Otomops martiensseni* p. 180

Identification: 6½", tail 1½", wingspan 19". Distinguished at once from all other African free-tailed bats by its large size and very large ears, 1½" long. Above and below rich mahogany brown of various shades; narrowly edged white on the back.

Distribution and Habitat: The headquarters of this rare bat is in caves on Mount Suswa, Kedong Valley, Kenya: elsewhere it has been recorded from Nairobi and the Shimba Hills, Kenya, and in northeastern Tanzania near Tanga. At Suswa large colonies exist in deep, remote caves. Flight exceptionally strong and direct.

Pottos, Galagos, Monkeys and Great Apes: *Primates*

This order, the one in which man belongs, is divided into four groups in East Africa. These are the nocturnal pottos and galagos, and the diurnal monkeys and baboons and the great apes.

POTTO *Perodicticus potto* p. 192

Identification: 18", tail 3". A thickset, arboreal mammal resembling a galago in general appearance but with a very short tail. Unlike the galagos its movements are slow and deliberate. Greyish brown to rufous-brown, often with a grizzled appearance on back and flanks: fur soft and thick.

Distribution and Habitat: Locally not uncommon in the forests of

Uganda, and also found in the Kakamega Forest, Western Kenya. Solitary, arboreal and nocturnal. Confined to areas of rain forest. Easily located at night with a powerful torch, when its eyes shine brightly in the torch beam.

GREATER GALAGO   *Galago crassicaudatus*   p. 181

Identification: 25″, tail 11″. Arboreal, nocturnal primate with dense grey-brown fur and a long bushy tail: large oval ears and relatively pointed profile. Eyes large and round. The Bush Baby is a much smaller animal (15″) with a relatively longer and thinner tail. Black and silver-grey forms occur in Western Kenya.

Distribution and Habitat: Widely distributed in Kenya and Tanzania, and on Pemba and Zanzibar; most abundant in coastal districts. Found in woodlands and coastal bush, and in cultivated areas where there are trees. Very noisy at night.

BUSH BABY   *Galago senegalensis*   p. 181

Identification: 16″, tail 9″. A smaller, more slimly built animal than the Greater Galago with a rounder face and ears and eyes relatively larger. Fur thick and woolly, but tail thin at base, becoming bushy towards tip. Conspicuous white stripe down nose.

Distribution and Habitat: Widespread and common throughout most of East Africa, inhabiting a variety of habitats from coastal bush and acacia woodlands to forested areas. Like the Greater Galago nocturnal but less solitary; sometimes in small parties.

Allied Species: Demidoff's Galago (*Galago demidovi*) is a tiny species (12″, tail 7″) with a longer profile, found in forests of Western Uganda. A single record for this species from Uluguru Mountains, Tanzania needs confirmation.

BLACK MANGABEY   *Cercocebus albigena*   p. 181

Identification: 48-60″, tail 32-36″. An all blackish-brown monkey with the long hairs on the head forming an occipital crest. The hair on the tail instead of lying flat sticks out at right angles, imparting a very untidy appearance: a good field character.

Distribution and Habitat: Found locally in forests of Uganda and in the Bukoba district of north-western Tanzania. An arboreal species confined to forest.

Allied Species: The Tana Mangabey (*Cercocebus galeritus*) is a rare animal found in riverine forest along the Tana River in Kenya. It is smaller than the Black Mangabey and grey-brown in colour.

Plate 1 BATS

1 **STRAW-COLOURED FRUIT BAT** page 171
No white tufts at base of ears or on shoulders; yellowish-brown;
gregarious, in trees.

2 **HAMMER-HEADED FRUIT BAT** ♂ page 172
Large size, wingspan 3 feet; white tufts at base of ears;
enlarged nasal region in ♂; dark grey.

3 **YELLOW-BELLIED BAT** page 177
Yellow or brownish-yellow underparts; simple muzzle without
nose-leaf.

4 **LONG-EARED LEAF-NOSED BAT** page 176
Nose-leaf present; long ears; orange-brown or buff.

5 **GIANT LEAF-NOSED BAT** page 176
Large size, wingspan 2 feet; short haired; narrow pointed
ears; nose-leaf present.

6 **LESSER LEAF-NOSED BAT** page 176
Nose-leaf present; notched rounded ears.

7 **FALSE VAMPIRE BAT** page 175
No tail; large ears; oval nose-leaf; grey wings.

8 **WHITE-BELLIED FREE-TAILED BAT** page 177
Tail free; wings white or greyish-white.

9 **FLAT-HEADED FREE-TAILED BAT** page 178
Body and head much flattened; tail free.

10 **GIANT FREE-TAILED BAT** page 178
Large size, wingspan 19 inches; large ears; upperparts rich
mahogany-brown edged white.

Plate 2 PRIMATES, AARDVARK, PANGOLIN

1 **BUSH BABY** page 179
Size small, 16 inches; tail slender at base.

2 **GREATER GALAGO** page 179
Size large, 25 inches; tail thick and woolly.

3 **BLACK MANGABEY** page 179
Blackish-brown; tail appears dishevelled.

4a **BLACK AND WHITE COLOBUS** (*abyssinicus* group) page 184
Black and white; no thumb; short hair on face.

4b **BLACK AND WHITE COLOBUS** (*angolensis* group) page 184
Black and white; no thumb; long hair on face.

5 **CHIMPANZEE** page 184
Height 48 inches; no tail.

6 **MOUNTAIN GORILLA** page 185
Height ca. 60 inches; no tail; high crown in ♂.

7 **ANT BEAR or AARDVARK** page 197
Elongated snout; long pointed ears; strictly nocturnal.

8 **LESSER GROUND PANGOLIN** page 185
Tail shorter than head and body; length 36 to 46 inches

note: not drawn to scale

BLACK-FACED VERVET   *Cercopithecus aethiops*   p. 192

Identification: 48-56″, tail 22-28″; female smaller. A greyish monkey with an olive or yellowish tinge; whitish below; tail with black tip; face black with whitish cheek tufts and white bar above eyes.

Distribution and Habitat: Common and widespread in favourable areas throughout East Africa. It specially favours acacia woodland along streams, rivers and lakes. Both arboreal and terrestrial: diurnal. Gregarious, often in large troops.

BLUE or SYKES' MONKEYS   *Cercopithecus mitis*   p. 192

Identification: 55-62″, tail 34-38″; females smaller. An extremely variable monkey of which many geographical races have been described. Those races called "Blue Monkeys," of which *Cercopithecus mitis stuhlmanni* is a typical example, are deep blue-grey with the limbs, crown and end of tail black; eyebrow stripe whitish-grey. The "Sykes' Monkeys," example *Cercopithecus mitis kolbi*, differ in having a distinct white throat and chest patch and the back more or less tinged rufous. Most distinct race is the rare and beautiful Golden Monkey, *Cercopithecus mitis kandti*, which has the entire back greenish gold merging to orange on the flanks: crown, limbs and end of tail black.

Distribution and Habitat: This group of monkeys is widely distributed and common in forest areas throughout East Africa. "Blue Monkeys" occur in Uganda, Western Kenya and Mount Kilimanjaro and elsewhere in Tanzania. "Sykes' Monkeys" are found in Kenya east of the Rift Valley, in coastal districts of Kenya and Tanzania, and on Zanzibar. The Golden Monkey is confined, in East Africa, to mountain bamboo forest in south-western Kigezi, Uganda. The species is found in groups and is largely arboreal: diurnal.

Allied Species: The Brazza Monkey (*Cercopithecus neglectus*) is a pale blue-grey monkey with black limbs, an orange forehead band and a well-developed white beard. It is found in forests on Mount Elgon and the Cherengani Mountains, Western Kenya; and in forests near Busia and in the Bwamba Forest in Uganda. The semi-terrestrial Hoest's Monkey (*Cercopithecus l'hoesti*) is a large blackish species with white cheeks and throat. It is found in the Kayonza forest of south-western Kigezi, Uganda.

RED-TAILED or WHITE-NOSED MONKEY
Cercopithecus nictitans   p. 192

Identification: 46-56", tail 24-28"; females smaller. A dark, rich brown monkey, sometimes tinged olive above, with a conspicuous white nose and a bright chestnut-red tail; bare skin around eyes blue.

Distribution and Habitat: A common forest monkey in Uganda, Western Kenya and north-western Tanzania. This is essentially an arboreal species. Its long red tail and white nose are conspicuous in the field. Gregarious and diurnal.

PATAS MONKEY   *Erythrocebus patas*   p. 192

Identification: 66-72", tail 22-26"; females smaller. The Patas Monkey or Red Hussar, as it is often called, is a mainly terrestrial animal. It is a long legged monkey, bright ginger-red above and white below. Found in small troops: diurnal.

Distribution and Habitat: Locally distributed in bush and savannah country in northern Tanzania and Kenya (Nanyuki; Rumuruti; Eldoret-Kitale; Kongelai Escarpment, West Pokot), and more commonly in eastern and northern Uganda. A ground-dweller, this monkey uses trees and termite hills only as vantage points.

OLIVE BABOON   *Papio anubis*   p. 192

Identification: 50-56", tail 18"; females smaller than males. This is a heavy, thickset baboon, greyish or olive brown, with a well-developed mane in old males: profile long and dog-like; tail carried in a loop, the base held upright. Gregarious and diurnal.

Distribution and Habitat: A common species in Kenya excepting eastern areas, western Tanzania and Uganda. Occurs in a variety of habitats from rocky bush and savannah country and acacia woodland to open plains in vicinity of trees or rocky outcrops. Terrestrial and arboreal.

YELLOW BABOON   *Papio cynocephalus*   p. 192

Identification: 46-54", tail 18-20"; females smaller. This is a much lighter, slimmer built animal than the Olive Baboon, with conspicuously long legs. Colour yellowish olive-brown; profile shorter than that of Olive Baboon, and little trace of mane in old males. Gregarious; diurnal.

Distribution and Habitat: Locally common in eastern districts of Kenya and Tanzania. Inhabits bush country, baobab trees, rocky outcrops and woodland.

BLACK and **WHITE COLOBUS**   *Colobus polykomos*   p. 181
Identification: 66-76″, tail 30-36″; female smaller. The black and white colobus are divided into two groups of races, the *abyssinicus* section with short hair on the head, and the *angolensis* group with long hair (see plate 2).   General colour black with a white mantle and a more or less well developed bushy white termination of the tail. In the Kikuyu (Kenya) and Meru (Tanzania) races most of the tail is bushy and white. Gregarious, arboreal and diurnal. Colobus differ from other monkeys in lacking a thumb.
Distribution and Habitat: The Colobus is a forest monkey found from sea level to over 11,000 feet in mountain forest. In Tanzania the *abyssinicus* group is found in Mount Kilimanjaro and Mount Meru forests; various races of the *angolensis* group elsewhere. In Kenya the *angolensis* type occurs in coastal forests and those of the *abyssinicus* in inland high country areas. In Uganda most of the colobus are of the short-haired *abyssinicus* section, except on Ruwenzori where a race of *angolensis* occurs.

RED COLOBUS   *Colobus badius*   p. 192
Identification: 48-52″, tail 26-30″; females a little smaller than males. This is a reddish-brown colobus, with a greyish cape and whitish underparts. Crown uniform deep reddish-brown; frontal band and tail blackish-brown.
Distribution and Habitat: This is a much rarer animal than the Black and White Colobus. It occurs in forests of western Uganda, western and north-western Tanzania, and in Kenya in some of the coastal forests and forests along the Tana River. On Zanzibar there exists a very distinct race which is coloured red, white and black, known as Kirk's Red Colobus (*Colobus badius kirkii*).

CHIMPANZEE   *Pan troglodytes*   p. 181
Identification: Height c.48″; tail-less ape covered with black hair. Large protruding ears of human shape. The race found in East Africa is the Long-haired Chimpanzee (*Pan troglodytes schweinfurthi*) which has long hair all over the body and a full cheek beard prominent in adult males.
Distribution and Habitat: Not uncommon in many forests in western Uganda; specially numerous in the Budongo Forest near Masindi. In Tanzania found east of Lake Tanganyika, from the Urundi border, south to the Mahari Mountains and Ubende. Chimpanzees occur

usually in small groups or family parties: diurnal, arboreal and terrestrial.

MOUNTAIN GORILLA   *Gorilla gorilla*   p. 181
Identification: Height c.60″; females smaller. A huge tail-less ape covered with black hair. Old males develop a high crown and heavy brow ridge and a silvery mantle. Body thickset with relatively short, weak legs but long and powerful arms. The race found in Uganda is the Mountain Gorilla (*Gorilla gorilla berengei*), which differs from the West African forest gorilla in its larger size and denser pelage. Diurnal. **Distribution and Habitat:** In East Africa found only in the mountain forest and bamboo zone of the Bufumbiro volcanoes—Mgahinga, Muhavura and Sabinio—and the Impenetrable-Kayonza forests, Kigezi district, south-western Uganda. Occurs in small family groups; arboreal and terrestrial.

Pangolins: *Pholidota*

Pangolins, or Scaly Ant-Eaters as they are sometimes called, are an order of reptilian-looking mammals with small heads and long broad tails which have the upper surface of the body covered with horny, over-lapping scales. They have no external ears and are toothless. Termites and ants form their diet which they pick up with their extremely long, sticky tongues. Forelimbs have large digging claws. When disturbed the animal rolls itself into a ball for protection.

LESSER GROUND PANGOLIN   *Manis temmincki*   p. 181
Identification: 36-46,″ tail 16-20″. Tail shorter than head and body; scales average 1½″ in width. Terrestrial, nocturnal and solitary.
Distribution and Habitat: Occurs throughout East Africa, but every-where extremely uncommon and local. Most frequent in southern Tanzania. Inhabits open country, bush and light woodland. Sleeps during day in a hole in the ground. Strictly nocturnal and seldom observed.
Allied Species: The Tree Pangolin (*Manis tricuspis*) is a much smaller and more slender species, 20-24″ with a tail longer than the head and body, and scales less than 1″ wide. It is a semi-arboreal mammal found in rain forest in Uganda and western Kenya: nocturnal and solitary.

Carnivores: *Carnivora*

For purposes of field identification the carnivores may be divided into two groups: those with the general appearance dog-like, the jackals, foxes, hyaenas and aard-wolf; and those which are not dog-like, the cats, otters, mongooses and allies.

HUNTING DOG   *Lycaon pictus*   p. 208

Identification: 48-50″, tail 15″, height at shoulder 24-30″. A rather long-legged, dog-like animal with massive jaws and very large, erect, rounded ears: tail bushy with white tip. Colour black with uneven rufous and white blotches: much individual variation in colour and markings. Diurnal; gregarious, hunting in small packs.

Distribution and Habitat: Locally distributed in small numbers throughout the big game areas of East Africa. Occurs both in open plains country and in sparse bush.

GOLDEN JACKAL   *Canis aureus*   p. 208

Identification: 34″, tail 12″, height at shoulder 17-18″. A dusky yellowish or rufous-grey jackal with an ill-defined darker back which merges into the colour of the sides; underparts and legs yellowish or rufous-grey; ears sandy-rufous; tail reddish-brown with dark tip. The Side-striped Jackal has a longer, more slender muzzle, dark brown ears, a pale stripe on the side, and usually a white-tipped tail. The Black-backed (Silver-backed) Jackal has a well-defined blackish back, more or less streaked silvery-grey, in marked contrast to rufous flanks and legs.

Distribution and Habitat: Status imperfectly known owing to confusion with other species. Occurs locally in Kenya—recorded Laikipia, Naivasha, Loita Plains, Sotik and Mount Suswa—and known from Serengeti Plains and elsewhere in northern Tanzania. Probably occurs Karamoja district, Uganda. Frequents open plains and bush country; solitary or in pairs, nocturnal and sometimes diurnal.

BLACK-BACKED or SILVER-BACKED JACKAL
Canis mesomelas   p. 208

Identification: 34-38″, tail 12″, height at shoulder 16-17″. This is the jackal with a well-defined blackish back contrasting strongly with rufous sides: ears rufous: tail bushy with dark tip.

Distribution and Habitat: The commonest of the East African jackals, found in suitable habitats in Kenya, Uganda and Tanzania. Occurs in open plains and bush country and light woodlands; solitary or in pairs or family parties; diurnal and nocturnal.

SIDE-STRIPED JACKAL   *Canis adustus*   p. 208

Identification: 34-38″, tail 12-14″, height at shoulder 18″. Uniform grizzled brownish-grey without dark "saddle"; indistinct pale stripe on side of body; ears dark brown, not rufous; tail bushy, dark brown, usually with distinct white tip. Nocturnal, sometimes diurnal; solitary or in pairs.

Distribution and Habitat: Common and widespread in Tanzania; in Kenya much less common than Black-backed Jackal and very local; in Uganda found in area around Lake Victoria and in south-western Uganda. Found in both wooded and open plains country.

BAT-EARED FOX   *Otocyon megalotis*   p. 208

Identification: 32″, tail 12″, height at shoulder 12-13″. Has field appearance of small, short-legged, greyish-brown jackal with enormous ears, black face and legs, and black tipped bushy tail.

Distribution and Habitat: Widely distributed in East Africa, but local and generally uncommon. Most frequent Serengeti Plains, northern Tanzania and localities in Rift Valley of Kenya. Nocturnal and diurnal. Often seen sunning themselves outside burrows in small groups or family parties. Frequents open country or sparse bush.

ZORILLA   *Ictonyx striatus*   p. 188

Identification: 24″, tail 9″. General appearance skunk-like; above longitudinally striped black and white; long-haired, tail bushy; underparts and limbs black. Solitary or in pairs; nocturnal.

Distribution and Habitat: Widely distributed East Africa, but seldom seen because of its strictly nocturnal habits. Occurs in a variety of habitats—plains, woodlands and bush.

Allied Species: The African Striped Weasel (*Poecilogale albinucha*) is a smaller, shorter-legged and more slender animal, short-haired, with yellowish-white and black stripes. Of wide distribution but everywhere rare. Occurs in both wooded and forested areas. Nocturnal and diurnal (rarely). Found in pairs or small groups. Even less often observed than the Zorilla.

Plate 3 MUSTELIDS, MONGOOSES, PORCUPINE

1 **ZORILLA** page 187
24 inches; back striped black and white; tail bushy.

2 **RATEL or HONEY BADGER** page 190
28 to 32 inches; pale grey back; black underparts.

3 **CLAWLESS OTTER** page 190
60 inches; throat unspotted; toes without claws.

4 **DWARF MONGOOSE** page 191
12 to 13 inches; tail short; reddish-brown.

5 **LARGE GREY MONGOOSE** page 191
48 inches; tail tufted.

6 **BLACK-TIPPED MONGOOSE** page 194
28 inches; black-tipped tail.

7 **WHITE-TAILED MONGOOSE** page 194
40 inches; thick white (rarely pale grey) tail.

8 **PORCUPINE** page 223
30 to 34 inches; long black and white quills.

Plate 4 BIG GAME, ZEBRAS

RATEL or HONEY BADGER   *Mellivora capensis*   p. 188
Identification: 28-32″, tail 4″, height at shoulder 8″. A thickset, short-legged badger-like animal with small ears and a short, slightly bushy tail; pale grey above, whitish on crown and sides, black below. Solitary or in pairs; terrestrial, normally nocturnal.
Distribution and Habitat: Widespread in East Africa, but everywhere very uncommon and rarely observed. May be found in almost every type of habitat, including open plains and forested country.

CLAWLESS OTTER   *Aonyx capensis*   p. 188
Identification: 60″ tail 25″, height at shoulder 7″. A short-limbed aquatic animal, rich brown with a white chin and throat; small rounded ears and flattened tail; toes not webbed and clawless.
Distribution and Habitat: Widespread but local in suitable localities Kenya and Tanzania; much less frequent in Uganda where commoner in the west, its place being taken by the Spotted-necked Otter in Lake Victoria. Occurs in rivers, streams and swamps. Nocturnal and partially diurnal. Solitary or in family groups; shy and not often seen.
Allied Species: The Spotted-necked Otter (*Lutra maculicollis*) is a smaller species, 40″, tail 16″, with brown spots on its throat and fully-webbed feet. It occurs in Lake Victoria and other lakes in Uganda, being most numerous in Lake Bunyonyi in Kigezi.

AFRICAN CIVET   *Civettictis civetta*   p. 208
Identification: 42″, tail 16″, height at shoulder 15″. A long-bodied, long-haired animal with a pronounced dorsal crest and long bushy tail: grey, with vertical blackish blotches and stripes; ears small and round, white tipped; all-black specimens are not uncommon.
Distribution and Habitat: Widely distributed in suitable areas throughout East Africa, including Zanzibar. Usually solitary; terrestrial; secretive and nocturnal: although not an uncommon animal it is infrequently observed. Occurs in most types of country from forest to open bush.

NEUMANN'S or SMALL-SPOTTED GENET
Genetta genetta   p. 208
Identification: 36″, tail 16″. A long-bodied spotted cat-like animal with a long banded tail. The species may be recognised by a dorsal crest of erectile hairs along the back. Terrestrial and arboreal.
Distribution and Habitat: Widely distributed over Kenya and Tanzania, but less common in Uganda. Occurs in a variety of habitats but most

frequent in bush country and acacia woodland. Solitary, sometimes in pairs: nocturnal.

BUSH or LARGE-SPOTTED GENET   *Genetta tigrina*   p. 208
Identification: 36-40″, tail 16-18″. Differs from Neumann's Genet in lacking the dorsal crest: a shorter-furred animal, usually with larger body spots. Melanistic examples are frequent: terrestrial and arboreal.
Distribution and Habitat: A common species throughout East Africa, including Uganda. Nocturnal and solitary. Occurs in a variety of habitats, favouring woodlands and forest areas.

AFRICAN PALM CIVET   *Nandinia binotata*   p. 208
Identification: 36″, tail 18-20″. A thick coated rufous-brown animal with a long bushy tail: indistinctly spotted dark brown; whitish spot on each side of shoulder; tail indistinctly ringed. Solitary, mainly arboreal and nocturnal.
Distribution and Habitat: An uncommon species throughout East Africa. Found in heavily wooded and forest areas, including both rain forest and montane forest.

MARSH MONGOOSE   *Atilax paludinosus*   p. 208
Identification: 35″, tail 12″. A thickset dark reddish-brown or blackish-brown mongoose with long hair. In some lights looks completely black.
Distribution and Habitat: Found locally throughout East Africa. Occurs mainly in the immediate vicinity of water—marshes, swamps, lakes and rivers. Mainly nocturnal but sometimes appears in daylight: solitary; terrestrial.

DWARF MONGOOSE   *Helogale undulata*   p. 188
Identification: 12-13″, tail 4″. A very small, short-tailed, reddish-brown mongoose of diurnal habits; gregarious in small packs; terrestrial.
Distribution and Habitat: Common species in Kenya and Tanzania: in Uganda place taken by similar but slightly larger Percival's Dwarf Mongoose (*Helogale percivale*), 15″. Inhabits bush country and savannah.

LARGE GREY MONGOOSE   *Herpestes ichneumon*   p. 188
Identification: 48″, tail 17″. A large greyish-brown mongoose with a long relatively slender tail which terminates with a black tuft. Solitary; diurnal and nocturnal.

Plate 5 PRIMATES, ELEPHANT SHREWS

1 **POTTO**   page 178
Short tail. Arboreal; nocturnal. Length 18 inches.

2 **YELLOW BABOON**   page 183
Relatively slim build; long legs. Length 46 to 54 inches.

3 **OLIVE BABOON**   page 183
Thickset build; legs relatively short and thick. Length 50 to
56 inches.

4 **BLACK-FACED VERVET**   page 182
Black face. Length 48 to 56 inches.

5 **BLUE MONKEY**   page 182
Dark throat and chest; Length 55 to 62 inches.

6 **GOLDEN MONKEY**   page 182
Orange back and thighs. Length 55 to 62 inches.

7 **SYKES' MONKEY**   page 182
White chest patch. Length 55 to 62 inches.

8 **RED-TAILED MONKEY**   page 183
Copper-red tail; white nose. Length 46 to 56 inches.

9 **PATAS MONKEY**   page 183
Orange-red back and legs; largely terrestrial. Length 66 to
72 inches.

10 **RED COLOBUS**   page 184
Red-brown cap; no thumb. Length 48 to 52 inches.

11 **YELLOW-RUMPED ELEPHANT SHREW**   page 168
Golden rump patch. Length 18 inches.

12 **KNOB-BRISTLED FOREST ELEPHANT SHREW**   page 168
White eye-ring; knob-tipped bristles along underside of tail.
Length 13 inches.

Plate 6 CARNIVORES (1)

1 **CHEETAH** page 195
Body markings round black spots, not rosettes. Height at shoulder 28 to 32 inches.

2 **CARACAL** page 195
Dark tufted ears. Height at shoulder 16 to 18 inches.

3 **AFRICAN WILD CAT** page 196
Indistinct bands on body and limbs. Height at shoulder 9 inches.

4 **SERVAL** page 196
Heavy black spots on body and limbs; short tail. Small-spotted and melanistic (black) forms occur. Height at shoulder 18 to 20 inches.

5 **GOLDEN CAT** page 196
Spotted belly. A grey form occurs. Height at shoulder 16 inches.

6 **LION** page 196
Well-developed mane in adult male; black tail tip. Height at shoulder 40 to 45 inches.

7 **LEOPARD** page 197
Body markings in form of rosettes. Height at shoulder 24 to 28 inches.

8 **AARD-WOLF** page 194
Well-developed dorsal mane; black stripes on body. Height at shoulder 18 to 20 inches.

9 **SPOTTED HYAENA** page 194
Sloping back; blackish-brown spots on body and limbs. Height at shoulder 27 to 36 inches.

10 **STRIPED HYAENA** page 195
Shaggy; striped not spotted. Height at shoulder 30 inches.

Distribution and Habitat: Occurs locally throughout East Africa. Frequents edges of lakes and swamps, woodlands and thick bush.

SLENDER or BLACK-TIPPED MONGOOSE
Herpestes sanguineus   p. 188

Identification: 28″, tail 14″. A slender, deep rufous-brown mongoose with a long black-tipped tail. Solitary; terrestrial; diurnal and nocturnal.

Distribution and Habitat: This is a common and widely distributed species found in a variety of habitats from woodlands to neglected cultivated ground.

WHITE-TAILED MONGOOSE   *Ichneumia albicauda*   p. 188

Identification: 40″, tail 18″. A rather large, thickset grey mongoose with shaggy hair and a white tail. Examples occur in which the tail is grey like the rest of the body: solitary or in pairs; terrestrial; nocturnal.

Distribution and Habitat: This is a common species over much of East Africa. It occurs in wooded areas, bush and even on open plains.

BANDED MONGOOSE   *Mungos mungo*   p. 208

Identification: 18″, tail 6″. This is a medium-sized greyish-brown mongoose with transverse dark bands along the body: occurs in small packs of up to a dozen or so; diurnal; terrestrial.

Distribution and Habitat: Widely distributed in East Africa, but local: inhabits bush country, open woodland and savannah.

AARD-WOLF   *Proteles cristatus*   p. 193

Identification: 35-38″, tail 8″, height at shoulder 18-20″. In general appearance resembles a very small striped hyaena. Sandy rufous with vertical dark stripes, a dorsal mane and a bushy tail. Solitary or in pairs or family parties; terrestrial; nocturnal.

Distribution and Habitat: Of wide distribution throughout East Africa, but everywhere local, rare and seldom seen. It inhabits arid and semi-arid country and plains.

SPOTTED HYAENA   *Crocuta crocuta*   p. 193

Identification: 55-65″, tail 12″, height at shoulder 27-36″. A large dog-like animal with a sloping back, large rounded ears and massive jaws. Varies in colour from reddish-brown to drab grey, with dark spots. Mainly nocturnal but may be seen during daytime and active at dawn and dusk. Solitary or gregarious; terrestrial. Produces eerie, wailing call at night.

Distribution and Habitat: A common animal throughout East Africa where conditions are favourable, but especially frequent in big game country. Habitat varied.

STRIPED HYAENA   *Hyaena hyaena*   p. 193

Identification: 54", tail 12", height at shoulder 30". Slighter in build than Spotted Hyaena, long-haired with dorsal mane and bushy tail; ears pointed and upright, not rounded; body grey or sandy grey with vertical black stripes. Mainly nocturnal but can be seen during day. Solitary, sometimes in pairs or even larger groups; terrestrial. Produces an eerie series of calls from moans to shrieks.

Distribution and Habitat: Wide distribution but everywhere very uncommon. Occurs in a variety of habitats, but favours dry, broken bush country. This is a much rarer animal than the Spotted Hyaena.

CHEETAH   *Acinonyx jubatus*   p. 193

Identification: 84", tail 30", height at shoulder 28-32". A lanky, small-headed, tawny yellow and black-spotted cat-type animal with an ill-defined short mane on the hindneck and shoulders. Stands higher than a leopard with rounded spots dotted over the body, not grouped in rosettes like a leopard's spots; tail ringed with black and has white tip. The cheetah is remarkable among the cats in being unable to retract its claws. Diurnal; solitary or in family groups; terrestrial.

Distribution and Habitat: Fairly widely distributed but uncommon in Kenya and Tanzania; in Uganda found only in Karamoja. Inhabits open plains country and dry, open bush. Probably much less common than leopard, but on account of its diurnal habits more often seen.

CARACAL   *Felis caracal*   p. 193

Identification: 26-36", tail 6", height at shoulder 16-18". A sleek red-brown cat with tufted ears and a short tail: some examples are tawny in colour and completely melanistic specimens have been recorded. Usually solitary; nocturnal, but sometimes observed by day; mainly terrestrial but can climb trees.

Distribution and Habitat: Widely distributed but nowhere common in Kenya and Tanzania: in Uganda confined to drier areas, being most frequent in Karamoja. Inhabits open woodlands and semi-arid bush country and plains country at the edge of bush.

AFRICAN WILD CAT *Felis lybica* p. 193

Identification: 28-32″, tail 7″, height at shoulder 9″. Resembles a thick-set broad-headed domestic tabby cat, but tail relatively shorter and body markings less distinct; backs of ears rufous. Solitary; nocturnal, but sometimes observed by day; terrestrial but partly arboreal.

Distribution and Habitat: Found throughout East Africa but not common. In the vicinity of human habitations often interbreeds with domestic cats. Inhabits a variety of country from wooded areas to semi-arid bush.

SERVAL *Felis serval* p. 193

Identification: 40-48″, tail 8″, height at shoulder 18-20″. A large tawny-yellow, black-spotted cat with a short, black-ringed tail, long legs and large oval ears. A colour variety with very small black spots is known as the Servaline. All black melanistic examples are not infrequent, especially from high country in Kenya. Mainly nocturnal; terrestrial, but can climb trees; solitary.

Distribution and Habitat: Widespread in suitable areas in East Africa. Found in many different types of country but specially favours areas of scattered bush and tall grass and dry reedbeds near streams; also not uncommon on montane moorlands.

GOLDEN CAT *Felis aurata* p. 193

Identification: 40″, tail 8″, height at shoulder 16″. A large, wild cat which may be either bright red-brown or grey-brown in general colour; usually with dark spots on flanks and underparts. Solitary; mainly terrestrial; nocturnal.

Distribution and Habitat: A rare animal in East Africa, found only in the Mau forest, western Kenya, and the forests of the Ruwenzori range and south-western Kigezi in western Uganda; perhaps most frequent on the alpine moorlands of the Ruwenzori Mountains. This is a forest species which is rarely encountered.

LION *Panthera leo* p. 193

Identification: 90-110″, tail 30-32″, height at shoulder 40-45″; lionesses are smaller, averaging 34″ at shoulder. Largest of African cat family, tawny in colour with a black tail tuft. Adult males develop manes which may be pale sandy-rufous to black. Usually gregarious; nocturnal and diurnal; normally terrestrial, but some—for example near Manyara, Tanzania and in the Queen Elizabeth Park, Uganda—do climb trees.

Distribution and Habitat: Found in suitable localities, mainly game areas in the National Parks and Reserves, throughout East Africa; but in much smaller numbers than formerly. Frequents lightly-wooded country, thickets, dry bush and broken rocky country and open plains.

LEOPARD *Panthera pardus* p. 193
Identification: 80-94″, tail 34″, height at shoulder 24-28″. A more powerfully built and thickset animal than the cheetah with thicker, shorter legs and relatively larger head. Black spots tend to form rosettes; tail spotted and usually black at tip. Mainly nocturnal; terrestrial but to some extend arboreal; solitary.
Distribution and Habitat: Widespread but not common in suitable areas in East Africa. Far less often seen than the cheetah, although a commoner animal. Inhabits a wide variety of country from forest to rocky outcrops in arid bush: favours riverine forest and woodlands.

Ant Bear: *Tubulidentata*

ANT BEAR or AARDVARK *Orycteropus afer* p. 181
Identification: 48-54″, tail 17-24″, height at shoulder 15-16″. A grotesque, thickset animal with strong digging claws; greyish or reddish-brown in colour with very sparse bristly hairs; head narrow with an elongated snout; long pointed ears. Tail thick at base but tapering to a point. Feeds upon ants and termites which it sweeps up with its extremely long viscid tongue. Strictly nocturnal and although common seldom seen; solitary; terrestrial.
Distribution and Habitat: Widespread in East Africa in localities where there are termite hills. Its diggings are often the only indication that the animal is present.

Hyraxes: *Hyracoidea*

Rabbit-sized animals without tails, dark brown or grey in colour, resembling gigantic guinea-pigs. They possess three toes on fore feet, four on hind feet, short ears and a narrow cream-coloured streak down the centre of the back, not always visible in the field. Species difficult to identify in field, when habitat—trees or rocks—is best guide to determination.

TREE HYRAX   *Dendrohyrax arboreus*   p. 209
  Identification: 16″. Tree Hyraxes vary from grizzled grey to deep brown in colour. They differ externally from the Rock Hyraxes in having longer and much softer fur. Both groups possess a dorsal line of pale cream-coloured fur. In general tree hyraxes live in trees and are nocturnal, whilst rock hyraxes live among boulders and are mainly diurnal. However the race of tree hyrax found in the Ruwenzori Mountains, Uganda, lives mainly among rocks. Occurs solitary, in pairs or in small groups; mainly nocturnal, drawing attention to its presence by its deep croaking and creaking calls and harsh strident screams: mainly arboreal.
  Distribution and Habitat: Tree Hyraxes of this or closely related species are locally common in suitable areas over most of East Africa. They are specially numerous in the Mau Forest in the western Kenya highlands. They occur in forested country and woodland along streams and rivers.

ROCK HYRAX   *Heterohyrax brucei*   p. 209
  Identification: 15-18″. Thickset, tail-less animals looking like giant grey or brown guinea-pigs, often seen sunbathing on rocks and boulders. Much shorter-haired than tree hyrax and hair coarser and stiffer, not soft and silky. Dorsal patch of buff or rufous-buff hair present, but not always conspicuous. Gregarious, lives in colonies; mainly terrestrial, but able to climb trees. Mainly diurnal but feeds usually at night.
  Distribution and Habitat: Wide ranging over East Africa where rocky outcrops, boulders and stony hills afford cover.

Elephants: *Proboscidea*

Remarkable for their great size and their trunks—an elongated nose—with which they convey food and water to their mouths, blow dust or water over themselves. Both sexes may grow tusks, but those of females smaller than in male; tuskless elephants occur in both sexes.

AFRICAN ELEPHANT   *Loxodonta africana*   p. 189
  Identification: 9-11½′ at shoulder: males larger than females. Tusks of adult males weigh between fifty and one hundred pounds each, but much larger tusks have been recorded. Gregarious in small or large herds, but bulls often solitary.
  Distribution and Habitat: Occurs in all types of country from mountain

forest to semi-arid bush and savannah country. Common in many National Parks and Game Reserves, and in other areas in East Africa. Very large tuskers occur on Marsabit Mountain in northern Kenya.

Odd-toed Ungulates: *Perissodactyla*

Ungulates are large hoofed mammals which feed on a vegetable diet. The present group includes the Rhinoceroses and the Zebras.

BLACK RHINOCEROS   *Diceros bicornis*   p. 189
Identification: 11′ in length from snout to base of tail, 5½′ at shoulder; females smaller. Front horns measure on average between 20 and 35″, rear horns up to 21″, but larger measurements have been recorded. Differs from larger Square-lipped or White Rhinoceros in having a pointed and prehensile upper lip: feet relatively small, three toes on each foot. The Black Rhinoceros is mainly a browser, whilst the Square-lipped Rhinoceros is a grazer.
Distribution and Habitat: Generally but locally distributed in suitable localities in East Africa, but exterminated from much of its previous range. Inhabits many types of country from semi-arid bush to montane forest. Most frequent in the National Parks where it can receive protection. Weight from one to two and a half tons.

SQUARE-LIPPED or WHITE RHINOCEROS *Diceros simus* p. 189
Identification: 11½-14′ in length from snout to base of tail, 5½-6′ at shoulder. Front horns measure on average 20-38″, rear horns up to 21″. Differs from much commoner Black Rhinoceros in its square-mouthed muzzle which has no prehensile upper lip; its enormous head; its front horn with an expanded square base and flat front surface; and its characteristic shoulder hump. When walking or resting the head is held low to the ground. After the elephants the Square-lipped Rhinoceros is the largest of the land mammals, weighing about three and a half tons. The Square-lipped Rhinoceros is not white in colour, the name being derived from the Dutch *"weit"*—wide—referring to the wide square muzzle. Occurs solitary or in small groups.
Distribution and Habitat: In East Africa found only in the West Nile district of north-western Uganda. The species has been introduced successfully into the Murchison Falls National Park, where both species of Rhino may now be observed. The Square-lipped Rhinoceros is a

more docile animal than the Black Rhinoceros, less likely to charge an intruder. It inhabits grassy savannah country and is a grazer.

GREVY'S ZEBRA   *Equus grevyi*   p. 189

Identification: Height at shoulder 5′. Mule-like; tallest and most beautiful of the zebras. Very narrow and close-set black or dark brown stripes on a white or cream ground; broad dorsal stripe; belly white, without stripes; mane thick and high extending on to the withers; ears large, rounded and heavily fringed. Gregarious, often associated with Burchell's Zebra and various antelopes.

Distribution and Habitat: Confined in East Africa to the northern districts of Kenya from the Tana River north-westwards to the eastern shores of Lake Rudolf and northwards. Inhabits dry open plains and arid grass-bush country.

BURCHELL'S or COMMON ZEBRA   *Equus burchelli*   p. 189

Identification: Height at shoulder 4′ 2″. Pony-like: stripes broad, especially on rump and hindquarters; ears relatively short and narrow; mane relatively short. Two distinct races of Burchell's Zebra occur in East Africa; Grant's Zebra in northern Kenya strikingly black and white without greyish "shadow stripes" between the black and white stripes, and Boehm's Zebra in southern Kenya southwards which has "shadow stripes." Gregarious, in herds.

Distribution and Habitat: Widespread in Kenya and Tanzania, but much less common in Uganda, where confined mainly to Karamoja. Occurs on open grassy plains, savannah grasslands and semi-arid grass-bush.

Even-toed Ungulates: *Artiodactyla*

The Even-toed ungulates include the pigs, hippopotamus, giraffes and antelopes. All the members of this order have hoofs with an even number of toes. With the exception of the hippopotamus all are cloven-hoofed.

HIPPOPOTAMUS   *Hippopotamus amphibius*   p. 189

Identification: Length 14′, height at shoulder 4′ 10″. A huge aquatic pig-like mammal with enormous head and broad square muzzle. General colour blackish-brown, merging to pink on sides of face and underparts. Gregarious as a rule, but old males sometimes solitary.

Distribution and Habitat: Widespread and common in suitable inland waters and swamps throughout East Africa. Inhabits lakes, swamps and rivers with sufficient water. Especially abundant in the Queen Elizabeth and Murchison Falls Parks in Uganda; may be observed under ideal conditions in the crystal clear waters of Mzima Springs in the Tsavo National Park, Kenya.

GIANT FOREST HOG *Hylochoerus meinertzhageni* p. 209
Identification: Length 48-50", height at shoulder 32". A very large, thickset pig, covered with coarse black hair; tusks well developed; boars possess extensive wart-like swelling below the eyes. The noticeable field character of this animal is its bulk, and when glimpsed in forest undergrowth, it can be mistaken for a young buffalo. Solitary or gregarious in small sounders and family groups; mainly nocturnal.
Distribution and Habitat: In Kenya occurs in small numbers in forests of Mount Kenya and Aberdare Mountains, and in forests of western districts; in Uganda it occurs in the Ruwenzori forests and in other forests in western Uganda; in Tanzania it is known from Mount Oldeani, and it probably occurs on Mount Meru. Inhabits highland and rain forest areas from 5,000 to 10,000 feet.

WARTHOG *Phacochoerus aethiopicus* p. 209
Identification: 36-40", height at shoulder 30". Boars larger than sows. A naked-skinned, greyish wild pig with bristles down back of neck and shoulders. Large wart-like growths present on sides of face; tusks well developed. Holds its tail straight up when running or about to move. Gregarious, usually in family parties; old males often solitary; diurnal.
Distribution and Habitat: Widespread and common in suitable areas throughout East Africa. Inhabits open plains and grasslands, savannah country and semi-arid grass-bush.

BUSH PIG *Potamochoerus porcus* p. 209
Identification: 34-36", height at shoulder 28-30". Variable in general colour from bright rufous to dark rufous-brown with white dorsal mane. Tusks relatively short and knife-like; ears tipped with tufts of long hair. Gregarious or solitary; nocturnal. Although a common animal in many areas it is seldom seen owing to its nocturnal habits.
Distribution and Habitat: Wide ranging in East Africa and often common, but rarely seen. Inhabits highland and rain forest, riverine woodlands and dense bush from sea level to over 10,000 feet.

COMMON GIRAFFE   *Giraffa camelopardalis*   p. 209

Identification: Height 15-18′, females smaller than males. With their long neck and limbs and blotched markings giraffes are unmistakable. Two races of the Common Giraffe occur in East Africa, the Masai Giraffe, *Giraffa camelopardalis tippelskirchi* with two (sometimes three) horns on the head; yellowish-buff with jagged-edged pale or dark rufous markings and legs more or less spotted below the knees; and the Uganda or Rothschild's Giraffe, *Giraffa camelopardalis rothschildi*, a paler more thickset animal with less jagged markings, having three or five horns (one in front of normal horns and sometimes two extra ones behind) and legs usually unmarked below the knees.

Distribution and Habitat: The Masai Giraffe occurs in Kenya south-west of the Athi, southwards through Tanzania. The Rothschild's Giraffe is found in western Kenya in the Trans-Nzoia and Lake Baringo districts, extending north-westwards to Karamoja and northern Uganda. Giraffes are found in open acacia woodland, desert grass-bush and scrub and coastal forest.

RETICULATED GIRAFFE   *Giraffa reticulata*   p. 209

Identification: Height 15-17′, females smaller than males. The most handsome of the giraffes, liver-red in colour marked with a network of white lines, quite different from the jagged blotches or rounded markings of the Common Giraffe.

Distribution and Habitat: Found in the Northern Frontier region of Kenya, north of the Tana River. Giraffe occurring between the Tana and Athi Rivers are more or less intermediate in appearance between the Reticulated and Masai Giraffe and are probably of hybrid origin. The Reticulated Giraffe lives in dry acacia woodland, desert grass-bush and in forest on Mount Marsabit.

COKE'S HARTEBEEST or KONGONI

Alcelaphus buselaphus cokii   p. 213

Identification: Height at shoulder 48″. A long-faced, fawn-coloured, hump-shouldered antelope with a whitish rump; horns bracket-shaped, short and relatively thick; present in both sexes. On account of the existence in western Kenya of populations apparently of hybrid origin between Coke's and Jackson's Hartebeests these two antelopes are at present considered to be races of a single species, in spite of their very different general appearance.

Distribution and Habitat: Widespread and common in southern Kenya

THE MAMMALS 203

and in Tanzania. Occurs on open grassy plains and tree-grassland from
sea level to 6,500 feet.

JACKSON'S HARTEBEEST
Alcelaphus buselaphus jacksoni   p. 213

Identification: Height at shoulder 52". Typical hartebeest appearance:
a larger animal than Coke's Hartebeest and quite different in colour,
being uniform tawny-red not fawn. Horns on high pedicle, less bracket-
shaped, more upright than in Coke's Hartebeest. In the closely related
Lelwel Hartebeest, *Alcelaphus buselaphus lelwel*, the horns incline outwards at the tips and dark markings are present on the lower part of
the legs.

Distribution and Habitat: Occurs commonly but locally in northern and
eastern Uganda, and in western Uganda as far south as the Semliki
Valley: in Kenya confined to areas near Lake Victoria: in Tanzania
occurs south-west of Lake Victoria. Inhabits open plains and grasslands,
and grasslands with scattered bush and trees. The Lelwel Hartebeest
occurs in East Africa only in a small region of arid bush and grassland
in extreme north-west Kenya.

LICHTENSTEIN'S HARTEBEEST
Alcelaphus lichtensteinii   p. 213

Identification: Height at shoulder 50-52". Horn pedicle short, the horns
much flattened and incurved. Rufous-tawny in colour with black
markings on legs.

Distribution and Habitat: Found locally in Tanzania, north to Biharamulo and western Mwanza. Inhabits open plains and bush and wooded
grasslands.

WHITE-BEARDED GNU or WILDEBEEST
Connochaetes taurinus   p. 213

Identification: Height at shoulder 52". A rather thickset, ungainly-
looking antelope with a humped back, buffalo-like horns and a lax,
long-haired black mane and tail; dun-grey or brown with darker
vertical stripes on body; distinct beard on throat, white in northern
races, dark in race in southern Tanzania, the Nyasa Blue Wildebeest.

Distribution and Habitat: Locally abundant in southern Kenya and in
Tanzania: not found in Uganda: inhabits open plains and tree-grasslands from 2,000 to 6,000 feet. Gregarious in large or small herds;
bulls sometimes solitary. Often associated with zebra and sometimes
other game animals.

HUNTER'S HARTEBEEST or HIROLA *Damaliscus hunteri* p. 213

Identification: Height at shoulder 42-46". This species differs from the true hartebeest, which it somewhat resembles, in lacking a horn-pedicle: uniform pale rufous-fawn with white chevron on forehead and white tail tuft: horns with a simple curve, not unlike those of an impala.
Distribution and Habitat: A local and very uncommon species in eastern Kenya, from north of the Tana River to the Somali border. Inhabits desert grass-bush in small herds. In recent years a small number has been introduced into the Tsavo National Park, south of the species' normal range.

TOPI   *Damaliscus korrigum*   p. 213

Identification: Height at shoulder 48-50". A hartebeest-like robust antelope, rich deep rufous in colour with a satin-like sheen; blackish patches on limbs: stout ridged horns which curve backwards and up-wards.
Distribution and Habitat: Local but usually common where it occurs. In Kenya found abundantly in the Mara Game Reserve, south-western Kenya. Also occurs in the coastal districts, mainly north of the Tana River; in the Northern Frontier east of Lake Rudolf and rarely east of Mount Elgon. The closely related race, the Tiang (*Damaliscus korrigum tiang*) is recorded from northern Turkana, north-west of Lake Rudolf. In Tanzania the Topi is widespread but local south to the Rukwa. In Uganda it occurs in the north-east and south-west of the country: abundant in the Kigezi section of the Queen Elizabeth Park. Inhabits open grassy plains, tree-grassland, open coastal forest, bush and scrub. Gregarious, often in large herds.

ZANZIBAR DUIKER   *Cephalophus adersi*   p. 212

Identification: Height at shoulder 14". A tiny bright chestnut antelope with white underparts, a broad white band around upper part of hind leg to the rump, and white mottling on lower limbs; small horns present in both sexes.
Distribution and Habitat: Described from Zanzibar, but present status there unknown. Also occurs rarely in Sokoke-Arabuku Forest, Kenya coast. Usually in pairs: at least partly nocturnal. Rare, shy and seldom observed.

RED DUIKER *Cephalophus harveyi* p. 212
Identification: Height at shoulder 16-17". Thickset bright mahogany-red antelope, black down the centre line of the face and on the hind legs: fore legs dark brown. Short horns, present in both sexes, extend backwards in line of head. Crest between horns bright red-brown; tail grizzled dark brown.
Distribution and Habitat: Widespread but local in East Africa, usually in localities below 8,000 feet to sea level. Inhabits forested areas, riverine forest and areas which afford thick cover. In pairs or solitary; mainly crepuscular or nocturnal.
Allied Species: The Natal Red Duiker, *Cephalophus natalensis*, occurs in the Southern Province of Tanzania. It is a more uniformly coloured animal than the Red Duiker without the dark face marking. The classification of the red duikers found in East Africa is far from satisfactory and the group is in need of revision. Some authorities unite the Red Duiker and the Natal Red Duiker as one species; and the relationship between certain races of the former and the Black-fronted Duiker are not fully understood. It is not impossible that undescribed species of duikers await discovery in East Africa.

BLACK-FRONTED DUIKER *Cephalophus nigrifrons* p. 212
Identification: Height at shoulder 19-20". Larger and relatively longer-legged than Red Duiker. A uniform deep rufous-brown duiker with a black face and crest; tail tip white: lower part of limbs dark brown. Short horns, extending backwards in line with face, present in both sexes. Coat redder in western Uganda animals than those in Kenya.
Distribution and Habitat: Occurs above 8,000 feet on Mount Kenya and Mount Elgon in Kenya, and on the Ruwenzori range and the mountains of south-western Kigezi, Uganda. Inhabits montane forest and bamboo zone, and also alpine moorlands where there is bush cover.

YELLOW-BACKED DUIKER *Cephalophus sylvicultor* p. 212
Identification: Height at shoulder 34". A very large, heavy, thickset duiker, blackish-brown in colour with a yellowish dorsal stripe from the middle of the back, broadening out over the rump to form a triangle. Horns present in both sexes, extending straight back in line with the head; crest between horns reddish-brown. Holds head low when moving.
Distribution and Habitat: The Yellow-backed Duiker is a local and elusive species found in montane forest in western Uganda, and in the

Mau Forest of the western Kenya highlands. Inhabits dense mountain forest and bamboo. Occurs singly or in family groups: mainly nocturnal and seldom seen.

ABBOT'S DUIKER   *Cephalophus spadix*   p. 212

Identification: Height at shoulder 30″. Resembles a smaller edition of the Yellow-backed Duiker, but without the yellow dorsal stripe. Uniform dark brown or dark reddish-brown with small bare grey patch on rump above tail. Horns present in both sexes.

Distribution and Habitat: Known only from high altitude forests on Mount Kilimanjaro and other ranges in north-eastern Tanzania. Inhabits dense forest: shy and seldom observed: nocturnal.

BLUE DUIKER   *Cephalophus monticola*   p. 212

Identification: Height at shoulder 13″. A hare-sized grey duiker tinged with brown on the back, face and limbs. Small horns set well back on the skull, pointing slightly upwards, almost hidden by tuft of hair. Horns present in both sexes in some races, absent from females in others.

Distribution and Habitat: Widely distributed in East Africa, but local. Inhabits forests, thickets and dense coastal scrub. Occurs singly or in pairs: diurnal and nocturnal.

BUSH DUIKER   *Sylvicapra grimmia*   p. 212

Identification: Height at shoulder 22-25″. A medium-sized grizzled-fawn or yellowish-fawn antelope with a dark stripe down centre of face. Horns present in males only: rufous hair tuft between horns.

Distribution and Habitat: The Bush Duiker is widely distributed and often common throughout most of East Africa. Occurs in a variety of habitats from alpine moorlands and forest to woodlands, scrub and bush country. Solitary or in pairs: usually nocturnal, but partly diurnal.

KLIPSPRINGER   *Oreotragus oreotragus*   p. 212

Identification: Height at shoulder 20-22″. A rather thickset, rough-coated yellowish olive-brown antelope associated with rocky outcrops. Horns present in both sexes in Masai race: in males only in other races.

Distribution and Habitat: Locally distributed in Tanzania, in southern, central and western Kenya and in northern districts and Ankole in Uganda. Occurs on rocky hills and outcrops, often isolated: sometimes descends to adjacent flat ground. Occurs singly or in small parties.

SUNI   *Nesotragus moschatus*   p. 212

Identification: Height at shoulder 12-13″. A tiny, graceful antelope brownish-grey with a white belly; horns ringed almost to tips, present in male only; no tuft of hair on crown between horns.

Distribution and Habitat: Occurs locally in Kenya and the northern half of Tanzania. Inhabits coastal forest and bush, highland forest and scrub. Occurs singly or in pairs: mainly nocturnal.

Allied Species: Livingstone's Suni, *Nesotragus livingstonianus*, is a larger animal, 14-15″ at shoulder, rufous-fawn, paler on sides; underparts white; lower part of limbs black. Occurs in thickets and forest-glades in southern region, Tanzania. Solitary or pairs: nocturnal; uncommon.

Fig. 15 Head and horns of Suni

ORIBI   *Ourebia ourebi*   p. 212

Identification: Height at shoulder 24″. A graceful small antelope with a relatively long neck and straight, upstanding horns in the male. Colour varies in different races from drab fawn-grey to bright rufous: bare black glandular patch below ear; short black-tipped tail and black knee tufts. Like the Duikers the Oribis are in need of revision. Some authors consider that there are several species of oribi in East Africa: others that the various populations are local races of a single species.

Distribution and Habitat: In Kenya most numerous in western areas: occurs also in coastal districts, especially north of the Tana River, in south-western Kenya and the extreme north-west. In Tanzania found in the north, north-west and south. In Uganda plentiful locally in north and west, and especially abundant in the Murchison Falls National Park. Occurs singly, or in pairs and small groups, inhabiting grasslands, mixed grass and bush, coastal bush and forest and tree-grassland, from sea level to 8,000 feet. Diurnal.

Plate 7 CARNIVORES (2)

1 **GOLDEN JACKAL**   page 186
Uniform colour; rufous ears; dark tail tip. Height at shoulder
17 to 18 inches.

2 **SIDE-STRIPED JACKAL**   page 187
Pale side stripe; dark ears; white tail tip. Height at shoulder
18 inches.

3 **BLACK-BACKED or SILVER-BACKED JACKAL**   page 186
Dark back; rufous ears; dark tail tip. Height at shoulder 16 to 17
inches.

4 **HUNTING DOG**   page 186
Large rounded ears; variable colour pattern. Height at
shoulder 24 to 30 inches.

5 **BAT-EARED FOX**   page 187
Very large ears; dark tail tip. Height at shoulder 12 to 13 inches.

6 **AFRICAN CIVET**   page 190
Thick banded tail; dorsal crest. Melanistic examples occur.
Height at shoulder 15 inches.

7 **LARGE-SPOTTED GENET**   page 191
Large dark spots; no distinct dorsal crest. Melanistic examples
occur. Length 36 to 40 inches.

8 **SMALL-SPOTTED GENET**   page 190
Small dark spots; distinct dorsal crest. Length 36 inches.

9 **BANDED MONGOOSE**   page 194
Distinct bands on body. Length 18 inches.

10 **MARSH MONGOOSE**   page 191
Large head; thick tail; uniform colour. Length 35 inches.

11 **AFRICAN PALM CIVET**   page 191
Thick long tail; pale spot on each side of shoulders. Length
36 inches.

Plate 8 PIGS, HYRAXES, GIRAFFES

1 **GIANT FOREST HOG**   page 201
   Covered with thick black hair; oval facial wart. Height at
   shoulder 34 inches.

2 **WARTHOG**   page 201
   Grey, sparsely haired; carries tail upright when moving.
   Height at shoulder 30 inches.

3 **BUSH PIG**   page 201
   Body rufous or brown; white mane and whiskers. Height at
   shoulder 28 to 30 inches.

4 **TREE HYRAX**   page 198
   Cream dorsal stripe; fur long and soft; occurs usually in trees.
   Length 16 inches.

5 **ROCK HYRAX**   page 198
   Cream dorsal stripe; fur short and harsh; occurs usually among
   rocks. Length 15 to 18 inches.

6 **MASAI GIRAFFE**   page 202
   Normally two horns; body and neck pattern broken; spotted
   shanks. Height 15 to 18 feet.

7 **ROTHSCHILD'S GIRAFFE**   page 202
   Normally three or five horns; body and neck pattern broken;
   unspotted shanks; thickset. Height 15 to 18 feet.

8 **RETICULATED GIRAFFE**   page 202
   Normally two horns; reticulated body and neck pattern.
   Height 15 to 17 feet.

STEINBOK   *Raphicerus campestris*   p. 220

Identification: Height at shoulder 22". A bright reddish-fawn antelope with very large ears: slender vertical horns present in male only. No lateral hoofs.

Distribution and Habitat: In Kenya frequent in central, southern and coastal districts; widespread in Uganda and Tanzania. Inhabits grasslands, open bush, coastal bush and forest and desert grass-bush from sea level to 8,000 feet. Occurs singly or in pairs and family parties; diurnal.

SHARPE'S GRYSBOK   *Raphicerus sharpei*   p. 220

Identification: Height at shoulder 18-20". Rich tawny-rufous in general colour with white streaking: sides of muzzle greyish-white, cheeks and sides of neck fawn: dark crescent-shaped mark on crown. Very large black-edged ears. Short vertical horns present in male only. No lateral hoofs.

Distribution and Habitat: An uncommon little antelope restricted in East Africa to the southern region of Tanzania. Frequents thin bush and open hilly country: diurnal: solitary or in pairs.

KIRK'S DIKDIK   *Rhynchotragus kirkii*   p. 220

Identification: Height at shoulder 14-15". A small grizzled grey-brown antelope, yellowish-rufous on flanks to reddish-fulvous on limbs; elongated trunk-like nose with hair growing right up to the nostrils; extensive tuft of hair on crown; horns present in both sexes.

Distribution and Habitat: Widely distributed in Kenya and Tanzania: in Uganda found in Karamoja and north-east Acholi. Inhabits desert grass-bush and scrub and coastal bush, and mixed grass-woodland. Occurs usually in pairs or family parties: diurnal.

GUENTHER'S DIKDIK   *Rhynchotragus guentheri*   p. 220

Identification: Height at shoulder 15-16". A slightly larger and more uniformly grey animal than Kirk's Dikdik with a more elongated, trunk-like nose. Limbs fawn, not reddish. Horns present in both sexes.

Distribution and Habitat: In East Africa confined to northern districts of Kenya from north of Lake Baringo and the Northern Uaso Nyiro river. Inhabits arid bush country and mixed grass-bush. Occurs singly or in pairs: diurnal.

UGANDA KOB   *Adenota kob*   p. 220
  Identification: Height at shoulder 36″. A relatively thickset antelope, bright red-brown with black and white markings on the face and legs, including a complete white ring around eye: horns, present in male only, lyrate in shape.
  Distribution and Habitat: The Uganda Kob is now confined mainly to the Murchison Falls and Queen Elizabeth National Parks and the Semliki Valley in western Uganda, being far less common than previously outside these areas. In Kenya a few remain along the Nzoia river in western Kenya. No recent record of the species from Tanzania. Frequents open grassy plains and tree-grasslands: gregarious, in herds: diurnal.

PUKU   *Adenota vardonii*   p. 220
  Identification: Height at shoulder 39″. Similar in general appearance to Uganda Kob, but with no black markings on forelegs. Horns, present in male only, lyrate in shape, shorter than those of Uganda Kob.
  Distribution and Habitat: In East Africa restricted to the southern region of Tanzania, where it is generally uncommon and local. Frequents mixed grass and woodlands, flood plains, usually in vicinity of water. Gregarious in small or large herds; diurnal: sometimes associated with Impala.

COMMON WATERBUCK   *Kobus ellipsiprymnus*   p. 220
  Identification: Height at shoulder 48-54″. Robust, thickset antelope with shaggy grey-brown coat with a white ring round buttocks. Horns, heavily ringed, curve backwards, outwards and upwards: present in males only. The Defassa Waterbuck differs only in having a double white patch on the buttocks instead of an elliptical white ring.
  Distribution and Habitat: Widespread in suitable areas of south-central, south-eastern, north-eastern, northern and central districts of Tanzania. In Kenya found in eastern, central and southern districts. Both the Common and the Defassa Waterbuck occur on the southern and northern Uasio Nyiro rivers and on the Athi River including the Nairobi National Park, where apparently hybrid animals may be found. Occurs in riverine woodland and bush and well-watered tree-grassland. Gregarious in herds: diurnal.

DEFASSA WATERBUCK   *Kobus defassa*   p. 220
  Identification: Height at shoulder 48-54″. Robust thickset antelope with shaggy grey-brown to brown coat with double white patch on

Plate 9 ANTELOPES (1)

1 **ZANZIBAR or ADERS' DUIKER**   page 204
   White stripe across hindquarters; white spots on legs. Height
   at shoulder 14 inches.

2 **HARVEY'S or RED DUIKER**   page 205
   Body bright mahogany-red; blackish legs and face stripe;
   crown tuft rufous. Height at shoulder 17 to 18 inches.

3 **BLACK-FRONTED DUIKER**   page 205
   Body rufous-brown; dark legs; black face stripe. Height at
   shoulder 19 inches.

4 **BLUE DUIKER**   page 206
   Grey or brown in general colour; legs sandy. Height at
   shoulder 14 inches.

5 **YELLOW-BACKED DUIKER**   page 205
   Creamy-yellow rump patch. Height at shoulder 34 inches.

6 **SUNI**   page 207
   Horns ringed nearly to tips. Height at shoulder 13 to 14 inches.

7 **BUSH DUIKER**   page 206
   Narrow dark face stripe; slender crest on crown. Height at
   shoulder 17 to 18 inches.

8 **ABBOT'S DUIKER**   page 206
   Uniform dark brown body. Height at shoulder 27 inches.

9 **KLIPSPRINGER**   page 206
   Large ears; coarse greenish or yellowish-tinged fur. Inhabits
   rocky outcrops and hills. Height at shoulder 20 to 22 inches.

10 **ORIBI**   page 207
   Bare black patch below ears; black-tipped tail. Height at
   shoulder 24 inches.

Plate 10 ANTELOPES (2)

buttocks. Horns, heavily ringed, curve backwards, outwards and up-wards. Distinguishable from Common Waterbuck only by white buttocks.

Distribution and Habitat: In Tanzania occurs in Bukoba district, the Serengeti plains and southwards to Rungwe, western Mbeya and Ufipa districts. In Kenya occurs in central south-western and western districts, and recorded from eastern Lake Rudolf. In Uganda locally common, especially in Queen Elizabeth Park where finest heads in Africa are found. Inhabits grassy areas near water and riverine wood-land. Gregarious, in herds, but bulls often solitary: diurnal.

BOHOR REEDBUCK　　*Redunca redunca*　　p. 220

Identification: Height at shoulder 28-30″. A uniformly sandy-rufous antelope with a white belly and a bushy tail white below, conspicuous when the animal runs. Horns, present in male only, sharply hooked forwards. Reedbuck have a curious bare patch on each side of the head immediately below the ear.

Distribution and Habitat: Common locally in southern half of Kenya, and in Tanzania and Uganda. The Bohor Reedbuck favours marshy surroundings and areas of lush grass. Occurs singly or in small groups: during day lies down in tall grass or rushes, flushing only when nearly trodden on.

Allied Species: The Southern Reedbuck, *Redunca arundinum* (p. 220) is a larger animal 36″ at the shoulder: horns of male curved forwards without terminal hook. It is widespread in southern Tanzania, in-habiting flood plains and upland grasslands.

CHANDLER'S MOUNTAIN REEDBUCK
Redunca fulvorufula　　p. 220

Identification: Height at shoulder 28″. Similar to Bohor Reedbuck but greyer with sandy thighs and legs. Males have relatively short, sharply forward-hooked horns. Tail very bushy, greyish fawn above, white below.

Distribution and Habitat: Occurs locally, mainly in central and western districts of Kenya: in Uganda it is found locally in Karamoja: in Tanzania confined to hilly country in northern districts. Inhabits open grasslands on hills and mountains up to 12,000 feet. Diurnal, usually in small groups. Species best distinguished from Bohor Reedbuck by greyer colour and by habitat.

IMPALA   *Aepyceros melampus*   p. 213
  Identification: Height at shoulder 36-42". A graceful rufous-fawn antelope, darker above with well-defined line of demarcation along flanks; white on abdomen. Rump white with a black streak on either side. Horns, in male only, wide and lyre-shaped.
  Distribution and Habitat: Common and widespread in south-western half of Kenya and widely distributed throughout Tanzania in suitable areas. In Uganda very uncommon and confined to Ankole and eastern Karamoja. Inhabits grass-woodland, riverine bush and arid grass-bush from near sea level to 6,500 feet. Gregarious in herds, but old males often solitary. Diurnal and nocturnal.

THOMSON'S GAZELLE   *Gazella thomsonii*   p. 213
  Identification: Height at shoulder 25-27". A rich rufous gazelle with a distinct blackish lateral stripe between the rufous flanks and white belly. White on rump ends below tail: tail black, constantly in motion. Horns curve upwards and backwards with tips vertical or curved slightly forwards. Horns in female slender and straighter. This is a smaller animal than Grant's Gazelle with less extensive white on buttocks.
  Distribution and Habitat: Locally common or abundant central, southern and south-western Kenya and south through northern Tanzania to the Iringa district. Inhabits open grassy plains and scattered tree-grassland. Gregarious in herds, often associated with other plains game: diurnal.

GRANT'S GAZELLE   *Gazella granti*   p. 213
  Identification: Height at shoulder 32-35": females smaller. Fawn or sandy-rufous in general colour with white belly: white of buttocks extends on to rump above tail. In Thomson's Gazelle white ends below tail. Lateral stripe variable (but more pronounced and darker in females), in some races dark and well-defined, in others indicated merely by darker tone along flanks. Both sexes carry horns, those of male large and graceful, extending upwards and outwards, curving forward slightly at tips: those of females smaller and thinner. Many races of Grant's Gazelle have been described. These include "Roberts' Gazelle" from the Mwanza, western Masai and Musoma districts of Tanzania northwards to the Loita Plains, Kenya, in which the male's horns, in extreme cases, grow outwards and downwards at the tips (see p. 213): "Bright's Gazelle" from northern Turkana, Kenya and north-eastern Karamoja, Uganda, which is small and pale without lateral stripes and

with small almost parallel horns; and "Peters' Gazelle," also a small race, from eastern districts of Kenya, including the northern section of the Tsavo National Park, in which the fawn body colour extends backwards in a band to the root of the tail; horns short, narrow and nearly straight.

Distribution and Habitat: Common throughout most of Kenya, except in south-west; in Tanzania widely distributed from Dodoma northwards and in Uganda occurs in Karamoja. Inhabits a variety of habitats from open plains and tree-grassland to arid grass-bush and desert scrub.

GERENUK   *Litocranius walleri*   p. 213

Identification: Height at shoulder 36-41″. Rufous-fawn in general colour, white below. Neck very elongated; legs long. Only males carry horns, which are massive and heavily ringed.

Distribution and Habitat: Ranges northwards from Pare and eastern Masai districts of northern Tanzania through eastern half of Kenya. Inhabits arid grass-bush country and semi-desert scrub from sea level to 4,000 feet. Occurs usually in pairs or small family groups: diurnal.

ROAN ANTELOPE   *Hippotragus equinus*   p. 221

Identification: Height at shoulder 55-57″. A large grey to rufous-grey antelope with black and white facial markings; short mane on back of neck and long tufted ears. Thick, heavily ridged, scimitar-curved horns present in both sexes, but those of female smaller.

Distribution and Habitat: Widespread in suitable areas of Tanzania; in Kenya extremely local and uncommon, confined mainly to south-west. In Uganda local and uncommon in Karamoja, Acholi and Ankole. Inhabits open wooded country and grass-woodlands. Occurs in small herds, sometimes associated with eland and other game animals.

SABLE ANTELOPE   *Hippotragus niger*   p. 221

Identification: Height at shoulder 50-54″. Males black or reddish-black with contrasting white underparts and white facial markings: females chestnut-brown. Very long scimitar-curved horns present in both sexes.

Distribution and Habitat: Widespread in suitable localities in Tanzania: in Kenya found only in the Shimba Hills, near Mombasa, Kenya coast. Gregarious, in small or large herds: inhabits open woodlands and tree-grasslands.

ORYX   *Oryx beisa*   p. 221

Identification: Height at shoulder 48". A thickset pale grey antelope, more or less tinged rufous, with black and white markings on the face; long, straight, rapier-like horns present in both sexes. Two well-defined races occur in East Africa, the Beisa Oryx (*Oryx beisa beisa*) (p. 221) having pointed ears with no tuft of black hair at tips, and the Fringe-eared Oryx (*Oryx beisa callotis*) (p. 221) which has a conspicuous fringe of black hair at the tips of its ears.

Distribution and Habitat: The Beisa Oryx inhabits Kenya north of the Tana River westwards to north-eastern Karamoja, Uganda. The Fringe-eared Oryx occurs south-east of the Tana River and south of the Aberdare Mountains, Kenya, southwards into northern Tanzania, where it is widespread in Masailand east of the Rift Valley. The Beisa Oryx inhabits arid, semi-desert bush and scrub: the Fringe-eared Oryx is found in similar country and in open grass-woodlands and grass country. Gregarious, in small or large herds: diurnal.

BONGO   *Boocercus eurycerus*   p. 221

Identification: Height at shoulder 44-50": females smaller than male. A thickset bright chestnut antelope with the body marked with vertical white stripes. Open spiral horns present in both sexes, those of female less massive.

Distribution and Habitat: In Kenya occurs in mountain forest on Mount Kenya, the Aberdares, the Mau Forest and the Cherengani Hills. In Uganda it is reputed to occur in hill forest on the Acholi-Sudan border. Bongo inhabit dense mountain forest and mixed bamboo forest. They are extremely shy animals which are seldom observed under ordinary circumstances. Occur in family parties as a rule, but bulls may be solitary.

SITATUNGA   *Tragelaphus spekei*   p. 221

Identification: Height at shoulder 43-46". The Sitatunga is an aquatic antelope, in general appearance resembling a shaggy-coated bushbuck, but unlike bushbuck tail not bushy. Males dark greyish-brown or brown, with a white chevron mark between eyes. Females are redder. Only the male carries horns; these are longer and more twisted than those of the bushbuck, with yellowish tips. Has long, splayed-out hoofs, enabling it to move freely on the surface of boggy swamps.

Distribution and Habitat: Very uncommon and local in Kenya, known only from Trans Nzoia and the papyrus swamps of Lake Victoria. In Uganda most frequent in the papyrus swamps surrounding the Sese

Islands and other localities fringing Lake Victoria and Lake George. In Tanzania local but widespread in suitable areas. Inhabits dense papyrus swamps: shy and difficult to observe. When alarmed often submerges below the surface, exposing only the nostrils above water. Occurs singly or in family parties.

BUSHBUCK   *Tragelaphus scriptus*   p. 221

Identification: Height at shoulder 30-36". A rufous-brown antelope with variable white spots and vertical stripes and a white band at base of neck: tail bushy, brown above, white below. Males of some races may be almost black with restricted white markings. Horns, present in males only, spiral in form. Many races of bushbuck have been described, varying in size and general body colour and markings. When running bushbuck raise the tail showing the striking white underside.

Distribution and Habitat: Widely distributed in southern half of Kenya, extending northwards to Marsabit, Kulal and other isolated mountain forests. Widespread and common in Uganda and Tanzania. Inhabits forests, riverine thickets and bush where there is thick cover. Occurs singly or in small groups; shy: mainly nocturnal.

GREATER KUDU   *Tragelaphus strepsiceros*   p. 221

Identification: Height at shoulder 55-60"; females smaller than males. A large and majestic antelope, grey or fawn with several narrow white vertical stripes on the body, and, in the male, wide-spreading open spiral horns and a heavy fringe of hair along the throat to the chest; shoulders humped, tail bushy and ears very large. The Lesser Kudu is a much smaller animal without a throat fringe.

Distribution and Habitat: Widely distributed in Tanzania; much less common in Kenya where widely distributed but very local, most frequent on Matthews Range and on Mount Marsabit in Northern Frontier Province. In Uganda equally uncommon and confined mainly to Mount Moroto and other hills in north-eastern Karamoja. Inhabits woodland and thickets, especially in broken, hilly country in semi-desert bush. Gregarious, in small herds: males often in separate groups or solitary.

LESSER KUDU   *Strepsiceros imberbis*   p. 221

Identification: Height at shoulder 39-40". A dark or light-grey antelope with vertical white stripes along the body; ears large. White patch on throat and white band across lower neck: tail bushy, dark above, white below. When running the tail is fanned and raised and is extremely conspicuous. Horns present in male only; these grow in three graceful spirals. The Greater Kudu is a much larger animal with a well-developed neck fringe which is lacking in the Lesser Kudu.

Distribution and Habitat: In Kenya widespread and locally not uncommon in eastern and northern districts. In Uganda it is a much rarer animal, known from Karamoja. In Tanzania generally distributed in Masailand east of the Rift Valley. Inhabits arid bush country and coastal bush from sea level to 4,000 feet. Occurs in small parties or singly.

ELAND *Taurotragus oryx* p. 221

Identification: Height at shoulder 69-72″; females smaller. The largest of the antelopes, cattle-like in build with thick, spiralled horns present in both sexes. Rufous-fawn to fawn in general colour with narrow white stripes down flanks. Well-developed, tufted dewlap hangs below the neck.

Distribution and Habitat: Widely distributed in Kenya, mainly south of Lake Rudolf. In Uganda found in Karamoja and parts of Acholi and Ankole. In Tanzania frequent in suitable areas. Inhabits open plains country, highland grassland, tree-grassland and semi-desert grass-bush. Gregarious, usually in small herds.

AFRICAN BUFFALO *Syncerus caffer* p. 189

Identification: Height at shoulder 57-60″. A massive, blackish bovine-type animal with greatly developed downward spreading, widely curved horns, the bases of which meet on the forehead to form a heavy boss. Rufous-coloured beasts occur in western Uganda, especially in the Queen Elizabeth Park. These may be of hybrid origin between the present species and the Dwarf Forest Buffalo of the Congo.

Distribution and Habitat: Widely distributed and often common in suitable areas throughout East Africa. Inhabits a variety of habitats from forested country to open grassy plains and reed beds bordering rivers and swamps. Gregarious, often in large herds: old bulls sometimes solitary: nocturnal and diurnal.

Plate 11 ANTELOPES (3)

1 **STEINBOK**   page 210
Bright rufous upperparts and limbs; large ears. Height at
shoulder 22 inches.

2 **SHARPE'S GRYSBOK**   page 210
Rufous-fawn upperparts flecked with white; large ears. Height
at shoulder 20 inches.

3 **KIRK'S DIKDIK**   page 210
Snout only slightly elongated; flanks and legs mainly rufous.
Height at shoulder 13 inches.

4 **GUENTHER'S DIKDIK**   page 210
Snout greatly elongated; legs tinged pale rufous. Height at
shoulder 13 to 15 inches.

5 **UGANDA KOB**   page 211
White eye ring; black stripe on forelegs; horns ringed almost to
tips. Height at shoulder 35 inches.

6 **PUKU**   page 211
No black stripe on forelegs; ears tipped black; horns ringed
almost to tips. Height at shoulder 39 to 40 inches.

7 **COMMON WATERBUCK**   page 211
White ring on rump. Height at shoulder 48 to 53 inches.

8 **DEFASSA WATERBUCK**   page 211
Buttocks white. Height at shoulder 48 inches.

9 **CHANDLER'S MOUNTAIN REEDBUCK**   page 214
Body colour greyish-rufous; forward curving horns relatively
short; bare patch skin below ears. Height at shoulder 28 inches.

10 **BOHOR REEDBUCK**   page 214
Body colour rufous not greyish; forward curving horns strongly
hooked towards tips; bare patch of skin below ears. Height at
shoulder 28 to 30 inches.

11 **SOUTHERN REEDBUCK**   page 214
General colour yellowish-rufous; forward curving horns diverge
upwards and outwards; bare patch of skin below ears. Height at
shoulder 36 to 37 inches.

Plate 12 ANTELOPES (4)

1 **SABLE ANTELOPE**   page 216
   Long scimitar-curved horns; adult males blackish, females
   rufous-brown. Height at shoulder 50 to 54 inches.

2 **ROAN ANTELOPE**   page 216
   Thick scimitar-curved horns; long tufted ears. Height at
   shoulder 55 to 57 inches.

3 **BONGO**   page 217
   General colour bright chestnut-red with vertical white stripes;
   horns open spiral in shape. Height at shoulder 44 to 50 inches.

4 **BEISA ORYX**   page 217
   Long straight horns; no ear tufts. Height at shoulder 48 inches.

5 **FRINGE-EARED ORYX**   page 217
   Long straight horns; ears tufted. Height at shoulder 48 inches.

6 **GREATER KUDU**   page 218
   Open spiral horns; large ears; fringe of hair on throat. Height at
   shoulder 60 inches.

7 **LESSER KUDU**   page 218
   No fringe of hair on throat. Height at shoulder 39 to 40 inches.

8 **SITATUNGA**   page 217
   Shaggy coat; spiral horns; very elongated hoofs. An aquatic
   antelope which inhabits swamps. Height at shoulder 43 to 46
   inches.

9 **ELAND**   page 219
   Spiral horns; dewlap from throat. Height at shoulder 69 to 72
   inches.

10 **BUSHBUCK**   page 218
   Males vary from rufous to black; females rufous; spiral horns;
   high rump. Height at shoulder 30 to 36 inches.

Hares and Rabbits: *Lagomorpha*

This familiar group is characterised by long, narrow ears, soft fur and short, woolly tails which are white below.

AFRICAN HARE *Lepus capensis* p. 224
  Identification: Length 20″, ear 3″. Above grizzled black and buff; nape, ears and legs rufous; tail dark brown above, sides and below white. There is need for a revision of the various species and races of hares described from East Africa.
  Distribution and Habitat: Widely distributed in suitable localities throughout East Africa. Frequents more or less open ground, including grasslands, bush and sparse woodland. Solitary: nocturnal.

BUNYORO RABBIT *Pronolagus marjorita* p. 224
  Identification: Length 20″, ear 2½″. General colour grizzled buff; flanks buffy-yellow merging to white on belly. Distinguished from African Hare by much shorter ears and legs, and in having the sides of the tail grizzled brown, not white.
  Distribution and Habitat: Locally not uncommon in north-western Uganda, including the Murchison Falls National Park. Can always be seen on the Masindi-Butiaba road after dark. Occurs in open grass-bush country: solitary: nocturnal.

Rodents: *Rodentia*

The Rodents or Gnawing mammals may be recognised by their large chisel-like incisor teeth. With the exception of species such as the porcupine and Spring Hare most members of this order are small or very small. It is not the intention of the present Field Guide to describe in detail the host of rats, mice and related small rodents found in East Africa—creatures seldom seen unless specially searched for and trapped. Only those species of special interest and the larger members of the order likely to be encountered in our National Parks have been described and illustrated.

CANE RAT *Thryonomys swinderianus* p. 224
  Identification: Length 15-18″, tail 3″. A heavy-looking, thickset rodent with coarse, bristle-like hair. Uniform brown: incisor teeth orange.

Distribution and Habitat: Locally common in suitable haunts in East Africa. Inhabits elephant grass and similar vegetation, including sugar-cane cultivation. Either solitary or in small parties: terrestrial: mainly nocturnal.

PORCUPINE *Hystrix galeata* p. 188
Identification: Length 30-34″, tail 6″. Easily recognised by its covering of long black and white quills.

Distribution and Habitat: Common and widespread in East Africa, but owing to its nocturnal habits not often seen. Inhabits all types of country apart from swampy areas; favours rocky scrub-covered hills. Solitary; terrestrial and strictly nocturnal.

STRIPED GROUND SQUIRREL *Xerus erythropus* p. 224
Identification: Length 18½-20″, tail 8″. Ground squirrels have aban-doned the arboreal habits of the rest of the family and are terrestrial, living in burrows. Their fur is coarse and bristly. The present species may be recognised by the presence of a white longitudinal flank-stripe: general colour rufous brown.

Distribution and Habitat: Common and widespread in sandy bush country in Kenya and in the vicinity of Lake Victoria, on Mount Elgon and in Bunyoro, Uganda. Inhabits arid bush country where a sandy soil exists: usually in pairs; terrestrial; diurnal.

UNSTRIPED GROUND SQUIRREL *Xerus rutilus* p. 224
Identification: Length 16″, tail 8″. Easily distinguished by absence of conspicuous white flank stripe. General colour pinkish-rufous; paler below.

Distribution and Habitat: Widespread in Kenya in arid, sandy areas, being abundant locally in the Northern Frontier Province. In Tanzania frequent in north-eastern districts, and common in Karamoja, Uganda. Inhabits sandy, semi-desert bush country; solitary or in pairs; terres-trial; diurnal.

BUSH SQUIRREL *Paraxerus ochraceus* fig. 16
Identification: Length 14″, tail 7″. A small olive-grey squirrel with a yellowish tinge on legs and underparts.

Distribution and Habitat: Widespread and locally common in Kenya and Tanzania. Inhabits bush and secondary growth at the edges of forest: seldom seen in large trees. Occurs usually in pairs: arboreal; diurnal.

Plate 13 RODENTS

1 **BUNYORO RABBIT** page 222
  20 inches; short ears and legs.

2 **AFRICAN HARE** page 222
  20 inches; long ears and legs.

3 **CANE RAT** page 222
  15 to 18 inches; coarse bristle-like hair.

4 **SPRING HARE** page 227
  45 inches; hind legs very long; tail thick and bushy; progresses by kangaroo-like leaps.

5 **SCALY-TAILED FLYING SQUIRREL** page 226
  22 inches; fore and hind limbs connected by gliding membrane.

6 **CRESTED RAT** page 227
  15 to 16 inches; Black and white with distinct flank stripe.

7 **GIANT RAT** page 228
  27 inches; terminal third of tail white.

8 **UNSTRIPED GROUND SQUIRREL** page 223
  16 inches; rufous; no side stripe.

9 **STRIPED GROUND SQUIRREL** page 223
  18 to 20 inches; white flank stripe.

Plate 14 CORMORANT, GODWITS

1   UGANDA CORMORANT   page 230
    Black throat and chest.

2   MONTANE FRANCOLIN   page 233
    Round black spots on chest.

3   WHITE-CHEEKED TERN   page 236
    Marine species; white face stripe.

4   EGYPTIAN PLOVER   page 235
    Black chest band.

5   STRIPED CRAKE   page 233
    White edgings to back feathers.

6   SPOTTED REDSHANK   page 234
    Long orange-red legs; no white wing patch.

7   BAR-TAILED GODWIT   page 235
    Barred tail; no white wing bar.

8   BLACK-TAILED GODWIT   page 234
    Black tail; white wing bar.

Allied Species: The East African Red Squirrel, *Paraxerus palliatus*, with tail and underparts fiery orange-red, occurs in eastern districts of Kenya and Tanzania. It is most frequent in strips of riverine forest and coastal forests.

GIANT FOREST SQUIRREL *Protoxerus stangeri* fig. 17

Identification: Length 26″, tail 14″. Underparts blackish-brown speckled with buff; below reddish-buff; legs bright rufous; tail very bushy, blackish with pale bands.

Distribution and Habitat: An uncommon species inhabiting forests in the western Kenya highlands and Kakamega; in Uganda recorded from forests of Buganda, Toro and Busoga. Inhabits the tops of high forest trees, usually in pairs: diurnal.

Fig. 16 Bush Squirrel

Fig. 17 Giant Forest Squirrel

Allied Species: The Sun Squirrel, *Heliosciurus rufobrachium*, closely resembles the Giant Forest Squirrel but is smaller, total length 19-20″, tail 10″. It occurs in forests on Mount Kenya and western areas of Kenya, and widely in Uganda.

SCALY-TAILED FLYING SQUIRREL *Anomalurus fraseri* p. 224

Identification: Length 22″, tail 10″. Scaly-tails may be recognised by the presence of a gliding membrane attached to fore and hind limbs which enables the animal to glide fifty or sixty feet from one tree to another. The underside of the tail has an area of rough scales which assists the animal to obtain a better purchase on a tree trunk when climbing. Above dark grey; below creamy-white; fur soft and silky.

Distribution and Habitat: In Kenya found in the Kakamega Forest and on Mount Elgon. In Uganda recorded from forests in Buganda, Bunyoro and Toro. In Tanzania recorded from the eastern Usambara Mountains, and the Upper Ruvuma River. Inhabits dense rain forests: generally nocturnal but sometimes observed by day: solitary or in pairs.

SPRING HARE   *Pedetes cafer*   p. 224
   Identification: Length 45″, tail 21″. A pale rufous-brown animal with a
   bushy, black-tipped tail. Hind legs very long and adapted for jumping:
   forelegs short. Spring hares progress by rapid jumps in the manner of
   a kangaroo.
   Distribution and Habitat: Widespread but local in Kenya and Tanzania. Inhabits grass plains and open bush country: gregarious, living
   in small colonies: nocturnal.

AFRICAN DORMOUSE   *Graphiurus murinus*   fig. 18
   Identification: Length 5½-6″,
   tail 3″. Small soft-furred rodent
   with long bushy tail, resembling a diminutive squirrel.
   General colour grey or buffy-
   grey, paler on the belly.
   Distribution and Habitat:
   Widely distributed in East
   Africa. Inhabits hollow trees
   in wooded and forest areas:
   frequent in buildings. Usually
   solitary; arboreal and terrestrial; nocturnal.

CRESTED RAT
   Lophiomys imhausi   p. 224
   Identification: Length 15-16″,
   tail 4″. A thickset animal, not   *Fig. 18 African Dormouse*
   in the least rat-like in spite of
its name, covered with long, silky black and white fur; distinct
whitish flank stripe and a conspicuous crest along the back and tail:
ears nearly concealed in long fur.
   Distribution and Habitat: Confined to forests of the Kenya highlands,
from Mount Kenya westwards to Mount Elgon. Uncommon and shy,
and seldom observed. Slow moving, but both arboreal and terrestrial
in its habits: nocturnal.

GIANT RAT   *Cricetomys gambianus*   p. 224
   Identification: Length 27″, tail 14″. A very large short-haired rat,
   brownish-grey in colour, with belly, feet and terminal third of the tail
   white; face pointed and oval ears prominent.

Distribution and Habitat: Widely distributed in Kenya, Tanzania and Uganda. Inhabits forests, wooded areas and dense bush. Occurs singly as a rule; terrestrial; nocturnal.

KENYA MOLE RAT   *Tachyoryctes ibeanus*   fig. 19

Identification: Total length 7-8″, tail 1″. A thickset burrowing rodent, covered with rather long and soft, dense fur: reddish or golden brown darker on belly: immature animals blackish-brown: incisor teeth bright orange. Many different species of *Tachyoryctes* have been described, most of which are probably conspecific with the present species.

Distribution and Habitat: This and closely related forms are locally distributed in the highlands of Kenya and northern Tanzania, and in Uganda. Their presence is betrayed by the mounds of earth which they throw up from their burrows.

Allied Species: The Mount Kenya Mole Rat, *Tachyoryctes rex*, from the alpine moorlands of Mount Kenya is a giant species 10-12″ in length.

Fig. 19 Kenya Mole Rat   *Fig. 20 Naked Mole Rat*

NAKED MOLE RAT   *Heterocephalus glaber*   fig. 20

Identification: Length 5″, tail 1″. This is one of the most remarkable rodents in the world, completely naked with just a few isolated hairs scattered over the body and on the tail: colour of skin pinkish-grey; incisor teeth white.

Distribution and Habitat: Confined to a few localities in eastern Kenya: it is perhaps most frequent in the Tsavo National Park, near Voi, and near Isiolo in the Northern Frontier Province. The Naked Mole Rat is completely fossorial, digging its burrows in sandy soil in semi-desert bush country. When digging it throws up puffs of fine earth resembling tiny geysers. Erupting every few moments to nearly a foot above the surface, these betray its whereabouts.

Part 3

The Rarer Birds of the
National Parks of East Africa

The Rarer Birds
of the National Parks of East Africa

This guide to the field identification of the birds of the East African National Parks is, in effect, a supplement to my previous book *A Field Guide to the Birds of East and Central Africa*. In order to conserve space the present volume deals fully only with those species not described and illustrated in the original Field Guide.

It does, however, mention many birds dealt with in the previous book, and they are indicated both here and in Part 1 by a number preceded by an asterisk: these numbers refer to the page in the original Field Guide on which the bird in question is described.

Numbers without the asterisk are references to the present volume—to plates if in **bold** type, otherwise to pages.

The birds are taken in systematic order, starting with the non-passerine families and finishing with the passers. The style followed and the symbols used are the same as those in the original Field Guide. Under "Identification" the length of the bird is given in inches, followed by an enumeration of the essential field characters: then follows a description of its call and song under "Voice." The heading "Distribution and Habitat" is self-explanatory. Related birds which are not illustrated are described under the heading "Allied Species." The symbols ♂ and ♀ indicate male and female respectively. "M" intimates that the species is a Palaearctic migrant.

Cormorants: *Phalacrocoracidae*

Cormorants are blackish-plumaged, moderately long-necked water birds with strong hooked bills and webbed feet: small goose or duck-sized; swim and dive to capture food, mainly fish and frogs.

UGANDA CORMORANT   *Phalacrocorax carbo patricki*   p. 225
   Identification: 36″. Large blackish water bird with striking white head and white thigh patches; chin and cheeks pale brown; eyes green; non-breeding plumage entirely blackish, sometimes (perhaps immature birds) with brownish foreneck. The White-necked Cormorant (*20)

lacks white head and has throat and chest white and in immature dress
entire underparts white. The Long-tailed Cormorant (*21) is much
smaller, 22-24″, and has relatively long tail and red eyes; immature
dusky white below. The discovery of this new cormorant, obviously a
race of the European Cormorant, necessitates a revision of the
status of the White-necked Cormorant. This was previously considered
a race of the European bird but must now be recognised as a distinct
species, *Phalacrocorax lucidus*.
Voice: None recorded.
Distribution and Habitat: Known only from Lakes George and Edward,
and the Kazinga Channel which connects these lakes, Western Uganda.
Occurs in small numbers alongside the White-necked Cormorant;
generally seen resting on sand banks at water's edge. Birds noted in full
breeding dress in January.

Falcons, Eagles, Buzzards, Sparrow-Hawks and allies: *Falconidae*

Falcons are characterised by their thickset build, sharply pointed wings
and often extremely fast flight; they generally kill their prey by swooping
on it at high speed.

Eagles are medium or large birds of prey with legs feathered to the toes,
but harrier-eagles have bare tarsus. In flight heads appear larger than
vultures' heads.

Buzzards resemble small eagles but have bare legs and much broader
wings: all buzzards except Mountain Buzzard are often seen perched on
telegraph poles.

Sparrow-hawks and allies are smaller than buzzards and have short,
rounded wings and usually long tails.

ELEONORA'S FALCON   *Falco eleonorae*   fig. 21
Identification: 15″. In general appearance resembles a giant European
Hobby (*46) or a small immature Peregrine (*45); bill and feet heavy
and tail long. Slate-grey above, rufous-buff below with heavy black
streaking; white throat and narrow moustache stripes. Melanistic form
occurs which is entirely dark slate-grey, with or without a white chin.
Voice: Not recorded in East Africa.
Distribution and Habitat: Recorded in recent years as a passage migrant
in the Ruaha National Park, Tanzania, and as a vagrant on Pemba
Island north of Zanzibar. The breeding range of the species is islands
and cliffs in the Mediterranean.

Allied Species: The Booted Eagle (*Hieraetus pennatus*), 18-21″, is a small eagle with heavily feathered tarsi, smaller than Wahlberg's Eagle (*55). Upperparts mottled dark brown, often with paler, reddish head; below either dark brown or whitish. In pale phase, in flight, dark primaries and secondaries contrast with whitish under wing-coverts. Passage migrant and winter visitor in small numbers to East Africa. Cassin's Hawk Eagle (*Cassinaetus africanus*), 22″, is a black and white forest eagle resembling Ayres' Hawk Eagle (*56) but with underparts white with black flank patches. In East Africa recorded from Impenetrable-Kayonza Forest, south west Uganda. The Long-legged Buzzard (*Buteo rufinus*), 24-26″, is a large pale rufous buzzard, rarely melanistic. Tail unbarred rufous in adult. In flight looks very pale below, except for dark wing-tips and thighs. Uncommon winter visitor northern Kenya and Karamoja, Uganda. The Long-tailed Hawk (*Urotriorchis macrourus*), 24-26″, is a very long-tailed hawk, grey above, chestnut below. Known from Bwamba Forest, Toro, Uganda.

Fig. 21 *Eleonora's Falcon*

Game Birds: *Phasianidae*

This family includes the francolins, quails, guinea-fowls and related species. All are chicken-like, terrestrial birds with moderate or short tails: sexes usually alike in African species.

MONTANE FRANCOLIN *Francolinus psilolaemus* p. 225

Identification: 12-13″. Related to the Red-wing Francolin (*72) and like that species has much rich chestnut in the wings and a rufous hind-neck patch; its belly is buff, mottled with chestnut and black. It may be distinguished from related francolins by its rufous upper chest band which is heavily spotted with round black spots. Previously this bird was thought to be an alpine race of Shelley's Francolin (*72), but recent research conducted at the British Museum (Natural History) into the relationships of African francolins has proved conclusively that the Montane Francolin is in fact a distinct species.

Voice: Relatively silent birds, but towards dusk before roosting frequently utter a three or four note strident grating call.

Distribution and Habitat: In East Africa confined to the alpine moorlands of Mount Kenya, the Aberdares, the Mau and Mount Elgon. Occurs on high level grasslands and among rocky outcrops immediately above the forest and bamboo zone.

Allied Species: The Grey-wing Francolin, *Francolinus afer* (*72), is shown by the British Museum revision to be a species confined to South Africa. The bird called by this name in earlier East African bird books is a race of Shelley's Francolin. "Grey-wing Francolin" must be deleted from the list of francolins found in East Africa.

Crakes, Rails and allies: *Rallidae*

Most of the rails and crakes are marsh or water-haunting birds with rounded wings and of apparently weak flight, with legs dangling. Toes long and slender; tails short and often carried cocked up. Crakes have relatively short and thick bills; rails have longer and more slender bills.

STRIPED CRAKE *Porzana marginalis* p. 225

Identification: 6-7″. An olive-brown crake with feathers of the upperparts edged white, imparting a striped appearance; below greyish.

Voice: A deep "grrrrr," like a snore; also utters a rapid churring call resembling a tree-frog's croaks.

Distribution and Habitat: An extremely uncommon species with a wide distribution in Africa. Is at least a partial migrant within Africa and many records refer to migrating birds which have flown into telegraph wires and lighted windows at night. Inhabits swamps and marshes: shy and elusive.

Snipe, Curlews and Sandpipers: *Scolopacidae*

A group of small to medium-sized wading birds, with long legs, slender bills and pointed and angular wings. In many species summer (breeding) and winter plumages differ greatly. Most of the members of this family occurring in East Africa are non-breeding visitors only, their chief nesting grounds being in Arctic or sub-Arctic regions. Many species highly gregarious in winter quarters in Africa.

SPOTTED REDSHANK   *Tringa erythropus* (M)   p. 225
   Identification: 12″. In winter plumage a pale grey wading bird with very long orange-red legs and a long, slender bill with a slight downward kink near the tip; underparts white; rump white; tail barred black and white. Longer legs and bill than Redshank (*106) and does not possess that bird's striking white wing patch. Winter-plumaged Ruff sometimes has orange legs but browner and rump brown, not white. Summer plumage entirely sooty black, speckled white on upperparts.
   Voice: A clear, loud "tchuit" or "tuiwit."
   Distribution and Habitat: Uncommon winter visitor Kenya and Uganda: rarely to northern Tanzania. Frequents shallow inland waters with muddy bottoms; very uncommon on coast. Birds in full summer plumage recorded on spring migration Lake Rudolf, northern Kenya.

BLACK-TAILED GODWIT   *Limosa limosa* (M)   p. 225
   Identification: 15-16″. In winter plumage a rather pale grey wader with a whitish belly: very long straight bill and long, blackish legs which trail well beyond tail in flight: wide terminal black band on pure white tail and broad white wing bar; white rump. In breeding plumage head, breast and some feathers of upperparts rufous; flanks and belly white with blackish bars. Juvenile like winter dress but with buff suffusion. Distinguished from Bar-tailed Godwit by black tail, white wing-bar and much longer legs.
   Voice: In winter quarters usually silent, but sometimes, especially in flight, utters a tittering "chiu, tee, chiu" or a harsh double note.
   Distribution and Habitat: Uncommon winter visitor, south to northern Tanzania: regular in small numbers Ferguson's Gulf, Lake Rudolf; Lake Naivasha and Lake Nakuru, where breeding-plumaged birds may be seen in April. Rare on coast. Inhabits edges of lakes, swamps and marshes.

BAR-TAILED GODWIT   *Limosa lapponica* (M)   p. 225

Identification: 15″. In winter dress a brownish-grey, rather mottled wader with a pale belly; long slightly upturned bill; barred grey and white tail; no white wing-bar; white rump. Legs dark grey and long, but barely project beyond end of tail in flight. In summer, male is rich reddish-chestnut; female not conspicuously different from winter plumage. Juvenile has buffy wash over strongly streaked breast. May be distinguished from Black-tailed Godwit by barred tail, lack of white wing-bar and shorter legs.

Voice: Usually silent in winter quarters, but utters a harsh "kirrik," sometimes repeated several times, in flight.

Distribution and Habitat: Uncommon winter visitor south to eastern Tanzania; unlike the Black-tailed Godwit much commoner on coastal mudflats than on inland waters. A few usually winter on the vast mud-flats of Mida Creek on the Kenya coast.

Coursers, Pratincoles and allies: *Glareolidae*

This is a group of small to medium-sized birds allied to the plovers with relatively short arched bills.

EGYPTIAN PLOVER   *Pluvianus aegyptius*   p. 225

Identification: 8″. A short-legged plover-like bird with crown, back and band on chest black; white stripe above eye to nape; chest and belly creamy-buff; wings grey. This strikingly patterned species is the well-known "crocodile bird" of the writings of Herodotus, but present day observations of it entering a sleeping crocodile's mouth to pick food from between the reptile's teeth are lacking.

Voice: A weak sand-plover type of call "teep, teep, teep."

Distribution and Habitat: In East Africa occurs very locally along rivers in northern Uganda, especially where there are sandbars. As a rule found in pairs or family parties: often tame and fearless of man.

Gulls and Terns: *Laridae*

The gulls and terns are medium or large-sized swimming birds. Gulls are more robust and wider-winged than the terns with slightly hooked bills; tails usually square or rounded: gregarious. Terns are more slender and graceful and usually have strongly-forked tails: also gregarious in habits.

WHITE-CHEEKED TERN   *Sterna repressa*   p. 225

Identification: 14″. A marine tern, generally grey, including the underparts, with a black cap and a broad white streak from the base of the bill extending below the eye to the nape: bill black to dusky-red towards base; tail strongly forked and outer tail feathers long and slender. The Roseate Tern has rosy-white underparts; the Little Tern is smaller, 9″, with a straw-yellow, black-tipped bill. The European Common Tern has paler grey upperparts and is white below.

Voice: Typical harsh tern call "kreert, kreert."

Distribution and Habitat: Occurs in coastal areas of Kenya and Tanzania, including Zanzibar and Pemba Islands, nesting on islands of Kiunga Archipelago off the northern Kenya coast. Outside East Africa it occurs along the Somali coast to the shores of the Red Sea and the Persian Gulf. Often seen in flocks resting on sandy beaches at low water.

Allied Species: The European Common Tern (*Sterna hirundo*), 14″, is much paler grey above than the White-cheeked Tern and has white underparts. It is an uncommon and spasmodic visitor to East African shores. The Roseate Tern (*Sterna dougallii*), 15″, is rosy-white below and much whiter in general appearance with very long tail streamers. It occurs all along the East African seaboard and nests on various offshore islands. Other marine terns found along the East African coast include the wholly sooty-brown Noddy (*Anous stolidus*), 16″, with a pale grey crown; the large Swift Tern (*Sterna bergii*), 19-20″, with grey back, black cap and yellow bill; and the Sooty Tern (*Sterna fuscata*), 16″, and the similar Bridled Tern (*Sterna anaethetus*), 14″; both these species have the upperparts and wings dark brownish-grey, underparts greyish-white and a black cap: the Bridled Tern has a white collar on the hind neck, the Sooty Tern lacks the white collar. The Little Tern (*Sterna albifrons*), 9″, occurs both on coastal and on inland waters: easily recognised by diminutive size, black-tipped yellow bill, yellow legs and white forehead.

Doves and Pigeons: *Columbidae*

Medium-sized, plump birds with small rounded heads and the base of the bill swollen: flight rapid. Many species have characteristic deep cooing calls. The terms "dove" and "pigeon" are loosely used to indicate size, the smaller species being called doves, the larger pigeons.

WHITE-NAPED PIGEON   *Columba albinucha*   p. 241

Identification: 13-14″. A vinous-maroon pigeon with grey underparts, spotted white on the chest and a white or very pale grey patch on the back of the head; bill and feet red. Distinguished from the similar but larger Olive Pigeon (*119) by its bright red not yellow bill and legs, lack of pale spots on upper wing coverts and whitish nape patch.

Voice: A deep, quavering "cuu-uuu" followed by three or four shorter coos.

Distribution and Habitat: A rare and little-known species found in the eastern Congo and extreme western Uganda, where it is recorded from the Bwamba forest and the forest bordering the Congo in the Queen Elizabeth Park. In the former locality this bird visits the hot springs at Mongiro together with other species of pigeons.

LEMON DOVE   *Aplopelia larvata*   p. 241

Identification: 10″. A thickset dark-backed dove with vinous-rufous underparts; forehead, sides of face and throat whitish. The juvenile has rufous edgings to the feathers of the upperparts.

Voice: Sometimes utters a short "coo," but generally a silent bird.

Distribution and Habitat: Widely distributed, but uncommon and often overlooked, in forests of Kenya, westwards to Mount Elgon, and in Tanzania. Inhabits thick forests, where it feeds on the ground in the undergrowth.

Allied Species: The Western Lemon Dover (*Aplopelia simplex*), 9-10″, is paler below with crown, hind neck and upper back iridescent green and pink; chest and breast grey with vinous wash. Similar in habits to Lemon Dove, inhabiting dense forest undergrowth and feeding on ground. Occurs in western and southern Uganda and on the Kungwe-Mahare Mountains, western Tanzania. The Vinaceous Dove (*Streptopelia vinacea*), 10″, may be distinguished from other ring-necked doves by its pink forehead. It is found in northern and north-western Uganda; inhabits savannah woodland and bush, and in cultivation where there are trees. The Black-billed Blue-spotted Wood Dove (*Turtur abyssinicus*), 7″, is also found in northern Uganda in savannah and bush country. It is a paler bird than the Blue-spotted Wood Dove (*122) with a black bill. Delalande's Green Pigeon (*Treron delalandii*), 10-11″, differs from the Green Pigeon (*122) in having the chest olivaceous-grey not green. Found in eastern and southern Tanzania in open woodland.

Cuckoos and Coucals: *Cuculidae*

The cuckoos are medium-sized, slim birds with long tails: one of their chief external characters is that their first and fourth toes are directed backwards. Most species are parasitic in their breeding habits, laying their eggs in the nests of foster parents. The coucals (*Centropus*) build their own nests and rear their own young.

SENEGAL COUCAL
Centropus senegalensis
Identification: 16″. A black-crowned coucal with rufous back and wings, a blackish tail and buffy-white underparts. Differs from Blue-headed Coucal (*127) in smaller size and dull black, not iridescent navy-blue crown.
Voice: Bubbling flute-like notes similar to call of White-browed Coucal (*126).
Distribution and Habitat: Local resident western Kenya in Kakamega area and near Tororo, and in northern half of Uganda. Inhabits bush and thick cover mainly in savannah woodland, often near water.

Fig. 22 Senegal Coucal

Turacos or Louries: *Musophagidae*

The turacos, louries, plantain-eaters and go-away-birds, as they are variously called, are a group of medium or large-sized arboreal birds confined to Africa. The forest species are remarkable for their brightly coloured plumage and long tails; many species possess rich red flight feathers. Most have loud, harsh calls.

SCHALOW'S TURACO *Tauraco schalowi* p. 244

Identification: 16″. Plumage mainly green with deep red flight feathers, a violet-purple glossed tail and a long attenuated, white-tipped crest: bill green at base to red at tip. The closely related Livingstone's Turaco (*127) has a green-glossed tail and a shorter, broadly white-tipped crest.

Voice: Typical turaco harsh, far-carrying "kar, kar, kar."

Distribution and Habitat: Local and usually uncommon in south-western Kenya (Mara River forest) and western Tanzania. Inhabits riverine forest and woodland-savannah country.

BLACK-BILLED TURACO *Tauraco schuttii* p. 244

Identification: 16″. Plumage mainly green with red flight feathers: distinguished from related species by short, rounded, white-tipped crest and black bill.

Voice: Typical turaco "kars."

Distribution and Habitat: In East Africa found in Uganda, western Kenya and north-western Tanzania. Inhabits forest tree-tops: most in evidence in fruiting fig trees.

RUWENZORI TURACO *Ruwenzorornis johnstoni* p. 244

Identification: 16″. A red-winged green and blue turaco with a deep red patch on the hind neck and a red patch in the centre of the chest. Bare yellow skin around the eye in the Ruwenzori race, but skin around eye feathered in the race found in south-western Uganda.

Voice: A guttural "kow, kow, kow, kow."

Distribution and Habitat: In East Africa occurs on the Ruwenzori mountains, western Uganda, and in the Impenetrable Forest and Birunga Volcanoes of south-western Uganda. Inhabits mountain forest over 7,000 feet.

EASTERN GREY PLANTAIN-EATER *Crinifer zonurus* p. 244

Identification: 20″. A greyish-brown turaco without red in the wings, outer tail feathers whitish with broad black terminal band; white-tipped feathers on neck, forming a mane; belly white; bill greenish-yellow; white wing bar.

Voice: A variety of guttural, cackling "kok-kok-kok-kok-koks" and other sounds.

Distribution and Habitat: A common and widely distributed species in Uganda, western Kenya near Lake Victoria and in north-eastern

Plate 15 HORNBILLS, HOOPOE, OWLS

1 WHITE-TAILED HORNBILL   page 254
Tail white except for black central feathers; dark patch on sides of bill.

2 WHITE-THIGHED HORNBILL   page 254
Tail white with black band.

3 WHITE-CRESTED HORNBILL   page 254
Very long graduated tail; white crest.

4 WATTLED BLACK HORNBILL   page 255
Blue face and throat wattles; ♂ black, ♀ with brown head.

5 HEMPRICH'S HORNBILL   page 255
Bill dusky red; outer pair tail feathers black, next two pairs white.

6 FOREST WOOD HOOPOE   page 255
No white on wings or tail; head usually pale brown.

7 ABYSSINIAN LONG-EARED OWL   page 258
Long ear tufts; upright slender stance.

8 MACKINDER'S EAGLE OWL   page 258
Fiery orange eyes.

Plate 16 LARKS, SWIFT, NIGHTJARS, PIGEONS

1 **NORTHERN WHITE-TAILED BUSH LARK**   page 266
   Heavy bill; outer two pairs tail feathers white.

2 **PINK-BREASTED LARK**   page 267
   Slim build; long tail; breast mottled rufous-pink.

3 **SHORT-TAILED LARK**   page 267
   Short tail; Y-shaped black marking below eye; long heavy bill.

4 **MASKED LARK**   page 267
   Heavy pinkish bill; blackish face markings.

5 **SCARCE SWIFT**   page 265
   Dark brown with greyish-brown throat; long tail feathers (see
   text).

6 **SABINE'S SPINETAIL**   page 265
   Very long white upper tail coverts.

7 **NUBIAN NIGHTJAR**   page 259
   Mottled above golden-buff and pale grey; indistinct rufous hind
   collar.

8 **FIERY-NECKED NIGHTJAR**   page 259
   Broad rufous collar and cheeks; outer tail feathers with wide
   white tips.

9 **WHITE-NAPED PIGEON**   page 237
   White or pale grey nape patch; red bill and feet.

10 **LEMON DOVE**   page 237
   Rufous-pink underparts; face whitish.
   N.P.E.A.   Q

Tanzania. Inhabits open country where there are scattered trees, open woodland and savannah.

GO-AWAY-BIRD   *Corythaixoides concolor*   p. 244

Identification: 20″. An all-grey turaco without red in the wings; bill black; head with lax crest. Grey underparts distinguish this species from allied turacos.

Voice: A penetrating, rude-sounding "waar" or "go-waar" and various chuckles and groaning sounds.

Distribution and Habitat: Locally common in southern half of Tanzania, roughly from south of the Rufiji River. Inhabits woodland and open riverine forest, and bush and acacia country. Occurs in parties or pairs, following one another from tree to tree.

BARE-FACED GO-AWAY-BIRD *Gymnoschizorhis personata* p. 244

Identification: 20″. A grey-backed, white-breasted turaco without red in wings, with a bare black face: greenish patch in middle of chest; head crested. The bare black face is a good field character.

Voice: A series of deep bleating calls, and wild ringing chuckles.

Distribution and Habitat: Widely distributed and locally common in Uganda, western and southern Kenya and in Tanzania. Inhabits bush country and woodland-savannah, especially where there are euphorbia trees. Found in pairs or small parties.

Parrots: *Psittacidae*

Parrots form a group of small or medium-sized birds with powerful hooked bills with a cere at base; first and fourth toes directed backwards: flight direct with rapid short wing-beats.

GREY PARROT   *Psittacus erithacus*   p. 244

Identification: 12-13″. A relatively large grey parrot with a bright scarlet tail and under tail coverts.

Voice: Typical parrot chattering, screams and whistles.

Distribution and Habitat: Locally distributed Uganda, western Kenya and north-western Tanzania. Reports that Grey Parrots occur on Mount Kilimanjaro have never been confirmed. Inhabits forest areas; especially plentiful Sese Islands in Lake Victoria off Entebbe, Uganda.

BROWN-NECKED PARROT *Poicephalus robustus* p. 244

Identification: 13-14". A greyish-green parrot with a grey head and a very heavy pale-coloured bill: red on shoulders of wings and sometimes on forehead. The Red-headed Parrot (*133) is smaller and much greener with a bright red forehead.

Voice: Typical harsh parrot screams.

Distribution and Habitat: Occurs locally in southern Tanzania, south of Morogoro and Tabora. Frequents edges of forest and open woodland and where there are baobab trees.

Allied Species: The Rose-ringed Parrakeet (*Psittacula krameri*), 18-20", is a long-tailed yellowish-green parrot with a crimson bill, and a tomato-red half collar on each side of the neck. It occurs from the Sudan into north-western Uganda and the Bwamba forest, western Uganda.

RED-HEADED LOVEBIRD *Agapornis pullaria* p. 244

Identification: 5". A vivid green lovebird with a red forehead, face and throat: blue patch on rump; bases of tail feathers red with a sub-terminal black band.

Voice: A high-pitched twittering call.

Distribution and Habitat: A very local species found in the country around Mount Elgon in western Kenya, in Uganda where not uncommon near Entebbe, and in northern and western Tanzania as far south as Kigoma. Inhabits woodland savannah, cultivated areas where there are trees and along edges of forest.

BLACK-COLLARED LOVEBIRD *Agapornis swinderniana* p. 244

Identification: 5". A green lovebird with a black and orange-red collar on the hind neck; rump deep blue; tail feathers red at base with sub-terminal black band.

Voice: Relatively subdued twittering calls; shriller calls uttered in flight.

Distribution and Habitat: A West African and Congo species which reaches western Uganda at two points, the Bwamba forest and the forest at the western edge of the Queen Elizabeth Park. This is a forest species, mostly in evidence in fruiting fig trees. Usually silent when feeding and easily overlooked.

Plate 17 PARROTS, TURACOS

Plate 18 KINGFISHERS, ROLLERS

Rollers: *Coraciidae*

The rollers are thickset, medium-sized birds of brilliant plumage. Most species occur singly or in pairs unless migrating, when they form loose flocks. They are usually observed perched on some vantage point, such as a telegraph pole, dead branch or termite hill, from which they scan the ground for large insects and lizards which form their diet. The name roller derives from their aerial manoeuvres during mating display.

ABYSSINIAN ROLLER   *Coracias abyssinica*   p. 245
   Identification: 15-16″. A vivid blue roller, brighter than the European Roller (*135), with a pale rufous brown back; outer tail feathers elongated to form two long streamers four or five inches beyond end of tail: bill strongly hooked.
   Voice: A series of harsh chattering notes "kraark-kraark-kraark-ak-ak-ak."
   Distribution and Habitat: In East Africa occurs in Turkana, northwestern Kenya, and in northern Uganda. Inhabits dry bush country and savannah: often associated with tall termite hills, in which it nests.

RACQUET-TAILED ROLLER   *Coracias spatulata*   p. 245
   Identification: 14-15″. A pale-blue roller with a cinnamon lower back and white forehead: outer tail feathers elongated with broad racquet-shaped tips.
   Voice: Typical harsh roller calls.
   Distribution and Habitat: In East Africa confined to Tanzania, occurring south of Korogwe. Inhabits brachystegia woodland and to a lesser extent mopane woodland.

BLUE-THROATED ROLLER   *Eurystomus gularis*   p. 245
   Identification: 9-10″. A small, thickset, bright deep chestnut roller with a forked tail and a blue throat-patch; bill wide and yellow. The Broad-billed Roller (*137) lacks the blue throat and forked tail.
   Voice: A shrill, high-pitched "kwe-kwe-kwe-kwe"; most vocal at dusk.
   Distribution and Habitat: A West African and Congo species which occurs in the forests of western Uganda. Inhabits forest areas: often selects branch of a dead tree as a lookout.

Kingfishers: *Alcedinidae*

The kingfishers are a distinct family of small or medium-sized birds most of which are brightly coloured. Not all species prey upon fish: some feed largely upon large insects and lizards and occur in habitats far from water.

HALF-COLLARED KINGFISHER *Alcedo semitorquata* p. 245
Identification: 6½". A cobalt-blue kingfisher with a cinnamon breast and a blue patch on each side of the foreneck; bill black. The closely-related Shining-blue Kingfisher is bright ultramarine-blue above and bright chestnut below.
Voice: A shrill pipe, but bird usually silent.
Distribution and Habitat: In East Africa occurs uncommonly in Kenya and Tanzania. Frequents streams in forest or woodland, and rivers where there is abundant vegetation along the banks.

SHINING-BLUE KINGFISHER *Alcedo quadribrachys* p. 245
Identification: 6½-7". An ultramarine-blue kingfisher with bright chestnut-red underparts; bill black. The Half-collared Kingfisher is cobalt-blue above and cinnamon below.
Voice: A shrill peeping call.
Distribution and Habitat: A Congo species found in western and south-western Uganda and north-western Tanzania. Inhabits thickly wooded and forested streams, rivers and lakes.

WHITE-BREASTED KINGFISHER
Corythornis leucogaster p. 245
Identification: 4½". A small ultramarine-blue kingfisher with a dusky-red bill; below throat and belly white, flanks and band across chest bright fiery-chestnut.
Voice: A shrill, but not very loud, peeping call uttered in flight.
Distribution and Habitat: A rare species, in East Africa found only in the Bwamba forest and the western edge of the Queen Elizabeth Park. Inhabits swamp forest and streams in dense forest.

DWARF KINGFISHER *Myioceyx lecontei* p. 245
Identification: 4". Upperparts dark ultramarine-blue; crown chestnut; forehead black; below rufous; bill flattened and red. The Pygmy

Kingfisher (*139) has a barred black and ultramarine crown and the bill is not flattened.

Voice: A weak but high-pitched peep.

Distribution and Habitat: In East Africa confined to western Uganda where it inhabits thick forest, not always near water.

MANGROVE KINGFISHER   *Halcyon senegaloides*   p. 245
Identification: 8″. A thickset greenish-blue kingfisher, greyer on the head; underparts whitish to pale grey on breast; bill entirely red. The very similar Woodland Kingfisher (*139) has a differently coloured bill, the mandible black and the maxilla bright red.

Voice: A series of harsh, drawn out notes.

Distribution and Habitat: Confined to the coastal districts of Kenya and Tanzania. Frequents mangrove swamps, coastal bush and open woodland and where there are baobab trees.

BLUE-BREASTED KINGFISHER   *Halcyon malimbicus*   p. 245
Identification: 9½″. Resembles a larger edition of the Woodland Kingfisher (*139) but wide breast-band vivid pale blue: bill black and red.

Voice: A very vocal kingfisher producing a wide range of loud whistles, followed by slower notes "keeoo, keeoo, keeoo, keeoo."

Distribution and Habitat: Found locally in Uganda and western Tanzania; common in the Budongo Forest, western Uganda. This is a forest-haunting kingfisher, often found a long way from water.

BROWN-HOODED KINGFISHER   *Halcyon albiventris*   p. 245
Identification: 8-8½″. A black-backed kingfisher with a greyish-brown or brown head, buff-tinged flanks (sometimes buff on chest) and an all red bill. The Mangrove Kingfisher has a blue-grey back.

Voice: A shrill piping call.

Distribution and Habitat: Locally distributed in Kenya and Tanzania; occurs along rivers and in wooded and savannah country.

CHOCOLATE-BACKED KINGFISHER   *Halcyon badius*   p. 245
Identification: 7½-8″. Easily recognised by deep chocolate-rufous head, back and wing-coverts; below white, creamy-buff tinge on chest; blue wing bar and blue and black tail; bill dusky red.

Voice: Produces a series of relatively slow, descending whistles.

Distribution and Habitat: A West African species found in some of the forests of western and central Uganda. Not uncommon in Budongo Forest. Usually seen perched above forest trails.

Bee-eaters: *Meropidae*

Bee-eaters are medium-sized, slim birds of brilliant plumage; bills long and slightly decurved; legs short and wings sharply pointed. So named from their diet of bees, wasps and hornets which they swallow with impunity being apparently immune to the sting.

BLUE-CHEEKED BEE-EATER   *Merops persicus* (M)   p. 252
Identification: 11-12″. A bright green bee-eater with long central tail feathers; top of head green with a blue wash; forehead and cheeks, above and below black eye streak, bluish; chin yellow to chestnut on throat. The Madagascar Bee-eater is a darker, duller-plumaged bird with a dark olive-brown crown and a white forehead and cheeks.
Voice: A distinctive, liquid "pruuk," uttered in flight.
Distribution and Habitat: A winter visitor and passage migrant throughout East Africa, often associated with the European Bee-eater. Frequents open country with scattered trees and bush, swamps, lakes and rivers and cultivated areas.

MADAGASCAR BEE-EATER   *Merops superciliosus*   p. 252
Identification: 11-11½″. A dull green bee-eater with long central tail feathers; top of head dark olive-brown; white forehead and cheek streaks; chestnut on throat. A much duller and browner-looking bird than the Blue-cheeked Bee-eater and dark crown conspicuous in field.
Voice: A sharp clear "teeek," not unlike that of European Bee-eater.
Distribution and Habitat: Widely distributed in East Africa, but commonest in coastal districts of Kenya and Tanzania. Resident birds augmented between May and September by Madagascar population which migrates to Africa. Inhabits mangrove swamps, and open and bush country.

SOUTHERN CARMINE BEE-EATER   *Merops nubicoides*   p. 252
Identification: 13-14″. A brilliant carmine-pink bee-eater with very long central tail feathers: crown dark greenish-blue; entire underparts, including throat, carmine-pink. The Carmine Bee-eater (*141) has the throat dark greenish-blue, not pink.
Voice: A loud, deep "teek-teek."
Distribution and Habitat: A migrant to the southern half of eastern Tanzania and to south-western Lake Victoria between April and

September. Inhabits open bush country, woodland bush and savannah country: usually in flocks. Often attracted to bush fires when it preys upon insects escaping from the flames.

BOEHM'S BEE-EATER   *Aerops boehmi*   p. 252
Identification: 9″. A medium-sized bee-eater with very long central tail feathers slightly spatulate at tips; crown and throat rufous-brown; blue streak below black eye stripe.
Voice: A soft liquid trill and single "tssp" notes.
Distribution and Habitat: An uncommon and non-gregarious bee-eater found in east, central and south-western Tanzania. Frequents bush and woodland along streams and fairly open bush and savannah.

CINNAMON-CHESTED BEE-EATER
Melittophagus oreobates   p. 252
Identification: 8½″. Central tail feathers not elongated, tail square; upperparts green; below, yellow throat, black throat band and cinnamon-chestnut belly. The Blue-breasted Bee-eater is slightly smaller and has cinnamon-chestnut confined to area immediately below blue-black throat band: also habitat difference.
Voice: A three-note, sharp "tee-see-seep."
Distribution and Habitat: Widespread in Kenya and Uganda, and in north-eastern Tanzania, usually at altitudes over 4,000 feet. Inhabits woodland and edges of forest, and along roads through forest: perches usually in branches of trees. The closely related Blue-breasted Bee-eater inhabits mixed grass and bush, rarely settling in trees.

BLUE-BREASTED BEE-EATER   *Melittophagus variegatus*   p. 252
Identification: 7-7½″. Central tail feathers not elongated; tail square. A medium-sized bee-eater with a yellow throat, blue-black neck band, cinnamon-chestnut breast patch merging to pale greenish buff on belly; white patch below black eye streak conspicuous in field.
Voice: Loud, sharp "teeep," similar to call of Little Bee-eater (*142).
Distribution and Habitat: A local species in Uganda and north-western and south-western Tanzania. Inhabits open grass country with scattered bush and vegetation near water.

SOMALI BEE-EATER   *Melittophagus revoilii*   p. 252
Identification: 6½″. A pale green, square-tailed bee-eater with a cinnamon-buff breast; silvery-blue rump conspicuous when bird flies.
Voice: A brief, clear trill of three to five notes.

Distribution and Habitat: A Somalia species which extends into the
Northern Frontier Province of Kenya. Inhabits relatively open arid
bush country; perches on bushes, usually near the ground.

RED-THROATED BEE-EATER   *Melittophagus bulocki*   p. 252
Identification: $8\frac{1}{2}$". A bright green, square-tailed species with a brilliant
red throat; rufous on hind neck and belly. Differs from the larger
White-fronted Bee-eater (*143) in having green, not frosted-white
crown.
Voice: Clear, liquid trill.
Distribution and Habitat: In East Africa locally common in northern
Uganda; often seen in the Murchison Falls Park. Inhabits open grass
and bush savannah and partial to deep, eroded gullies.

BLUE-HEADED BEE-EATER   *Melittophagus mulleri*   p. 252
Identification: 7-$7\frac{1}{2}$". A square-tailed bee-eater with a deep chestnut
back; crown and nape ultramarine-blue merging to cobalt-blue and
white on the forehead; chin bright scarlet; lower throat blue-black to
deep blue on rest of underparts and tail.
Voice: A weak "tssp."
Distribution and Habitat: A very uncommon and local bird found in
Uganda and the Kakamega Forest, western Kenya. A forest species
living in glades in dense forest, perching in dead trees.

BLACK BEE-EATER   *Melittophagus gularis*   p. 252
Identification: $7\frac{1}{2}$". A square-tailed black bee-eater with a vivid scarlet
throat; lower back, rump and spots on underparts bright cobalt-blue.
Voice: A sustained, clear liquid trill, interspersed with sharp, high-
pitched "tssps."
Distribution and Habitat: A West African and Congo species which
ranges to the forests of western Uganda. Inhabits forests: unlike the
other forest species, the Blue-headed Bee-eater, it is usually found in
the vicinity of forest swamps and streams rather than glades.

Hornbills: *Bucerotidae*

The hornbills are a very distinct group of birds of medium or large size,
characterised by their very large curved bills which in some species possess
casque-like structures on the culmens. The family has remarkable nesting
habits, the female in most cases sealing herself inside the nesting chamber

Plate 19 BEE-EATERS, BARBETS

1 **BLUE-CHEEKED BEE-EATER**   page 249
   Green crown; blue forehead.

2 **MADAGASCAR BEE-EATER**   page 249
   Olive-brown crown.

3 **SOUTHERN CARMINE BEE-EATER**   page 249
   Carmine-pink throat.

4 **BOEHM'S BEE-EATER**   page 250
   Rufous crown and throat; blue streak below eye.

5 **CINNAMON-CHESTED BEE-EATER**   page 250
   Deep cinnamon chest and belly; frequents woods and forests.

6 **BLUE-BREASTED BEE-EATER**   page 250
   Deep cinnamon restricted to chest; frequents open bush and
   grasslands.

7 **BLACK BEE-EATER**   page 251
   Black upperparts; red throat.

8 **SOMALI BEE-EATER**   page 250
   Generally pale plumage; silvery blue rump.

9 **BLUE-HEADED BEE-EATER**   page 251
   Back deep chestnut; throat red.

10 **RED-THROATED BEE-EATER**   page 251
   Green crown; red throat.

11 **BLACK-BILLED BARBET**   page 260
   Black bill; red throat.

12 **RED-FACED BARBET**   page 260
   Horn-coloured bill; black throat.

Plate 20 BARBETS, WOODPECKERS, HONEY-GUIDES

1 **BLACK-BACKED BARBET** page 261
White V on back; salmon-pink abdomen.

2 **RED-FRONTED BARBET** page 261
Red forehead; yellow eye-stripe.

3 **YELLOW-SPOTTED BARBET** page 261
Yellow-spotted black upperparts; red crown.

4 **YELLOW-BILLED BARBET** page 261
Bare yellow face and bill; inhabits forests.

5 **BROWN-EARED WOODPECKER** page 262
Brown ear coverts; buff breast spots.

6 **YELLOW-CRESTED WOODPECKER** page 264
Black crown; with yellow streaks in male.

7 **BUFF-SPOTTED WOODPECKER** page 263
Pale olive-grey ear coverts; buff-spotted underparts.

8 **LITTLE SPOTTED WOODPECKER** page 263
Yellowish-green spots on back.

9 **OLIVE WOODPECKER** page 264
Chest and breast olive-green.

10 **ELLIOT'S WOODPECKER** page 264
Black forehead.

11 **SPOTTED HONEY-GUIDE** page 262
Greenish-yellow spots on breast.

12 **THICK-BILLED HONEY-GUIDE** page 262
Thick bill; dark grey underparts.

with dung and mud brought by the male, leaving only a narrow slit through which she is fed by her mate.

WHITE-TAILED HORNBILL   *Bycanistes sharpii*   p. 240

Identification: 22-24″. A relatively small black and white hornbill with an ivory-white bill with blackish patch on side, and low casque present in male. Plumage black on back and chest; large white wing-patch and white breast, abdomen and rump; tail, central pair feathers black, rest white. Small size and completely white outer tail feathers best field characters.

Voice: A shrill, high-pitched "keep-keep-keep-keep" and more guttural "ark, ark, ark" noises.

Distribution and Habitat: A West African and Congo species which extends eastwards to the Bwamba forest, western Uganda, where it is not uncommon. A forest hornbill most in evidence when figs and other trees are in fruit.

WHITE-THIGHED HORNBILL   *Bycanistes albotibialis*   p. 240

Identification: 27-28″. A large, black and white hornbill best distinguished from allied species by its tail pattern—entirely white with a black band across the centre. Bill greyish-white and casque, in male, decurved and pointed; breast black, lower abdomen and thighs white.

Voice: Various loud raucous cries typical of this genus of hornbills.

Distribution and Habitat: Another West African and Congo species which reaches some of the western Uganda forests: most frequent in Bwamba and Budongo forests. Inhabits tree-tops, most in evidence when fig trees are fruiting.

WHITE-CRESTED HORNBILL   *Tropicranus albocristatus*   p. 240

Identification: 26″, tail 17″. A black hornbill with an unmistakable long, graduated, white-tipped black tail; forehead to nape white, the feathers long and lax forming a crest; white tips to greater wing coverts forming a wing bar.

Voice: A plaintive "oo-oo-oo-oo-ah," soft but far-carrying: also reputed to utter chicken-like squarks.

Distribution and Habitat: Another West African species which extends eastwards to the Bwamba forest, western Uganda. A forest species often associated with troops of colobus monkeys, preying upon insects disturbed by the animals.

WATTLED BLACK HORNBILL   *Ceratogymna atrata*   p. 240
   Identification: ♂ 32″, ♀ 30″. A large black hornbill with broad white tips to tail feathers; bill with high pointed casque; bright cobalt-blue neck wattles; female differs in chestnut head and neck and smaller size.
   Voice: A loud nasal squark and drawn-out whistles.
   Distribution and Habitat: This is yet another West African hornbill which occurs in the Bwamba forest, western Uganda. The species inhabits rain forest and attracts attention by the loud swishing noise made by its wings in flight.
   Allied Species: Two other Congo forest hornbills are recorded from the Bwamba forest, western Uganda: the Red-billed Dwarf Hornbill (*Tockus camurus*), 14″, pale brown with a white belly, a bright red bill and a double white wing bar; and the Black Dwarf Hornbill (*Tockus hartlaubi*), 14″, with black upperparts, a white streak from above eye to nape and a red and black bill; below grey on throat to whitish on belly.

HEMPRICH'S HORNBILL   *Tockus hemprichii*   p. 240
   Identification: 22″. In general appearance blackish-grey with a white belly and white edgings to wing-coverts and scapulars; bill dusky-red; outer pair tail feathers, blackish next two pairs white, central tail feathers black. Differs from related Crowned Hornbill (*149) in lacking white streaks on side of head and nape and in having two pairs tail feathers wholly white.
   Voice: A two- or three-note piping call.
   Distribution and Habitat: In East Africa found in north-eastern Uganda and north-western Kenya as far south as Lake Baringo. Nearly always associated with rocky, broken country and inland cliffs.

Wood Hoopoes: *Phoeniculidae*

The wood hoopoes are medium-sized, slender birds with black plumage glossed green, blue or purple. Tails long and graduated; bills long and down-curved. Arboreal, usually in small flocks: noisy birds keeping up a constant chatter.

FOREST WOOD HOOPOE   *Scoptelus castaneiceps*   p. 240
   Identification: 10½″, tail 6″. A black wood hoopoe without white spots on the wings and tail; body glossed bottle green, tail glossed violet;

Plate 21 PIPITS, BABBLERS, BULBULS

Plate 22 FLYCATCHERS, WATTLE-EYE

bill blackish with a yellow streak along cutting edges. Some males, the female and immatures have pale brown heads.

Voice: A plaintive, "Wah, wah, wah, wah," repeated over and over.

Distribution and Habitat: A local and very uncommon species in Uganda. Inhabits forest and secondary growth at the edge of forest: usually in pairs or small family parties.

Allied Species: The Violet Wood Hoopoe (*Phoeniculus damarensis*), 15", has white spots on the wings and tail, and a red bill and legs: it differs from the Green Wood Hoopoe (*152) in being violet-purple, not green, in gloss colour. It occurs locally in Kenya, being common along the Tana River. The Black-billed Wood Hoopoe (*Phoeniculus somaliensis*), 15", resembles the Violet Wood Hoopoe but has a black bill and dusky-red feet. It is found in north-eastern Kenya. The Black Wood Hoopoe (*Scoptelus aterrimus*), 8½", is a violet-black species, with a white bar across the flight feathers and a greyish-yellow bill and blackish feet. It occurs in acacia woodland and savannah country in the northern half of Uganda.

Owls: *Strigidae*

Nocturnal birds of prey characterised by large heads, rather flattened faces with conspicuous "facial discs" and forward facing eyes. Plumage soft and downy and flight noiseless: ear-tufts present in many species; hooked bills and powerful claws.

MACKINDER'S EAGLE OWL   *Bubo capensis*   p. 240

Identification: 22". A thickset mottled orange-buff, dark-brown and white eagle owl with conspicuous ear-tufts and fiery-orange eyes. The Spotted Eagle Owl (*155) has no orange-buff in the plumage and its eyes are either dark brown or pale greenish-yellow.

Voice: A deep resonant hoot, not very loud but far-carrying.

Distribution and Habitat: A high altitude species recorded locally in Kenya and Tanzania. In Kenya not uncommon on Mount Kenya, the Aberdare range and Mount Elgon. Inhabits rocky cliffs and escarpments, but often hunts in more open country.

ABYSSINIAN LONG-EARED OWL   *Asio abyssinicus*   p. 240

Identification: 18". A rather slim, sooty-brown owl with some buff markings; below blotched and barred dark-brown and white on a buff ground; ear-tufts well developed. This owl is a larger edition of the familiar Long-eared Owl of Europe, and has the same upright, slender stance.

Voice: Undescribed: a series of brief hoots on a descending scale heard on Mount Kenya may have been uttered by this bird.

Distribution and Habitat: A rare and little-known owl, in East Africa recorded from Mount Kenya, Kenya and the Ruwenzori Mountains, Uganda. Inhabits the top edge of mountain forest and the heath zone on the alpine moorlands.

Allied Species: Another species found in mountain forest is the Red-chested Owlet (*Glaucidium tephronotum*), 9″, with umber-brown upper-parts, a white collar on hind neck, and rufous-brown chest and flanks. It is known from Mount Elgon in Kenya and the Impenetrable Forest, south-western Uganda.

Nightjars: *Caprimulgidae*

Nightjars are nocturnal, insectivorous birds with small weak bills but huge gapes, large eyes, tiny feet and long wings. Plumage of "dead-leaf" pattern which gives excellent camouflage when bird immobile during day.

FIERY-NECKED NIGHTJAR   *Caprimulgus fervidus*   p. 241
Identification: 9½″. General colour warm vinous brown with bold black and buff markings; very broad rufous collar, the rufous extending on to sides of neck; first four primaries with white spots; apical third of two outermost tail feathers white; underparts with warm vinous wash. Best field characters are the very broad rufous hind neck and cheeks, and the wide white tips to outer tail feathers.

Voice: A beautiful liquid call, "too-dee, he, he, heeer," repeated slowly over and over again.

Distribution and Habitat: Widely distributed and not uncommon locally in Uganda and Tanzania. Inhabits forest edges, open woodland and bush country.

NUBIAN NIGHTJAR   *Caprimulgus nubicus*   p. 241
Identification: 8½″. General colour, mottled pale golden-buff and pale grey; indistinct rufous hind collar; first four primaries with white spots, apical third of two pairs outer tail feathers white. Female lacks white in wings and tips of tail feathers are buff. Best recognised by its pale coloration.

Voice: A liquid "chucker, chucker, chucker, chucker."

Distribution and Habitat: In East Africa occurs in eastern Kenya, where common in Tsavo National Park. Inhabits arid bush country.

Allied Species: The Usambara Nightjar (*Caprimulgus guttifer*), 8″, has very dark rufous plumage with apical third of two outer pairs tail feathers white. It is a bird of mountain grasslands and forest edges from north-eastern to southern Tanzania. The Star-spotted Nightjar (*Caprimulgus stellatus*), 8½″, is a large-headed grey or rufous-grey nightjar with star-shaped black and buff marks on the crown and scapulars. It occurs in the Northern Frontier Province of Kenya, but is everywhere uncommon.

Barbets: *Capitonidae*

The barbets are related to the woodpeckers and like them have the first and fourth toes directed backwards; birds thickset with short heavy bills: extremely variable plumage characters. Barbets are mainly fruit eaters, and are often numerous in fruiting fig and other fruit-bearing trees.

BLACK-BILLED BARBET   *Lybius guifsobalito*   p. 252

Identification: 6″. A black barbet with a red crown, face and throat and a black bill; wing feathers edged yellowish. The closely related Red-faced Barbet has no red on the throat or crown and the bill is greyish-white.

Voice: A metallic "awk, awk, awk."

Distribution and Habitat: A local and rather uncommon species in extreme western Kenya and in Uganda. Inhabits open savannah woodland and bush country.

RED-FACED BARBET   *Lybius rubrifacies*   p. 252

Identification: 6″. A black barbet with a red face and a pale grey bill; yellowish edgings to wing feathers. Lack of red on crown and throat distinguishes it from Black-billed Barbet.

Voice: A low nasal "yak" repeated several times.

Distribution and Habitat: A very uncommon species found only in south-western Uganda and north-western Tanzania. Inhabits savannah woodland, especially where there are euphorbia trees.

BLACK-BACKED BARBET   *Lybius minor*   p. 253
Identification: 6". Upperparts black with white V on back and red
forehead; below white to bright salmon-pink on abdomen; bill whitish-
horn.
Voice: A penetrating but not very loud "tonk-tonk."
Distribution and Habitat: North-eastern, eastern and south-western
Tanzania: in woodland and along edges of forest: a very uncommon
species, usually seen singly or in pairs.

RED-FRONTED BARBET   *Tricholaema diadematum*   p. 253
Identification: 5". A blackish-brown-backed barbet with yellow
streaks and yellow edging to wings and tail: forehead red; yellow eye
stripe; below yellowish white more or less spotted brown.
Voice: A plaintive, rather drawn-out "twa, twa, twa, twa," or a harsh
double-note "ki, waa."
Distribution and Habitat: It occurs locally in Kenya and Uganda, south
to central Tanzania. Inhabits acacia woodland and scrub.

YELLOW-SPOTTED BARBET   *Buccanodon duchaillui*   p. 253
Identification: 6". Upperparts black, heavily spotted yellow; crown
deep crimson; below mottled black and yellow.
Voice: A deep, far-carrying trill.
Distribution and Habitat: An uncommon and local barbet in western
Kenya to western and southern Uganda. Inhabits forest tree-tops;
most noticeable when visiting fruiting fig trees.

YELLOW-BILLED BARBET   *Trachylaemus purpuratus*   p. 253
Identification: 9". A rather long-tailed barbet, shiny black above;
belly mottled yellow; forehead and throat deep crimson; face and bill
bright yellow—conspicuous in field.
Voice: A deep, frog-like croaking, followed by sharp clinking notes.
Distribution and Habitat: Local and uncommon western Kenya,
Uganda and north-western Tanzania. A bird of the forest tree-tops,
easily overlooked until its call is recognised.

Honey-guides: *Indicatoridae*

A family of rather small birds, 4½-8" long, of sombre brown, olive, grey
and white plumage. All species have a considerable amount of white in the
three outer pairs of tail feathers, a conspicuous field character when the

bird is in flight. They are parasitic in their nesting habits, laying their eggs in the nests of birds such as bee-eaters, barbets and woodpeckers. Honey-guides feed largely upon bees' wax and bee larvae and are often encountered near African beehives hung in trees. They can be attracted by nailing lumps of bees' comb to tree trunks. The Greater Honey-guide (*170) has developed a most remarkable habit of guiding humans to the nests of wild bees in order to feed upon the honeycomb and grubs when the nest is chopped out.

SPOTTED HONEY-GUIDE   *Indicator maculatus*   p. 253
  Identification: 7½". An olive-green honey-guide with round, yellowish-green spots over the chest and belly. Immature birds have the underparts streaked, not spotted.
  Voice: A curious mewing call, just like the sound produced by a small kitten.
  Distribution and Habitat: A West African species found in a few forests in western Uganda. Inhabits dense forest where it usually keeps to the high tree-tops.

THICK-BILLED HONEY-GUIDE   *Indicator conirostris*   p. 253
  Identification: 6". A bright olive-green honey-guide with ill-defined dark streaks on upperparts and wings; below grey, darker than Lesser Honey-guide (*171), with black streaks sometimes present on throat; bill noticeably thick and heavy.
  Voice: A rather sharp "tssp-tssp."
  Distribution and Habitat: A very local and uncommon species in western Kenya, where recorded Kakamega Forests and Mount Elgon, and Uganda. Inhabits forest: sometimes seen at wild bees' nests.

Woodpeckers: *Picidae*

This is a family of chisel-billed, wood-boring birds with powerful feet (two toes directed forwards, two backwards) and stiff tails which act as props in climbing tree trunks and branches: flight undulating. Woodpeckers nest in holes which they excavate in trees.

BROWN-EARED WOODPECKER   *Campethera caroli*   p. 253
  Identification: 7½". Upperparts bright golden-olive without markings; crown dark olive with crimson streaks in male; below olive, with dense,

round yellowish-white spots; ear coverts and band down side of neck chestnut-brown.

Voice: A silent bird, no call recorded.

Distribution and Habitat: A very local species in western Kenya, Uganda and north-western Tanzania. A forest woodpecker which usually keeps high in the tree-tops.

Allied Species: The Green-backed Woodpecker (*Campethera permista*), 7″, has the upperparts unmarked green; crown red in male, white-spotted with red nape in female; below greenish with heavy black bars. The related Fine-banded Woodpecker (*172) has narrow, close-set bars on underparts. The Green-backed Woodpecker is a rare bird in East Africa recorded only from the Bwamba Forest, western Uganda.

BUFF-SPOTTED WOODPECKER   *Campethera nivosa*   p. 253

Identification: 5½″. A bright olive-green woodpecker without markings on back; nape of male red, crown and nape of female uniform olive; below, throat yellowish-white streaked olive, breast and belly olive with round yellowish-white spots.

Voice: Mainly silent, but sometimes utters a soft, metallic "ting, ting, ting."

Distribution and Habitat: An uncommon species in East Africa recorded from the Kakamega Forest, western Kenya and from Uganda. Inhabits forests, where it may be found both in the tree-tops and in heavy undergrowth near the ground.

LITTLE SPOTTED WOODPECKER
Campethera cailliautii   p. 253

Identification: 6½″. Bright green upperparts, spotted with yellowish-white; crown scarlet in male, in female crown black with white spots and nape scarlet; below yellowish-white, spotted black.

Voice: A high-pitched "tee-tee-tee-tee."

Distribution and Habitat: Of wide distribution in southern Kenya, southern Uganda and throughout Tanzania. Inhabits woodlands, savannah country and at the coast often seen in coconut plantations.

Allied Species: Bennett's Woodpecker (*Campethera bennettii*), 8″, is greenish above with dark and pale barring; underparts yellowish-white with black spots; crown red in male. The female has a white-spotted crown with red nape, chocolate stripe below eye and a chocolate throat patch. This is a very uncommon woodpecker found in woodland and savannah bush in Tanzania. The Spotted-throated Woodpecker (*Campethera scriptoricauda*), 7″, is another "ladder-backed" greenish woodpecker with spotted underparts, closely resembling a Nubian Woodpecker (*172) from which it may be distinguished by its black-spotted throat. It is found in brachystegia woodland in the Morogoro district, Tanzania. Another rare Tanzania woodpecker is Stierling's Woodpecker (*Ipophilus stierlingi*), 6", with uniform olive-brown upperparts and a black nape patch; crown of male red, of female olive-brown; underparts greenish-white streaked and barred with black. It appears to be confined, in East Africa, to south-western Tanzania.

OLIVE WOODPECKER   *Mesopicos griseocephalus*   p. 253
Identification: 7-7½". General colour golden-olive-green, unmarked above and below, with a grey head; upper tail coverts and centre of belly deep bright red; crown of male streaked deep wine-red, crown of female grey. The related Grey Woodpecker (*174) has the breast grey, not olive-green, and male has bright red crown.
Voice: A churring call, "chi-r-r-r-ee."
Distribution and Habitat: A local species found at altitudes over 6,000 feet in western Uganda and the highlands of Tanzania. A mountain forest bird found both in the tree-tops and near the ground.

YELLOW-CRESTED WOODPECKER
Mesopicos xantholophus   p. 253
Identification: 8½". A large, thickset woodpecker: uniform dark olive back; crown black in female, streaked, especially towards nape, yellow in male; underparts dark olive with round whitish spots, whitish on chin.
Voice: A shrill, churring "pirit," often repeated several times, but generally a silent bird.
Distribution and Habitat: An uncommon and local species in Uganda. Also recorded from the Kakamega Forest, western Kenya. Inhabits forest, where it keeps mainly to the tree-tops.

ELLIOT'S WOODPECKER   *Mesopicos elliotii*   p. 253
Identification: 6½". A rather slim woodpecker with a bright green back and the front half of the crown black. Hind crown and nape scarlet in male; entire crown and nape black in female; underparts pale greenish-yellow with black streaks.
Voice: A shrill "tssp-tssp."
Distribution and Habitat: A very uncommon species in western Uganda. Inhabits forest tree-tops: most frequent in Mpanga Forest near Fort Portal and the Bwamba Forest.

Swifts: *Apodidae*

In general appearance swifts are swallow-like but may be distinguished by the formation of their wings which are more slender and scythe-shaped, their usually short tails and their manner of flight which is rapid and direct, often gliding considerable distances without flapping wings. Structurally quite distinct from swallows with flat skulls and a foot in which all four toes point forwards.

SCARCE SWIFT   *Apus myoptilus*   p. 241

Identification: 6½". An entirely dark-brown swift with a slightly paler greyish-brown throat; outer tail feathers elongated and attenuated. In flight the tail is often kept closed, when the two long outer tail feathers project behind the bird like a spike. Flight very rapid and wing-beats fast for a swift.

Voice: Usually silent; call unrecorded.

Distribution and Habitat: Extremely uncommon and local. In Kenya recorded from Mount Kenya and the Aberdares, from the Cherengani Mountains and from Mount Elgon. In Uganda it occurs on the Ruwenzori range and in south-west Kigezi. This is a highlands species which flies high, seen only when thunder-storms or cloud force them to fly lower than usual.

SABINE'S SPINETAIL   *Chaetura sabini*   p. 241

Identification: 4". A glossy blue-black swift with a white rump and white upper tail coverts which reach almost to the tip of the tail; below throat and chest blue-black, breast, belly and under tail coverts white.

Voice: Unrecorded.

Distribution and Habitat: This is a rare West African and Congo swift which has been recorded in East Africa in the Kakamega Forest, western Kenya, and in the Budongo and Bwamba forests, western Uganda. It is a forest swift which flies high over the tree-tops and is attracted low only when termites or some other food supply is on the wing near ground level.

Larks: *Alaudidae*

A group of ground-loving song birds: often gregarious in non-breeding season. Hind claw often elongated and more or less straight. Build usually heavier and bills more robust than pipits and wagtails which are also terrestrial in their habits.

NORTHERN WHITE-TAILED BUSH LARK

Mirafra albicauda   p. 241

Identification: 5". A rather thickset, heavy-billed lark with blackish upperparts and rufous edged wings; below with dense mottling on the chest; outer two pairs tail feathers pure white, these are very conspicuous when bird is in flight. Very dark upperparts and white tail feathers best field characters.

Voice: A sweet, musical song uttered on the wing as it flies in circles above its nesting place.

Distribution and Habitat: Widespread but local throughout East Africa. Frequents open grasslands and mixed grass and bush usually on black cotton soil. A secretive bird, terrestrial in habits, keeping to long grass from which it may be flushed. Rarely perches on bushes—in spite of its name!

Allied Species: The Singing Bush Lark (*Mirafra cantillans*), 5", also has the outer tail feathers white, but is a fawn-coloured bird with noticeably rufous wings in flight. It too indulges in a song flight in circles above its nesting ground. This species inhabits grasslands and grass-bush on sandy soil. Locally common in Kenya, Uganda and north and central Tanzania. Williams' Bush Lark (*Mirafra williamsi*), 5½", also has white outer tail feathers: upperparts dark vinous brown or dark vinous grey with narrow pale tips to the feathers; below white with heavy rufous and dark brown mottling on the chest and flanks; bill relatively heavy. This is a rare bird known at present only from three localities in Kenya; these are Mount Marsabit, the Dida Galgalla Desert and black lava desert thirty miles east of Isiolo, all localities in the Northern Frontier Province. The Fawn-coloured Lark (*Mirafra africanoides*), 5½", has upperparts rufous tawny with broad blackish streaks; a pronounced creamy-white eye stripe; below pale buff, streaked dark brown on chest; outer webs and tips of outer tail feathers whitish. Widespread in dry bush country in Kenya, eastern Uganda and north and central Tanzania. In the field looks like a diminutive

Rufous-naped Lark (*180): often perches on bushes and small trees.
The Athi Short-toed Lark (*Calandrella rufescens*), 5″, is a mottled
greyish lark with a moderately heavy bill, heavy streaking on chest and
no chestnut or rufous in wings. Often in flocks, flight low and undulating. This is a very local species found on the Athi Plains and in the
Nairobi National Park, Kenya.

PINK-BREASTED LARK   *Mirafra poecilosterna*   p. 241
Identification: 6″. A rather slim, relatively long-tailed lark which
habitually perches on small trees and bushes. Upperparts fawn brown,
greyer on the crown; wings and tail ashy-brown; below rufous-white
with deeper pink-rufous mottling on chest and flanks.
Voice: Song, a soft trill, uttered from perch on bush or tree. Call note a
thin "tweet" often repeated several times.
Distribution and Habitat: Widespread in drier areas of Kenya and
north-eastern Tanzania. Inhabits arid bush country, usually on sandy
soil.

SHORT-TAILED LARK   *Pseudalaemon fremantlii*   p. 241
Identification: 5½″. A short-tailed lark with much the appearance of a
European Wood Lark. Upperparts grey to pinkish-grey mottled and
streaked blackish-brown; distinct white eye stripe and Y-shaped black
marking below eye; bill long and heavy for size of bird; below white
with dark patch each side of chest; rufous wash on chest and flanks,
overlaid on chest with short blackish streaks.
Voice: A liquid three note whistle.
Distribution and Habitat: Extremely local, but common in flocks where
it occurs. Recorded from the Athi-Kapiti plains and the Nairobi
National Park and on Marsabit in Kenya and the Arusha area in
northern Tanzania. Inhabits open grassy plains: feeds largely on bulbs
and corms which it digs up with its heavy bill.

MASKED LARK   *Aethocorys personata*   p. 241
Identification: 5½-6″. Upperparts, wings and tail uniform ash-brown,
tail with pale cinnamon edges to outer feathers; bill large and heavy,
pinkish-white; black patch in front of and below eyes and black patch
on each side of chin; throat white; chest grey merging to warm vinous
brown on belly and under tail coverts. Best field characters are black
face mask and pink bill.
Voice: A series of liquid, far-carrying notes, not unlike those of Short-
tailed Lark.

Distribution and Habitat: In East Africa known only from three localities in the Northern Frontier Province of Kenya, the Isiolo district,
Mount Marsabit and the black lava desert of the Dida Galgalla.
Inhabits open bush country and sparse grass on black cotton soil and
black lava desert.

Wagtails and Pipits: *Motacillidae*

This is a group of graceful, slender terrestrial birds which run and walk.
The pipits are generally brown above, with or without streaks: they resemble larks but are more slender and have a different and more upright
carriage, and their bills are thin. Wagtails have long tails and strongly-
marked patterns, often with much yellow: they fall into two groups, those
which occur singly or in pairs on or near water, and those which occur
in flocks and are associated with cattle and herds of other domestic
animals whose passage disturbs insects upon which the wagtails feed.

PLAIN-BACKED PIPIT   *Anthus leucophrys*   p. 256
Identification: 6″. A slim pipit having the back dark brown or dark
rufous-brown without streaks on upperparts and without white in tail;
below warm rufous or buffy-brown with some indistinct streaks or
spots on chest. The related Richard's Pipit (*184) has streaked upperparts and white in the outer tail feathers.
Voice: A rather weak "tssp" or "tssp, tssp," uttered when the bird
takes wing.
Distribution and Habitat: Locally common in Uganda, western Kenya
and Tanzania except eastern districts. Inhabits open plains and flats
adjacent to inland lakes.
Allied Species: The Sandy Plain-backed Pipit (*Anthus vaalensis*), 6″, is
a paler coloured bird than the Plain-backed Pipit and has only a trace
of streaking on chest: there are also differences in structure of flight-
feathers between the two but this is not a field character. This is a local
bird found east of the Rift Valley in Kenya. The Malindi Pipit (*Anthus
melindae*), 5½″, is a rare species found in coastal districts of Kenya and
Tanzania. Above, it is grey-brown; below, dull white with heavy
blackish streaks on chest and flanks; no white on outer tail feathers.
The Sokoke Pipit (*Anthus sokokensis*), 5″, has unusual habits for a
pipit, favouring glades and bush in the coastal forests of Kenya and
Tanzania. It is a warm buff with heavy black streaking above; below,
yellowish-white with black streaks on chest and flank. The Striped Pipit

(*Anthus lineiventris*), 6½″, is olive-brown above with dark streaking; wing coverts, flight and tail feathers edged green; below, buff with close dark streaks; outer tail feathers partly white. Inhabits rocky hills with scattered bush and scrub in southern Kenya and Tanzania.

LITTLE TAWNY PIPIT   *Anthus caffer*   p. 256
Identification: 4½″. A very small brown pipit with heavy dark streaking on upperparts and chest; outer tail feathers white on outer edges and tips.

Voice: A soft two-note whistle uttered when flushed.

Distribution and Habitat: A very uncommon and local species in southern Kenya and northern and central Tanzania. Inhabits open grasslands and acacia grassland. Common at Seronera in Serengeti National Park.

Allied Species: The Short-tailed Pipit (*Anthus brachyurus*), 4½″, is very dark above with olive-brown streaking; below, whitish with heavy chest and flank streaks. Found in western Uganda to north-western and south-central Tanzania. Inhabits mixed acacia-grasslands. A much darker bird than the Little Tawny Pipit, though similar in size.

Babblers, Chatterers and allies: *Turdoididae*

The babblers, chatterers and related species are an ill-defined group of thrush-like birds. Some species—babblers and chatterers—occur in noisy parties in bush and thorn-bush country. The Illadopsis group and the Hill Babblers are forest species, more or less solitary and shy. Plumages are usually dull grey, brown, olive or rufous; wings rounded.

SCALY BABBLER   *Turdoides squamulata*   p. 256
Identification: 8½″. A stocky greyish bird with a relatively long tail and bright orange eyes. Distinguished from related Arrow-marked Babbler (*187) by white chin and black lores and ear coverts. The similar Black-lored Babbler (*187) has bluish-white eyes and pale ear coverts.

Voice: Various harsh babbling calls. Birds move in small flocks through thick scrub but draw attention to themselves by their grating call-notes.

Distribution and Habitat: The Scaly Babbler has a restricted distribution, found in Kenya only in coastal bush and scrub, and the riverine belt along the Tana River as far inland as Garissa. Keeps to thick cover; uncommon and local. Occurs in noisy parties.

Allied Species: The Brown Babbler (*Turdoides plebeja*), 9″, is a dark, greyish-brown species with a whitish chin, yellow eyes and very small whitish points on breast feathers. It occurs in bush savannah in Uganda and western Kenya. The White-rumped Babbler (*Turdoides leucopygia*), 8½″, is grey-brown with a more or less well-developed white rump: known in East Africa from the Ufipa Plateau, south-western Tanzania. Hinde's Pied Babbler (*Turdoides hindei*), 8″, is sooty-brown with patches of white feathers of varying extent appearing on the head and body giving the appearance of a semi-albino! A very uncommon species from central Kenya, known from the Fort Hall and Machakos districts. The Scaly Chatterer (*Argya aylmeri*), 7″, resembles an ash-brown edition of the Rufous Chatterer (*187). It occurs in dry bush country in Kenya and Tanzania.

MOUNTAIN ILLADOPSIS   *Malacocincla pyrrhopterus*   p. 256

Identification: 5½″. The Illadopsis group are rather small, relatively plump thrush-like birds with shortish tails, rounded wings and long legs, which live on the forest floor. All are drab plumaged in greys, browns and whites, solitary and shy. The present species may be recognised by its grey throat and breast: above, dark rufous olive-brown, greyer on crown.

Voice: A brief warbling song.

Distribution and Habitat: In East Africa known from the highlands of western Kenya and Uganda. Lives on the forest floor among dense undergrowth: seldom seen.

Allied Species: The Brown Illadopsis (*Malacocincla fulvescens*), 6″, occurs in pairs or small groups. It has a pale greyish-white throat and warm brown upperparts: inhabits forests of Uganda, western Kenya and western Tanzania. The Pale-breasted Illadopsis (*Malacocincla rufipennis*), 5½″, has a whitish throat and abdomen; rest of plumage tawny-brown. Found in forests of Uganda, western Kenya and north-eastern Tanzania. The Scaly-breasted Illadopsis (*Malacocincla albipectus*), 5½″, also has a white throat and belly, but pale chest feathers edged blackish giving a scaly appearance. Found in Uganda and western Kenya forests. The Grey-chested Illadopsis (*Malacocincla poliothorax*), 6½″, is a rufous-chestnut above, grey below. It occurs in the Kakamega Forest and Mount Elgon in western Kenya, and the Ruwenzori range and the highland forests of south-west Kigezi in Uganda.

ABYSSINIAN HILL BABBLER *Pseudoalcippe abyssinicus* p. 256
Identification: 5″. The Abyssinian Hill Babbler looks and behaves like
a large thickset warbler: back, wings and tail olive-rufous; head and
underparts grey. The southern Tanzania race has black streaks on the
throat; the western Uganda race has a black crown.
Voice: A clear two-note whistle, various clucking sounds and a melodious warbling song.
Distribution and Habitat: Widespread in East Africa, inhabiting mountain forest. It forages in the foliage of trees and amongst hanging
creepers.

Bulbuls: *Pycnonotidae*

The bulbuls are a group of thrush-like birds of plain green, yellow, grey
and brown plumage: tarsus very short; arboreal in habits and most
species are inhabitants of forest and woodland; food mainly fruits with
some insects; many species are outstanding songsters.

WHITE-EARED BULBUL *Pycnonotus dodsoni* p. 256
Identification: 6″. A drab-grey, white and blackish bulbul with yellow
under tail coverts and a conspicuous white patch on each side of the
neck below the ear coverts. The Dark-capped Bulbul (*188) is larger
and lacks the white neck patch.
Voice: A clear, liquid "tee, dee, doo, doo" and various other notes.
Distribution and Habitat: The dry bush country of eastern Kenya and
north-eastern Tanzania: a common species in the Tsavo National Park.

BRISTLE-BILL *Bleda syndactyla* p. 256
Identification: 8½″. An olive-green bulbul with bright yellow underparts, a chestnut-red tail and a bare blue patch around the eyes.
Voice: A monotonous "chr, chr, chr, chr" and a sharp "pritt-pritt."
Distribution and Habitat: Frequent in the Kakamega Forest, western
Kenya, and in Uganda. Inhabits the undergrowth and small trees in
dense forest.
Allied Species: The Green-tailed Bristle-bill (*Bleda eximia*), 7½″, has a
green tail with yellow tips to outer pairs tail feathers. It occurs in the
forests of western and southern Uganda. Other bulbuls with yellow
underparts are the Joyful Greenbul (*Chlorocichla laetissima*), 9″, with
green upperparts, wings and tail, and bright yellow below; found in

Plate 23 CHATS, ROBINS, THRUSHES

Plate 24 WARBLERS, APALIS, CISTICOLAS

forests of western Kenya and Uganda: and the Yellow-bellied Greenbul (*Chlorocichla flaviventris*), 8½″, deep olive-brown above, buffy-yellow below; widely distributed in Tanzania and eastern half of Kenya occurring in forests and coastal scrub. The smaller Xavier's Greenbul (*Phyllastrephus xavieri*), 6½″, is olive-green above with a rufous wash on the wings and tail: found locally in forests in western Uganda.

YELLOW-THROATED LEAF-LOVE *Pyrrhurus flavicollis* p. 256
Identification: 8½″. Above dark olive-grey; creamy-yellow throat; remainder underparts pale dull yellowish-olive.

Voice: Utters a scolding chatter and mewing calls.

Distribution and Habitat: Occurs locally in Uganda, western Kenya and western Tanzania. Frequents forest, secondary growth and gardens. A common bird at Entebbe, Uganda.

Allied Species: The White-tailed Greenbul (*Thescelocichla leucopleura*), 9″, differs from the Yellow-throated Leaf-love in having broad white tips to its outer pairs of tail feathers and a grey chest. It occurs in forests of western Uganda. The Honey-guide Greenbul (*Baeopogon indicator*), 7″, is olive with the outer tail feathers white. It inhabits forests in western Kenya and Uganda. The Leaf-love (*Pyrrhurus scandens*), 8″, is greyish brown with whitish underparts: wings and tail cinnamon-rufous. Inhabits forest tree-tops in Uganda and western Tanzania. The Spotted Greenbul (*Ixonotus guttatus*), 7″, is greenish-grey above and white below, with conspicuous white spots on upper-parts. Found in forests in western Uganda.

NORTHERN BROWNBUL *Phyllastrephus strepitans* p. 256
Identification: 6½″. A rather slim, russet-brown bulbul with dark rufous rump and upper tail coverts; below warm brown, whitish on throat and centre of belly; eyes red-brown.

Voice: A clear chattering call.

Distribution and Habitat: Wide ranging in drier areas of Kenya and eastern Tanzania. Inhabits bush country, riverine thickets and coastal scrub. Often in small parties: feeds near the ground.

Allied Species: The very similar Brownbul (*Phyllastrephus terrestris*), 7″, has olive-brown back, white throat, greyish chest and flanks, a creamy-white belly and yellow eyes. It is found in coastal areas of Kenya and in Tanzania. This also is a bird of thick scrub and bush. The Zanzibar Sombre Greenbul (*Andropadus importunus*), 7″, is a common bird of coastal scrub in Kenya and Tanzania. It is olive-green on upperparts, wings and tail, paler below and yellowish in centre of belly: eye creamy-white.

OLIVE-BREASTED MOUNTAIN GREENBUL

Arizelocichla tephrolaema p. 256

Identification: 7″. This is a green bulbul with a clear-grey head and throat and white eye-ring; yellowish in centre of belly.

Voice: Produces a variety of clucking notes and has a sustained thrush-like song.

Distribution and Habitat: Inhabits mountain and highland forest areas in Uganda and Kenya. Found in undergrowth, in the foliage of smaller trees and in creepers.

Allied Species: The similar Mountain Greenbul (*Arizelocichla nigriceps*), 7″, is found in mountain forest in Tanzania: the northern race, on Kilimanjaro and Meru, has a blackish crown: other races possess dark grey crowns and are best distinguished from Olive-breasted Mountain Greenbul by lack of yellow in centre of belly.

Flycatchers: *Muscicapidae*

This is a large family of small or medium-sized birds, usually with flattened bills and well-developed bristles at gape: immature plumages spotted. Many species perch upright on some vantage point, such as a dead branch or wire fence, from which short erratic flights are made after their insect prey. Some other species hunt insect food amongst foliage in manner of warblers.

LITTLE GREY FLYCATCHER *Bradornis pumilus* p. 257

Identification: 4½″. A pale grey flycatcher with a white throat and belly and indistinct dark streaks on crown. Upright stance, usually perches on branch of acacia bush. The Grey Flycatcher (*191) is darker and slightly larger, 5″.

Voice: Usually silent but sometimes utters a weak chirp.

Distribution and Habitat: Locally common in dry bush country of eastern Uganda and in Kenya west of the Rift Valley. A bird of semi-desert acacia bush: common in Turkana, Kenya.

BANDED TIT-FLYCATCHER *Parisoma bohmi* p. 257

Identification: 4½″. A rather plump little bird, tit or warbler-like in its habits: upperparts grey; tail blackish, edged white on outer feathers;

Plate 25 WARBLERS, CUCKOO SHRIKE, HELMET SHRIKE, DRONGO

1 **STOUT CISTICOLA** page 294
Thickset; heavily streaked on back; crown rufous.

2 **TINKLING CISTICOLA** page 294
Slim; very heavily streaked on back; crown and wing edging bright rufous.

3 **WHITE-CHINNED PRINIA** page 295
Conspicuous white throat.

4 **BLACK-FACED RUFOUS WARBLER** page 295
Face, throat and chest black.

5 **BANDED PRINIA** page 295
Barred flanks; white spotted wings.

6 **MOUSTACHE WARBLER** page 295
Black malar stripe.

7 **BLUE SWALLOW** page 296
Uniform blue-black; long outer tail feathers.

8 **PETIT'S CUCKOO SHRIKE** page 297
Sexes dissimilar; yellow gape wattles; underparts ♀ bright yellow with little barring.

9 **RED-BILLED SHRIKE** page 298
Pale blue-grey head; rufous breast.

10 **VELVET-MANTLED DRONGO** page 297
Tail long and forked; back velvety black, not glossy.

Plate 26 SHRIKES, RAVEN

1 **SOUZA'S SHRIKE**   page 298
Barred brown mantle with white **V.**

2 **YELLOW-BILLED SHRIKE**   page 299
Clear yellow bill; rufous wing patch.

3 **WHITE-WINGED BABBLING STARLING**   page 306
White wing patch; black throat stripe.

4 **BROAD-RINGED WHITE-EYE**   page 309
Large white eye-ring; no yellow on forehead.

5 **RED-NAPED BUSH SHRIKE**   page 299
Bright red patch on hind crown and nape.

6 **LUHDER'S BUSH SHRIKE**   page 299
Chestnut crown; throat and breast orange-rufous.

7 **ZANZIBAR PUFF-BACK SHRIKE**   page 300
Wings not edged white.

8 **BLACK-FRONTED BUSH SHRIKE**   page 301
Black forehead; underparts variable—orange, red, pinkish-buff
or greenish.

9 **THREE-STREAKED BUSH SHRIKE**   page 300
Black streak down centre of crown and black streaks over eye.

10 **NICATOR**   page 301
Yellow spots on wings.

11 **DWARF RAVEN**   page 303
Tail extends beyond wing tips.

note: not drawn to scale

below white with indistinct dark spotting on throat and black band across chest; flanks tawny; eye yellow.

Voice: A short trilling song, often repeated, and loud double-note call "tik-wirra, tik-wirra."

Distribution and Habitat: Northern and eastern Kenya, south to central Tanzania. Found in acacia woodland and bush in drier areas.

Allied Species: The Grey Tit-Flycatcher (*Parisoma plumbeum*), $4\frac{1}{2}''$, lacks the black chest-band and tawny flanks and has the outer tail feathers white: it resembles the Ashy Flycatcher (*191) except for its white outer tail feathers. It has a wide range in East Africa occurring in wooded country and bush. The Brown Tit-Flycatcher (*Parisoma lugens*), $4\frac{1}{2}''$, is a dark smoky-brown, warbler-like bird with a whitish belly; outermost tail feathers edged and tipped with white. Occurs locally in Kenya and Tanzania, favouring acacia woodland and savannah woodland. Boehm's Flycatcher (*Myopornis bohmi*), $4\frac{1}{2}''$, is brown, streaked with blackish above; below, white with wedge-shaped blackish spotting on chest and flanks. It occurs in western and southern Tanzania.

YELLOW FLYCATCHER *Chloropeta natalensis* p. 257

Identification: 5″. A yellow-breasted, green flycatcher of warbler-like habits: broad bill; crown olive-brown.

Voice: A warbling trill: also utters a harsh churr.

Distribution and Habitat: Widely distributed but local over much of East Africa. Inhabits thick bushy areas and swampy places, often at the edge of forests. Keeps low down in thick cover.

Allied Species: The Mountain Yellow Flycatcher (*Chloropeta similis*), 5″, is uniformly green above without a darker crown. It is found in thick undergrowth at the edges of mountain forest in East Africa. The Little Yellow Flycatcher (*Chloropetella holochlora*), $3\frac{1}{2}''$, is a tiny yellow flycatcher, greenish on upperparts, which looks and behaves like a white-eye. Occurs in coastal forests of Kenya and Tanzania.

CHESTNUT-CAP FLYCATCHER *Erythrocercus mccallii* p. 257

Identification: $3\frac{1}{2}''$. An olive-brown flycatcher with a bright chestnut tail, which is constantly fanned; crown chestnut with white streaks; below, rufous-buff to buffish-white on abdomen.

Voice: A high-pitched "tsssp."

Distribution and Habitat: A forest species found in western Uganda. Frequents the foliage of medium-sized trees, often in small parties.

Allied Species: Livingstone's Flycatcher (*Erythrocercus livingstonei*),

$3\frac{1}{2}''$, has a bright chestnut-red tail with a black sub-terminal band, again constantly fanned; upperparts green; below, yellowish-green. Occurs locally in southern Tanzania in woodland and scrub: usually in small parties.

RUFOUS FLYCATCHER   *Stizorhina fraseri*   p. 257

Identification: 7″. General colour chestnut-brown, brighter on wings and tail. Not unlike a smaller edition of the Red-tailed Ant Thrush (p. 000) but tail shorter and bill wider and shorter.

Voice: A three-note whistle.

Distribution and Habitat: A local bird in forests of western and southern Uganda. Frequents forest tree-tops where it searches for insect prey among foliage like a puff-backed shrike.

Allied Species: The Shrike Flycatcher (*Megabyas flammulatus*), $6\frac{1}{2}''$, is found in the Kakamega Forest, western Kenya and in forests of western and southern Uganda. Male black above with pure white rump and underparts; female is earth-brown above, below white streaked brown. When perched both sexes wag the tail slowly up and down. The Black and White Flycatcher (*Bias musicus*), 6″, has black upperparts and chest in the male; belly white. The female is cinnamon-rufous with white and tawny underparts. Found in forests of Uganda, Kenya and eastern Tanzania.

YELLOW-BELLIED FLYCATCHER   *Hyliota flavigaster*   p. 257

Identification: $4\frac{1}{2}''$. An iridescent blue-black flycatcher with a white wing-stripe and bright tawny-yellow underparts. Female grey above.

Voice: A tit-like double whistle.

Distribution and Habitat: Widespread in East Africa but everywhere uncommon and local. Found in wooded and lightly forested areas where it frequents foliage of trees, hunting insects in the manner of a tit or warbler.

Allied Species: The Southern Yellow-bellied Flycatcher (*Hyliota australis*), $4\frac{1}{2}''$, is dull velvety-black above, not blue-black; female brownish-grey above. Occurs in western Uganda, western Kenya, and Tanzania. Inhabits woodland tree-tops.

PYGMY PUFF-BACK FLYCATCHER   *Batis perkeo*   p. 257

Identification: 3″. The smallest of the puff-back flycatchers, a group characterised by black and white plumage; male with grey crown and narrow black chest-band; female has tawny chest-band.

Voice: Various "peeps" and a harsh "churr."

Distribution and Habitat: Northern districts of Kenya, including Turkana. Inhabits arid acacia country; most in evidence in acacia trees bordering dry watercourses.

Allied Species: In the Ruwenzori Puff-back Flycatcher (*Batis diops*), 4½″, the sexes are alike, both male and female having a very broad black chest-band. This species occurs in mountain forest of western and south-western Uganda. The Grey-headed Puff-back Flycatcher (*Batis orientalis*), 4″, resembles a larger edition of the Pygmy Puff-back Flycatcher but female has a chestnut, not a tawny breast-band. It occurs in extreme northern Kenya in bush country. The Black-headed Puff-back Flycatcher (*Batis minor*), 4″, has the crown black, not grey; female with dark chestnut breast-band. Occurs in coastal areas of Kenya and Tanzania. The Puff-back Flycatcher (*Batis capensis*), 4½″, has a grey crown, a black stripe through the eye and a wide black breast-band; female has throat and chest rich rufous-brown. Occurs in eastern districts of Kenya and Tanzania in wooded areas.

JAMESON'S WATTLE-EYE   *Dyaphorophyia jamesoni*   p. 257

Identification: 3″. A plump very short-tailed flycatcher, glossy greenish-black above and on throat and chest; chestnut patch on each side of neck; belly pure white; large turquoise-blue eye wattles. Female slightly greyer on upperparts.

Voice: A sharp "brrrp" and various clicking sounds.

Distribution and Habitat: Forests of western Kenya and Uganda. Inhabits dense undergrowth; shy and not often seen, but draws attention to its presence by the sharp "brrrp" it produces.

Allied Species: The Yellow-bellied Wattle-eye (*Dyaphorophyia concreta*) 3¾″, is olive-green above with a chestnut-yellow belly; eye wattle bright green. Found in forest undergrowth in western Kenya, western Uganda and the Kungwe-Mahare Mountains, western Tanzania.

CRESTED FLYCATCHER   *Trochocercus cyanomelas*   p. 257

Identification: 4½″. The crested flycatchers draw attention to themselves by their restless behaviour, constantly flitting about and fanning and closing their tails: in colour they are various combinations of black, grey and white; heads crested. The present species has the head and chest blue-black, the mantle bluish-slate; narrow white bands on wing; breast and abdomen white; no white on tail. Female duller and greyer.

Voice: Rasping "zeet-zeet."

Distribution and Habitat: Local but widespread in East Africa. Inhabits thick cover in forests, woodland and dense coastal thickets.

Allied Species: The White-tailed Crested Flycatcher (*Trochocercus albonotatus*), 4″, has a black head and crest and broad white tips to the tail feathers. It inhabits forested areas in western Kenya, Uganda and Tanzania. The Blue-headed Crested Flycatcher (*Trochocercus nitens*), 4½″, has the upperparts, head and chest glossy blue-black; breast and abdomen grey; tail dark. It frequents the forests of western and southern Uganda. The Dusky Crested Flycatcher (*Trochocercus nigromitratus*), 3½″, is pale slate-grey with crown and crest dull black. It occurs in the Kakamega Forest, western Kenya and in forests in Uganda.

Thrushes, Wheatears, Chats and allies: *Turdidae*

A group of rather long-legged birds of upright stance: eyes inclined to be large and bills usually pointed and relatively slender: juvenile plumages spotted. Most species spend much time on the ground and feed mainly upon insects.

AFRICAN THRUSH   *Turdus pelios*   p. 272

Identification: 9″. A pale, washed-out-looking thrush, brownish-grey above with a pale ashy-grey chest; throat streaked ash-brown; breast and abdomen whitish, tinged cinnamon-buff on flanks. In general appearance very like Kurrichane Thrush (*196) but grey on chest, not palebuff.

Voice: A clear, loud, typical thrush song, and a two-note whistle.

Distribution and Habitat: Widespread in Uganda, Tanzania and western Kenya. Inhabits forested and wooded areas, and in Uganda often seen in gardens.

Allied Species: The Red-tailed Ant-Thrush (*Neocossyphus rufus*), 8″, is dark rufous-brown above, paler on the rump, tail, wings and underparts: tail relatively long. Occurs locally in western Uganda, eastern Kenya and north-eastern Tanzania, including Zanzibar: frequents coastal scrub and forest.

ABYSSINIAN GROUND THRUSH   *Geokichla piaggiae*   p. 272

Identification: 7½″. A stocky orange-rufous thrush with forehead orange-brown; white ring around eye and white spots on wings; belly white.

Voice: A three or four-note liquid whistle, and a more prolonged song.

Distribution and Habitat: Highland forest of Kenya, Uganda and northern Tanzania. Inhabits mountain forest, especially where inter-mixed with bamboo. Feeds mainly on ground.

Allied Species: The Orange Ground Thrush (*Geokichla gurneyi*), $7\frac{1}{2}''$, is a less rufous bird being olive-brown on upperparts and crown; white eye-ring incomplete; below bright orange-rufous, white in centre of abdomen. Found in mountain forest in northern and eastern Tanzania and on Teita and Chyulu Hills and Mount Kenya in Kenya.

HILL or MOUNTAIN CHAT   *Pinarochroa sordida*   p. 272

Identification: $6\frac{1}{2}''$. A stocky, English Robin-like bird, dull greyish-brown, paler on the belly; tail feathers mainly white.

Voice: Various soft metallic calls, but usually silent.

Distribution and Habitat: Alpine zone of mountains in Kenya and northern Tanzania (Mount Kilimanjaro and Mount Olimoti). In-habits alpine meadows and scrub: very tame and fearless little bird.

CLIFF CHAT   *Thamnolea cinnamomeiventris*   p. 272

Identification: $7''$. Male a striking bird, upperparts, head, wings, tail and chest glossy black; white wing shoulders; chestnut-red rump and belly; female is grey above and on chest and lacks white wing shoulders.

Voice: A clear double whistle and a warbling song.

Distribution and Habitat: Widespread in East Africa but very local. Confined to rocky cliffs and hills, hillsides with rocky outcrops, quarries and ruins. Usually in pairs.

BLUE-SHOULDERED ROBIN CHAT
Cossypha cyanocampter   p. 272

Identification: $6\frac{1}{2}''$. Thrush-like, but smaller and with relatively long tail. Upperparts black on crown to dark slate on mantle; wings blackish with clear blue shoulders; white stripe over eye; below orange buff; tail rufous with blackish central feathers.

Voice: A sustained warbling song of high quality: clucking notes.

Distribution and Habitat: Forests of western Kenya and Uganda. Inhabits undergrowth of forests and thick cover along rivers.

Allied Species: The Grey-winged Robin Chat (*Cossypha polioptera*), $6''$, has a grey crown, a black eye-stripe and a white stripe above eye; back olive-brown; rump, tail and underparts rufous; wings grey to olive-brown. Occurs in thick cover, usually in forest undergrowth, in western Kenya, Uganda and north-western Tanzania.

EQUATORIAL AKALAT *Sheppardia aequatorialis* p. 272
Identification: 5″. A plump, English Robin-like bird, olive-brown above with russet-brown rump and tail; below bright orange-brown on throat, chest and flanks, whitish in centre of belly.
Voice: A series of croaking calls.
Distribution and Habitat: Found in Uganda and western Kenya. Inhabits the undergrowth of forests: shy and not often seen although not uncommon.
Allied Species: The Akalat (*Sheppardia cyornithopsis*), 5″, is a much rarer bird, found in western Uganda forests. It differs from the Equatorial Akalat in having orange-brown confined to chest; flanks pale olive-brown to grey, belly white; under tail coverts white. The East Coast Akalat (*Sheppardia gunningi*), 4½″, is bright yellowish-buff below and has slate-coloured wings. It occurs in coastal forests of Kenya and Tanzania. Sharpe's Akalat (*Sheppardia sharpei*), 4½-5″, is olivaceous-buff on throat, breast and flanks and wings are olive-brown. It occurs in mountain forests in eastern Tanzania.

FOREST ROBIN *Stiphrornis erythrothorax* p. 272
Identification: 4″. Another small robin-like bird, olive-brown above with russet tail; throat, chest and breast brilliant chrome-orange, belly white.
Voice: Usually a croaking churr, but also produces a clear, soft warbling song.
Distribution and Habitat: Widespread and locally not uncommon in forests of Uganda, but very shy and not often observed. Inhabits dense cover of forest undergrowth.

BROWN-CHESTED ALETHE *Alethe poliocephala* p. 272
Identification: 6″. Alethes are long-legged, thrush-like birds which inhabit forest undergrowth: they are most in evidence in the vicinity of safari ant parties, preying on the insects disturbed by the ants. The present species is warm russet-brown above, with a whitish stripe from bill to above eye; below, throat white, chest buff, paler on flanks.
Voice: A repeated two or three-note whistle.
Distribution and Habitat: Widespread in Uganda, westwards to Mount Kenya, Kenya and in western and south-western Tanzania. Inhabits high-level and mountain forest: shy and elusive.
Allied Species: The Firecrest Alethe (*Alethe castanea*), 6½-7″, is warm dark-brown above with a tawny-orange streak down centre of crown; below white, greyish on chest and flanks. Occurs in the forests of

Plate 27 TITS, WEAVERS SILVER-BILLS

1 **RED-THROATED TIT**   page 302
   Rufous collar on hind neck.

2 **MOUSE-COLOURED PENDULINE TIT**   page 302
   Buffy-white underparts; sharp tapering bill.

3 **GREEN HYLIA**   page 320
   Greenish-yellow eye stripe.

4 **BLACK-CAPPED SOCIAL WEAVER**   page 321
   Black crown; greenish-white bill.

5 **RUFOUS SPARROW**   page 322
   Whitish cheeks; black stripe through eye.

6 **YELLOW-SPOTTED PETRONIA**   page 323
   Pale yellow spot on throat; narrow white eye ring.

7 **SPECKLE-FRONTED WEAVER**   page 323
   Crown black speckled with white; rufous hind neck.

8 **GREY-HEADED SILVER-BILL**   page 331
   White rump; pinkish-brown back.

9 **SILVER-BILL**   page 331
   Black tail and flight feathers.

10 **BLACK AND WHITE MANNIKIN**   page 331
   Black back and head.

11 **QUAIL FINCH**   page 335
   Very short tail; inhabits open plains perching on ground.

Plate 28 WAXBILLS, CANARIES

western and southern Uganda. The Red-throated Alethe (*Alethe poliophrys*), 6½″, may be distinguished by its deep rufous throat patch. It occurs in the mountain forests of western Uganda. The White-chested Alethe (*Alethe fulleborni*), 7½″, is a stocky species, russet-brown above, with pure white underparts and a russet-olive patch on each side of the chest. It occurs in mountain forest in north-eastern, eastern and southern Tanzania.

EASTERN BEARDED SCRUB ROBIN

Erythropygia quadrivirgata   p. 272

Identification: 6½″. Upperparts rufous-brown; black streak on each side of the crown, immediately above white eye-stripe; tail black with white tips; below white, tawny-buff on chest and flanks.

Voice: Utters loud clear whistles; also a sustained warbling song.

Distribution and Habitat: Widespread in eastern districts of Kenya and Tanzania, including Zanzibar. Inhabits coastal scrub and bush: shy and elusive.

Allied Species: The closely related Bearded Scrub Robin (*Erythropygia barbata*), 6½″, differs in having paler streaks on sides of crown and white outer tail feathers. It occurs in south-western Tanzania, frequenting thick cover in scrub and riverine forest.

WHITE-THROATED ROBIN   *Irania gutturalis* (M)   p. 272

Identification: 6½″. Slim build, resembling a robin chat but with a black tail. Upperparts grey; white stripe over eye; sides of face and neck black with a white stripe down centre of throat; breast and flanks rufous; belly white.

Voice: Mainly silent in winter quarters.

Distribution and Habitat: Winter visitor to Kenya and northern half of Tanzania. Inhabits dense scrub along dry river beds in arid bush country: shy and skulking, but comes out of cover in late evening.

Allied Species: The European Nightingale (*Luscinia megarhynchos*), 6½″, is warm-brown, underparts whitish-brown; brownish-chestnut tail. It is a winter visitor to East Africa as far south as north-eastern Tanzania: shy and skulking, keeps to thick cover in bush country. The Sprosser (*Luscinia luscinia*), 6½″, is another winter visitor, extending throughout East Africa. It differs from the Nightingale in being darker, more olive-brown in general colour with a brownish-mottled breast. It inhabits dense thickets, both in dry bush country and in the vicinity of swamps and marshes.

Warblers: *Sylviidae*

A large family of small, active insectivorous birds of slim build: related to thrushes and flycatchers but bills slender and juvenile plumages unspotted. Many species, especially among the "leaf warblers," *Phylloscopus*, and the Cisticola Warblers, *Cisticola*, lack distinctive markings and may appear confusingly alike. Voice, behaviour, habitat and distribution are important in their identification.

GREATER SWAMP WARBLER *Calamocichla gracilirostris* p. 273
    Identification: 6½". A uniformly warm olive-brown warbler with a graduated tail; gape, deep orange. Found only in papyrus and reed beds by or over water.
    Voice: Various loud chattering and scolding calls—a very vocal bird. A clear warbling song.
    Distribution and Habitat: Widespread in Uganda, Kenya and western and northern Tanzania. Inhabits dense reed and papyrus beds, drawing attention to its presence by constant calls and song. Especially abundant at Lake Naivasha, Kenya.
    Allied Species: The Lesser Swamp Warbler (*Calamocichla leptorhyncha*), 5½", is more russet-brown on the back and whiter below. It has a wide range in East Africa, in reed and papyrus beds, but is usually a less common and more skulking species than the Greater Swamp Warbler. Fox's Swamp Warbler (*Calamocichla foxi*), 7", is dark earth-brown above, greyish on the throat, chest and flanks, whitish on belly. Best recognised by large size and dark colour. Occurs in reed-beds around lakes in south-western Uganda. The Yellow Swamp Warbler (*Calamonastides gracilirostris*), 5½", is olive-green above with a russet rump; below, yellow with brownish flanks. It occurs in swamps around Lake George in western Uganda. The African Reed Warbler (*Acrocephalus baeticatus*), 4½", is pale-brown above with buff underparts, white in centre of belly. Found locally in East Africa: in addition to swamps also occurs in thick bush and scrub, gardens, mangrove swamps and coastal thickets.

    Among European migrants found in winter in East Africa are the following. The Great Reed Warbler (*Acrocephalus arundinaceus*), 7½", with uniform russet-brown upperparts, long stout bill, and usually a bold eye-stripe. The European Reed Warbler (*Acrocephalus scirpaceus*), 5" with uniform russet-brown upperparts, clear buffish-

Plate 29 STARLINGS, SUNBIRDS

1 **GREY-CHINNED SUNBIRD**   page 318
Grey chin; short bill.

2 **KENYA VIOLET-BACKED SUNBIRD**   page 319
White breast; violet-blue tail.

3 **ANCHIETA'S SUNBIRD**   page 319
Scarlet breast stripe; brown upperparts.

4 **AMANI SUNBIRD**   page 320
White belly; dark throat.

5 **ORANGE-TUFTED SUNBIRD**   page 314
Maroon chest band; brown belly; orange pectoral tufts.

6 **MAGPIE STARLING**   page 306
Orange-red eyes; inhabits arid bush country.

7 **ABBOT'S STARLING**   page 306
Yellow eye; inhabits mountain forest.

8 **GREY-HEADED SUNBIRD**   page 320
Grey head; orange pectoral tufts.

9 **PURPLE-HEADED STARLING**   page 307
Velvety crown feathers; inhabits forest treetops.

10 **BLACK BREASTED GLOSSY STARLING**   page 307
Dark oily green plumage; black belly.

11 **FISCHER'S STARLING**   page 309
Grey chest; white belly.

12 **PURPLE GLOSSY STARLING**   page 307
Conspicuous large yellow eyes.

13 **ASHY STARLING**   page 308
Long tail; ash-brown plumage.

14 **SLENDER BILLED CHESTNUT-WING STARLING**   page 308
Thin bill; chestnut flight feathers.

15 **BRONZE-TAILED STARLING**   page 306
Central tail feathers with bronze sheen.

16 **BRISTLE-CROWNED STARLING**   page 308
Cushion of velvety feathers on forehead; long tail.

Plate 30 SUNBIRDS

white underparts and whitish ring around eye. The European Marsh Warbler (*Acrocephalus palustris*), 5″, difficult to distinguish from European Reed Warbler, but upperparts and rump more olive than russet. The European Sedge Warbler (*Acrocephalus schoenobaenus*), 5″, with conspicuous cream-coloured eye-stripe and boldly streaked upperparts. The European Whitethroat (*Sylvia communis*), 5½″, is rusty-brown above with pinkish-buff underparts and a pure white throat; crown pale grey in male; female duller, brownish on head. The Barred Warbler (*Sylvia nisoria*), 6″, ashy-brown above, white below with dark crescent-shaped barring. The Olive-tree Warbler (*Hippolais olivetorum*), 6″, has no outstanding field mark—a greyish-brown warbler with a slight olivaceous wash, below whitish with yellowish-buff tinge on breast; legs dull blue-grey. Common in arid bush country of northern Kenya in winter.

RED-FACED WOODLAND WARBLER   *Seicercus laetus*   p. 273
Identification: 3½″. A small "leaf warbler" with bright green upperparts, wings and tail; forehead, stripe over eye, face and throat rufous-buff; belly white.
Voice: A low warbling song; a double-note call "tssp-tssp."
Distribution and Habitat: Mountain forest in western and south-western Uganda. Active little birds, often in small parties, in foliage of forest trees and in bamboo.
Allied Species: The Yellow-throated Woodland Warbler (*Seicercus ruficapillus*), 4″, has a russet-olive head and green back; below, throat bright greenish-yellow; grey on chest and flanks; belly creamy-white. It occurs in forest on the Teita Hills, south-eastern Kenya and in mountain forests in Tanzania. The Uganda Woodland Warbler (*Seicercus budongoensis*), 4″, has green upperparts and a white stripe over the eye above a blackish stripe through eye; below white, tinged greenish on flanks. Found in forests of Uganda and western Kenya.

BARRED WREN-WARBLER   *Calamonastes fasciolatus*   p. 273
Identification: 5″. An olivaceous-brown, dark-tailed warbler with underparts barred black and white. Tail often fanned up and down.
Voice: A Camaroptera-like "pleet-pleet" and a loud trilling song.
Distribution and Habitat: Southern Tanzania. Usually found in bush and undergrowth in brachystegia woodland; in pairs or small parties.

FAN-TAILED WARBLER   *Schoenicola brevirostris*   p. 273
  Identification: 6½″, tail 3½″. A small russet-brown warbler with buffy-white underparts and a long and very broad black tail.
  Voice: A loud "whist-whist-r, r, r, r, r"; also a shrill piping call.
  Distribution and Habitat: Widespread but very local in East Africa. Inhabits areas of lush tall grasslands and bush-grasslands, frequenting marshy hollows and vegetation along streams, and also in long grass away from water: tail very conspicuous in field.

GREY APALIS   *Apalis cinerea*   p. 273
  Identification: 5″. The Apalis group of warblers are slim with long graduated tails: most are forest or woodland dwellers which obtain their insect food in either the tree-tops or the undergrowth. The Grey Apalis is grey above with an indistinct brownish crown; below, creamy-white; outer three pairs tail feathers white.
  Voice: "Peek-it peek-it" repeated constantly.
  Distribution and Habitat: Mountain forests of Uganda, western and central Kenya and north-eastern Tanzania. Usually in pairs in tree-tops but sometimes found in undergrowth.
  Allied Species: The Brown-headed Apalis (*Apalis alticola*), 5″, has a much browner head and white-tipped grey outer tail feathers. Occurs in mountain forest in north-eastern to south-western Tanzania.

BLACK-HEADED APALIS   *Apalis melanocephala*   p. 273
  Identification: 5-5½″. Upperparts dusky-grey to blackish-brown with black or dark brown crown; below, creamy-white; tail grey with whitish tips.
  Voice: A sharp "territ-territ," often repeated, and a brief trill.
  Distribution and Habitat: Occurs in both mountain and coastal forests in central and southern Kenya and in Tanzania. Frequents both tree-tops and undergrowth; often in small groups, or members of mixed bird parties.

BLACK-BACKED APALIS   *Apalis rufogularis*   p. 273
  Identification: 4½-5″. Adult male has upperparts blackish-brown; below, creamy-white; outer four pairs tail feathers white. Female uniform dark-grey above; below, greyish-white, throat and chest orange-buff; four pairs outer tail feathers white. In several books of reference dealing with East African birds, the male and female of this apalis have been incorrectly designated as separate species, the male being called *Apalis nigrescens,* and the female *Apalis rufogularis.*

Voice: A clear, two-note "tssp-ee, tssp-ee."

Distribution and Habitat: Forests of western Kenya and Uganda. A local and uncommon little bird found mainly in the tree-tops.

Allied Species: The Collared Apalis (*Apalis ruwenzorii*), 4", has pale grey upperparts; below, rufous-buff on throat, breast and flanks and a grey chest-band. Found in mountain forests of western and south-western Uganda. The Green-tailed Apalis (*Apalis caniceps*), 4", is green-backed with a grey crown; wings and tail green; below, white with broad, greenish-yellow chest patch. Occurs in woodland and savannah country in Uganda, western and eastern Kenya and eastern and southern Tanzania. Often in small flocks in woodland trees, behaving like White-eyes. The Masked Apalis (*Apalis binotata*), 4", is green above, with green wings and tail; grey crown and face; throat and chest black with a white patch on each side of the neck; breast and abdomen white, greenish on flanks. A forest species found both in the tree-tops and in the undergrowth: occurs locally in Uganda and on Mount Elgon, western Kenya. The Black-capped Apalis (*Apalis nigriceps*), 4", is one of the most beautiful African warblers: above, bright green with a jet black crown and face and a pure yellow nape collar; below, white with a black crescent on the lower throat. A forest tree-tops species found in western and southern Uganda.

CHESTNUT-THROATED APALIS *Apalis porphyrolaema* p. 273

Identification: 5". Upperparts, wings and tail ash-grey; pale tips to tail feathers; below, grey on lower throat, breast and flanks; white in centre of abdomen; chestnut-red patch on chin and upper throat.

Voice: A single "tssp" note.

Distribution and Habitat: Highland forest in western and south-western Uganda, western and central Kenya and north-eastern Tanzania.

RED-FACED APALIS   *Apalis rufifrons*   p. 273

Identification: 4½". A pale ash-brown Apalis with a black, white-tipped tail; forehead rufous; below, white with buff-tinged flanks and sometimes indistinct blackish mottling on chest. Cocks its tail up at right angles and also waves it from side to side.

Voice: A clear, chirping song.

Distribution and Habitat: Northern and eastern Kenya, and north-eastern Tanzania. A bird of desert-bush and scrub country: usually in pairs, low down in bushes. Their tails are always in motion.

WHITE-BROWED CROMBEC *Sylvietta leucophrys* p. 273
Identification: 3″. The crombecs are plump little warblers with such short tails that they appear almost tail-less in the field. The present species has a green back, wings and tail; crown and stripe through eye russet-brown; a broad white streak above eye; below greyish-white; under tail coverts greenish-yellow.
Voice: A brief soft trill.
Distribution and Habitat: Mountain and high level forest in central and western Kenya, Uganda and western Tanzania. Frequents dense undergrowth of forest and margins of forest; white eye-stripe very conspicuous in field.
Allied Species: The Green Crombec (*Sylvietta virens*), 3″, is a dull, dark greenish-grey species with greyish-white underparts, washed brownish-buff on throat and chest. Occurs locally in undergrowth of forests in Uganda and of Kakamega Forest, western Kenya. In some ways resembles a Grey-backed Camaroptera (*210) but has very much shorter tail.

WING-SNAPPING CISTICOLA *Cisticola ayresii* p. 273
Identification: 3″. A tiny, stumpy-tailed Cisticola with heavily streaked crown and upperparts; below, whitish with a slight tawny wash. Differs from the Pectoral-patch Cisticola in lacking dusky streaks on each side of chest. In Kenya a bird of highland grasslands, usually over 7,000 feet. At lower altitudes elsewhere.
Voice: Indulges in display flight over nesting grounds during which utters shrill whistling song accompanied by loud wing-snapping.
Distribution and Habitat: Locally distributed in the highlands of Kenya, southern, western and south-western Uganda and southern Tanzania. Inhabits open grasslands.

HUNTER'S CISTICOLA *Cisticola hunteri* p. 273
Identification: 5½″. A dark-looking cisticola found in highland areas, over 6,000 feet, which draws attention to itself by its habit of dueting. Two, three or more birds will gather together and start singing in duet. Upperparts dark brown, slightly russet on the head, with ill-defined streaking; below grey, paler on the throat.
Voice: The species sings in duet, a loud, clear, babbling warble.
Distribution and Habitat: Found in localities over 6,000 feet in the Kenya highlands, on Mount Elgon in Uganda and in northern Tanzania. Inhabits scrub and bush, often along forest margins: occurs up to at least 13,000 feet.

Allied Species: Chubb's Cisticola (*Cisticola chubbi*), 5½", resembles
Hunter's Cisticola and also indulges in dueting: it differs in having
plain upperparts without streaking and a russet cap. Occurs in western
Kenya, Uganda and north-western Tanzania. Inhabits forest glades
and margins, and thick vegetation along streams and rivers.

STOUT CISTICOLA   *Cisticola robusta*   p. 276
Identification: 4½-5½": Male larger than female. A rather thickset
cisticola with brownish-grey mantle and rufous crown, both heavily
streaked with black; below, buffy-white. Heavy streaking and rufous
crown conspicuous in field.
Voice: A distinctive piping whistle.
Distribution and Habitat: Widely distributed though local in many
areas of East Africa; less common in Tanzania where found in north-
east, north-west and south-west. Inhabits mixed grass-bush country;
sometimes in lush cover at the edge of marshes and swamps.
Allied Species: The Winding Cisticola (*Cisticola galactotes*), 5", is also
heavily streaked above and has a rufous crown, but is a slimmer bird
with much rufous edging in the wing feathers. It is wide-ranging and
common in East Africa: frequents swamps, marshes, lush grasslands
and grassland-bush. The Croaking Cisticola (*Cisticola natalensis*),
5-5½", is also streaked above and on the crown, but does not have a
rufous cap. Found locally in grasslands and mixed grass-bush over
much of East Africa.

TINKLING CISTICOLA   *Cisticola tinniens*   p. 276
Identification: 5½". A rather slim cisticola with a relatively long tail:
above, very heavily and broadly streaked black so that mantle often
appears blackish; crown, edges of wing feathers and edges of blackish
tail feathers bright rufous; below, buffy-white.
Voice: A far-carrying, tinkling whistle.
Distribution and Habitat: Found in the central highlands of Kenya,
where it inhabits the rank vegetation at the margins of swamps, dams
and streams.
Allied Species: The Ashy Cisticola (*Cisticola cinereola*), 5½", is a rather
pale grey cisticola with narrow dark streaking on crown and upperparts: below, creamy-white. Found in dry bush country and dry bush-
grass in eastern and southern Kenya and in north-eastern Tanzania.
The Tiny Cisticola (*Cisticola nana*), 3½", is a short-tailed species, greyish-
brown above without streaking, and with a rufous crown; below,
pale buff. Inhabits mixed grass and bush and savannah in eastern

Kenya and in northern and central Tanzania. The Foxy Cisticola (*Cisticola troglodytes*), 4″, is uniform bright rufous-brown above, buff below. Found in mixed bush and grass in north-western Kenya and in northern Uganda.

WHITE-CHINNED PRINIA *Prinia leucopogon* p. 276
Identification: 5½″. A grey warbler with a long slender tail, white or buffy-white throat and buff abdomen.
Voice: A sharp two-note call; also has a quavering, warbling song.
Distribution and Habitat: Forest areas and adjacent secondary growth in Uganda, western Kenya and north-western Tanzania. In pairs or small parties in dense undergrowth or other lush vegetation at forest margins and in neglected cultivation. Male often raises tail high over back; white chin conspicuous in field.

BANDED PRINIA *Prinia bairdii* p. 276
Identification: 4½″. Upperparts, wings and tail brownish-black, wings spotted and tail tipped with white; below, throat black, chest and flanks boldly barred black and white; abdomen white; eye yellow.
Voice: A shrill, rapid "plee-plee-plee-plee."
Distribution and Habitat: A local and generally uncommon forest bird found in western Kenya and in Uganda. Inhabits dense forest undergrowth, often feeding on or just above the ground.

MOUSTACHE WARBLER *Melocichla mentalis* p. 276
Identification: 7-7½″. A very large, heavy-looking bird for a warbler: at first sight may be mistaken for a bulbul. Upperparts warm dark brown; forehead and ear coverts chestnut-brown; white stripe over eye: cheeks and throat white with a distinct black malar stripe; breast to under tail coverts pale russet-brown.
Voice: A rasping "te-te-te-te" and a rapid, warbling song.
Distribution and Habitat: Widespread but local, Uganda, western, central and southern Kenya and Tanzania. Inhabits rank grass and mixed grass and bush.

BLACK-FACED RUFOUS WARBLER
Bathmocercus rufus p. 276
Identification: 5″. Male has upperparts, wings, tail and sides of breast bright foxy-red; forehead, face, throat, chest and streak down breast,

black; abdomen grey. The female resembles the male but is olivaceous-grey instead of foxy-red.

Voice: A constant "tss-pt, tss-pt, tss-pt."

Distribution and Habitat: Forests of Uganda and western Kenya. Usually in pairs; frequents dense forest undergrowth.

Swallows and Martins: *Hirundinidae*

Swallows and their allies are a well-marked group of birds which capture their insect food on the wing. They bear a superficial resemblance to swifts, but wing formation differs in being less slender and scythe-like. Build slim and flight graceful, less direct and rapid than swifts. Many species possess long and slender outer tail feathers; feet very small; bill short with wide gape.

BLUE SWALLOW *Hirundo atrocaerulea* p. 276

Identification: 8″, outer tail feathers 5″. Entire plumage glossy blue-black; outer tail feathers very long and slender.

Voice: Typical swallow-type twittering.

Distribution and Habitat: A very local species found in western Kenya, Uganda and southern highlands, Tanzania. Frequents grasslands and mixed bush and grass; hawks low over the grass, often settling on isolated bushes and even on grass stems.

Allied Species: The Pearl-breasted Swallow (*Hirundo dimidiata*), 6″, has uniform violet-blue-black upperparts without rufous on crown or rump; tail blue-black without white spots; below white with grey wash on chest. Recorded from south-western Tanzania; in open grass-bush country and near water. The European House Martin (*Delichon urbica*), 5″, is blue-black above with a contrasting white rump; tail relatively short and forked; underparts white. This is a winter visitor and passage migrant in small numbers in East Africa.

Cuckoo Shrikes: *Campephagidae*

The cuckoo shrikes are a group of medium-sized, shrike-like birds inhabiting forests and woodland. In some species sexes very dissimilar, the males being black and the females yellow, white and olive-grey. In the hand cuckoo shrikes may always be identified by stiff pointed feather shafts of lower back and rump: these give the impression of spines when brushed upwards.

PETIT'S CUCKOO SHRIKE *Campephaga petiti* p. 276
Identification: 8″. Sexes dissimilar, male entirely black with a bluish gloss; yellow gape, wattles large, conspicuous in field. Female wholly bright canary-yellow below with some blackish bars on chest; above yellowish-olive, barred dusky, yellower on rump; tail dusky-olive, broadly tipped yellow on three pairs outer feathers. Male differs from the Black Cuckoo Shrike (*215) in having much larger yellow gape wattles and wash on inner webs of flight feathers—noticeable when bird flies—grey, not yellow. Female's yellow underparts quite different from mottled white, black and yellow underparts of female Black Cuckoo Shrike.
Voice: A soft whistle repeated two or three times, but bird usually silent.
Distribution and Habitat: A very local and uncommon bird found in Kakamega Forest, western Kenya and in forests in Uganda. A tree-top species, often member of mixed bird parties.
Allied Species: The Red-shouldered Cuckoo Shrike (*Campephaga phoenicea*), 8″, is a black species with the wing shoulder bright scarlet or orange-red. Female resembles female Black Cuckoo Shrike but more olive above; sometimes has little red on shoulders. Found in forest and wooded country in western Kenya and in Uganda.

Drongos: *Dicruridae*

Medium-sized black, shrike-like birds with hooked bills and more or less forked tails, the outer tail feathers curving outwards towards the tip in "fish-tail" fashion. Feeding habits resemble those of some species of fly-catchers—catching insects in flight and returning to same perch.

VELVET-MANTLED DRONGO *Dicrurus modestus* p. 276
Identification: 9½-10″, tail 4½″. An all black drongo; tail noticeably long and strongly "fish-tailed." Feathers of mantle not glossy but velvety in appearance. The closely related Drongo (*216) has a glossy back and a shorter tail. Present species best recognised in field by long tail and habit of perching on bare branches of tall forest trees.
Voice: Harsh, scolding chatter.
Distribution and Habitat: Forests of western Kenya and Uganda. A

very local and uncommon species inhabiting forest clearings and glades, where the commoner drongo is not likely to be found. Keeps to tree tops, perching on bare branches.

Helmet Shrikes: *Prionopidae*

A group of medium-sized, shrike-like birds with hooked bills. One of their main characteristics is their extreme sociability, being found always in small flocks, even during the nesting season. Flight graceful and butterfly-like. Calls also distinctive, a loud communal chattering and bill-snapping. In most species feathers of forehead project forwards and there is a fleshy wattle around eye.

RED-BILLED SHRIKE   *Sigmodus caniceps*   **p. 276**
Identification: 7″. A thickset, forest-tree-tops helmet shrike always in parties. Back, wings and tail black with an oily, dark-green sheen; head pale blue-grey with large triangular black patch on throat; chest greyish-white; breast and belly rich rufous; bill crimson-red; eyes yellowish-brown, eye-lids flesh; feet coral-red.
Voice: A constant soft chattering, interspersed with curious swishing and bill-clicking sounds.
Distribution and Habitat: Forests of western Uganda: most frequent in Bwamba Forest, Toro. Inhabits the tree-tops in small groups: draws attention to presence by chattering notes. Red bill contrasting with pale bluish head very noticeable in life.

Shrikes: *Laniidae*

Conspicuously coloured medium-sized birds with strong hooked bills. Some species perch on vantage points from which they can pounce on their prey: others, more skulking, feed among foliage of trees and bushes. Call-notes usually harsh but songs sometimes surprisingly musical.

SOUZA'S SHRIKE   *Lanius souzae*   **p. 277**
Identification: 6½″. A grey-capped shrike with a barred brown mantle; scapulars white, forming a conspicuous V on the back; ear coverts black; tail narrow, dark brown tipped white; underparts greyish-white.
Voice: A low "teee-teee" repeated slowly; usually silent.
Distribution and Habitat: In East Africa found in western and south-

western Tanzania. A bird of brachystegia woodlands: local and un-common.

Allied Species: Emin's Shrike (*Lanius gubernator*), 6½″, is a red-backed shrike with a grey head and a broad, black forehead and eye-stripe; be-low tawny, throat and belly white. Looks like a European Red-backed Shrike but has rump and upper tail coverts chestnut, not grey. Found in savannah country in northern Uganda. The Woodchat Shrike (*Lanius senator*), 6½″, is a black and white shrike with rich chestnut-red crown and nape, and a white rump which is conspicuous in flight; below, whitish. This is an uncommon European winter visitor to Kenya and Uganda.

YELLOW-BILLED SHRIKE   *Corvinella corvina*   p. 277
Identification: 12″, tail 7″. A drab brownish-grey shrike, paler on under-parts, with narrow black streaking above and below; dark brown ear coverts; bill clear chrome-yellow; chestnut patch in wings, conspicu-ous in flight.

Voice: An often repeated "scis-scis."

Distribution and Habitat: Northern and eastern Uganda, and in western Kenya: frequents acacia woodland and bush, especially near water and where there is a lush undergrowth. Sometimes in pairs, otherwise in small groups. Hunts prey in typical shrike fashion, from a vantage point.

RED-NAPED BUSH SHRIKE   *Laniarius ruficeps*   p. 277
Identification: 6½″. Shrikes of the genus *Laniarius* hunt their prey amongst foliage. The present species is black and white with a bright red patch on the hind crown and nape; below, white.

Voice: Various harsh scolding calls, one bird calling, the other answer-ing.

Distribution and Habitat: An uncommon species in eastern and coastal districts of Kenya. Inhabits arid bush country: skulking in habit and not often seen; red nape patch conspicuous in field. Not uncommon in the dense bush near the Galana River in the Tsavo National Park.

LUHDER'S BUSH SHRIKE   *Laniarius luhderi*   p. 277
Identification: 7-7½″. Upperparts and tail black; crown chestnut; band through eye and ear coverts black; below, throat and breast orange-rufous, belly white.

Voice: A liquid "chee-oo-ch, ch," perhaps uttered by pair of birds.

Distribution and Habitat: Forests of western Kenya, Uganda and western Tanzania. Inhabits thick cover near forest or undergrowth in forest: shy and not often seen.

ZANZIBAR PUFF-BACK SHRIKE   *Dryoscopus affinis*   p. 277

Identification: 6-6½". Crown, mantle, wings and tail glossy black; lower back, rump and underparts white; no white edging to flight feathers. Female has white streak from nostrils to over eye. The Black-backed Puff-Back Shrike (*223) has whitish edgings to wings and its white rump and underparts have a slight grey tinge.

Voice: A series of loud whistling "chee-ows." Also produces wing-snapping noises in flight.

Distribution and Habitat: Occurs in coastal districts of Kenya and Tanzania, and in forests of western Uganda. A forest and woodland bird which obtains its insect food among the foliage of trees.

Allied Species: Pringle's Puff-back Shrike (*Dryoscopus pringlii*), 5-5½", is a small species with a glossy-black head, mantle and tail; outer tail feathers edged and tipped whitish; rump and underparts greyish-white; heavy black bill with yellowish base to mandible. A bird of arid bush country in northern and eastern Kenya. The Puff-back Shrike (*Dryoscopus gambensis*), 7", differs in having a duller black mantle, pale buffy-grey scapulars and edgings to flight feathers and a greyish rump; below whitish-grey. The female is brown above with a grey rump; below, pale tawny buff. A forest tree-top species found in Kenya and Uganda. The Pink-footed Puff-back Shrike (*Dryoscopus angolensis*), 6", male has the crown and upper back dark slate; mantle, wings and tail ash-grey; rump and underparts pale grey; feet pink; the female has the crown and upper back pale grey; mantle, wings and tail olive-brown and rump greyish-brown; below rufous-buff, centre of belly white: legs pink. A forest tree-tops bird found in western Kenya and in Uganda.

THREE-STREAKED BUSH SHRIKE   *Tchagra jamesi*   p. 277

Identification: 6½". An ashy-grey bush shrike with rufous wings and a white-tipped dark tail; black streak down centre of crown and black streak through eye along sides of head; underparts pale grey, whiter on throat and belly.

Voice: A loud trill on a descending scale.

Distribution and Habitat: Occurs in arid bush country of northern and eastern Kenya, including Turkana and country north of Mount Elgon. Inhabits thorn thickets and similar cover: red wings very conspicuous in flight.

BLACK-FRONTED BUSH SHRIKE

Chlorophoneus nigrifrons   p. 277

Identification: 7-7½″. Crown and upper back blue-grey, a black forehead and a wide black stripe through eye; back, wings and tail bright green; underparts variable, rich orange-yellow, scarlet, salmon-pink or blackish-green. The orange-yellow form is the most usual.

Voice: A loud whistle "who-koo" and various harsh scolding calls.

Distribution and Habitat: A local and usually uncommon species in western and central Kenya, south through Tanzania. Mainly a bird of mountain or high level forest: frequents tree-tops and often a member of mixed bird parties.

Allied Species: The Grey-green Bush Shrike (*Chlorophoneus bocagei*), 6″, has the crown and upper mantle black; lower back, rump and wings olive-grey; tail black with narrow white tips; forehead and stripe over eye white; below, white, washed buff on breast. Frequents foliage of tall forest trees: found in western Kenya and in Uganda. White eye-stripe and forehead conspicuous in field.

NICATOR   *Nicator chloris*   p. 277

Identification: 8″. A green shrike with yellow spots on the wings and yellow tips to tail feathers; underparts greenish-grey, paler on throat and centre of belly; under tail coverts greenish-yellow.

Voice: Harsh, guttural notes and a loud "zokh": also utters deep liquid notes.

Distribution and Habitat: A forest and thick woodland species found in Uganda, in northern and eastern Kenya and in Tanzania. Inhabits forest undergrowth and the lower branches of forest trees, singly or in pairs.

Allied Species: The Yellow-throated Nicator (*Nicator vireo*), 5½″, is like a miniature Nicator but has a yellow patch on the throat. It occurs both in undergrowth and among the branches of forest trees in western Uganda.

Tits: *Paridae*

A group of small, rather plump birds of distinctive structure and habits: extremely active and acrobatic when feeding, frequently hanging upside down while searching for insects in foliage. Often members of mixed bird parties.

RED-THROATED TIT   *Parus fringillinus*   p. 284

Identification: 4½". A grey-backed tit with rather pale rufous-buff underparts and conspicuous broad rufous collar on hind neck; crown grey, wing feathers and tail broadly edged white. The Cinnamon-breasted Tit (*226) has no rufous collar on hind neck.

Voice: A typical tit "preet-chu-chee-chee."

Distribution and Habitat: A local and uncommon species found in southern Kenya and northern Tanzania. Most frequent in Masai country. Inhabits open acacia woodland and plains country with scattered bush: usually in pairs or family parties.

Allied Species: The Stripe-breasted Tit (*Parus fasciiventer*), 4½", is a grey-backed tit with a blackish head and chest and a blackish stripe down the centre of the breast. It is a mountain forest bird found on the Ruwenzori Mountains and the forested mountains of south-western Uganda.

MOUSE-COLOURED PENDULINE TIT

Anthoscopus musculus   p. 284

Identification: 3". A tiny short-tailed tit with a tapering sharp bill; above pale grey, slightly darker on wings and tail; below creamy-white, tinged buff on belly. The closely related African Penduline Tit (*226) has a pale buff forehead and the underparts cinnamon-buff.

Voice: A high-pitched "teep, teep" frequently repeated.

Distribution and Habitat: A very local species found in acacia bush and woodland in Kenya, northern Uganda and north-eastern Tanzania. Usually in small flocks or pairs.

Orioles: *Oriolidae*

A group of active, thrush-sized birds, usually of brilliant yellow plumage, inhabiting tree-tops in woodland and forest. Calls are loud, clear, melodious whistles.

BLACK-WINGED ORIOLE   *Oriolus nigripennis*

Identification: 9½". A bright yellow oriole with a black head and yellow-tipped black tail: central tail feathers all black: wings blackish with yellowish-green or whitish edgings. The closely related Black-headed Oriole (*227) has central tail feathers green.

Voice: Three soft, liquid whistles.

Distribution and Habitat: A forest tree-top species, most frequent in highland forest: occurs in central and western Kenya, in Uganda and in mountain forest on Mahare Mountains, western Tanzania.

Allied Species: The Western Black-headed Oriole (*Oriolus brachyrhynchus*), 8½-9", has green central tail feathers: it differs from the Black-headed Oriole (*227) in having edges of outer secondaries grey, not whitish. It occurs in forests of western Uganda and in the Kakamega Forest, western Kenya. Like other orioles it inhabits the tree-tops. The Green-headed Oriole (*Oriolus chlorocephalus*), 9½", is another yellow oriole, but with the head and chest moss-green, not black; wing feathers edged blue-grey; tail green with yellow tips to outer feathers. It occurs in mountain forest on the Usambara, Nguru and Uluguru Mountains, north-easten Tanzania, and on the Rondo plateau, southern Tanzania.

Crows: *Corvidae*

The largest of the perching birds: plumages of most species black or black and white. Bills usually heavy with nostrils covered by forward-pointing bristles. Feed mainly on the ground: omnivorous.

LESSER BROWN-NECKED or DWARF RAVEN
Corvus edithae p. 277

Identification: 18". An all black raven with a moderately long tail: closely resembles an all black Pied Crow (*230). The Fan-tailed Raven (*230) has an extremely short tail and very broad wings.

Voice: A series of guttural croaks.

Distribution and Habitat: A locally common species in the northern frontier province of Kenya: often associates with Fan-tailed Ravens, but more gregarious than that species. Nests in colonies in trees, not on cliff faces like many ravens. Attracted to human camps and settlements as a scavenger.

Starlings: *Sturnidae*

A group of medium-sized usually gregarious birds: many species possess brilliantly metallic plumage, greens, blues and purples predominating. Most are noisy and conspicuous.

Plate 31 WEAVERS

1   **CHESTNUT SPARROW**   page 322
Small size; chestnut back and underparts.

2   **RUFOUS-TAILED WEAVER**   page 321
Cinnamon-rufous wings and tail feathers.

3   **CLARKE'S WEAVER**   page 323
Black head, mantle and chest; black bill.

4   **NORTHERN BROWN-THROATED WEAVER**   page 325
Chestnut-brown face.

5   **DARK-BACKED WEAVER** (Western Kenya race)   page 325
Grey back.

6   **DARK-BACKED WEAVER** (Kenya coastal race)   page 325
Black back.

7   **BLACK-BILLED WEAVER**   page 327
Yellow face.

8   **TAVETA GOLDEN WEAVER**   page 325
Chestnut patch on nape.

9   **ORANGE WEAVER**   page 325
Orange-yellow head and underparts; pale bill.

10   **GOLDEN WEAVER**   page 326
Brownish-yellow head; red eyes.

11   **BROWN-CAPPED WEAVER**   page 328
Yellow mantle streak; chestnut cap in male.

12   **YELLOW-MANTLED WEAVER**   page 328
Yellow collar on hind neck.

13   **LITTLE WEAVER**   page 324
Black face; relatively thick bill.

14   **STUHLMANN'S WEAVER**   page 327
Black crown; streaky green back.

15   **COMPACT WEAVER**   page 328
Dusky underparts; yellow crown; thick bill.

16   **SLENDER-BILLED WEAVER**   page 326
Black face; bill slender.

Plate 32 WEAVERS, WAXBILLS

WHITE-WINGED BABBLING STARLING

Neocichla gutturalis   p. 277

Identification: 8″. A pale-looking brownish-grey starling with dark wings and tail and a conspicuous white wing-patch; below, pinkish-buff with black patch on throat. Found in small groups, nearly always in brachystegia woodland: not very starling-like in appearance; flight heavy, resembling that of helmet-shrikes.

Voice: Harsh, strident call-notes.

Distribution and Habitat: A very local and uncommon bird found in central and south-western Tanzania. Inhabits brachystegia woodlands, especially where trees well spaced and large. Occurs in tree-tops and also feeds on the ground. White wing patches noticeable in flight.

ABBOT'S STARLING   *Pholia femoralis*   p. 288

Identification: 6-6½″. A rather stumpy-looking blue-black starling with a white breast and abdomen; eye yellow; sexes alike. The similar Sharpe's Starling (*232) has the breast and abdomen rufous-buff.

Voice: Various, rather high-pitched whistles.

Distribution and Habitat: A local and very uncommon starling found in southern Kenya and north-eastern Tanzania. Inhabits mountain forest, keeping to the tree-tops. Perhaps most frequent in forests on Kilimanjaro, where it associates with another tree-top species, Kenrick's Starling (see page 308).

MAGPIE STARLING   *Speculipastor bicolor*   p. 288

Identification: 7-7½″. Male: upperparts, head, chest, wings and tail bluish-black; white patch on flight feathers; breast and abdomen creamy-white; eye red. Female differs in having head and chest grey, not black.

Voice: Various shrill whistles.

Distribution and Habitat: Local and often of irregular appearance in northern arid districts of Kenya, south to the country around Lake Baringo. Most frequent in northern Turkana, where it is locally common, especially in those areas where large termite hills are a feature of the landscape. Also recorded eastern Karamoja, Uganda.

BRONZE-TAILED STARLING   *Lamprocolius chalcurus*   p. 288

Identification: 8½-9″. A metallic bluish-green starling with deep violet-blue ear coverts; eye yellow; central tail feathers bronzy-violet or blue. Very similar to Blue-eared Glossy Starling (*232) in field and unless good view is obtained difficult to distinguish: best field characters are contrasting violet-blue ear coverts and violet central tail feathers.

Voice: Various musical whistles, but less vocal than Blue-eared Glossy Starling.

Distribution and Habitat: Locally distributed northern and eastern Uganda: less common western Kenya. Found usually in open savannah woodland and in bush country where there are scattered trees.

PURPLE GLOSSY STARLING   *Lamprocolius purpureus*   p. 288

Identification: 10½″. A thickset, brightly metallic bluish-green starling with violet-blue underparts; eye orange-yellow, conspicuously large. Violet-blue underparts and large eye distinguish it from smaller Blue-eared Glossy Starling (*232). The larger Splendid Glossy Starling (*233) has velvety black bands across the closed wing and tail.

Voice: Various chattering calls and soft whistles.

Distribution and Habitat: Locally not uncommon in Uganda; local and uncommon western Kenya. Inhabits savannah woodlands, edges of forest and open bush country with scattered trees. Frequently gregarious in large flocks: feeds in trees and on the ground.

PURPLE-HEADED GLOSSY STARLING
                                Lamprocolius purpureiceps   p. 288

Identification: 7″. A thickset, short-tailed, metallic-green starling with a purple head and throat; eye dark brown; crown feathers velvety in texture. This is a forest tree-top species, best identified by its short-tailed, chunky appearance and its dark, not yellow eye.

Voice: Various short, liquid whistles.

Distribution and Habitat: Local, but not uncommon in forests of western Uganda. Frequents fruiting fig trees in forest, often in large flocks.

BLACK-BREASTED GLOSSY STARLING
                                Lamprocolius corruscus   p. 288

Identification: 7-8″. A rather slim, relatively long-tailed starling, with dull metallic oily-green upperparts and chest; breast violet, merging to black on belly; eye bright orange.

Voice: Various harsh chatterings and warblings.

Distribution and Habitat: Eastern and central districts Kenya and eastern Tanzania, most frequent in coastal districts and along Tana River in Kenya. Frequents bush, open woodland and riverine forest often in large flocks when Salvadora bushes along Tana are in fruit.

ASHY STARLING   *Cosmopsarus unicolor*   p. 288
Identification: 12". An entirely brownish-grey starling with a very long tail; eye pale yellow.
Voice: Soft, whistling calls.
Distribution and Habitat: Locally common in bush country in Tanzania. Pale eye conspicuous in field: occurs in pairs or small flocks.

SLENDER-BILLED CHESTNUT-WING STARLING
Onychognathus tenuirostris   p. 288
Identification: 10-11". A slim, blue-black starling with conspicuous reddish flight feathers; tail long; bill slender: female differs from male in having greyish head and chest.
Voice: Shrill, liquid whistles and some chattering notes.
Distribution and Habitat: A high-level species found both in mountain forest and on alpine moorlands in Kenya, Uganda and Tanzania. Not uncommon alpine zone of Mount Kenya where birds search giant lobelias for snails. A more lightly built, slender bird than the Redwing Starling (*234).
Allied Species: The Narrow-tailed Starling (*Poeoptera lugubris*), 7", is a very slender, blue-black starling with a long, slender and graduated tail; female greyer, with chestnut in wings. It occurs in forest tree-tops in western Uganda. Stuhlmann's Starling (*Stilbopsar stuhlmanni*), 6", is a small slender species, blue-black in male; female grey with chestnut flight feathers. Differs from Narrow-tailed Starling in smaller size and thicker, shorter tail. Found in forests of western Kenya and Uganda. Kenrick's Starling (*Stilbopsar kenricki*), 6", resembles Stuhlmann's Starling but is dull black without blue sheen. Found in mountain forest in Kenya and north-eastern Tanzania. Waller's Chestnut-wing Starling (*Onychognathus walleri*), 8", is a short-tailed, thickset blue-black starling with chestnut flight feathers; female greyish on head. This is another forest tree-top species found in highlands of East Africa.

BRISTLE-CROWNED STARLING   *Galeopsar salvadorii*   p. 288
Identification: 15-16". A large, very long-tailed blue-black starling with bright chestnut in wing feathers and a rounded cushion of velvety-black feathers on fore-crown; eye red.
Voice: Various loud, liquid whistles.
Distribution and Habitat: Local and uncommon north-eastern Uganda; northern Kenya as far south as Lake Baringo and Isiolo. Inhabits

inland cliffs and rocky country. In pairs or small flocks. Velvety forehead conspicuous in field.

FISCHER'S STARLING   *Spreo fischeri*   p. 288
Identification: 7″. A plump, short-tailed, pale grey starling, with a
white belly and a pale grey crown. Often seen on the ground: general
appearance that of a Superb Starling (*235) but quite different in colour
Eye, pale cream.
Voice: Various whistles and chattering calls.
Distribution and Habitat: Local and generally uncommon in eastern
Kenya and north-eastern Tanzania. Inhabits dry bush country. Often
seen in Tsavo National Park.
Allied Species: The White-crowned Starling (*Spreo albicapillus*), 9″, is
an ashy-brown starling with a relatively long, dark tail; crown and
abdomen white; white streaks on breast. This species has been dis-
covered recently near North Horr, Northern Frontier Province of
Kenya. It inhabits arid bush country.

White-eyes: *Zosteropidae*

A group of small green or yellowish-green warbler-like birds, with conspicuous white rings around their eyes. Gregarious, in flocks even during
the nesting season. Often associated with mixed bird parties. The classification of these birds is still unsatisfactory; different populations vary greatly
and the status of some races and species is uncertain.

BROAD-RINGED WHITE-EYE *Zosterops eurycricotus*   p. 277
Identification: 5″. A deep green white-eye with a very large and conspicuous white eye-ring; below, olive-yellow, yellower on throat and
abdomen. The Kikuyu White-eye (*238) differs in having a broad
yellow forehead.
Voice: High-pitched, plaintive "tsssp, tsssp" and brief warbling song.
Distribution and Habitat: Mountain forest in northern Tanzania, including Mounts Meru and Kilimanjaro.
Allied Species: The Teita White-eye (*Zosterops silvanus*), 5″, is another
species with a very large white eye-ring, but has the breast, abdomen
and flanks grey. It occurs in forests on the Teita Hills, south-eastern
Kenya. The Pale White-eye (*Zosterops pallidus*), 4½-5″, has a small

white eye-ring and a pale grey belly, often yellowish in the centre. It occurs in the forests of Mount Kulal, Northern Frontier Province, Kenya and on the Pare Mountains, north-eastern Tanzania.

Sunbirds: *Nectariniidae*

A distinct family of small birds with slender curved bills and, in most species, brilliant metallic plumage in males. In some species male has dull female-like non-breeding plumage. Some females are difficult to identify in field and are best recognised by their associated males. Flight very erratic and rapid. Most species visit flowering trees, such as *Erythrina*, in which they may be observed at close quarters. The best way to see several of the rarer forest species is to wait in the vicinity of a flowering tree for the birds to appear.

SCARLET-TUFTED MALACHITE SUNBIRD
Nectarinia johnstoni   p. 289

Identification: Male 10-12″, tail 6-8″; female 5½-6″. A brilliant metallic-green sunbird with very long central tail feathers and bright red pectoral tufts. In non-breeding dress, body feathers blackish-brown. Female dark-brown, paler in centre of belly, without elongated tail feathers but with red pectoral tufts. The Malachite Sunbird (*239) has yellow pectoral tufts in male: female paler and lacks tufts.

Voice: Call note a sharp "tssik"; also has warbling song.

Distribution and Habitat: A species confined to alpine moorlands. In Kenya known from Mount Kenya and the Aberdare range; in Uganda on the Ruwenzori range and the Birunga volcanoes in south-western Kigezi; in Tanzania on Mount Kilimanjaro in the north, and on the Livingstone range in the south.

PURPLE-BREASTED SUNBIRD
Nectarinia purpureiventris   p. 289

Identification: Male 9-10″, tail 5½-6½″; female 5″, tail 2″. A long-tailed sunbird of rainbow hues; crown and throat velvety metallic violet, hind neck metallic-greenish-blue to violet-pink and golden-bronze on back; throat bronze-green to deep purplish-violet remainder under-parts. Non-breeding males have body plumage dull greenish-grey but retain metallic wing coverts and rump feathers. Female olive-green with grey head, paler on throat; central tail feathers extend half an inch beyond rest.

Voice: A relatively weak, typical sunbird "tssp": male has soft but rapid warbling song.

Distribution and Habitat: In East Africa known only from forests on the Ruwenzori range and the Impenetrable-Kayonza forests, south-western Kigezi, Uganda. This is a forest tree-tops sunbird which, unlike related species, rarely descends to feed at flowers near the ground. It favours the globular red flowers of a tree, *Symphonia gabonensis*: these from the ground look like red berries, nearly an inch across, growing along the branches. The Regal and Blue-headed Sunbirds also feed at these blossoms. Seen in silhouette the long tail and relatively small body size are distinctive.

RED-CHESTED SUNBIRD *Nectarinia erythrocerca* p. 289

Identification: Male 5½-6", tail 2½"; female 4½". A metallic bluish-green sunbird with a deep red chest-band and a black belly; central tail feathers elongated ¾" beyond rest; no pectoral tufts: no non-breeding plumage. Female darkish olive-brown above; no pale eye-stripe; below, dull yellowish-white with dark mottling on neck and chest.

Voice: A sharp, sunbird-type "tsssp" or "tink, tink."

Distribution and Habitat: Locally common western Kenya, Uganda and north-western Tanzania. This is a common sunbird in Uganda, most frequent in the vicinity of water. Often seen in gardens and parks where attracted by flowers.

SMALLER BLACK-BELLIED SUNBIRD
Nectarinia nectarinioides p. 289

Identification: Male 4½", tail 2"; female 3½". The smallest of the long-tailed sunbirds: central feathers extend ¾" beyond rest. Plumage metallic green; bright red breast-band, sometimes with trace of yellow feathering at edges; belly black: no non-breeding plumage. Female olive-grey with indistinct pale eye-stripe; below, dull creamy-white with dusky-olive streaking on throat, chest and flanks. Female indistinguishable in field from female Tsavo Purple-banded Sunbird. The black-bellied race of the Beautiful Sunbird (*243) is larger and has a yellow patch on each side of the red breast-band.

Voice: Jangling song of double "tee-tss, tee-tss" and various high-pitched, typical sunbird notes.

Distribution and Habitat: Local and uncommon eastern districts of Kenya and north-eastern Tanzania. Most frequent along the Tana River in Kenya. Inhabits arid bush country; most in evidence in acacias bordering rivers or dry river beds, where it feeds among acacia blossoms or in the red flowers of *Loranthus*, parasitic on the acacias.

PYGMY SUNBIRD   *Hedydipna platura*   p. 289

Identification: Male 6½-7″, tail 3½-4″; female 3½″. A metallic green sunbird with a bright, yellow breast and abdomen and very long spatulate central tail feathers; bill very short for sunbird. Female pale grey above, pale yellow below; central tail feathers not elongated. Male in non-breeding dress moults long tail feathers and resembles female except for metallic wing coverts.

Voice: A warbler-like "teep-teep": song a soft, warbling trill.

Distribution and Habitat: Local, but not uncommon in some areas: occurs in northern Uganda and in north-western Kenya where it appears only to be a visitor during the nesting season, arriving in August and departing by February. Inhabits arid thorn-bush and acacia woodland, especially along dry river beds: much attracted by fruiting *Salvadora* bushes.

SUPERB SUNBIRD   *Cinnyris superbus*   p. 289

Identification: 5½″. A large, rather heavy-looking sunbird with a relatively short, square tail and a long bill. Male metallic green above, bluer on crown; wings and tail black; throat and chest metallic violet-blue; breast and abdomen deep maroon-red; no pectoral tufts; no non-breeding plumage. Female olive-green above with pale stripe over eye; below, dull yellow, under tail coverts orange.

Voice: A sharp, typical sunbird "tsssp": also brief warbling song.

Distribution and Habitat: Widespread but local and uncommon in Uganda: has been recorded Kakamega Forest, western Kenya. A forest tree-top sunbird often attracted to flowering *Erythrina* trees near forest; also often visits banana cultivation to feed on nectar in flowers.

COPPER SUNBIRD   *Cinnyris cupreus*   p. 289

Identification: 4½″. Male brilliant metallic copper with violet and red reflections; breast and abdomen black; no pectoral tufts. Female olive-brown above, dull yellowish below; wings olive-brown; tail black with grey tips to outer feathers. The non-breeding dress of the male resembles the female but wings black and metallic wing coverts retained.

Voice: A sharp, but not very loud "tssp."

Distribution and Habitat: Locally common in Uganda, western Kenya and locally in Tanzania, mainly in western and southern districts.

Inhabits bush country, open savannah woodland, cultivated areas where there are trees and bushes, and gardens. Much attracted to clumps of orange-flowered *Leonotis*.

SHINING SUNBIRD *Cinnyris habessinicus* p. 289
Identification: 5″. Male brilliant metallic green, often with golden sheen on back; crown purple; bright red breast-band, yellow pectoral tufts, black belly. No non-breeding dress. Female uniform pale grey with whitish eye-stripe; wings and tail dark grey with pale edgings.
Voice: Rather harsh sunbird "tssps" and a sustained, warbling song.
Distribution and Habitat: Local and uncommon northern Kenya, except in Turkana where common sunbird, and in eastern Karamoja, Uganda. Inhabits dry thorn-bush country: much attracted to flowering acacia trees and bushes and to fruiting *Salvadora* bushes. The male's red breast, yellow tufts and black abdomen are good field marks.
Allied Species: The Splendid Sunbird (*Cinnyris coccinigaster*), 5″, has the red breast-band suffused with metallic violet, and female has indistinct greenish streaking on chest, otherwise similar to Shining Sunbird. It has been recorded from the north of West Nile Province, Uganda.

TSAVO PURPLE-BANDED SUNBIRD *Cinnyris tsavoensis* p. 289
Identification: 4″. A metallic, bluish green sunbird with black belly; purplish band across chest and narrow maroon line below; no pectoral tufts; no non-breeding plumage. Female olive-grey above; below, dusky-yellowish with olive streaking on chest and flanks. The Little Purple-banded Sunbird (*245) has a broad maroon band across the chest.
Voice: Usual sunbird "tssps."
Distribution and Habitat: Dry bush country of eastern Kenya and eastern Tanzania, but not on the coast.
Allied Species: The Violet-breasted Sunbird (*Cinnyris chalcomelas*),4½″, is also metallic green with a black belly; band across chest deep violet-purple; no maroon band; no pectoral tufts; female paler below and has a well-defined pale streak above eye. Found in eastern and coastal districts of Kenya: frequents bush and coastal thickets. Shelley's Double-collared Sunbird (*Cinnyris shelleyi*), 4½″, is also green with a black belly but has broad scarlet band across chest—not purple or maroon. Female olive above, yellowish-white below, with heavy olive mottling on chest and some feathers tipped dull red. This

is a rare sunbird found in brachystegia woodland of Morogoro district, Tanzania. It feeds from clumps of *Loranthus* growing in trees.

ORANGE-TUFTED SUNBIRD   *Cinnyris bouvieri*   p. 288

Identification: 4½″. A metallic green sunbird with a dark brown belly; forehead bluish-purple; violet chest-band and maroon stripe below; pectoral tufts yellow and orange. No non-breeding plumage. Female olive above; yellowish-olive below with very indistinct olive streaking on throat, chest and flanks.

Voice: Usually a soft three-note "tssp, tssp, tssp," less harsh than most sunbirds.

Distribution and Habitat: A very uncommon forest sunbird found in Uganda; and recorded Kakamega Forest, western Kenya. Usually seen when visiting flowering *Erythrina* trees at forest edge.

Allied Species: The Northern Orange-tufted Sunbird (*Cinnyris oseus*), 4″, has been recorded in West Nile Province, Uganda. It is a metallic bluish-green sunbird with a violet-blue chest and black belly; pectoral tufts, orange and pale yellow. Female greyish-olive, paler below; not streaked.

GREATER DOUBLE-COLLARED SUNBIRD

Cinnyris afer   p. 289

Identification: 5-5½″. A metallic green sunbird with a graduated black tail, a very broad red breast-band, yellow pectoral tufts and an olive-grey belly; upper tail-coverts purple: no non-breeding plumage. Female uniform olive, paler in centre of belly. The Northern Double-collared Sunbird is very similar but much smaller.

Voice: A short, sharp "tsp," often repeated; also a sustained warbling song.

Distribution and Habitat: Frequents mountain forest and bamboo zone at high altitudes: known in East Africa from high forest on the Ruwenzori range and Birunga Volcanoes in western and south-western Uganda.

NOTE: The Birunga Volcanoes race, *Cinnyris afer graueri*, is wrongly classified as a race of Southern Double-collared Sunbird in some other works on East African birds.

Allied Species: Moreau's Sunbird (*Cinnyris moreaui*), has restricted red on the chest and yellow pectoral tufts extend as a half-band across chest on each side of red breast-band. This is a rare bird known only from the high forest of the Nguru Mountains, north-eastern Tanzania.

SOUTHERN DOUBLE-COLLARED SUNBIRD
Cinnyris intermedius p. 289

Identification: 4½-5″. NOTE: This is the sunbird which in other orni-thological books is classified as a race of *Cinnyris chalybeus*. *Cinnyris intermedius* and its Rhodesian race *bractiatus* differ from *chalybeus* in having grey wings and non-metallic grey rumps and their habitat and habits are different. *Cinnyris chalybeus* and *Cinnyris mediocris* (*245) are conspecific. Male Southern Double-collared Sunbird is metallic yellowish-green on back, head and throat; rump non-metallic grey; upper tail feathers tipped green or violet; narrow purple line across chest followed by scarlet breast-band; pectoral tufts yellow; belly pale grey. No non-breeding plumage. Female olive-grey, paler on belly, short pale stripe above eye. This is the common sunbird with a red breast-band found in brachystegia woodland in Tanzania.
Voice: A relatively weak double "tssp-tssp." Also soft, warbling song.
Distribution and Habitat: A common species in the brachystegia woodland of central and southern Tanzania. Often a member of mixed bird parties.

NORTHERN DOUBLE-COLLARED SUNBIRD
Cinnyris reichenowi p. 289

Identification: 4″. A bright metallic-green sunbird with a narrow purple chest-band followed by a very broad, deep red breast-band; belly dark olive; upper tail coverts violet. No non-breeding plumage. Female uniform olive, paler on belly. Except for much smaller size, very similar to Greater Double-collared Sunbird. The Eastern Double-collared Sunbird (*245) has a much narrower red breast-band and blue upper-tail coverts.
Voice: The usual soft sunbird "tssp" and a warbling song.
Distribution and Habitat: Found in mountain forest usually below 8,000 feet, in the Kenya highlands, Mount Elgon and in western and south-western Uganda. Best identified on small size and very wide red breast-band.

OLIVE-BELLIED SUNBIRD *Cinnyris chloropygius* p. 289

Identification: 4″. A metallic-green sunbird with a broad scarlet breast-band, an olive belly, very large yellow pectoral tufts; upper tail coverts green like the back. No non-breeding plumage. Female dark olive above and on wings; tail blackish; below, bright greenish-yellow with heavy olive streaking on throat, breast and flanks; chin whitish.
Voice: A weak "tsp, tsp, tsp, tsp, tsp" and a sustained warbling song.

Distribution and Habitat: A locally common sunbird in Uganda and north-western Tanzania. Frequents forest, margins of forest and secondary growth and lush bush near swamps. Much attracted by flowering *Erythrina* trees.

Allied Species: The Tiny Sunbird (*Cinnyris minullus*), 3½", is a small edition of the Olive-bellied Sunbird; the male has sub-terminal blue bars on red breast-band and a darker, olive belly: the female differs only in its smaller size. An uncommon forest sunbird found in western Uganda.

REGAL SUNBIRD   *Cinnyris regius*   p. 289

Identification: 4-4½". Male metallic green with graduated black tail; breast and abdomen bright chrome-yellow with scarlet stripe down centre; under tail coverts red; no non-breeding plumage. Female uniform olive-green above; yellowish-olive below; wings olive; tail blackish.

Voice: Loud, clear "tssp" and a rapid warbling song.

Distribution and Habitat: Occurs in western and south-western Uganda and on the Kungwe-Mahare Mountains of western Tanzania. Inhabits mountain forest up to 12,000 feet.

Allied Species: Loveridge's Sunbird (*Cinnyris loveridgei*), 4½-5", is a thickset, rather short-tailed sunbird confined to mountain forest of Uluguru Mountains, Tanzania. Male metallic green with yellowish-olive breast and belly; orange-red suffusion on breast. Female olive with slight metallic-grey wash on upperparts.

GREEN-THROATED SUNBIRD   *Chalcomitra rubescens*   p. 289

Identification: 4½-5". Male a square-tailed, velvety-black sunbird having metallic green throat patch edged at bottom metallic violet and blue; crown metallic green, edged violet towards nape: no non-breeding plumage. Female dark olive-brown with yellowish streak above eye; below, yellowish with dark olive streaking on breast and flanks. Sunbirds of the genus *Chalcomitra* are easily recognised by their square-tipped tails and velvety-black or dark brown plumage in males.

Voice: A loud and distinctive "tssp-tee" not unlike that of Scarlet-chested Sunbird (*246).

Distribution and Habitat: A rather local species found in Uganda, western Kenya and north-western Tanzania. A forest tree-top bird, much attracted to flowering *Erythrina* and Nandi Flame trees.

HUNTER'S SUNBIRD *Chalcomitra hunteri* p. 289

Identification: 5-5½″. A rather thickset, square-tailed sunbird, velvety blackish-brown with a brilliant scarlet chest; non-metallic black chin; metallic green crown; metallic violet shoulders and rump: no non-breeding dress. Female brown, paler below, heavily mottled dark brown on throat and rest of underparts. The Scarlet-chested Sunbird (*246) is larger with a metallic green chin, lacks the metallic violet rump, and has sub-terminal blue bars in scarlet chest patch. Hunter's Sunbird is also known as the Somali Scarlet-chested Sunbird.

Voice: A variety of loud and clear "tssp-teee-tees" and a brief warbling song. Much like calls of Scarlet-chested Sunbird.

Distribution and Habitat: Northern and eastern districts Kenya, extreme north-eastern Karamoja, Uganda and north-eastern Tanzania. A bird of arid bush country: much attracted to flowering *Erythrina* trees, acacias and aloes.

MOUSE-COLOURED SUNBIRD *Cyanomitra veroxii* p. 289

Identification: 4½″. Sexes alike. A grey sunbird with slight bluish-green metallic wash on upperparts; below pale greyish-white; red and creamy-yellow pectoral tufts. Bird has habit of constantly flicking its wings, a habit also shared by Olive Sunbird.

Voice: A loud, clear warbling song; call a rather drawn-out, plaintive "teeee."

Distribution and Habitat: Coastal areas of Kenya and Tanzania, including Zanzibar. Inhabits dense coastal scrub and also mangrove swamps.

BLUE-HEADED SUNBIRD *Cyanomitra alinae* p. 289

Identification: 5″. Sexes alike. Crown, head, throat and chest metallic violet-blue; back orange-brown; belly sooty black; pectoral tufts pale yellow, present in male only; eyes red. No non-breeding dress. The commoner Green-headed Sunbird (*246) has the head and chest metallic green, the back olive-green and the underparts grey.

Voice: A three or four-note "tchee, tchee, tchee" and a sustained, warbling song.

Distribution and Habitat: A mountain forest sunbird found in the Ruwenzori range and the Kigezi highland forests, Uganda. Much attracted to clumps of the parasitic *Loranthus* growing in forest trees.

BLUE-THROATED BROWN SUNBIRD

Cyanomitra cyanolaema   p. 289

Identification: 5½″. Male a dull-looking sooty-brown sunbird, paler on belly; crown and throat patch metallic-steel-blue; pectoral tufts pale yellow; no non-breeding dress. Female olive above and on wings and tail; pale stripe above and below eye; chin whitish merging to pale brown on throat; remainder underparts whitish, mottled olive-grey on breast and flanks.

Voice: A harsh, repeated "teep, teep, teep, teep."

Distribution and Habitat: A common sunbird in Uganda and recorded from Kakamega Forest, western Kenya. A forest species, keeping to the tree-tops: attracted to flowering *Erythrina* and Nandi Flame trees.

OLIVE SUNBIRD   *Cyanomitra olivacea*   p. 289

Identification: 5-6″. Several races of Olive Sunbird occur in East Africa, varying in size, possession or lack of pectoral tufts in female and presence or absence of pale patch at base of mandible. Sexes alike; a rather slim olive-green sunbird, paler below, without metallic plumage; yellow pectoral tufts present in male, and in some races also in female. Has habit of constantly flicking wings.

Voice: A high-pitched "teek, teek" and a variety of harsh churring calls. Also a sustained warbling song.

Distribution and Habitat: Widespread in East Africa, mainly in forests, heavy woodland and scrub. Occurs both in tree-tops and in undergrowth. An especially common forest sunbird in Uganda. Often member of mixed bird parties.

GREY-CHINNED SUNBIRD   *Anthreptes tephrolaema*   p. 288

Identification: 4″. A thickset, stumpy sunbird with a relatively short bill. Male upperparts metallic golden-green; rump and upper tail coverts non-metallic olive-green; wings and tail dark olive-brown; chin grey; throat and chest metallic green; narrow dull orange band across chest; remainder underparts greyish; yellow pectoral tufts; no non-breeding plumage. Female uniform olive-green, paler below; no pectoral tufts. This sunbird is placed as a race of the Gambian *Anthreptes rectirostris* in some East African bird books, but it is unlikely that the two are conspecific.

Voice: A weak, zosterops-like "tssp, tssp" frequently repeated.

Distribution and Habitat: A forest tree-tops sunbird found locally in Uganda and in western Kenya. Often associated with Apalis warblers and other tree-top species. Visits fruiting figs and other trees and feeds to some extent on fruits.

Allied Species: The Banded Green Sunbird (*Anthreptes rubritorques*), 4", differs in having the chin and throat grey, and a narrow scarlet band across chest: female metallic green above, dull yellowish-olive below. Found in the forests of eastern Usambara and Nguru Mountains of north-eastern Tanzania: rare and little known.

KENYA VIOLET-BACKED SUNBIRD

Anthreptes orientalis p. 288

Identification: 5-6". Male metallic violet-blue above and on tail and chin; wings grey; underparts white; yellow pectoral tufts; no non-breeding plumage. Female grey above with white streak above eye; tail violet-black; wings grey; underparts white. The Violet-backed Sunbird (*247) is larger and greyish below in male, yellowish on belly in female.

Voice: A high-pitched but not very loud chirping call and a sharper "teeep."

Distribution and Habitat: Locally common north-eastern Uganda, northern and eastern Kenya and north-eastern and central districts of Tanzania. Inhabits arid and semi-dry bush country: especially attracted to flowering acacia trees and bushes.

Allied Species: The Uluguru Violet-backed Sunbird (*Anthreptes neglectus*), 5½-6", is dusky brownish-grey below; blackish non-metallic collar on hind neck; female resembles male but lacks metallic violet chin; grey below, bright yellow on abdomen. This is a forest sunbird recorded from the Tana River forest and Teita Hills in Kenya and forests on the Eastern Usambara, Nguru and Uluguru Mountains in north-eastern Tanzania.

ANCHIETA'S SUNBIRD   *Anthreptes anchietae*   p. 288

Identification: 4½". Sexes alike; upperparts dark sooty-brown; forehead, throat and chest metallic dark blue; centre of breast and belly scarlet, bordered on each side yellow; abdomen pale grey, under tail coverts red.

Voice: A plaintive single note "tee," often repeated: weak warbling song.

Distribution and Habitat: Local and uncommon in south-western and southern Tanzania: occurs in brachystegia woodland. Sometimes associates with mixed bird parties: warbler-like in feeding habits, less attracted to flowering trees than many sunbirds.

AMANI or PALE-BELLIED SUNBIRD

Anthreptes pallidigaster p. 288

Identification: 3½". A tiny, rather thickset sunbird with a short tail. Male upperparts and throat metallic dark bottle-green; breast and abdomen white; red pectoral tufts; no non-breeding plumage. Female grey above with slight metallic wash; below greyish-white, tinged yellow in centre of belly.

Voice: Very weak "tsss" calls and a soft warbling song of short duration.

Distribution and Habitat: A very uncommon and local sunbird known from the Sokoke-Arabuku Forest, Kenya coast and the forests of eastern Usambara Mountains, north-eastern Tanzania. A bird of the tree-tops, warbler-like in feeding habits.

GREY-HEADED SUNBIRD   *Anthreptes axillaris*   p. 288

Identification: 4½-5". Sexes alike; a green warbler-like sunbird with a grey head; bill horn-coloured, relatively straight for sunbird; orange-red pectoral tufts in male; no non-breeding plumage.

Voice: A high-pitched "peet," but usually silent.

Distribution and Habitat: A forest tree-top species found locally in Uganda; most frequent in western districts. Feeds on insects and insect larvae captured among foliage in manner of warbler, seldom visiting flowers.

Allied Species: The Little Green Sunbird (*Anthreptes seimundi*), 3½", is a short-tailed all green sunbird without pectoral tufts. This is another tree-top forest species found locally in Uganda. The Plain-backed Sunbird (*Anthreptes reichenowi*), 4", occurs in coastal forests of Kenya and north-eastern Tanzania. The male is non-metallic green, paler and yellower on belly, with a metallic dark blue forehead and throat and lemon-yellow pectoral tufts: the female lacks the metallic forehead and throat, and has no pectoral tufts; below pale greenish-yellow.

GREEN HYLIA   *Hylia prasina*   p. 284

Identification: 4½". Sexes alike; a dark olive-green bird with a broad greenish-yellow stripe above eye; wings and tail green; below pale olive-grey; bill short and slightly curved. This is a bird of uncertain status, at present placed among the sunbirds.

Voice: A harsh, grating "grr-grr" quite unlike any sunbird call: a loud warbling song with high notes.

Distribution and Habitat: A common but rather shy forest bird, usually found in undergrowth but sometimes a member of bird parties in tree-tops. Found in Uganda and in western Kenya.

Weavers, Sparrows, Waxbills and allies: *Ploceidae*

This is one of the largest bird families in Africa. Most but not all are seed-eaters with short heavy bills. They resemble true finches in general appearance but have ten, not nine primaries. Finches build open nests; weavers and allies build domed structures with a side, top or bottom entrance. Many species are highly gregarious, nesting in colonies. Some have female-like non-breeding plumage.

RUFOUS-TAILED WEAVER   *Histurgops ruficauda*   p. 304
   Identification: 8″. Sexes alike; upperparts greyish-brown with whitish edgings to feathers giving a scaly effect: wings dark brown with inner webs pale chestnut; tail pale chestnut except central feathers which are brown; underparts creamy-white mottled with brown; eye, pale blue. Field appearance a mottled brown buffalo weaver; rufous in wings and tail conspicuous in flight.
   Voice: Harsh chattering calls, especially at nesting colonies.
   Distribution and Habitat: Occurs locally in northern Tanzania; relatively common in Serengeti National Park. Inhabits open plains where there are groups of acacia trees. Often feeds on the ground, sometimes in company of starlings.
   Allied Species: The Chestnut-crowned Sparrow Weaver (*Plocepasser superciliosus*), 6″, is a pale brown, sparrow-like bird with a chestnut crown; white stripe over eye and black stripe down each side of throat; two whitish wing-bars; below, greyish-white. A very silent and unobtrusive bird, found in small parties or pairs in bush and savannah woodland: often feeds on the ground. Found in north-western Kenya from Kapenguria northwards and in northern Uganda.

BLACK-CAPPED SOCIAL WEAVER
Pseudonigrita cabanisi   p. 284
   Identification: 5″. Sexes alike; a pale brown weaver with a black crown and a black tail; underparts white with some black in centre of breast and on flanks; bill greenish-white.
   Voice: Subdued chattering calls.
   Distribution and Habitat: A very local bird in northern and eastern Kenya and north-eastern Tanzania. Inhabits dry bush country where

there are acacias in which it nests in colonies. This is a common bird in the Samburu Game Reserve, northern Kenya.

RUFOUS SPARROW   *Passer motitensis*   p. 284

Identification: 6". Typical sparrow: male with black-streaked rufous back and unmarked rufous rump; crown grey, pale rufous stripe from eye to nape; black streak through eye to upper ear coverts; cheeks white; chin and throat patch black; rest underparts whitish or grey on flanks. Female has chin and throat patch grey. The closely related Kenya Rufous Sparrow (*250) lacks the black eye-stripe and has grey cheeks.

Voice: Typical sparrow chirping.

Distribution and Habitat: In East Africa found locally in northern half of Uganda. Inhabits open thorn-bush country, usually near human habitations, and cultivated land. Often feeds on the ground.

Allied Species: The Indian race of the House Sparrow (*Passer domesticus*), 5½", is an introduced species found in Mombasa, Kenya and on Zanzibar; species best distinguished from Rufous Sparrow by dark chestnut stripe over eye. The Somali Sparrow (*Passer castanopterus*), 5", differs from the Rufous Sparrow in having the top of the head tawny-rufous and the underparts washed yellow. It occurs locally in northern Kenya, most frequent in northern Turkana.

CHESTNUT SPARROW   *Sorella eminibey*   p. 304

Identification: 4½". Male, uniform deep chestnut; wings and tail brown with pale edgings. Female and non-breeding male, earth-brown above with black streaking on mantle; pale rufous stripe over eye; underparts pale buffy-grey to whitish on belly. Adult males in breeding dress unmistakable; females and non-breeding males best identified by small size.

Voice: Subdued chirping calls, not unlike flock calls of queleas.

Distribution and Habitat: Locally common in eastern Uganda, Kenya and northern Tanzania. Inhabits arid bush country: gregarious, often associated with Red-billed Quelea and other weavers.

Allied Species: The Parrot-billed Sparrow (*Passer gongonensis*), 7", has a greyish head, unstreaked tawny-brown mantle and rufous rump; below, greyish; bill very large and heavy. General appearance a giant edition of the Grey-headed Sparrow (*250). Inhabits open country with scattered trees and bush: found in central, eastern and southern Kenya; most frequent at the coast. The Swahili Sparrow (*Passer suahelicus*), 6", differs from both the Grey-headed and Parrot-billed

Sparrows in having the head and mantle the same colour, brownish-grey. It occurs locally in open acacia and other woodland and bush country in southern Kenya and in Tanzania.

YELLOW-SPOTTED PETRONIA *Petronia xanthosterna* p. 284
Identification: 6″. A grey, sparrow-like bird with greyish-white underparts; pale yellow spot in centre of throat, not always conspicuous in field; narrow white ring around eye: pale stripe above eye. Occurs in pairs or small flocks: feeds mainly on ground.
Voice: Sparrow-like chirps, but usually silent.
Distribution and Habitat: Occurs in eastern Uganda, Kenya and north-eastern Tanzania. Found in arid bush country, open savannah country and cultivated areas where there are bushes and trees.
Allied Species: The Yellow-throated Petronia (*Petronia superciliaris*), 5½″, is darker in general colour with heavy blackish streaking on upperparts. It is locally common in woodland and bush country in Tanzania. The Bush Petronia (*Petronia dentata*), 5″, is unstreaked above, smaller and paler than the Yellow-spotted Petronia with a greyish crown and a pale, russet-brown mantle. It occurs in northern Uganda.

SPECKLE-FRONTED WEAVER *Sporopipes frontalis* p. 284
Identification: 4½–5″. A pale greyish-brown, sparrow-like bird with a bright rufous hind neck; crown and stripe on each side of throat black, speckled with white; below, greyish-white.
Voice: A liquid "tsssk" and a finch-like twittering song.
Distribution and Habitat: Locally common in the drier areas of Kenya, Uganda and northern and central Tanzania. Found in arid bush country, woodland and marginal cultivation. Gregarious or in pairs.

CLARKE'S WEAVER *Ploceus golandi* p. 304
Identification: 5″. Male a black weaver with a bright yellow breast and abdomen; wings black, edged with yellow; rump and tail dark olive-green. Female bright green above with black streaks on mantle; wings black with yellow edgings; tail dark olive; underparts bright canary-yellow, merging to buffy-white on belly.
Voice: Undescribed.
Distribution and Habitat: A very rare and local weaver, known only from the Sokoke-Arabuku forest on the Kenya coast. Found in small flocks in tree-tops, often associated with other birds in mixed bird parties.
Allied Species: Fox's Weaver (*Ploceus spekeoides*), 6″, is another rare

and local weaver found in north-western to central Uganda in or near swamps. It is a yellow weaver with a black face and chin, yellow crown and dusky mottled back; similar to Speke's Weaver (*251), but with a conspicuous yellow rump and shorter tail: female olive-yellow above with dusky streaks; rump yellow; underparts yellowish. Heughlin's Masked Weaver (*Ploceus heuglini*), 5″, also has a black face-mask and yellow crown, but has mantle yellowish-green, not mottled black. Female with black-streaked olive upperparts; below, yellow with buff wash on breast. Found in savannah bush and woodland, often near water, in eastern and central Uganda and in western Kenya. The Northern Masked Weaver (*Ploceus taeniopterus*), 5½″, also has yellow underparts and a black face-mask, similar to the Vitelline Weaver (*252), but has much less black on the cheeks and extensive chestnut on head and throat. The female is olive-buff above, streaked blackish; below pale yellowish-buff. It occurs locally in northern Uganda, usually near swamps. The Tanganyika Masked Weaver (*Ploceus reichardi*), 5½″, also resembles the Vitelline Weaver but has a broad black band on forehead and chestnut flanks; the female is less distinctly streaked above than related species. This is another very local species found in southern Tanzania, usually in vicinity of water and swamps. The Baglafecht Weaver (*Ploceus baglafecht*), 6½″, is a green-backed, yellow-breasted weaver with a golden-yellow forehead and black ear coverts; belly white. In East Africa it has been recorded from northern Uganda: it frequents lush bush and grass near water.

LITTLE WEAVER   *Ploceus luteolus*   p. 304

Identification: 4½″. Male, upperparts yellowish-green; below, yellow; black forehead, face and throat: female greenish-grey above with dusky streaking; below, yellowish, white on belly; bill stumpy. Small size and stumpy black bill best characters for distinguishing this species. The Slender-billed Weaver has a longer, more slender bill and female much yellower and unstreaked.

Voice: A rather soft, churring note, but relatively silent for a weaver.

Distribution and Habitat: Occurs locally in Uganda, western and northern Kenya and in northern Tanzania. Inhabits open acacia woodland and bush and cultivation in drier areas. Found either in pairs in acacias or in flocks. Nests singly, not in colonies.

NORTHERN BROWN-THROATED WEAVER
Ploceus castanops   p. 304

Identification: 5½". Male a bright golden-yellow weaver with a green back; forehead, front half of face and throat rich chestnut; female olive-buff with dusky streaking on back; below yellowish-buff.
Voice: Various subdued chattering calls.
Distribution and Habitat: Found locally in Uganda and along the shore of Lake Victoria, western Kenya. Frequents papyrus and reed beds and other waterside vegetation. Not uncommon along the Kazinga Channel in the Queen Elizabeth Park: usually gregarious in small flocks, sometimes associated with Yellow-collared and Golden-backed Weavers (*253).

TAVETA GOLDEN WEAVER   *Ploceus castaneiceps*   p. 304

Identification: 5½". Male a bright yellow weaver with a greenish-yellow back and greenish wings and tail; chestnut patch on nape and chestnut wash on chest: female yellowish-olive with dusky streaks on mantle; yellowish stripe above eye; below, pale buffy-yellow.
Voice: A constant low chattering.
Distribution and Habitat: An extremely local species but often common where it does occur. Found in south-eastern Kenya and north-eastern Tanzania: abundant around camps and park lodge at Amboseli Game Reserve. Inhabits open acacia woodland where there is bushy undergrowth, and lush vegetation in the vicinity of water.

ORANGE WEAVER   *Ploceus aurantius*   p. 304

Identification: 5". A brilliant orange-yellow weaver with a greenish-yellow back and golden rump; wings and tail blackish-olive; bill horn-coloured, not black. Female unstreaked green above; below, white with greenish wash on throat and chest; bill pale horn.
Voice: Usual chattering weaver calls.
Distribution and Habitat: Local in Uganda and north-western Tanzania, mainly around Lake Victoria and in nearby swamps. Inhabits reed beds, papyrus, and lush lake shore vegetation: gregarious, often associated with other species of weavers.

DARK-BACKED WEAVER   *Symplectes bicolor*   p. 304

Identification: 6". Sexes alike: a thickset black and golden-yellow weaver with a bluish- or greenish-white bill and red eyes. The race found along the Kenya-Tanzania coast south to Dar es Salaam has the head, upper-parts, wings and tail jet-black and the breast and abdomen bright golden yellow. Elsewhere the mantle is greyish, the wings and tail paler and the underparts less golden.

Voice: A double "weet-weet" and various high-pitched squeaky notes. **Distribution and Habitat:** Locally distributed coastal and western Kenya, Uganda and Tanzania. Inhabits coastal forest and scrub, rain forests and woodland. A tree-top species usually found in pairs; sometimes associated with mixed bird parties.

Allied Species: The Olive-headed Golden Weaver (*Hyphanturgus olivaceiceps*), 5½", has yellowish-green upperparts, head and throat; yellow underparts with a chestnut patch on the chest. It is a rare and local weaver found in brachystegia woodland in south-western Tanzania. It inhabits tree-tops singly or in pairs. The Strange Weaver (*Hyphanturgus alienus*), 6", has upperparts, wings and tail green, head and throat black; breast and abdomen yellow with a chestnut patch on chest. It occurs singly or in pairs in tree-tops of mountain forest in western and south-western Uganda. The Usambara Weaver (*Hyphanturgus nicolli*), 6", has brownish-black upperparts, wings and tail; a dusky olive head and throat, dull yellow on forehead; below, yellow with chestnut patch on chest. Another very uncommon and local forest weaver, known only from the Usambara Mountains, north-eastern Tanzania.

GOLDEN WEAVER   *Xanthophilus subaureus*   p. 304

Identification: 6". Male a yellow weaver, slightly greenish on back, with a pale chestnut wash on head and throat; eye pale red. Female, green above with very indistinct olive striping; below yellow, paler on the belly; eye pale red. The Golden Palm Weaver (*254) has a brilliant orange head and dark brown eyes.

Voice: Various chattering calls.

Distribution and Habitat: Locally distributed central and eastern Kenya and in Tanzania, including Zanzibar: commonest in coastal areas where often exists alongside the Golden Palm Weaver. Gregarious. Inhabits coconut plantations, coastal scrub and bush, along rivers and in cultivation where there are trees.

SLENDER-BILLED WEAVER   *Icteropsis pelzelni*   p. 304

Identification: 4½". A small yellow weaver, greenish on back, with a black face and throat and a slender black bill. Female, bright yellow with greenish back. The similar Little Weaver has a shorter, more stumpy bill and has a different habitat—acacia woodlands.

Voice: Subdued chattering calls, but relatively quiet for a weaver.

Distribution and Habitat: Locally common in western Kenya, Uganda and northern Tanzania around Lake Victoria. Inhabits lake-shore vegetation, swamps and damp woodlands. Common at Entebbe, where often seen in gardens. Slender black bill conspicuous in field.

BLACK-BILLED WEAVER *Heterhyphantes melanogaster* p. 304
Identification: 5½-6". An all black weaver with golden-yellow fore-crown and cheeks; female has fore-crown, face and throat yellow.
Voice: A rather high-pitched chirp, but usually silent.
Distribution and Habitat: An uncommon forest weaver found in Uganda and western Kenya. Inhabits both tree-tops and dense under-growth of forests; usually in pairs.
Allied Species: Weyns' Weaver (*Melanopteryx wenysi*), 6", has black upperparts, head and chest; breast and abdomen yellow, flanks rich chestnut; wings black with yellow edgings; tail dark olive. Female dark olive with indistinct dusky streaking; below, whitish with olive wash on throat, chest and flanks; wings blackish-olive with distinct pale yellow edgings; tail olive. This is a rare and local forest weaver found in Uganda. It is most frequent near Entebbe where it may be found in both forest and lush lakeside scrub. Emin's Weaver (*Othyphantes emini*), 6", has upper parts grey, streaked black; yellow fore-head and black ear coverts; wings and tail dusky olive with greenish edging; below yellow on throat and chest; breast and belly whitish. The female has the crown entirely black. This is a very uncommon and local species in the northern half of Uganda; also recorded from Turkana, north-western Kenya. Inhabits open savannah woodland, usually near water.

STUHLMANN'S WEAVER *Othyphantes stuhlmanni* p. 304
Identification: 6". Sexes alike; crown and face black, rest upperparts, wings and tail green with narrow black streaking on mantle; under-parts bright yellow.
Voice: Various chirping calls.
Distribution and Habitat: Locally common central Uganda south-wards to southern Tanzania. Occurs in open bush and woodland savannah and in cultivation where there are trees. Found singly or in pairs.
Allied Species: Bertram's Weaver (*Xanthoploceus bertrandi*), 6", has a yellow crown and yellowish-green upperparts, wings and tail; nape patch, face and chin black; below yellow. The female has the crown black. An uncommon and very local bird in the highlands of eastern

and southern Tanzania, from the Nguru and Uluguru Mountains southwards. Favours vegetation along mountain streams and hillsides with mixed grass, bush and trees.

COMPACT WEAVER   *Pachyphantes pachyrhynchus*   p. 304

Identification: 5″. A thickset, short-tailed weaver with a heavy bill; upperparts dark olive with very indistinct dark mottling; forehead chestnut, merging to yellow on hind crown; wings dark brown; face and throat black; remainder underparts yellow to white on belly. Female like male but has crown blackish and a golden-yellow stripe over eye.

Voice: A rather harsh "cheee," followed by a series of double notes.

Distribution and Habitat: Locally common in Uganda, western Kenya and north-western Tanzania. Inhabits open park-like country with scattered bush and trees, where there is long grass. Gregarious in small flocks in grassland.

BROWN-CAPPED WEAVER   *Phormoplectes insignis*   p. 304

Identification: 6″. A black and yellow forest weaver, the male of which has a bright chestnut cap. General colour bright yellow with black wings and tail, and a black face and chin: female has crown black not chestnut.

Voice: Usually silent, but sometimes utters a sharp "tssst."

Distribution and Habitat: A local and uncommon forest species found in Uganda, central and western Kenya and northern and western Tanzania, south to the Kungwe-Mahare Mountains. Inhabits the forest tree-tops, usually in pairs or family parties, searching the branches for insects in the manner of a tit. The broad yellow stripe down the back and the male's chestnut crown are conspicuous in the field.

YELLOW-MANTLED WEAVER   *Melanoploceus tricolor*   p. 304

Identification: 6″. A black weaver with a bright yellow collar on the hind neck; breast and abdomen deep chestnut. Female has sooty-brown underparts, otherwise like male.

Voice: A sharp "tssst" or "chirr-it", but usually silent.

Distribution and Habitat: A very uncommon and local forest weaver found in Uganda and in the Kakamega Forest, western Kenya. Habits woodpecker or tit-like, climbing about over branches of tall forest trees searching for insects. Usually in pairs or family parties.

Allied Species: Maxwell's Black Weaver (*Melanoploceus albinucha*), 5″, is a relatively small all black forest weaver with white eyes: smaller than Vieillot's Black Weaver (*255) and female black, not olive with streaked underparts. This is a rare tree-top weaver in East Africa, recorded from the Bwamba Forest, Toro, Uganda. Gray's Malimbe (*Malimbus nitens*), 6½″, is a black weaver with a deep red throat and chest and a bluish-white bill; found in the Bwamba Forest, western Uganda. This species is distinguished from the Crested and Red-headed Malimbes (*258) by less extensive red and a white, not black, bill. The Red-bellied Malimbe (*Malimbus erythrogaster*), 7″, has a red crown, breast and abdomen. It also has been recorded from the Bwamba Forest, western Uganda.

BLACK BISHOP   *Euplectes gierowii*   p. 305

Identification: 6″. A black bishop weaver with an orange-red chest-band, nape and hind neck; mantle orange-red or yellow. Female, non-breeding male and immature sparrow-like, streaked dusky above, best recognised in field by size and by association with adult male.

Voice: Various subdued twittering calls.

Distribution and Habitat: A very local and generally uncommon species found in Uganda, southern Kenya and northern Tanzania in the vicinity of Lake Victoria. Inhabits swampy areas of bush and tall grass, elephant grass and margins of swamps. Not highly gregarious, but sometimes in small flocks, especially at roost.

FIRE-FRONTED BISHOP   *Euplectes diademata*   p. 305

Identification: 4″. A black-breasted bishop with a red forehead and a bright chrome-yellow lower back and rump; wings and tail brown. Female, non-breeding male and immature sparrow-like and streaky, not identifiable in field except in association with adult male.

Voice: A sharp "zeep-zeep."

Distribution and Habitat: Occurs very locally in drier parts of eastern Kenya and north-eastern Tanzania, inhabiting areas of tall grass or marshy hollows in arid bush country: relatively gregarious, nesting in small scattered colonies. Not uncommon in the Voi area of the Tsavo National Park.

YELLOW-CROWNED BISHOP   *Euplectes afra*   p. 305

Identification: 4½″. A black bishop with a bright canary-yellow crown, back and rump. Female, non-breeding male and immature sparrow-like, streaky and in field best identified by association with adult male. The Yellow Bishop (*261) has a black crown.

Voice: A rather slowly uttered "zeet, zeet": male often calls when flying in circles above swampy nesting ground.

Distribution and Habitat: Found locally in Uganda, western, central and southern Kenya and eastern northern and extreme southern Tanzania. Inhabits swamps and marshes where there is rank grass and sedges. Nests in small scattered colonies.

YELLOW-SHOULDERED WIDOW-BIRD
Coliuspasser macrocercus   p. 305

Identification: Male 10-12", female 5½". An all black, relatively long-tailed widow-bird with canary-yellow shoulders. Male in non-breeding dress streaky and sparrow-like, but retains yellow shoulders: female and immature sparrow-like, best recognised by association with males.

Voice: A thin piping "zee-zee-zee" or "zeet."

Distribution and Habitat: Locally not uncommon in Uganda and western Kenya. Inhabits areas of marshland with lush grass and scattered bush and drier areas of grass and bush. Not specially gregarious, but sometimes in flocks at roosts and in smaller groups when feeding.

Allied Species: Hartlaub's Marsh Widow-bird (*Coliuspasser hartlaubi*), 12-14", 6", is a heavy-looking black widow-bird with orange-buff shoulders: female sparrow-like. It frequents areas of extensive marsh with lush grass in Uganda and western Kenya; everywhere uncommon, but most frequent in marsh along the Eldoret-Tororo road in western Kenya. The Marsh Widow-bird (*Coliuspasser psammocromius*), 20", 12", occurs in marshy valleys in the southern highlands of Tanzania. The male is all black with a very long tail and pale yellow and buff shoulders: female streaky and sparrow-like. The Long-tailed Widow-bird (*263) has a longer tail and red and buff shoulders.

YELLOW-MANTLED WIDOW-BIRD
Coliuspasser macrourus   p. 305

Identification: Male 10-12", female 5½". An all black widow-bird with yellow shoulders and mantle. The non-breeding male retains its yellow shoulders when it may be distinguished from the non-breeding Yellow-shouldered Widow-bird by slightly duller dark streaking of upperparts: female and immature streaky and sparrow-like, not identifiable in field unless associated with adult male.

Voice: Various "zeeting" calls, not unlike those of some cisticola warblers.

Distribution and Habitat: Locally common in Uganda, western Kenya

and Tanzania. Inhabits open grassy plains, marshy areas of lush grass
and bush, and swampy low-lying districts.

BLACK AND WHITE MANNIKIN   *Spermestes poensis*   **p. 284**
   Identification: 4″. Rather thickset, heavy-billed seed-eater with upperparts, head, throat and chest glossy black; breast and abdomen white,
   barred black on flanks. Gregarious, feeding on seeding grasses in
   small flocks. The Bronze Mannikin (*264) has a greyish-brown back;
   the Rufous-backed Mannikin (*264) has a bright chestnut-brown back.
   Voice: Various subdued chirping calls.
   Distribution and Habitat: Locally common Uganda, western Kenya and
   north-western Tanzania. Frequents grassy margins and glades of
   forests and savannah woodland.
   Allied Species: The Magpie Mannikin (*Amauresthes fringilloides*), 5″,
   resembles a large edition of the Black and White Mannikin, but has
   the mantle brown with black centres to the feathers and white shaft
   stripes. Uncommon and local in East Africa; most frequent in north-
   eastern Tanzania. Found in lush bush and grass, often at forest edge.

SILVER-BILL   *Euodice malabarica*   **p. 284**
   Identification: 4″. A pale, ashy-brown seed-eater with flight feathers,
   rump and tail black; throat and chest ashy-buff; breast and abdomen
   white; bill pale blue-grey. Gregarious, in small flocks.
   Voice: Soft double note and a longer, weak trill.
   Distribution and Habitat: Locally common in arid bush country in
   Kenya, Uganda and northern half of Tanzania.

GREY-HEADED SILVER-BILL   *Odontospiza caniceps*   **p. 284**
   Identification: 4½″. A seed-eater with a vinous-pink back, conspicuous
   white rump and black wings and tail; head grey, sides of face and throat
   speckled with white; breast and belly vinous-brown.
   Voice: High-pitched, weak trill.
   Distribution and Habitat: A very local and uncommon bird of dry bush
   country with a wide range in East Africa: the contrasting pinkish-
   brown back, white rump and black tail are good field characters:
   gregarious in small flocks. Most frequent in the Dodoma district of
   Tanzania and in southern Kenya.

GREY-HEADED NEGRO FINCH *Nigrita canicapilla* p. 305
Identification: 5". Upperparts grey; forehead, face, wings, tail and underparts black; white spots on wing coverts. Black underparts and grey mantle best field characters.
Voice: A soft, three-note whistle.
Distribution and Habitat: Local and usually uncommon Uganda, western, central and southern Kenya and northern Tanzania. Inhabits forest areas and woodland, usually seen along margins or in glades of forest: frequents both foliage of forest trees and undergrowth.
Allied Species: The Chestnut-breasted Negro Finch (*Nigrita bicolor*), 4", has the forehead and underparts deep maroon; mantle sooty-brown. It is found in forests in Uganda and western Kenya (Kakamega Forest). The White-breasted Negro Finch (*Nigrita fusconota*), 4", has white underparts, a pale brown back and black head, rump and tail. It also is found in the Kakamega Forest, western Kenya and in Uganda. Both species may be observed in either the foliage of tall forest trees or in the undergrowth.

RED-HEADED BLUE-BILL *Spermophaga ruficapilla* p. 305
Identification: 6". A large black and red waxbill inhabiting forest undergrowth. Male, head, chest, flanks and upper tail coverts bright crimson-red, rest of plumage black; bill heavy, metallic-blue to pink along cutting edges; feet dark horn. Female, black replaced by dark grey and has round white spots on belly. The Black-bellied Seed-cracker has a differently shaped blue-grey bill and yellowish legs: the female is brown and red and has no white spots on underparts.
Voice: A series of barely audible clinking notes.
Distribution and Habitat: Locally not uncommon in Uganda, western Kenya and north-western Tanzania as far south as the Kungwe-Mahare Mountains. Inhabits dense forest undergrowth: sometimes comes to the edge of forest to bask in sun, especially after heavy rain storms.
Allied Species: The Usambara Red-headed Blue-bill (*Spermophaga cana*), 5½", is slate-grey not black in the male, and the female is paler. It occurs in forests on the Usambara Mountains, north-eastern Tanzania. Grant's Blue-bill (*Spermophaga poliogenys*), 5½", resembles the Red-headed Blue-bill but red much brighter and on crown red confined to forehead; female has top and sides of head grey; chin to breast red; remainder of underparts grey with round white spots. A rare and seldom seen species recorded from the Bwamba Forest, western Uganda. The Brown Twin-spot (*Clytospiza monteiri*), 5", has the head grey,

back and wings brown, rump crimson, tail blackish; below, crimson streak on throat in male, white streak in female; breast and abdomen pale chestnut with round white spots. Found in forest undergrowth and dense scrub near forest. An uncommon and skulking bird found locally in Uganda.

BLACK-BELLIED SEED-CRACKER *Pirenestes ostrinus* p. 305
Identification: 6". Male head, chest, flanks, rump and central tail feathers crimson-red, rest of plumage black; bill blue-grey, feet yellowish. Female resembles male but black replaced by brown. Male distinguished from Red-headed Blue-bill by all grey bill, yellowish legs and crimson-washed tail: female lacks white spots on underparts and is brown not dark grey.
Voice: A soft tinkling call-note, but birds usually silent.
Distribution and Habitat: Found locally, but everywhere uncommon, in Uganda and in the Kakamega Forest, western Kenya. Inhabits dense forest undergrowth, especially the margins of forest and in glades; also in dense scrub and secondary growth near water.
Allied Species: Rothschild's Seed-cracker (*Pirenestes rothschildi*), 5½", differs from the Black-bellied Seed-cracker only in smaller size and smaller bill (width of lower mandible at base 12-13 mm. against 14-17 mm. in the Black-bellied Seed-cracker). A rare bird found in western Uganda in forest undergrowth. The Large-billed Seed-cracker (*Pirenestes maximus*), 6", differs from the Black-bellied Seed-cracker only in having a larger and heavier bill, 18-19 mm. wide at base of lower mandible. Recorded from western and north-western Uganda; frequents dense thickets in savannah woodland. The Lesser Seed-cracker (*Pirenestes minor*), 5", is an earth-brown species with the front half of crown, face, throat, chest, rump and central tail feathers crimson. Female has less red on the head and underparts. Found in eastern and southern Tanzania. Inhabits dense scrub along woodland streams. The closely related Urungu Seed-cracker (*Pirenestes frommi*), 5", has a larger and heavier bill (13.5-16 mm. width at base of lower mandible, against 9-12 mm. in Lesser Seed-cracker). Found in the Uluguru Mountains and south-western districts of Tanzania. This is a rare and little-known bird.

RED-FACED CRIMSON-WING *Cryptospiza reichenovii* p. 305
Identification: 4½". The crimson-wings are a group of plump crimson and olive or crimson and dark grey waxbills found in the undergrowth of highland forest. The present species is dusky olive with crimson-red

on the back, rump, wing coverts and flanks and a crimson-red patch round eye; bill dark leaden-grey: female similar to male but has pale olive eye patch.

Voice: A high-pitched "tzeet."

Distribution and Habitat: Found locally in the highland forests of Uganda and Tanzania. Inhabits dense undergrowth, usually in pairs or family groups: sometimes seen on forest paths in early morning or late evening. Red eye-patch of male conspicuous in field.

ABYSSINIAN CRIMSON-WING *Cryptospiza salvadorii* p. 305
Identification: $4\frac{1}{2}''$. Sexes alike. Head, nape, upper back and underparts greyish-olive; back, rump, flanks and wing-coverts crimson-red; bill dark leaden-grey. Best distinguished from Red-faced Crimson-wing by lack of eye-patch.

Voice: A soft "tzeep" or "tzeep, tzeep."

Distribution and Habitat: Locally common in highland forest and bamboo zones in Kenya, Uganda and north-eastern Tanzania. Inhabits undergrowth of forest and bamboo, often on forest track feeding on small seeds or picking up grit. Common on Mount Kenya and Aberdare Mountains, Kenya.

DUSKY CRIMSON-WING *Cryptospiza jacksoni* p. 305
Identification: $4\frac{1}{2}''$. Sexes alike. Dark grey with crown, face, mantle, rump, flanks and wing coverts crimson; bill dark leaden-grey. Easily distinguished from other species by dark grey and crimson plumage.

Voice: Usually silent: call a soft "tzeek."

Distribution and Habitat: Forests of the Ruwenzori range and highland forest of Kigezi, Uganda. Inhabits dense undergrowth, rarely apparent but sometimes seen on road margins through forest. Most frequent in the Impenetrable Forest, south-western Uganda.

SHELLEY'S CRIMSON-WING *Cryptospiza shelleyi* p. 305
Identification: $5''$. Male differs from other crimson-wings in having a red bill. Crown, cheeks and upperparts bright maroon-crimson; below, throat and breast pale olive, belly deep pinkish-olive; female differs in having pale olive head and a black and red bill.

Voice: A series of rapid twittering notes, not unlike the call of some small sunbird.

Distribution and Habitat: A rare and seldom seen species found in the mountain forests of western and south-western Uganda. Inhabits dense forest undergrowth: less frequently seen along road margins than related species.

QUAIL FINCH *Ortygospiza atricollis* p. 284

Identification: 3½″. Tiny short-tailed waxbills found in swampy depressions in open plains country. Male, forehead face and chin black; rest upperparts greyish-brown; chest, breast and flanks barred brown and white; centre of lower breast orange-brown; belly white; tail very short, outer feathers white-tipped; bill bright red. Female duller, has chin white and black on head replaced by grey.

Voice: Metallic chirruping calls made on wing.

Distribution and Habitat: Widespread but local Kenya, Uganda and Tanzania. Inhabits open plains country especially in the vicinity of swamps and marshes and the margins of pools. Birds perch almost always on the ground, flushing from underfoot: usually in pairs or in small flocks. Metallic call notes in flight characteristic.

Allied Species:: The Locust Finch (*Ortygospiza locustella*) has the same habits and habitat preference as the Quail Finch. General plumage blackish with white dots; face, throat and breast red; female whitish below. A very uncommon and local species found in southern Tanzania.

PETERS' TWIN-SPOT *Hypargos niveoguttatus* p. 285

Identification: 5″. A handsome black, crimson, brown and grey waxbill with round white spots on the belly. Male, crown greyish-brown, mantle, wings and wing coverts russet-brown; hind neck, rump, face, throat and chest, crimson; tail black with crimson wash; breast and belly black with round white spots; female paler and has chin to chest deep buff with crimson wash; breast and belly grey, spotted with white.

Voice: A weak, rather squeaky trill, but birds usually silent.

Distribution and Habitat: Widespread and sometimes common eastern Kenya and Tanzania, but skulking in habits and not often seen. Most frequent in coastal areas. Inhabits dense scrub and bush, coastal thickets and heavy undergrowth bordering streams.

Allied Species: The Green-backed Twin-spot (*Mandingoa nitidula*), 3½″, is a bright green finch-like bird with a blackish breast and belly heavily marked with round white spots; male has the face and chin tomato-red. Very local and inconspicuous little bird found in Kenya, Tanzania including Zanzibar and Pemba Islands and in western Uganda: inhabits dense undergrowth of forests, thickets and heavy vegetation along streams. The Red-winged Pytilia (*Pytilia phoenicoptera*),

5", is a red-billed grey finch-like bird with the wings, tail and rump crimson, and the flanks vermiculated grey and white. An uncommon species found in dense thickets in mixed grass and bush savannah, northern half of Uganda and northern Turkana, north-western Kenya. The Orange-winged Pytilia (*Pytilia afra*), 5", is another red-billed finch-like species with forehead, face, chin, rump and tail feathers crimson; crown, mantle and rump olive-green; edges of flight feathers and wing coverts orange; below, throat and neck grey to orange-washed olive on chest; remainder underparts barred olive and white. Distinguished from the Green-winged Pytilia or Melba Finch (*264) by its grey throat and orange wings. A species of wide distribution in East Africa, but everywhere uncommon. Skulking in habits, in thick bush and thickets in open savannah country. The Bar-breasted Fire Finch (*Lagonosticta rufopicta*), 4", is a small reddish waxbill with a red bill, dark brown back and crimson upper tail coverts; chin to breast vinous-crimson with broken white bars across chest. In East Africa found in open savannah bush in north-western Uganda: often seen around human habitations. The Dusky Fire Finch (*Lagonosticta cinereovinacea*), 4½", is brownish-grey above and on chest with deep maroon-red rump; tail black; breast and abdomen black with maroon-red flanks speckled with white. A bird of highland forest undergrowth, known from south-western Uganda. The Black-faced Fire Finch (*Lagonosticta larvata*), 4½", is a brownish-grey species with the crown, rump, tail and chest maroon-red; sides of face, chin and throat black: the female is paler and lacks the black face. Found in tall grass savannah in northern Uganda. The Parasitic Weaver (*Anomalospiza imberbis*), 5", is a short-tailed greenish-yellow finch-like bird with indistinct dark mottling on upperparts and a black bill: female more buffy in colour, less yellow. Has the appearance of some kind of short-tailed canary with a heavy black bill. Inhabits open grasslands where parasitic on cisticola warblers. Widely distributed in East Africa, but everywhere uncommon and often overlooked.

BLACK-HEADED WAXBILL   *Estrilda atricapilla*   p. 285
Identification: 4". A small vermiculated greyish waxbill with a black cap and tail, red rump and flanks and black under tail coverts; found in small flocks along edges of highland forest. Underparts, face, chin and breast greyish-white, merging to black on abdomen and under tail coverts; bill black; red on lower mandible. The very similar Black-crowned Waxbill is whiter on face and underparts, and pale grey on under tail coverts.

Distribution and Habitat: Highlands of Kenya and western and southern Uganda. Inhabits forested areas, most frequent along margins of forest, in glades and along forest tracks where there is an abundance of grasses. Occurs in small flocks.

BLACK-CROWNED WAXBILL *Estrilda nonnula* p. 285
Identification: 4″. A small black-capped waxbill with vermiculated greyish upperparts, red rump and flanks and whitish underparts to pale grey below tail; bill black and red. The Black-headed Waxbill has black on abdomen and under tail coverts.
Voice: Weak, twittering calls.
Distribution and Habitat: Locally common in western Kenya, Uganda and north-western Tanzania. Found in flocks in neglected cultivation, open bush and tall grass and in lush vegetation near water.
Allied Species: The Zebra Waxbill (*Estrilda subflava*), 3½″, is yellow or orange-yellow below with olive barred flanks; above, brown with a red stripe above eye and red upper tail-coverts. Found in open grasslands and marshy areas: a widespread species in Uganda, the southern half of Kenya and in Tanzania including Zanzibar and Pemba Islands. The Black-rumped Waxbill (*Estrilda troglodytes*), 3½″, is a pale brown waxbill with a red bill and a red streak through the eye; rump and tail black. The closely related Waxbill (*266) has a brown rump and tail. The Black-rumped Waxbill occurs in open savannah woodland and areas of tall grass and bush in north-western Uganda. The black rump and tail are conspicuous in the field. The Fawn-breasted Waxbill (*Estrilda paludicola*), 4½″, is a pale brown waxbill with a greyish head, red bill and red rump; below, creamy-white with a strong pink wash on the belly. A local species found in western Kenya, Uganda and Tanzania; found in areas of swampy grassland and bush, woodland and forest margins. Generally pale appearance, pink belly and red bill are best field characters. The Lavender Waxbill (*Estrilda perreini*), 4½″, is grey with a red rump, a black stripe through the eye, a black chin and a black tail. This is an uncommon and local waxbill of woodland and bush with tall grass, found in western and south-western Tanzania. The Black-bellied Waxbill (*Estrilda rara*), 5″, has the head, upperparts, chest and flanks vinous-red; breast and abdomen black; bill black, lower mandible pink. Female has vinous-buff underparts. This species resembles a large African Fire Finch (*265) but has black extending on to breast. Occurs locally in Uganda and western Kenya, inhabiting mixed grass and bush country and thick vegetation along streams.

BLACK-FACED WAXBILL   *Estrilda erythronotos*   p. 285

Identification: 5". A small, relatively long-tailed waxbill with black face, ear coverts and throat; general colour pale pinkish-grey with distinct blackish barring especially on wing coverts; rump and tail coverts red; below, pinkish-grey with indistinct barring, washed red on flanks, blackish on belly and under tail coverts: female, paler below. The closely related Black-cheeked Waxbill has little or no black on the throat and has under tail coverts pale grey, not black.

Voice: A series of soft, liquid "tsssps."

Distribution and Habitat: Locally not uncommon in acacia woodland and arid thornbush country of Kenya, southern Uganda and northern and central Tanzania. Frequents acacia trees and bushes, feeding on blossoms and insects attracted to the blossoms. Usually in pairs or small family groups.

Allied Species: The Black-cheeked Waxbill (*Estrilda charmosyna;* p. 285), 5", is very similar to the Black-faced Waxbill, but has little or no black on the chin and throat; below, pale pinkish-grey, narrowly and indistinctly barred with grey. This species has often been considered conspecific with the Black-faced Waxbill, but the two exist side by side in several localities in Kenya and northern Tanzania. The Black-cheeked Waxbill also occurs in acacia woodland and scrub, in Kenya and north-central Tanzania.

WHITE-COLLARED OLIVE-BACK   *Nesocharis ansorgei*   p. 285

Identification: 4½". A small waxbill with the habits of a warbler, searching in foliage of forest trees and undergrowth for insect food. Upperparts bright golden-olive; head and throat black; collar on hind neck grey; collar between neck and chest white; breast golden-olive; belly grey. Female has less pronounced grey collar on hind neck.

Voice: A soft, sunbird-like "tsssp."

Distribution and Habitat: An extremely local and uncommon bird in the forests of western Uganda. Found in pairs in foliage of trees, often along margin of forest, and sometimes members of mixed bird parties. The golden-olive back and white throat band are distinctive.

Allied Species: The Grey-headed Olive-back (*Nesocharis capistrata*), 5", has the top of the head and nape grey; mantle and tail olive-green; cheeks white; throat and line around cheeks black; rest underparts grey to golden-yellow on flanks. This is another waxbill with warbler-like habits, searching the foliage for insect food. It occurs in the forested areas of north-western Uganda.

PURPLE INDIGO-BIRD *Hypochera ultramarina* p. 285
Identification: 4½″. Male glossy blue-black with white bill and salmon-pink or orange legs; female and male in non-breeding plumage sparrow-like, upperparts brown with dark streaks; crown dark brown with broad buff stripe down centre; buff streak over eye; below dusky buff, whiter on belly. Several other species of Indigo-birds have been described, but the status of these is in doubt and most are not identifiable in the field.
Voice: A sharp "tk, tk" call: also sustained warbling song.
Distribution and Habitat: Locally distributed over much of Kenya, Uganda and Tanzania. Inhabits cultivated areas, gardens, open wood-land and bush. White bill and pink or orange legs conspicuous in field.
Allied Species: The South African Indigo-Bird (*Hypochera amaurop-teryx*), 4½″, differs from the Purple Indigo-Bird in having a red or pink bill. It has been recorded on the Kenya coast near Malindi and in central and south-western Tanzania.

Finches: *Fringillidae*

The finches are thick-billed seed-eating birds which resemble weavers but have nine visible primaries only, not ten. Nests unlike those of weavers, open and cup-shaped.

WHITE-BELLIED CANARY *Serinus dorsostriatus* p. 285
Identification: 5″. A greenish-yellow canary with dark streaks on the upperparts; relatively long forked tail; yellow throat and chest; white belly; bill relatively small; female is duller and brownish-green above, but also with white belly.
Voice: A loud warbling song: call a sharp "tweep."
Distribution and Habitat: Locally common in bush country in Uganda, Kenya and northern Tanzania. Relatively small horn-coloured bill and white belly conspicuous in field.
Allied Species: The Black-faced Canary (*Serinus capistratus*), 5″, resembles a White-bellied Canary but has a yellow belly and in the male a blackish or grey face and a yellow band on the forehead. It occurs in western Kenya and in central and southern Uganda. The African Citril (*Carduelis citrinelloides*), 4½″, differs from the Black-faced Canary in having no yellow band on forehead. It occurs in Uganda, northern, central and south-eastern Kenya and northern and western Tanzania.

YELLOW-CROWNED CANARY   *Serinus flavivertex*   p. 285
Identification: 5″. A high altitude canary, in East Africa usually found in localities over 7,000 feet. Male, crown golden-yellow; back green streaked with black; rump yellowish-green; wings dark with two conspicuous yellow bars; tail black edged with yellow, strongly forked (in western race tail yellow with dark shaft streaks); below greenish-yellow to white in centre of belly. Female duller and more heavily streaked above and below.
Voice: A sustained musical warbling song; flock call a sharp "twsstp."
Distribution and Habitat: Common in the highlands of Kenya and north-eastern and western Tanzania and in western Uganda. Occurs in open country and cultivation, especially in stands of exotic conifer trees planted as windbreaks.
Allied Species: The Grosbeak Canary (*Serinus donaldsoni*), 5½″, is a heavy-billed canary, green with dark streaks and a very bright chrome-yellow rump; yellow eye-stripe; bright yellow underparts; female ash-brown with dark streaks and bright yellow rump: below whitish with dark chest and flank streaks. Occurs in semi-desert country of eastern Kenya as far south as Voi. The Kenya Grosbeak Canary (*Serinus buchanani*), 6″, also has a very heavy bill, but is greener above and greenish-yellow below, not bright yellow; female streaked on chest. Occurs in arid bush country in southern Kenya south to central Tanzania.

THICK-BILLED SEED-EATER   *Serinus burtoni*   p. 285
Identification: 7½″. A large, heavily-built seed-eater with a thick bill. Upperparts dark brown with indistinct blackish streaking; white patch on forehead; wings and tail brown, edged green; below brownish-grey, mottled on chest, paler on belly.
Voice: Silent, unobtrusive birds, sometimes uttering a soft "pleet," and a brief warble.
Distribution and Habitat: A bird of highland forest and bush in the vicinity of forest; found in the highlands of Kenya, Uganda and Tanzania. Shy, elusive birds which are often overlooked.
Allied Species: The Streaky-headed Seed-eater (*Serinus gularis*), 6″, is a grey seed-eater with crown streaked black, ash-brown and white and a white stripe over eye; below white with streaking on chest and flanks. A common species in brachystegia woodland in Tanzania; less common in Kenya and Uganda where it inhabits open woodland and cultivation. The Oriole Finch (*Linurgus olivaceus*), 5″, is a golden-yellow or greenish-yellow seed-eater with an orange bill and a black

head and throat. The female is greenish-yellow and lacks the black head and throat. The orange bill is conspicuous in the field. The Oriole Finch inhabits forested mountains in Kenya, and highland forest in north-eastern to south-western Tanzania, and south-western Uganda.

Buntings: *Emberizidae*

Mainly ground-feeding, finch-like birds found singly, in pairs or in small parties. Distinguished from finches by bill structure, the cutting edge of the upper mandible being sinuated.

THREE-STREAKED BUNTING   *Emberiza orientalis*   p. 285
Identification: 6½". Upperparts grey and brown with distinct black streaks; crown black with white stripe down centre, white stripe over each eye; sides of face black; double white wing-bar; tail with white tips to outer feathers; underparts yellow: female has brownish crown and face and less distinct white streak down centre of crown. The Golden-breasted Bunting (*270) is similar but has a rufous back.
Voice: A shrill whistling song.
Distribution and Habitat: Locally not uncommon Tanzania, inhabiting brachystegia woodland, light bush country and cultivation.
Allied Species: Cabanis' Bunting (*Emberiza cabanisi*), 6½", resembles the Three-streaked Bunting but lacks the white stripe down centre of crown. Found in open bush and woodland in western Uganda. The Brown-rumped Bunting (*Emberiza forbesi*), 6", has a black crown with three white streaks and a chestnut-brown back and rump. The similar Golden-breasted Bunting (*270) has a grey rump. The Brown-rumped Bunting occurs in semi-arid bush country in northern Uganda. The House Bunting (*Fringillaria striolata*), 5", is a slim, reddish-brown bunting with a black and white-streaked crown and a white streak over the eye; throat grey, streaked black; rufous-brown on chest and belly. The Cinnamon-breasted Rock Bunting (*270) has the throat and chest black. In East Africa the House Bunting occurs in arid, rocky country in northern Turkana, and in north-eastern Karamoja, Uganda.

Index

INDEX OF PLACES

343

N.B. All the mammals are included in this index but only those birds which are described or illustrated in this book (i.e. between pages 230 and 341). Birds described in the author's earlier *Field Guide to the Birds of East and Central Africa*, which covers the commoner or more conspicuous species, are included where appropriate in the check-lists in Part I (pages 13 to 164), but do not appear in this index.

Numbers in bold type refer to pages facing illustrations